AMERICAN JUVENILE JUSTICE

Cases, Legislation and Comments

- College Edition -

Clifford Dorne

and

Kenneth Gewerth

AMERICAN JUVENILE JUSTICE

Cases, Legislation and Comments

- College Edition -

Clifford Dorne

and

Kenneth Gewerth

Austin & Winfield, Publishers
San Francisco - London - Bethesda
1998

Austin & Winfield, Publishers
4720 Boston Way
Lanham, Maryland 20706

12 Hid's Copse Rd.
Cumnor Hill, Oxford OX2 9JJ

Printed in the United States of America
British Library Cataloging in Publication Information Available

Library of Congress Cataloging-in-Publication Data

Dorne, Clifford K., 1957-
American juvenile justice : cases, legislation, and comments / Clifford Dorne and Kenneth Gewerth. - College ed.
p. cm.

Includes bibliographical references and index.
1. Juvenile justice, Administration of—United States—Cases. I. Gewerth, Kenneth. II. Title.
KF9778.D67 - 1998 345.73'08—dc21 98-5601 CIP

ISBN 978-1-5729-2100-9

™ The paper used in this publication meets the minimum requirements of American National Standard for Information Sciences—Permanence of Paper for Printed Library Materials, ANSI Z39.48—1984

Table of Contents

TABLE OF CASES

To my parents, Joel and Renee, and brother Curtis; and to my wife, Juanita.

— C.K.D. —

To my friends, Rita Egel, and Lori Wreggelsworth, who recently co-authored projects of their own, and to Susie Ross, who made sure I made my page quota every day. Thanks for all your help.

— K.E.G. —

PREFACE

The study of juvenile justice exists amidst philosophical and historical contradictions: free will versus determinism, philanthropy versus social Darwinism, tolerance/cultural relativism versus nativism/ethnocentrism, and public calls for retribution against delinquents versus public compassion for disadvantaged children.

Currently such conflicts are played out in political debates about the possible abolition of traditional (state benevolent) juvenile justice. They are also manifested in polemics about the extent to which juveniles should be diverted from adjudication for delinquency as well as the degree to which parents should be held legally accountable for the transgressions of their children. Heated debates about juvenile curfew laws (as a crime prevention policy) and the death penalty for juvenile murderers also serve to maintain juvenile justice policy discourse at politically visible levels.

There are certainly some textbooks that serve as excellent sources for the study of such profound ideological conflicts, but a legal casebook is clearly needed in this area. This motivated us to produce our 1995 edition of *American Juvenile Justice: Cases, Legislation and Comments*. This original edition is 1226 pages long and was designed mainly for law school classes, graduate classes, and, to a lessor extent, for advanced undergraduate study. We wanted to be as comprehensive as possible, giving the reader a realistic conception of the ways in which juvenile justice is reviewed by a wide variety of courts. We also intended to cover as many issues as space would permit. The original edition, however, may not be suitable for some undergraduate introductory courses due to its prodigious length.

We concur with some of our faculty colleagues and with our publisher that an undergraduate abridged edition is needed. Here, the goal is to provide undergraduate university students with an overview of the American juvenile justice system with a focus on judicial review (appellate cases). Most of our commentary from the 1995 edition has been retained here, but many of the less significant cases have been extracted, resulting in a casebook of 251 pages. This book is a perfect length to use as the main text in a 100 or 200 level juvenile justice course. It is also quite suitable for use alongside one or two regular textbooks at the advanced levels of undergraduate university study. Perhaps the most important attribute of this abridged casebook is that the actual case excerpts tend to be much more detailed and comprehensive when compared to presentations of such legal materials in other shorter juvenile justice casebooks that have recently been published.

Chapter 1 provides a macro-historical orientation covering the past century-and-a-half. Chapters 2, 3, 4, and 5 comprise cases and comments on police, court, and correctional agencies in juvenile justice. In the much larger 1995 edition, Chapter 6 covered a wide array of miscellaneous issues including child maltreatment cases and juveniles' rights in public schools. In this much shorter edition, however, we have reduced Chapter 6 solely to death penalty-related issues. In the interest of brevity, we were not originally planning to include a sixth chapter in this edition. But after much discussion, we decided to cover the death penalty in the last chapter. We did this because of the sheer intensity of ongoing political and scholarly debates surrounding this topic as they relate to defendants who committed first degree murder when they were between the ages of 16 and 21. We also believe that an analysis of the death penalty is a fitting coda to this casebook as it leaves the reader with many profound issues to ponder, including the question of what the future doctrinal and practical relationships should be between the adult criminal justice and the civil law juvenile justice system.

We believe that this abridged college edition, with its appellate cases, discussion questions, and commentary will serve undergraduate juvenile justice education well. While the book is primarily designed for classroom application, it should be useful to anyone interested in juvenile justice public policy.

Clifford Dorne, Ph.D., Associate Professor
Department of Criminal Justice
University of Southwestern Louisiana at Lafayette

Kenneth Gewerth, Ph.D., Professor
Department of Criminal Justice
Saginaw Valley State University
University Center, Michigan

ACKNOWLEDGMENTS

My work on this casebook began when I was a Department Chair at Texas A&M International University at Laredo. At this institution, many faculty members encouraged my work in juvenile justice as I researched and edited the cases for this book. Most notably, Professors Faridoun Farrokh, Patricia Manning, Gary Woods, and Nasser Momayezi were influential. Secretary Jane Sample was helpful as I did the original legal research. Moreover, Lucinda Farrokh and Bill Wisner, both of Laredo Community College provided much encouragement during my tenure in Laredo.

At the University of Southwestern Louisiana, my faculty colleagues in The Department of Criminal Justice urged me (and Ken Gewerth) to edit down the original edition from 1226 pages to this much shorter, abridged undergraduate volume. I thank Professors Michael Neustrom, Chris De Lay, Burk Foster, Paula Broussard, and secretary Billy Ault. They informally reviewed the original edition and also reported undergraduate student feedback to me. I also acknowledge the positive influence rendered by Professors Sunil Ahuja and Bryan-Paul Frost, both of the USL Political Science Department.

Ken and I greatly appreciate the strong secretarial support of Saun Strobel of Saginaw Valley State University for the extensive word processing and for helping us meet our publishing deadline. We also thank Dr. Robert West of Austin and Winfield Publishers for working with us towards the publication of this edition.

I thank my own family, parents Renee and Joel and brother Curtis, for their love and encouragement. I also thank my "local family" (in-laws) here in Louisiana: James ("Mitch"), Anita, and nephew David Mitchell for inspiring my work. My wife Juanita has provided powerful and consistent encouragement for my academic work and I will always be grateful to her.

C.K.D.

To begin with, we must acknowledge the tremendous intellectual debt we owe to H. Ted Rubin, Joseph Senna and Larry Siegel, John Whitehead, and Steven Lab. Their previous works on juvenile justice served as important case finding tools for us during our research for the present work.

This is the second huge project that I have undertaken while a member of the faculty at SVSU, and both have required the extraordinary assistance of a number of people who surely had no idea what they were getting into when they agreed to help. Yet, even after the enormity of the project became apparent, they dug right in and worked hard to get the job done, efficiently and with a tremendous amount of good cheer. Consequently, it with a great deal of thanks that I note the contributions of Saun Strobel, Linda Peterson, Nancy Rood, Darlene

Rademacher, Lorraine Kranz, Susan Welke, Valerie Taylor, Sue Schmidt, Kelly McCabe, Jennifer McKenna, Maria McCormack, Kristin Young, and Rebecca Kuiper. This work couldn't have been done without their efforts. Cliff and I are in their debt, and I'm sure that they will spend many hours over the next few years figuring out countless ways for us to pay them back.

K.E.G.

Chapter 1

The Historical Origins of the Juvenile Court

THE HISTORICAL ORIGINS OF THE JUVENILE COURT

INTRODUCTION

As human beings living in society, we exist in the midst of a complex web of interlocking organizations—both formal and informal—which act to guide, channel or constrain our behavior. As infants and children, we learn the basic rules of behavior from that most intimate of organizations, the family. Later, another set of organizations, schools and universities, teach us additional rules of behavior, and provide us with an organized body of knowledge that we will need for our survival. As we grow, we encounter in one way or another, a wide variety of other groups—churches, clubs, our place of employment, to name just a few—that teach us additional rules of behavior. For most of us, this process—known as socialization—takes hold quite nicely, and we live peacefully and productively. And, while it is true that most of us will break one of the rules that we have learned now and then, these lapses in our behavior tend to be isolated incidents, of relatively minor significance, without any long lasting impact on ourselves or others.

With some individuals, however, the socialization process does not seem to take hold as effectively. As a result, some people have difficulty conforming to the rules of society.[1]

When these rule violators are children, or when families are unable to adequately care for their children, a group of agencies (collectively known as the juvenile justice system) may be called upon to intervene, and somehow attempt to remedy the situation. Since the interventions of the juvenile justice system are backed by the coercive force of the law to compel behavior and its power to effect deprivations of liberty, the first step in understanding the operations of the juvenile justice system requires an examination of the legal mechanisms which guide the operations of this system.

---

[1]A detailed discussion of the factors which may cause this breakdown in the socialization process, is, of course, beyond the scope of this work. Here it is sufficient to note that the various academic disciplines explain defects in the socialization process in different ways. In some disciplines (*e.g.*, biology and psychology) the breakdown occurs because of factors located inside the person (for a more detailed discussion of these factors see, generally, Toch (ed.), *Psychology of Crime and Criminal Justice*, (New York: Holt, Reinhart and Winston, 1979); in other disciplines (*e.g.*, sociology, political science, economics) the breakdown in the socialization process occurs because of factors external to the individual (for a more detailed discussion of these factors, see, generally, Hirschi, *Causes of Delinquency*, (Berkeley, California: University of California Press, 1969); Nettler, *Explaining Crime* (3rd ed.), (New York: McGraw-Hill, Inc., 1984); Williams III and McShane, *Criminological Theory* (2d ed.), (New Jersey: Prentice Hall, 1994)).

Consequently, a thorough understanding of how the system operates requires that the laws, rules and procedures enforced by the juvenile justice agencies be examined in the context of much larger intellectual, social and historical forces. A few of the forces which triggered the establishment of the juvenile court, and shaped its early work, will be discussed below.

THE CLASSICAL MODEL OF HUMAN NATURE AND THE COMMON LAW STATUS OF CHILDREN

A. The Classical Model of Human Nature

One of the fundamental tasks of our legal system is to authoritatively express value judgments about a person's actions: in criminal cases, a defendant is found guilty or innocent of a criminal act; in civil cases, a defendant's behavior is judged to be wrongful, or it is vindicated. Under our system of laws, however, the motivations and intentions underlying a person's action are considered highly relevant to the question of whether those actions are wrongful or criminal. Thus, since the law must judge human intentions, it must make some assumptions about the nature of human beings and the ways they behave. Traditionally, the legal system has adopted the "classical" view of human nature.

In the classical view, human behavior was first and foremost, the product of *free will*. Supplanting earlier notions that human actions were predestined in accordance with some divine plan, the classical view suggested that people had the power to choose one course of action over another, to decide between right and wrong. Second, classical scholars argued that human beings were *rational*—they calculated the costs and benefits of a particular action, and behaved in the manner yielding the greatest personal benefit. The third element of the classical model of human nature was the notion that human beings had *a natural tendency to seek pleasure and avoid pain*.

Of course, the classical model of human nature applied to criminals as well. With free will like everyone else, they too were rational beings whose calculation of costs and benefits resulted in their decision to break the law. Beyond this, no further investigation of the causes of an individual's criminal behavior was necessary.

B. The Status of Children at Common Law

Tied as it was to the classical model of human nature, and therefore blind to the background and personal characteristics of the offender, it is not surprising that under the common law of England and pre-Revolutionary America, childhood was not recognized as special status before the law. Parents, beginning with the father, and then at his death, the mother, had a more or less absolute right to the custody of their child, regardless of the effect that this custody had on the child's welfare. ...to discipline children, and this included the right to inflict harsh corporal punishment. Since this right was apparently derived from a number of Biblical injunctions ("spare the rod, and spoil the child," *etc.*), courts rarely interferred.[2]

Nor did age afford special protection when a child was accused of a crime. Except for the principle that a child under the age of seven could not be held criminally responsible (a rule that apparently developed in Ancient Rome, and was carried over to the common law[3]), children were—at least theoretically—subject to the same courtroom procedures and criminal penalties as adults. Further, upon conviction, little or no attempt was made to separate juveniles from adults during incarceration in jails and prisons. Thus, the criminal law's continuing failure to adequately distinguish between children and adult offenders, both at trial and after conviction, led to the recognition that a special effort was necessary to deal with children who were neglected or misbehaved. To try and solve the problem, small groups of conservative, well-to-do reformers[4] in New York, Philadelphia and Boston established a new type of social institution known as the House of Refuge, in the early part of the nineteenth century.

EARLY NINETEENTH CENTURY DEVELOPMENTS: THE HOUSE OF REFUGE MOVEMENT

A. The House of Refuge as an Alternative Form of Confinement for Juveniles

The reformers' concern over the law's failure to separate adults and children during periods of confinement stemmed from their belief that, housed together, the bad habits and criminal tendencies of adults would be passed down to the children, thereby perpetuating the crime problem. Reformers also felt that with mixed confinement, public respect for, and confidence in the law was lessened. With no alternative to harsh jail or prison confinement for young offenders, juries and criminal justice officials were inclined to emotional, overly sympathetic responses to the juvenile's plight, which often caused them to overlook juvenile misdeeds or render unjustified not guilty verdicts.[5]

---

[2]McCarthy and Carr, *Juvenile Law and Its Processes*, 17-20 (Indianapolis: Bobbs-Merrill, 1980), *as cited in* Hahn, *The Juvenile Offender and the Law* (3rd ed.), 3 (Cincinnati: Anderson Publishing Co., 1984).

[3]Champion, *The Juvenile Justice System: Delinquency, Processing and the Law*, 7 (New York: MacMillan Publishing Co., 1992). For an account of how one jurisdiction is currently grappling with a difficult case involving the criminal responsiblity of a very young child, see, Bounds, "Can a 3-Year-Old Murder? Is the Court a Place to Decide?" *Wall Street Journal*, March 3, 1994, at A-1.

[4]As Mennel points out, the philanthropists behind the House of Refuge Movement were deeply religious people who felt they had a moral obligation as God's Elect to provide help to the misfortunate. Mennel, *Thorns and Thistles: Juvenile Delinquents in the U.S., 1825-1940*, 5 (Hanover: University Press of New England, 1973).

[5]Schlossman, *Love and the American Delinquent: The Theory and Practice of "Progressive" Juvenile Justice, 1825-1920*, 24 (Chicago: University of Chicago Press, 1977).

A new kind of institution, the House of Refuge, was intended to protect youth from the bad influences of adult offenders, and provide a place where youths would experience firm but fair discipline and receive an education.

However, Houses of Refuge quickly became not only a place to confine delinquents, but also a dumping ground for children who were impoverished, abused, neglected or simply beyond the control of their parents.

From the work of Mennel,[6] Rothman,[7] and others,[8] it is clear that, in operation, Houses of Refuge were much more like prisons than schools. Believing that an orderly existence was the key to well behaved children, Refuge officials tightly structured the childrens' daily activities into monotonous routine, broken only slightly on Sundays and holidays such as New Year's Day. In the New York House of Refuge, for example, the youths were typically awakened at sunrise, attended school briefly, and then worked in a variety of different workshops (menial labor) until five p.m. Following dinner, they studied until eight p.m., attended a brief prayer service and went to bed. Strict regimentation of behavior was also obtained through the use of military drill.

Refuge managers also believed that it was critical to impart a strong work ethic in children to insure their development into law abiding adults. To teach their charges the value of work, Refuge officials, like their counterparts in adult institutions, established contract labor and apprenticeship systems. Under the contract labor system, manufacturers of shoes, clothing and other items set up workshops on Refuge grounds; the goods children helped manufacture were then sold on the open market.

Under the apprenticeship system, children were sent to work on farms, sailing ships, or with skilled craftsmen in the area. The manifest goal of the apprenticeship system was to teach youths a trade that would allow them to live independent, law abiding lives, a goal which, in practice, was frequently unmet.[9] However, since Refuge officals could refuse to tell a parent the whereabouts of an apprenticed child, the apprenticeship system served the latent function of permanently severing children's relationships with their "unfit" parents, thereby extending the state's power over the lower class.[10]

---

[6]Mennel, *supra*.

[7]Rothman, *The Discovery of the Asylum: Social Order and Disorder in the New Republic*, (Boston: Little, Brown and Co., 1971, rev. ed. 1990); Rothman, *Conscience and Convenience: The Asylum and Its Alternatives in Progressive America*, (Boston: Little, Brown and Co., 1980).

[8]Schlossman, *supra*.

[9]Mennel, *supra*.

[10]Mennel, *supra*.

Despite the regimentation and brutality of Refuge confinement, proponents were quick to judge the institutions a success. Tocqueville and Beaumont, with benevolent understatement, said that children held in the Refuges were "merely deprived of fatal liberty,"[11] while Dorthea Dix called the institution she toured, "a blessing to its inmates and to society."[12]

The sanguine sentiments of Tocqueville and Beaumont and Dix were not shared by all, however. Anguished parents wrote to Refuge officials begging for the release of their children,[13] others turned to the law to try and force state appellate courts to justify the continued confinement of their children.

B. Court Challenges to the House of Refuge Movement

1. *Habeas Corpus Petitions*: Direct Challenges to the Confinement of Children

Faced with a legal challenge to the confinement of a child, most appellate courts relied on ancient English legal doctrine called *parens patriæ*, to affirm the state's power to establish Refuges and hold children in them. A few, however, found Refuge confinement in the absence of criminal behavior to be unconstitutional. The cases exerpted below illustrate both sides of this debate.

EX PARTE CROUSE.

* * *

This was a habeas corpus directed to the keeper and manager of the "House of Refuge," in the county of Philadelphia, requiring them to produce before the court one Mary Ann Crouse, an infant, detained in that institution. The petition for the habeas corpus was in the name of her father.

By the return to the writ it appeared, that the girl had been committed to the custody of the managers by virtue of a warrant...which recited that complaint and due proof had been made before him by Mary Crouse, the mother of the said Mary Ann Crouse, "that the said infant by reason of vicious conduct, has rendered her control beyond the power of the said complainant, and made it manifestly requisite that from regard to the moral and future welfare of the said infant she should be placed under the guardianship of the managers of the House of Refuge;" * * *

The House of Refuge was established by an Act of Assembly passed in March 1826. The sixth section of that act declared that the managers should, "at their discretion, receive into the said House of Refuge, such children who shall be taken up or committed as vagrants, or upon any criminal charge, or duly

[11]Beaumont and de Toqueville, *On the Penitentiary System in the United States*, trans. Francis Leiber, 115 (Philadelphia, 1833), *as cited in* Mennel, *supra*.

[12]Dix, *Remarks on Prison and Prison Discipline* (2d ed.), 94 (Philadelphia, 1845), as cited in Mennel, *supra*.

[13]Mennel, *supra*.

convicted of criminal offences." By a supplement to the act passed on the 10th day of April 1835, it was declared, that in lieu of the provisions of the act of 1826, it should be lawful for the managers of the House of Refuge "at their discretion, to receive into their care and guardianship, infants, males under the age of twenty-one years, and females under the age of eighteen years committed to their custody in either of the following modes, viz First: Infants committed by an alderman or justice of the peace on the complaint and due proof made to him by the parent, guardian or next friend of such infant, that by reason of incorrigible or vicious conduct such infant has rendered his or her control beyond the power of such parent, guardian or next friend, and made in manifestly requisite that from regard for the morals and future welfare of such infant, he or she should be placed under the guardianship of the managers of the House of Refuge. Second: Infants committed by the authority aforesaid, where complaint and due proof have been made that such infant is a proper subject of the guardianship of the managers of the House of Refuge, in consequence of vagrancy, or of incorrigible or vicious conduct, and that from the moral depravity or otherwise of the parent or next friend in whose custody such infant may be, such parent or next friend is incapable or unwilling to exercise the proper care and discipline over such incorrigible or vicious infant. Third: Infants committed by the courts of this Commonwealth in the mode provided by the act to which this is a supplement."

Mr. *W.L. Hirst*, for the petitioner, now contended, that these provisions, so far as they authorized the committal and detention of an infant without a trial by jury, were unconstitutional.

PER CURIAM.—The House of Refuge is not a prison, but a school. Where reformation, and not punishment, is the end, it may indeed be used as a prison for juvenile convicts who would else be committed to a common goal; and in respect to these, the constitutionality of the act which incorporated it, stands clear of controversy. It is only in respect of the application of its discipline to subjects admitted on the order of the court, a magistrate or the managers of the Almshouse, that a doubt is entertained. The object of the charity is reformation, by training its inmates to industry; by imbuing their minds with principles of morality and religion; by furnishing them with means to earn a living; and, above all, by separating them from the corrupting influence of improper associates. To this end may not the natural parents, when unequal to the task of education, or unworthy of it, be superseded by the *parens patriæ*, or common guardian of the community? It is to be remembered that the public has a paramount interest in the virtue and knowledge of its members, and that of strict right, the business of education belongs to it. That parents are ordinarily entrusted with it is because it can seldom be put into better hands; but where they are incompetent or corrupt, what is there to prevent the public from withdrawing their faculties, held, as they obviously are, at its sufferance? The right of parental control is a natural, but not an unalienable one. It is not excepted by the declaration of rights out of the subjects of ordinary legislation; and it consequently remains subject to the ordinary legislative power which, if wantonly or inconveniently used, would soon be constitutionally restricted, but the competency of which, as the government is constituted, cannot be doubted. As to abridgment of indefeasible rights by confinement of the person, it is no more than what is borne, to a greater or less extent, in every school; and we know of no natural right to exemption from restraints which conduce to an infant's welfare. Nor is there a doubt of the propriety of their application in the particular instance. The infant has been snatched from a course which must have ended in confirmed depravity; and, not only is the restraint of her person lawful, but it would be an act of extreme cruelty to release her from it.

REMANDED.

COMMONWEALTH V. FISHER, APPELLANT.

* * *

OPINION BY MR. JUSTICE BROWN, October 9, 1905:

In a proceeding conducted in the court of quarter sessions, Frank Fisher, the appellant, was committed by that court to the House of Refuge. The constitutionality of the act of 1903 was the sole question before the court in that case, and is renewed here. The objections of the appellant to the constitutionality of the act, as presented by counsel, are: *(a)* Under its provisions the defendant was not taken into court by due process of law; *(b)* he was denied his right of trial before a jury on the charge of the felony for which he had been arrested; *(c)* the tribunal before which he appeared and which heard the case and committed him to the house of refuge was an unconstitutional body and without jurisdiction; *(d)* the act provides different punishments for the same offense by a classification of individuals according to age; *(e)* the act contains more subjects than one, some of which are not expressed in the title. In considering these objections the order in which they are made will not be followed.

The act is entitled: "An act defining the powers of the several courts of quarter sessions of the peace, within this commonwealth, with reference to the care, treatment and control of dependent, neglected, incorrigible and delinquent children, under the age of sixteen years, and providing for the means in which such power may be exercised." By this title notice of the purpose of the act is distinctly given. It is a single one. It is to define what powers the state, as the general guardian of all of its children, commits to the several courts of quarter sessions in exercising special guardianship over children under the age of sixteen years needing the substitution of its guardianship for that of parents or others. This purpose is expressed in the title in as few words as are consistent with clearness. No one from reading the title can possibly misunderstand the purpose of the act that follows, and, Art. III, sec. 3, of the constitution is not offended, if, in passing to the body of the act, nothing is there found but this one single purpose. After defining the powers of the court the act proceeds to direct how they are to be exercised in giving effect to its purpose. Nothing in the first nine sections can be read as relating or germane to any other purpose than the one named; and there can be no surer test than this of compliance with the constitutional requirement of the singleness of purpose of an act of assembly.

The objection that "the act offends against a constitutional provision in creating, by its terms, different punishments for the same offense by a classification of individuals," overlooks the fact, hereafter to be noticed, that it is not for the punishment of offenders, but for the salvation of children, and points out the way by which the state undertakes to save, not particular children of a special class, but all children under a certain age, whose salvation may become the duty of the state in the absence of proper parental care or disregard of it by wayward children. No child under the age of sixteen years is excluded from its beneficent provisions. Its protecting arm is for all who have not attained that age and who may need its protection. It is for all children of the same class. That minors may be classified for their best interests and the public welfare, has never been questioned in the legislation relating to them. Under the act of 1887, the classification of females under sixteen years of age means felonious rape, with its severe penalties for what may be done one day, though on the next it remains simple fornication, to be expiated by a mere fine. Other acts forbid the employment of minors under twelve years of age in mills; of any boy under fourteen or any female in anthracite coal mines; of minors under fourteen in and about elevators; of a boy under twelve or any female in bituminous coal mines; others make it a misdemeanor to furnish intoxicating drinks, by sale, gift or otherwise, to one under twenty-one, and forbid the admission of any minor into certain places of amusement. Such classification is not prohibited by the constitution, and what has not been therein prohibited the legislature may enact.

No new court is created by the act under consideration. In its title it is called an act to define the powers of an already existing and ancient court. In caring for the neglected or unfortunate children of the commonwealth, and in defining the powers to be exercised by that court in connection with these children, recognized by the state as its wards requiring its care and protection, jurisdiction is conferred upon that court as the appropriate one, and not upon a new one created by the act. The court of quarter sessions is not simply a criminal court. Its existence antedates our colonial times, and, by the common law and statutes, both here and in England, it has for generations been a court of broad general police powers in no way connected with its criminal jurisdiction. Innumerable statutes upon our own books during the last two centuries attest this. With its jurisdiction unrestricted by the constitution, it is for the legislature to declare what shall be exercised by it as a general police court, and instead of creating a distinctively new court, the act of 1903 does nothing more than confer additional powers upon the old court and clearly define them. It might as well be said that the court of quarter sessions is not a court of quarter sessions, because it keeps a separate road docket, or, for convenience, a separate docket for desertion cases, or appoints days in which it will hear a certain class of cases, or as it is said in popular parlance, will hold a 'license court.' In the latter class of cases, where there is more than one court of common pleas within a county, it is usual for the courts themselves to designate the judges who shall hold what is known as the license court. It has never been claimed, so far as we know—certainly not successfully claimed—that such designation was in any sense unconstitutional or that, because of the designation, a separate court was created. It is no more so in the case under consideration than in any of the cases spoken of above." It is a mere convenient designation of the court of quarter sessions to call it, when caring for children, a juvenile court, but no such court, as an independent tribunal, is created.

In pressing the objection that the appellant was not taken into custody by due process of law, the assumption, running through the entire argument of the appellant, is continued, that the proceedings of the act of 1903 are of a criminal nature for the punishment of offenders for crimes committed, and that the appellant was so punished. But he was not, and he could not have been without due process of law, for the constitutional guaranty is that no one charged with a criminal offense shall be deprived of life, liberty or property without due process of law. To save a child from becoming a criminal, or from continuing in a career of crime, to end in maturer years in public punishment and disgrace, the legislature surely may provide for the salvation of such a child, if its parents or guardian be unable or unwilling to do so, by bringing it into one of the courts of the state without any process at all, for the purpose of subjecting it to the state's guardianship and protection. The natural parent needs no process to temporarily deprive his child of its liberty by confining it in his own home, to save it and to shield it from the consequences of persistence in a career of waywardness, nor is the state, when compelled, as parens patriæ, to take the place of the father for the same purpose, required to adopt any process as a means of placing its hands upon the child to lead it into one of its courts. When the child gets there and the court, with the power to save it, determines on its salvation, and not its punishment, it is immaterial how it got there. The act simply provides how children who ought to be saved may reach the court to be saved. If experience should show that there ought to be other ways for it to get there, the legislature can, and undoubtedly will, adopt them, and they will never be regarded as undue processes for depriving a child of its liberty or property as a penalty for crime committed.

The last reason to be noticed why the act should be declared unconstitutional is that it denies the appellant a trial by jury. Here again is the fallacy, that he was tried by the court for any offense. "The right of trial by jury shall remain inviolate," are the words of the bill of rights, and no act of the legislature can deny this right to any citizen, young or old, minor or adult, if he is to be tried for a crime against the commonwealth. But there was no trial for any crime here, and the act is operative only when there is to be no trial. The very purpose of the act is to prevent a trial, though, if the welfare of the public require that the minor should be tried, power to try it is not taken away from the court of quarter sessions, for the eleventh section expressly provides that nothing in the preceding sections "shall be in derogation of the powers of the courts of quarter sessions and oyer and terminer to try, upon an indictment, any delinquent child, who, in due course, may be brought to trial." This section was entirely unnecessary, for without it a delinquent child can be tried only by a jury for a crime charged; but, as already stated, the act is not for the trial of a child charged with a crime, but is mercifully to save it from such an ordeal, with the prison or penitentiary in its wake, if the child's own good and the best interests of the state justify such salvation. Whether the child deserves to be saved by the state is no more a question for a jury that whether the father, if able to save it, ought to save it. If the latter ought to save, but is powerless to do so, the former, by the act of 1903, undertakes the duty, and the legislature, in directing how that duty is to be performed in a proper case, denies the child no right of a trial by a jury, for the simple reason that, by the act, it is not to be tried for anything. The act is but an exercise by the state of its supreme power over the welfare of its children, a power under which it can take a child from its father, and let it go where it will, without committing it to any guardianship or any institution, if the welfare of the child, taking its age into consideration, can be thus best promoted.

* * *

"* * * There is no restraint upon the natural liberty of children contemplated by such a law,—none whatever; but rather the placing of them under the natural restraint, so far as practicable, that should be, but is not, exercised by parental authority. It is the mere conferring upon them that protection to which, under the circumstances, they are entitled as a matter of right. It is for their welfare and that of the community at large. The design is not punishment, nor the restraint imprisonment, any more than is the wholesome restraint which a parent exercises over his child. The severity in either case must necessarily be tempered to meet the necessities of the particular situation. There is no probability, in the proper administration of the law, of the child's liberty being unduly invaded. Every statute which is designed to give protection, care and training to children, as a needed substitute for parental authority and performance of parental duty, is but a recognition of the duty of the state, as the legitimate guardian and protector of children where other guardianship fails. No constitutional right is violated, but one of the most important duties which organized society owes to its helpless members is performed just in the measure that the law is framed with wisdom and is carefully administer."

None of the objections urged against the constitutionality of the act can prevail. The assignments of error are, therefore, all overruled and the order of the Superior Court, affirming the commitment below, is affirmed.

COMMONWEALTH V. FISHER

1. What was the logic of Justice Brown with respect to the denial of jury trial in the court of quarter sessions presiding as a juvenile court? Compare this reasoning with the McKiever case (in Chapter 4).

2. Critique Justice Brown's 1905 opinion from the perspective of the 1974 Juvenile Court Act, labeling theory, libertarian ideology, and from a strict due process perspective.

3. In sociologist Erving Goffman's famous book, *Asylum*, the perils of "total institutions" are examined. The student is referred to this work as an important and relevant reference in the study of corrections. Critique the outcome of the *Fisher* case taking into account the negative aspects of total institutions.

4. Systematically compare the principles of law and the holdings of the *Crouse* and *Fisher* cases.

MID-NINETEENTH CENTURY CHANGES: THE FAILURE OF THE HOUSES OF REFUGE, THE RISE OF DETERMINISM, PSYCHIATRY AND THE INVENTION OF CHILDHOOD

A. The Decline of the House of Refuge Movement

However misapplied the doctrine of *parens patriæ* was, the decisions in *Crouse* and *Fisher* were sufficient to forestall serious challenges to the confinement of juveniles, at least for a while. Most courts, swayed by the benevolent and protective language of these cases, used them as precedent to sanction the Refuge confinement of children. The period from 1850–1870 was marked by a gradually increasing criticism of the abusive conditions and prisonlike atmosphere in the Houses of Refuge.[14] Eventually, these criticisms could no longer be ignored.

B. Determinism: External Forces as Causes of Human Behavior

Besides the failure of the House of Refuge Movement, three other intellectual developments gave additional force to the movement to establish a separate juvenile court. The first was the rise of determinism as an alternative model for understanding human behavior; the second was the development psychiatry; and the third was the notion that the period from childhood through adolescence was a unique phase of human development. The growth of these ideas lent scientific credence to the juvenile court reform movement, increasing its credibility.

As an alternative to the classical, free will model of human nature, the deterministic view posited that human behavior was the product of hereditary or environmental forces over which the individual had little or no control. The origins of determinism can be traced back to Darwin's theory of evolution. According to Darwin, animal species (including humans) that existed in the present were more complex and better adapted than variations of species that had existed in the past. Although Darwin was primarily concerned with explaining the anatomical changes that occurred in a species over time, it was not long before those inspired by his work began to use it to explain not only human anatomy, but human behavior as well.

One person strongly influenced by Darwin's theory was an Italian criminologist named Cesare Lombroso. It was his belief that about one third of all criminals were biological regressions or "throwbacks" to an earlier, more primitive evolutionary stage.[15] In addition to these "born criminals"

---

[14]Empey, *The Progressive Legacy and the Concept of Childhood*, 26 in Empey (ed.) *Juvenile Justice: Progressive Legacy and Current Reforms*, (Charlottesville: University Press of Virginia, 1979).

[15]Lombroso-Ferrero, *Criminal Man, According to the Classification of Cesare Lombroso*, (New York: G.P. Putnam's Sons, 1911) *as cited in* Jacoby, *Classics of Criminology*, 76 (Prospect Heights, Illinois: Waveland Press, 1988).

another third of the criminal population was composed of minor offenders called "criminaloids" and finally, a group of "occasional and habitual offenders."[16]

Lombroso contended that the born criminal's link to more primitive biological species was evident in the offender's anatomy. Like "carnivores and savages," born criminals possessed "enormous jaws, strong canines, prominent zygomae and strongly developed orbital arches," as well as a number of apelike characteristics such as a scanty beard, excessive body hair, prehensile feet, unlined palms of the hands, cheek pouches, large middle incisors, flattened noses, angular shaped skulls, large eyes, and hooked noses, among others.[17] Subsequent revisions of Lombroso's theory[18] implicated a number of environmental factors such as poverty as well as biological factors as external, deterministic causes of crime.

The rise of determinism had profound implications for the nascent system of juvenile justice. By implicating factors external to the individual as causes of human behavior, such as poverty or a poor home environment, determinism cast doubt on the notions of free will and the individual's ability to choose between right and wrong, and, by extension, the legitimacy of the state's power to blame people and punish them for their wrongful choices. Implicitly, at the very least, determinism called into question both the criminal law's basic assumption about human nature, and its policy of not distinguishing between children and adults; it also put the weight of science behind the efforts of those seeking to create the juvenile court.

C. The Development of Psychiatry

Around the turn of the century, just as the juvenile court movement was gaining strength, psychiatry was developing as a distinct intellectual discipline. As a field of study, its focus was on how peoples' internal mental states and emotions influenced their behavior. In general, psychiatric theories took a very individualistic view of human behavior: each person was unique, and no two people behaved in exactly the same way for precisely the same reasons. As a result, in order to understand human behavior, and help people to change, one had to observe closely each individual case, and prescribe a unique treatment for each person's problems.

This new, and scientific view of human behavior quickly found favor among juvenile court advocates. The emphasis on individualized treatment of problem youth set the stage for the juvenile court's case by case approach for dealing with youthful misconduct.

---

[16]*Id.*

[17]*Id.*

[18]Ferri, *Criminal Sociology*, (Boston: Little, Brown, 1917).

D. The Invention of Childhood

The third intellectual force that helped to trigger the creation of the juvenile court was a growing popular interest in child development and the emergence of a child study movement within the academic community at the turn of the century.

Among those in the child study movement, children were viewed as fundamentally innocent.[19] However, as it developed, this concept of innocence could have two interpretations, negative or positive. Viewed negatively, as some did, innocence was seen as "a lack of responsibility for a particular act or event"[20] Children were innocent—*i.e.*, they could not be held responsible for their bad acts—because their faults and bad acts were an unavoidable part of the growth process. In this view, before children could reach a socialized state, it was necessary that they individually pass through various stages of development that mirrored the evolutionary development of the human species as a whole. The amoral acts of children, then, simply meant that they were reflecting a developmental state of amoral primitive humans, that would pass with time.

Others viewed childhood innocence more positively, as a time of pureness and goodness and guilelessness. Here, the bad acts of children were the result, not of amorality, but of true ignorance of the rules of behavior, which could be easily overcome since children had both an innate sense of "the great principles of right and wrong" and an "innate willingness to submit to authority.". Properly nurtured and developed, these naturally good tendencies would foster an upstanding, law abiding adult. Proper nurturance and development, of course, meant the benevolent, nonpunitive, helping approach of the juvenile court.[21]

THE CREATION OF THE JUVENILE COURT

Massachusetts, Colorado and Illinois can all lay claim to the establishment of the nation's first juvenile court, in one fashion or another. From 1869 to 1877, Massachusetts enacted a series of laws creating a rudimentary system of juvenile probation. Under these provisions, personnel from the State Board of Charities were authorized to conduct investigations in juvenile cases, recommend dispositions to the judge, and visit homes where delinquent children had been "placed out" in an early version of foster care. There were also separate hearings, dockets, and records of juvenile cases.[22] Later, in 1899, Colorado's Compulsory School Act,

---

[19]Rothman, *supra*.

[20]*Id*.

[21]Rothman, *supra*.

[22]Rothman, *supra*; Hahn, *supra*; McCarthy and Carr, *supra*.

> "[a]lthough...primarily targeted at youths who were habitually absent from school,...also encompassed juveniles who wandered the streets during school hours without any obvious business or occupation. These youths were termed 'juvenile disorderly persons' and they were legislatively placed within the purview of truant officers and law enforcement officers who could detain them and hold them for further action by other community agencies."[23]

The state of Illinois, however, is typically credited with the establishment of the nation's first juvenile court. An excert from the legislation authorizing the creation of the juvenile court is presented below.

1899 ILLINOIS JUVENILE COURT ACT

JUVENILE COURTS.

FOR DEPENDENT, NEGLECTED AND DELINQUENT CHILDREN.

AN ACT *to regulate the treatment and control of dependent, neglected and delinquent children.*

SECTION 1. *Be it enacted by the People of the State of Illinois, represented in the General Assembly:* DEFINITIONS.] This act shall apply only to children under the age of 16 years not now or hereafter inmates of a State institution, or any training school for boys or industrial school for girls or some institution incorporated under the laws of this State, except as provided in sections twelve (12) and eighteen (18). For the purposes of this act the words dependent child and neglected child shall mean any child who for any reason is destitute or homeless or abandoned; or dependent upon the public for support; or has not proper parental care or guardianship; or who habitually begs or receives alms; or who is found living in any house of ill fame or with any vicious or disreputable person; or whose home, by reason of neglect, cruelty or depravity on the part of its parents, guardian or other person in whose care it may be, is an unfit place for such a child; and any child under the age of 8 years who is found peddling or selling any articles or singing or playing any musical instrument upon the streets or giving any public entertainment. The words delinquent child shall include any child under the age of 15 years who violates any law of this State or any city or village ordinance. The word child or children may mean one or more children, and the word parent or parents may be held to mean one or both parents, when consistent with the intent of this act. The word association shall include any corporation which includes in its purposes the care of disposition of children coming within the meaning of this act.

§ 2. JURISDICTION.] The circuit and county courts of the several counties in this State shall have original jurisdiction in all cases coming within the terms of this act. In all trials under this act any person interested therein may demand a jury of six, or the judge of his own motion may order a jury of the same number, to try the case.

§ 3. JUVENILE COURT.] In counties having over 500,000 populations the judges of the circuit court shall, at such times as they shall determine, designate one or more of their number whose duty it shall be

[23]Champion, *supra*.

to hear all cases coming under this act. A special court room, to be designated as the juvenile court room, shall be provided for the hearing of such cases, and the findings of the court shall be entered in a book or books to be kept for that purpose and known as the "Juvenile Record," and the court may, for convenience, be called the "Juvenile Court."

§ 4. PETITION TO THE COURT.] Any reputable person, being resident in the county, having knowledge of a child in his county who appears to be either neglected, dependent or delinquent, may files with the clerk of a court having jurisdiction in the matter a petition in writing, setting forth the facts, verified by affidavit. It shall be sufficient that the affidavit is upon information and belief.

§ 5. SUMMONS.] Upon the filing of the petition a summons shall issue requiring the person having custody or control of the child, or with whom the child may be, to appear with the child at a place and time stated in the summons, which time shall be not less than 24 hours after service. The parents of the child, if living, and their residence is [if] known, or its legal guardian, if one there be, or if there is neither parent nor guardian, or if his or her residence is not known, then some relative, if there be one and his residence is known, shall be notified of the proceedings, and in any case the judge may appoint some suitable person to act in behalf of the child. If the person summoned as herein provided shall fail, without reasonable cause, to appear and abide the order of the court, or to bring the child, he may be proceeded against as in case of contempt of court. In case the summons can not be served or the party served fails to obey the same, and in any case when it shall be made to appear to the court that such summons will be ineffectual, a warrant may issue on the order of the court, either against the parent or guardian or the person having custody of the child or with whom the child may be, or against the child itself. On there turn of the summons or other process, or as soon thereafter as may be, the court shall proceed to hear and dispose of the case in a summary manner. Pending the final disposition of any case the child may be retained in the possession of the person having the charge of same, or may be kept in some suitable place provided by the city or county authorities.

§ 6. PROBATION OFFICERS.] The court shall have authority to appoint or designate one or more discreet persons of good character to serve as probation officers during the pleasure of the court; said probation officers to receive no compensation from the public treasury. In case a probation officer shall be appointed by any court, it shall be the duty of the clerk of the court, if practicable, to notify the said probation officer in advance when any child is to be brought before the said court; it shall be the duty of the said probation officer to make such investigation as may be required by the court; to be present in court in order to represent the interests of the child when the case is heard; to furnish to the court such information and assistance as the judge may require; and to take such charge of any child before and after trial as may be directed by the court.

§ 7. DEPENDENT AND NEGLECTED CHILDREN.] When any child under the age of sixteen (16) years shall be found to be dependent or neglected within the meaning of this act, the court may make an order committing the child to the care of some suitable State institution, or to the care of some reputable citizen of good moral character, or to the care of some training school or an industrial school, as provided by law, or to the care of some association willing to receive it embracing in its objects the purpose of caring or obtaining homes for dependent or neglected children, which association shall have been accredited as hereinafter provided.

§ 8. GUARDIANSHIP.] In any case where the court shall award a child to the care of any association or individual in accordance with the provisions of this act the child shall, unless otherwise ordered, become a ward and be subject to the guardianship of the association or individual to whose care it is committed. Such association or individual shall have authority to place such child in a family home, with or without indenture, and may be made party to any proceeding for the legal adoption of the child, and may be its or his attorney or agent appear in any court where such proceedings are pending and assent to such adoption. And such assent shall be sufficient to authorize the court to enter the proper order or decree of adoption. Such guardianship shall not include the guardianship of any estate of the child.

§ 9. DISPOSITION OF DELINQUENT CHILDREN.] In the case of a delinquent child the court may continue the hearing from time to time, and may commit the child to the care an guardianship of a probation officer duly appointed by the court, and may allow said child to remain in its own home, subject to the visitation of the probation officer; such child to report to the probation officer as often as may be require and subject to be returned to the court for further proceedings, whenever such action may appear to be necessary; or the court may commit the child to the care and guardianship of the probation officer, to be placed in a suitable family home, subject to the friendly supervision of such probation officer; or it may authorize the said probation officer to board out the said child in some suitable family home, in case provision is made by voluntary contribution or otherwise for the payment of the board of such child, until a suitable provision may be made of the child in a home without such payment; or the court may commit the child, if a boy, to a training school of boys, or if a girl, to an industrial school for girls. Or, if the child is found guilty of any criminal offense, and the judge is of the opinion that the best interest requires it, the court may commit the child to any institution within said county incorporated under the laws of this State for the care of delinquent children, or provided by a city for the care of such offenders, or may commit the child, if a boy over the age of ten years, to the State reformatory, or if a girl over the age of ten years, to the State Home for Juvenile Female Offenders. In no case shall a child be committed beyond his or her minority. A child committed to such institution shall be subject to the control of the board of manager thereof, and the said board shall have power to parole such child on such conditions as it may prescribe, and the court shall, on the recommendation f the board, have power to discharge such child from custody whenever in the judgment of the court his or her reformation shall be complete; or the court may commit the child to the care and custody of some association that will receive it embracing in its objects the care of neglected and dependent children and that has been duly accredited as hereinafter provided.

§ 10. TRANSFER FROM JUSTICES AND POLICE MAGISTRATES.] When, in any county where a court is held as provided in section three of this act, a child under the age of 16 years is arrested with or without warrant, such child may, instead of being taken before a justice of the peace or police magistrate, be taken directly before such court; or if the child is taken before a justice of the peace or police magistrate, it shall be the duty of such justice of the peace or police magistrate to transfer the care [case] to such court, and the officer having the child in charge to take such child before that court upon petition as herein provided. In any case the court shall require notice to be given and investigation to be made as in other cases under this act, and may adjourn the hearing from time to time for the purpose.

§ 11. CHILDREN UNDER TWELVE YEARS NOT TO BE COMMITTED TO JAIL.] No court or magistrate shall commit a child under twelve (12) years of age to a jail or police station, but if such child is unable to give bail it may be committed to the care of the sheriff, police officer or probation officer, who shall keep such child in some suitable place provided by the city or county outside of the inclosure of any jail or police station. When any child shall be sentenced to confinement in any institution to which adult convicts are sentenced it shall be unlawful to confine such child in the same building with such adult convicts, or to confine such child in the same yard or inclosure with such adult convicts, or to bring such child into any yard or building in which such adult convicts may be present.

§ 12. AGENTS OF JUVENILE REFORMATORIES.] It shall be the duty of the superintendent of the State Reformatory at Pontiac and the board of managers of the State Home for Juvenile Female Offenders at Geneva, and the board of managers of any other institution to which juvenile delinquents may be committed by the courts, to maintain an agent of such institution for the purpose of ascertaining and reporting to said court whether they are suitable homes; to assist children paroled or discharged from such institution in finding suitable employment, and to maintain a friendly supervision over paroled inmates during the continuance of their parole; such agents shall hold office subject tot he pleasure of the board making the appointment, and shall receive such compensation as such board may determine out of any funds appropriated for such institution applicable thereto.

* * *

§ 15. SURRENDER OF DEPENDENT CHILDREN—ADOPTION.] It shall be lawful for the parents, parent, guardian or other person having the right to dispose of a dependent or neglected child to enter into an agreement with any association or institution incorporated under any public or private law of this State of the purpose of aiding, caring for or placing in homes such children, and being approved as herein provided, for the surrender of such child to such association or institution, to be taken and cared for by such association or institution or put into a family house. Such agreement may contain any and all proper stipulations to that end, and may authorize the association or institution, by its attorney or agent, to appear in any proceeding for the legal adoption of such child, and consent to its adoption, and the order of the court made upon such consent shall be binding upon the child and its parents or guardian or other person the same as if such parents or guardian or other person were personally in court and consenting thereto, whether made party to the proceeding or not.

* * *

§ 17. RELIGIOUS PREFERENCES.] The court in committing children shall place them as far as practicable in the care and custody of some individual holding the same religious belief as the parents of said child, or with some association which is controlled by persons of like religious faith of the parents of the said child.

§ 18. COUNTY BOARDS OF VISITORS.] The county judge of each county may appoint a board of six reputable inhabitants, who will serve without compensation, to constitute a board of visitation, whose duty it shall be to visit as often as once a year all institutions, societies and associations receiving children under this act. Said visits shall be made by not less than two of the members of the board, who shall go together or make a joint report; the said board of visitors shall report to the court from time to time the condition of children received by or in the charge of such associations and institutions, and shall make an annual report to the Board of State Commissioners of Public Charities in such form as the board may prescribe. The county board may, at their discretion, make appropriations for the payment of the actual and necessary expenses incurred by the visitors in the discharge of their official duties.

§ 19. POWERS OF JUVENILE COURT.] The powers and duties herein provided to be exercised by the county court or the judges thereof may, in counties having over 500,000 population, be exercised by the circuit courts and their judges as hereinbefore provided for.

§ 20. INDUSTRIAL AND TRAINING SCHOOLS NOT AFFECTED.] Nothing in this act shall be construed to repeal any portion of the act to aid industrial school[s] for girls, the act to provide for and aid training schools for boys, the act to establish the Illinois State Reformatory or the act to provide for a State Home for Juvenile Female Offenders. And in all commitments to said institutions the acts in reference to said institutions shall govern the same.

§ 21. CONSTRUCTION OF THE ACT.] This act shall be liberally construed, to the end that its purpose may be carried out, to-wit: That the care, custody and discipline of a child shall approximate as nearly as may be that which should be given by its parents, and in all cases where it can properly be done the child be placed in an improved family home and become a member of the family by legal adoption or otherwise.

APPROVED APRIL 21, 1899.

A. The Role of Women's Clubs and Criminal Justice Agencies

Historical accounts by Platt,[24] Fox,[25] Rothman,[26] and others[27] properly credit a number of women's clubs in Chicago with leading the campaign to secure passage of the 1899 Illinois Juvenile Court Act. However, a central disagreement in the historical literature concerns the interpretation of the motives behind the push for the passage of the Juvenile Court Act. The traditional or orthodox view (well described by Rothman, for example) is that motives of the women and the other reformers were benevolent in nature: their only interest was in helping poor and unfortunate children and their families. In contrast, Platt and Fox present a "revisionist" view of juvenile court history in which they argue that the women's groups and other reformers acted out of a profound fear of the largely immigrant lower class families and their children. They pushed for the creation of the juvenile court because it offered a way to control this "dangerous class," and vested the women's efforts to inculcate rural middle class, protestant values in urban immigrant children with the authority of law.

In addition, it is important to note that while the herculean efforts of the women's clubs cannot be denied, the juvenile court legislation was supported by a broad coalition of organizations. Private child caring groups supported the legislation because they felt that the court's authority would allow them to provide help to children even if the parents objected to their efforts to intervene; superintendents of juvenile institutions favored the legislation because they felt that the juvenile court's authority would allow them to take not only delinquent, but also dependent and neglected children, into custody without fear that their decisions would be overruled by judges of other (non-juvenile) courts; police and correctional officials supported the legislation because they recognized the dangers inherent in the mixed confinement of adult and juvenile offenders, and believed that separate facilities for youth operated under the auspices of the juvenile court would prevent the contamination of impressionable young minds with the criminogenic ideas of older offenders, and allow for longer periods of confinement to bring about reform; and, at least one district attorney noted that the creation of the juvenile court would substantially reduce the caseload in his office.[28]

---

[24]Platt, *The Child Savers* (2nd ed.), (Chicago: University of Chicago Press, 1977).

[25]Fox, "Juvenile Justice Reform: An Historic Perspective," 22 *Stanford Law Review* 1187 (1970).

[26]Rothman, *supra*.

[27]Mennel, *supra*.

[28]Rothman, *supra*.

B. The Unique Operation and Structure of the Court

As envisioned by the Progressive era reformers, the day-to-day operations of the new juvenile court were to be fundamentally different then those of the adult criminal court. Suffused with benevolence, cognizant of the significance of envirnomental influences on youthful misconduct (urban vices, *etc.*), and guided by the scientific priniciples of psychiatry, court officials would work to transform wayward children into law abiding adults. To create an environment conducive to change, reformers renamed the various stages of the process, to convey the notion that the juvenile court actions were kinder, gentler, and less judgmental than the corresponding activites in the adult court. Thus, youthful misconduct was not criminal, it was delinquent. Juveniles were not arrested and taken to jail; instead they were taken into custody and detained. Rather than being formally accused of a crime by an indictment, juvenile court action was triggered by a petition. Court proceedings were not public trials, but rather private hearings. The outcome was not a finding of guilt and conviction, but rather a finding or an adjudication of delinquency. There were no sentences to be served as punishment as in adult court; instead the court crafted a disposition to bring about the rehabiltiation of the youth.

These changes in terminology were accompanied by modifications in procedures. For example, following the filing of a petition, but prior to the actual adjudicatory hearing, it was envisioned that probation officers would conduct detailed interviews with youths who had been taken into custody, to identify the root causes of their delinquent behavior and recommend appropriate interventions to treat the underlying problem. The purpose of these interviews were not to uncover evidence of guilt; it was to gather information that would be used to diagnose the youth's problem and form the basis for the court's disposition of the case.

The adjudicatory stages of the process were also radically different than the trial stage in adult court. Rather than formal confrontations between an accused offender and society, governed by strict evidentiary procedures, adjudicatory hearings in juvenile court were designed to be informal and non-adversarial in nature (sometimes referred to as the socialized juvenile court to distinguish it from its more modern constitutionalist or due process counterpart). As a result, various procedural safeguards, such as formal notice of charges, attorney representation of the offender, the confrontation and cross examination of witnesses—traditionally regarded as the cornerstones of a fair trial in adult court—were deemed unnecessary in juvenile court. The fear was that these formal procedures would create a hostile, accusatory and adversarial atmosphere which would impair the court's rehabilitative efforts. Instead, the probation officer (ideally the same one who conducted the preliminary diagnostic interview, and who was, therefore, most familiar with the case) was given the dual task of presenting the case and representing the youth before the court.

The role of the judge was drastically modified as well. Rather than acting as an impartial referee, well versed in both the substantive and procedural aspects of the law who carefully weighed competing versions of the facts and the law before deciding the question of guilt or innocence, the juvenile court judge was to function more like a kindly parent, fair but firm. Friendly, wise and charismatic, it was expected that the judge would, with gentleness, compassion and just the right amount of sternness, counsel the delinquent and then formulate an appropriate disposition in the case.

Reformers were also sensitive to the fact that public knowledge of a juvenile's misconduct might impair the court's rehabilitative efforts. As a consequence, courtroom procedures were modified to protect the juvenile's privacy: the names of juveniles taken into custody were not made public, adjudicatory hearings were closed to journalists and spectators, while juvenile court records were routinely sealed at the conclusion of the case, and inadmissible as evidence in any other court.[29]

At the dispositional stage, the goal was the individualized treatment of the offender. It was expected that probation would serve as the primary dispositional alternative; institutionalization was seen as a last resort to be reserved for only the most intractable delinquents. Like the judge at the adjudicatory hearing, the probation officer was to function as a watchful friend, carefully guiding the youth back into law abiding society.

Here, discussion of the fact that juvenile court remained this way until the 1960s when it adopted a more adversarial approach to adjudication—the constitutionalist or due process approach (see *In re Gault* in Chapter 3).

CONCLUSION

The preceding chapter focused on the historical forces that prompted Progressive era reformers to advocate and eventually persuade lawmakers to create a separate system of justice for children. Each of the chapters that follow will focus on a major processing point within the juvenile justice system, beginning, of course, with the police and their efforts to control juvenile crime.

---

[29]Some jurisdictions are apparently reassessing the need for, and value of juvenile court confidentiality. See Sullivan, "Witman Calls for Less Secrecy Surrounding Juvenile Offenses," *New York Times*, March 18, 1994, at B-5, and Eckholm, "When Does a Young Offender Lose the Right to Privacy?" *New York Times*, March 27, 1994, at D-4.

Chapter 2

The Police and Juvenile Justice

THE POLICE AND JUVENILE JUSTICE

INTRODUCTION

A. Law Enforcement, Order Maintenance and Service—The Nature of the Police Role

Probably no occupation in society is as varied as that of a police officer. Whether hunting for a serial killer, ensuring the smooth flow of traffic at a busy intersection, or providing directions to a confused tourist lost in a downtown metropolitan area, police officers are expected to aid citizens in a wide variety of situations, ranging from the mundane to the life threatening, twenty-four hours a day, seven days a week. Given its complexity, any attempt to describe the nature of police work unavoidably oversimplifies the job. Most generally, however, the police role consists of three basic tasks: law enforcement, order maintenance and the provision of service to those in need.[1] The law enforcement role consists of police efforts to detect and investigate crimes, and apprehend those responsible for committing them. In performing this task, the police conduct investigations in response to the complaints of crime victims, or, working undercover, create situations designed to prompt unwary criminals into committing crimes. The law enforcement task may also involve the interrogation of suspects, the collection of physical evidence at the scene of the crime, and the presentation of that evidence at trial.

The order maintenance role involves the police control of behavior "that either disturbs or threatens to disturb the public peace or [requires the resolution] of face-to-face conflict among two or more persons."[2] Police activities such as dispersing juveniles loitering on a street corner, telling the participants of a loud party to quiet down, or separating opposing factions at a political demonstration fall into the realm of order maintenance.

Finally, police officers fulfill the service function whenever they provide aid or assistance to people in need. Examples of service activities include: calling a tow truck for a stranded motorist, transporting abandoned or neglected children to a hospital or shelter facility, or delivering a baby whose parents didn't quite make it to the hospital on time.

---

[1]See generally, Wilson, *Varieties of Police Behavior: The Management of Law and Order in Eight Communities*, (Massachusetts: Harvard University Press, 1968).

[2]*Id.*.

The above typology of police activities should be regarded as a very general classification scheme, for at least two reasons. First, because it can be used to describe the actions of a single officer or the "style" of an entire department.[3] Second, the typology is general because the dividing line between the three roles can become fuzzy at times; what starts out as one type of activity may take on the character of another as the situation develops, or the resolution of a particular situation may require one or more officers to perform a combination of law enforcement, order maintenance or service functions.[4] For example, while the separation of opposing factions at a political demonstration may begin as an exercise in order maintenance, it may quickly evolve into a law enforcement task if the demonstration turns ugly and arrests become necessary. Similarly, while some officers are transporting a group of abandoned children to a hospital—a service function—others may be directed to locate the parents and initiate a child abuse investigation—a law enforcement function.

It appears that police officers do not undertake these three functions with equal degrees of enthusiasm. In general, officers view the law enforcement function as the primary task of any police agency.

In contrast, the order maintenance and service tasks are typically regarded with mixed feelings ranging from ambivalence to disdain.

Since the law enforcement, order maintenance, and service situations to which police officers must respond can differ on a number of dimensions (*e.g.*, criminal versus non-criminal, urgent versus routine, dangerous versus relatively safe, *etc.*), they are permitted to exercise a great deal of discretion—the ability to choose between different courses of action[5]—in the course of their day-to-day activities.[6] However, as

---

[3]For a discussion of how organizational factors can lead to the development of an organization-wide "style" of policing that emphasizes law enforcement, order maintenance or service, see Wilson, *supra*.

[4]Wilson attempts to distinguish between law enforcement and order maintenance situations by suggesting that the former involve clear violations of the law, which are resolved when the officer makes an arrest or issues a summons. In these situations, says Wilson, the suspect is both guilty and blameworthy. In contrast, order maintenance situations appear to involve less a determination of legal guilt than the identification of who is to blame. Wilson, *supra*.

Wilson's attempt to differentiate the two situations in this way, however, seems to be largely a case of a distinction without a difference. To say someone is to blame for something is to hold them at fault, to judge that they *are guilty*. Thus, it seems unreasonable to use the difference between the concepts of blame and guilt as a basis for classifying law enforcement and order maintenance situations.

[5]Davis, *Discretionary Justice: A Preliminary Inquiry*, 4 (Louisiana: Louisiana State University Press, 1979).

[6]The literature on the use, abuse and control of discretionary decisions in the criminal justice system is vast. Some of the classic references in this area are Davis, *supra*; Goldstein, *Policing A Free Society*, (Massachusetts: Ballinger Publishing); Goldstein, "Police Discretion Not to Invoke the Criminal Justice Process: Low Visibility Decisions in the Administration of Justice," 69 *Yale Law Journal* 543 (1960).

Goldstein[7] and Davis[8] have pointed out, the discretionary authority granted to police officers is unique in at least two respects. First, unlike other organizations, discretion in police organizations tends to flow downward. In traditional bureaucracies, the authority to make discretionary decisions is severely limited at the lowest levels of the organization and increases only at the higher levels of the organizational chart. In police agencies, however the opposite is true—the greatest amount of discretionary authority tends to concentrate at the lowest levels of the organization—in the person of the individual patrol officer.[9] Second, unlike traditional bureaucracies, where the actions of line personnel are subject to close scrutiny and tight control by supervisory staff, the discretionary decisions of police officers on patrol are "low visibility" decisions—typically made out of the sight of command personnel, and therefore frequently beyond their control. As a result of these unique features, much analytical effort has been devoted to examining the nature of police discretion, and developing ways to control it to prevent its abuse. The next section contains a brief description of police discretion as it relates to the various facets of the police role.

B. Law Enforcement, Order Maintenance, Service and Police Discretion

While the amount of discretionary latitude that police officers have available to them in any particular situation depends on a wide variety of factors,[10] it seems reasonable to suggest that their decisions are most circumscribed in law enforcement situations. This is because law enforcement situations involve the application of criminal laws to specific sets of facts. Since the criminal laws proscribe acts that are rather clear cut (murder, robbery or rape, for example), the only questions that officers must resolve are: (1) whether the act occurred; and, (2) whether there is sufficient evidence to justify the arrest (and eventually, the conviction) of the suspect. In most cases, the determination of these two issues can be readily made by police officers, with the subsequent steps of the criminal process following as a matter of course.[11] Law enforcement situations offer little room for debate about what police officers ought to do.

Order maintenance situations, in contrast, offer much greater opportunities for the exercise of police discretion. As Wilson suggests, this is because order maintenance (involving, for example, the application

---

[7]Goldstein, *Id.*

[8]Davis, *Police Discretion, supra.*

[9]Goldstein, *supra.*

[10]For example, Wilson, *supra*, discusses how local political conditions in a community contribute to the development of either a "legalistic," "watchman" or "service" style of police organization, and how the different organizational norms in these three types of departments shape the way police officers confront and resolve the problems encountered while on patrol.

[11]This statement should not be construed to suggest that the question of guilt or innocence in criminal cases is always unequivocal, or that police are always correct in their determinations that a crime occurred and a particular suspect is guilty. We merely suggest that these situations typically offer less room for such debates.

of disorderly conduct statutes,) frequently require the officer to make a subjective determination that a condition (the "public peace" or the "public order") rather than a law has been violated.

Finally, there appears to be little specific discussion in the literature about the exercise of police discretion in service situations, beyond the observation that they are regarded as "garbage calls." This may be due, in part, to the fact that calls for service (*e.g.*, rendering emergency first aid, helping a stranded motorist) do not typically require officers to reinforce their actions with coercive authority, in the way that may be necessary in dealing with law enforcement or order maintenance situations. What is clear from the literature, however, is a strong call for the re-evaluation of the police attitude of disdain for these types of calls, and the suggestion that the police response to requests for service might result, in the long run, in more effective law enforcement. Moore goes on to note that service calls may even be more significant than "harbinger[s] of future crimes." They may, in fact, represent what citizens regard as the primary police role or priority.[12] In other words, there may be a profound difference between how officers and how citizens view the primary police role, with the former emphasizing law enforcement and the latter wanting service.

Interestingly, Moore's latter point seems bolstered by the results of several research studies indicating that, of the three types of activities, comparatively little time is devoted to the law enforcement function. For example, from his analysis of calls handled by the Syracuse, New York police from June 3–9, 1966, Wilson found that 90 percent did *not* involve the exercise of the law enforcement function.[13] Similarly, from his classification of the patrol activities of five different types of departments, Lundman determined that overall, only 30 percent of the total number of calls involved a law enforcement matter; among the five departments, the proportion of law enforcement calls varied markedly, from 13 percent in a suburban department to 33 percent in an urban department.[14] However, Reiss found a somewhat higher proportion (58 percent) of law enforcement related calls made to the Chicago Police Department Central Communications Center during a one day period in 1966.[15]

Whatever its shortcomings, the conceptualization of the police role as either law enforcement, order maintenance, or service tasks does seem to provide a useful framework for the analysis of police decisionmaking in situations involving juvenile offenders. The sections that follow will focus on each of these three tasks as they relate to the processing of juveniles.

---

[12]*Id.*

[13]Wilson, *supra.*

[14]Lundman, "Police Patrol Work: A Comparative Perspective," 56 in Lundman (Ed.) *Police Behavior: A Sociological Perspective*, (New York: Oxford University Press, 1980).

[15]Reiss, *The Police and the Public*, (Connecticut: Yale University Press, 1971).

THE LAW ENFORCEMENT TASK

A. Parental Notification Following Arrest

In 1964 an Arizona youth named Gerald Gault was taken into custody by the Gila County Sheriff for allegedly making an obscene telephone call to a woman who lived in his neighborhood. At the time, both Gault's parents were at work, and neither was informed of his arrest by police or juvenile court officials; his mother was told of it several hours later, by Gerald's brother. The failure of police or juvenile court officials to provide adequate and timely notice of Gault's arrest to his parents, was noted only in passing by Justice Fortas, the author of the U.S. Supreme Court's landmark *Gault* decision.

It cannot really be said that the Court's passing reference to the Sheriff's failure to notify Gerald's parents of his arrest gave that fact constitutional significance. Nor does the statement serve as a clear signal that a similar failure to notify parents would, *by itself* amount to a denial of due process. However, the fact that it *was* mentioned, coupled with the Court's extensive discussion of how the failure to provide adequate notice of the charges against a juvenile at the adjudicatory stages of the process *did* amount to a denial of due process, may have prompted police agencies to examine their arrest procedures in cases involving juveniles, and develop specific policies to ensure the timely notification to parents in the event that a child is arrested. An example of one such policy statement, currently in use at the Saginaw County (Michigan) Sheriff's Department, is provided below.

SAGINAW COUNTY SHERIFF DEPARTMENT

POLICY AND PROCEDURE 09A [DRAFT]

SUBJECT: JUVENILE POLICY

PURPOSE: To establish policy and procedures to be followed by deputies of the Saginaw County Sheriff Department when taking juveniles into custody.

I. Juveniles can be taken into custody by any sworn officer when:

A. The juvenile is found violating any law or ordinance.

B. Conditions exist that would make an arrest lawful if the juvenile were an adult.

C. It is reasonably believed that the juvenile was evading legal custody.

D. Conditions exist which endanger the juvenile's health or welfare.

E. The deputy is continuing a lawful arrest by a citizen (*i.e.*, Retail Fraud cases).

II. Delinquency

A. Serious Delinquent Offenses

1. If a deputy takes custody of a juvenile for a serious offense, he/she may request detention if the offense that has occurred is so serious that release would endanger public safety or if any circumstances exist which would make detention advisable (*e.g.*, violation of a court order where arrest would be automatic if the subject were an adult).

2. When the arresting deputy intends to detain a juvenile, contact shall be made with the Juvenile Court Intake Officer or an alternate whose names and numbers appear in Appendix A.

3. If custody is authorized, the juvenile will be taken to Headquarters for processing.

4. Any juvenile taken into custody must be kept under visual supervision at all times.

5. **All juveniles taken into custody, for whatever reason, are to be kept separate (out of sight and hearing range) of any adult offender.**

6. Delinquent offenders may be handcuffed to a fixed object and may be kept in a locked or secured room. <u>Length of custody at headquarters may not exceed six (6) hours for processing. This time limit starts the moment a juvenile is handcuffed to a fixed object or placed in a secure room. The time stops once the juvenile is placed in someone else's custody.</u>

7. Prior to taking the juvenile to the Juvenile Center, the arresting deputy will take the juvenile's fingerprints.

    a. Fingerprints are to be taken at Headquarters.

    b. If an instant camera is available, photographs of the arrested juvenile may be taken. Place the photographs in a separate envelope and attach to the case report.

    c. Do not enter a juvenile's fingerprints or photograph into evidence.

8. Once obtained, fingerprints, photos and other forms of identification pertaining to juveniles will be filed separately from adult records.

9. After the juvenile has been fingerprinted and photographed, the deputy will immediately take the juvenile to the juvenile center for placement.

10. The arresting deputy will document the time of custody, the time contact was made with the Court Intake Officer, the time the juvenile was handcuffed to a fixed object or placed in a secure room (if applicable), the time of the fingerprinting and photographing, and the time of placement in the juvenile center.

    a. **Until the juvenile is placed into the custody of the juvenile center, the juvenile will not be questioned, even if a parent, guardian, or custodian is available.**

b. Questions regarding needed information normally attendant to arrest and custody may be asked such as: name, DOB, address, phone number, physical descriptors, *etc*.

11. The deputy will complete the juvenile court complaint and supplemental complaint forms and contact the child's parent, guardian, or custodian regarding placement. Notification will be given to the parent(s) of the time, date, and place of the hearing. This notification will also be noted in the deputy's incident report.

12. After the juvenile is placed at the Juvenile Center, an attempt to take a statement may be made. Miranda rights should be read to both the child and parent. Both must waive the rights before a statement can be taken.

13. If the request for detention is denied, an attempt to take a statement may be made at headquarters. The same Miranda rights outlined above will apply.

14. Anytime a juvenile is detained, fingerprints **MUST** be taken if the juvenile is charged with any of the following offenses:

Arson
Assault with Intent to Murder
Assault with Intent to do Great Bodily Harm less than Murder
Assault with Intent to Rob, unarmed or armed
Homicide
Attempted Murder
Breaking and Entering with Intent to Commit Larceny
Kidnapping
Larceny in a Building
UDAA
CSC — First, Second, or Third Degree
CSC — Second or Subsequent Offense
Assault W/I to Commit Sexual Penetration, 2nd Degree CSC
Armed Robbery
Controlled Substance — Delivery/Manufacture Cocaine 10 Grams or More
Controlled Substance — Possession of 650 or more Grams

15. Anytime a juvenile is detained for any of the following offenses, the Detective Sergeant should be contacted immediately since the law permits a waiver to adult court:

Murder — 1st and 2nd Degree

Assault W/I Intent to Murder

Attempted Murder

Armed Robbery

Assault W/I to Commit Sexual Penetration

Possession of 650 Grams or more of a Schedule I or Controlled Substance

a. All other stated procedures still apply

B. Minor Delinquent Offenses

1. When a juvenile is taken into custody for a minor offense, he/she may be taken home or a parent, guardian, or custodian may be summoned to headquarters or to the scene when the juvenile is being detained.

2. If the deputy is able to handle the problem by discussing it with a parent, guardian, or custodian, a case report will be written.

3. Positive identification shall be obtained from the person taking custody of the juvenile. The person's name, address, phone number, DOB, *etc.* shall be listed in the case report.

4. Any juvenile taken into custody must be kept under visual supervision at all times. Juveniles must be kept separate from adult offenders (out of sight and hearing range).

5. Once again, a juvenile charged with delinquent offenses may be kept in a locked or secured facility or room for up to six (6) hours staring with the time they are locked in the room or when they are handcuffed to a fixed object. The time stops when they are placed in someone else's custody.

III. Status Offenses

A. Deputies taking custody of a juvenile for a status offense (RAW, curfew violation, truancy, possession of alcohol, and/or any illegal conduct based solely on a child's age) will return the juvenile to the custody of a parent, guardian, or custodian, or a parent, guardian, or a custodian may be summoned to headquarters to pick up the juvenile.

1. If the juvenile refuses to stay at home, placement can be arraigned at Innerlink or with a relative if said relative is approved by the parents and the juvenile.

2. Anytime a juvenile is taken into custody for a status offense, a case report will be written.

3. Status offenders shall not be placed in a locked or secured facility or room while they are in custody.

4. Status offenders shall not be handcuffed to a fixed object such as a handcuffing bar. They man, however, be handcuffed to themselves.

5. Status offenders shall be kept under visual supervision at all times while in custody.

6. Status offenders, while in custody, must be kept separate from adult offenders (out of sight and hearing range).

IV. Child Abuse/Neglect

A. Taking a juvenile into custody **WITHOUT** a Court Order

1. When a deputy decides to take a juvenile into custody due to abuse or neglect, the deputy shall:

a. Take the juvenile to a hospital for an examination and treatment if there is abuse suspected or if the juvenile is in need of other medical attention.

b. If the juvenile has been abused, photographs of the injuries shall be taken.

2. Child Protective Services (DSS) **MUST** be contacted if a deputy takes a report of abuse or neglect; **this notification of DSS is required by law** even if the perpetrator is not a member of the same household as the victim. Child Protective Services of the DSS shall be contacted as soon as practical after the deputy originally receives the information regarding abuse or neglect.

3. Decisions as to whether a detective shall be called out on a abuse or neglect case shall be made on a case by case basis by the on-duty Patrol Sergeant.

4. The Juvenile Court Intake Officer must be contacted regarding placement in the Child Receiving Home.

a. If the juvenile was taken into custody for neglect or abuse and place in the Child Receiving Home, the court complaint and supplemental complaint must be completed. The Department of Social Services' form DSS 3200, generally available at the Child Receiving Home or hospital emergency rooms, will also be completed.

b. When the juvenile is placed in the Child Receiving Home, a hearing will be scheduled at the time that the Intake Officer authorizes placement. The deputy taking custody of the juvenile is responsible for attending the hearing and ordering the parents to attend. The deputy will supply the parents with the date, time, and location of the hearing.

c. If the juvenile has been left alone and there is someone available to take custody, the Juvenile Court Intake Officer should be advised of the situation before placement with that individual is made. The deputy must decide if the placement with the individual will provide for the juvenile's safety and security. A DSS Form 3200 must be completed and the Child Protective Services worker notified.

5. If the juvenile is taken to Headquarters, the juvenile must not be held in a locked room or facility, must be kept under visual supervision at all times, must be kept separate (out of sight and sound range) from adult offenders, and may not be handcuffed.

B. Taking a child into custody **WITH** a court order.

1. Temporary Order of Care

a. When a deputy is called upon to assist in removing a juvenile with a ***Temporary Order of Care***, the deputy will attempt to carry out the order. ***In this type of a situation, the deputy DOES NOT have the authority to enter a residence if entry is refused by those persons having control of the premises.***

2. Temporary Order of Custody

a. When a deputy is called on to assist in removing a juvenile using a ***Temporary Order of Custody, the deputy DOES HAVE the authority to enter the premises*** to effect the order. This order may also be used to take delinquent children into custody.

3. Authority to enter a private premise is stipulated and limited by each individual Order of Custody.

4. A parent or other adult may resent the execution of court orders and all attempts should be made as diplomatically as possible.

V. Rights of Juveniles

A. Juveniles are entitled to the same rights and privileges as adults.

B. Both the juvenile and the parent must be present and both must waive their rights against self-incrimination (Miranda). Neither the juvenile not the parent can independently waive the rights of the juvenile.

VI. Revision Responsibility

Responsibility for the continuous updating and revision of this policy and procedure lies with the office of the Sheriff. Continuous shall mean when necessary or when mandated by law.

VII. Application

Violations of this directive, if proven, may be used for administrative action and/or discipline.

In the event that this directive conflicts with or supersedes any previous departmental order, procedure, or directive, to that extent the conflicting or superseded order is cancelled.

B. Custodial Interrogation of Juveniles

Almost five decades ago, in *Haley v. Ohio*, 332 U.S. 596 (1947), the U.S. Supreme Court recognized that juvenile offenders, because of their youth and immaturity, were more susceptible to the potentially coercive atmosphere of a custodial interrogation. In *Haley*, a 15-year-old homicide suspect was arrested, subjected to intense interrogation from midnight until 5 a.m. the next morning, and prevented from seeing his mother or his attorney for more than 72 hours following his arrest. In the excerpt below, Justice Douglas vehemently condemns the use of such methods to extract a confession.

HALEY v. OHIO

* * *

OPINION OF DOUGLAS, J.

Mr. Justice Douglas announced the judgment of the Court and an opinion in which MR. JUSTICE BLACK, MR. JUSTICE MURPHY, and MR. JUSTICE RUTLEDGE join.

Petitioner was convicted in an Ohio court of murder in the first degree and sentenced to life imprisonment. The case is here on a petition for a writ of certiorari which we granted because we had doubts whether the ruling of the court below could be squared with *Chambers v. Florida*, 309 U.S. 227, *Malinski v. New York*, 324 U.S. 401, and like cases in this Court.

A confectionery store was robbed near midnight on October 14, 1945, and William Karam, its owner, was shot. It was the prosecutor's theory, supported by some evidence which it is unnecessary for us to relate, that petitioner, [a] boy aged 15, and two others, Willie Lowder, aged 16, and Al Parks, aged 17, committed the crime, petitioner acting as a lookout. Five days later—around midnight October 19, 1945—petitioner was arrested at his home and taken to police headquarters.

Taking only the undisputed testimony * * *, we have the following sequence of events. Beginning shortly after midnight this 15-year-old lad was questioned by the police for about five hours. Five or six of the police questioned him in relays of one or two each. During this time no friend or counsel of the boy was present. Around 5 a.m.—after being shown alleged confessions of Lowder and Parks—the boy confessed. A confession was typed in question and answer form by the police. At no time was this boy advised of his right to counsel; but the written confession started off with the following statement:

> "We want to inform you of your constitutional rights, the law gives you the right to make this statement or not as you see fit. It is made with the understanding that it may be used at a trial in court either for or against you or anyone else involved in this crime with you, of you own free will and accord, you are under no force or duress or compulsion and no promises are being made to you at this time whatsoever.
>
> "Do you still desire to make this statement and tell the truth after having had the above clause read to you?
>
> "A. Yes."

He was put in jail about 6 or 6:30 a.m. on Saturday, the 20th, shortly after the confession was signed. Between then and Tuesday, the 23d, he was held incommunicado. A lawyer retained by his mother tried to see him twice but was refused admission by the police. His mother was not allowed to see him until Thursday, the 25th. But a newspaper photographer was allowed to see him and take his picture in the early morning hours of the 20th, right after he had confessed. He was not taken before a magistrate and formally charged with a crime until the 23d—three days after the confession was signed.

We do not think the methods used in obtaining this confession can be squared with that due process of law which the Fourteenth Amendment commands.

What transpired would make us pause for careful inquiry if a mature man were involved. And when, as here, a mere child—an easy victim of the law is before us, special care in scrutinizing the record must be used. Age 15 is a tender and difficult age for a boy of any race. He cannot be judged by the more exacting standards of maturity. That which would leave a man cold and unimpressed can overawe and overwhelm a lad in his early teens. This is the period of great instability which the crisis of adolescence produces. A 15-year-old lad, questioned through the dead of night by relays of police, is a ready victim of the inquisition. Mature men possibly might stand the ordeal from midnight to 5 a.m. But we cannot believe that a lad of tender years is a match for the police in such a contest. He needs counsel and support if he is not to become the victim first of fear, then of panic. He needs someone on whom to lean lest the overpowering presence of the law, as he knows it, crush him. No friend stood at the side of this 15-year-old boy as the police, working in relays, questioned him hour after hour, from midnight until dawn. No lawyer stood guard to make sure that the police went so far and no farther, to see to it that they stopped short of the point where he became the victim of coercion. No counsel or friend was called during the critical hours of questioning. A photographer was admitted once this lad broke and confessed. But not even a gesture towards getting a lawyer for him was ever made.

This disregard of the standards of decency is underlined by the fact that he was kept incommunicado for over three days during which the lawyer retained to represent him twice tried to see him and twice was refused admission. A photographer was admitted at once; but his closest friend—his mother—was not allowed to see him for over five days after his arrest. It is said that these events are not germane to the present problem because they happened after the confession was made. But they show such a callous attitude of the police towards the safeguards which respect for ordinary standards of human relationships compels that we take with a grain of salt their present apologia that the five-hour grilling of this boy was conducted in a fair and dispassionate manner. When the police are so unmindful of these basic standards of conduct in their public dealings, their secret treatment of a 15-year-old boy behind closed doors in the dead of night become darkly suspicious.

The age of petitioner, the hours when he was grilled, the duration of his quizzing, the fact that he had no friend or counsel to advise him, the callous attitude of the police towards his rights combine to convince us that this was a confession wrung from a child by means which the law should not sanction. Neither man nor child can be allowed to stand condemned by methods which flout constitutional requirements of due process of law.

But we are told that this boy was advised of his constitutional rights before he signed the confession and that, knowing them, he nevertheless confessed. That assumes, however, that a boy of fifteen, without aid of counsel would have a full appreciation of that advice and that on the facts of this record he had a freedom of choice. We cannot indulge those assumptions. Moreover, we cannot give any weight to recitals which merely formalize constitutional requirements. Formulas of respect for constitutional safeguards cannot prevail over the fact of life which contradict them. They may not become a cloak for inquisitorial practices and make an empty form of the due process of law for which free men fought and died to obtain.

REVERSED.

BURTON, J., dissenting.

The question in this case is the simple one—was the confession in fact voluntary? As in many other cases it is difficult, because of conflicting testimony, to determine this controlling fact. It may not be possible to become absolutely certain of it. Self-serving perjury, however, must not be the pass-key to a mandatory exclusion of the confession from use as evidence. It is for the trial judge and the jury, under the safeguards of constitutional due process of criminal law, to apply evenhanded justice to the determination of the factual issues. To do this, they need every available lawful aid to help them test the credibility of the conflicting testimony.

Due process of law under the Fourteenth Amendment requires that the states use some fair means to determine the voluntary character of a confession like that in this case. The procedure may differ in each state. The form adopted by Ohio is not criticized by this Court. The sole question here is the validity of the application of the Ohio procedure to the facts of this case. That application can be tested in this Court only under the great handicap of attempting to appraise, by use of the printed record, the action of the trial court and jury taken in the light of the living record. In connection with every confession that is unaccompanied by testimony as to how it was secured, all sorts of conditions may be conjectured as to the methods used to secure it. To rely upon conjecture, either in favor of or against the accused, is not justice. It is not due process of law by any definition. Similarly, all sorts of conditions as to the methods which might have been used in obtaining such a confession may be conjectured by a witness and falsely testified to by him. Such action puts the true testimony into direct conflict with the false. In the present case, the conflict of testimony is so clear that it is evident that one or more of the witnesses must have committed perjury. The issue resolves itself, therefore, not into one of civil rights but into one of the truth or falsity of the testimony as to the methods used in obtaining Haley's confession.

The present case, turning as it does upon the credibility of the testimony as to the existence of the coercion, if any, that was used to secure the confession, is readily distinguishable from cases relied upon by the accused. For example, in the present case, this Court does not rely on any claim that the confession was elicited by unreasonably delaying the arraignment of the accused or even by any alleged delay in charging him with delinquency in the Juvenile Court. The confession of the accused was given, transcribed and signed by 5:30 a.m. on October 20, immediately following his arrest at about midnight. There is, accordingly, no basis for contending that there was unnecessary delay in taking the accused before a court or magistrate having jurisdiction of the offense insofar as such unnecessary delay, if any, had relation to the confession. Whatever delay there was occurred after the confession was made and it is obvious that it was not unreasonable to delay the taking of the accused before a court or magistrate at least until after 5:30 a.m. *United States v. Mitchell*, 322 U.S. 65. Cf. *Anderson v. United States*, 318 U.S. 350; *McNabb v. United States*, 318 U.S. 332.

If the unequivocal and consistent testimony of the several police officers is believed, including that of the Acting Chief of Police, the confession was clearly voluntary. The police officers were men of experience in the local detective service and, if inferences are to be indulged in, it may be inferred the they understood the necessity that the confession be uncoerced and voluntary if it was to be admissible in evidence.

* * *

Haley v. Ohio

1. This case occurred prior to the famous Miranda decision. Critique the police interrogation in *Haley* from the perspective of Miranda. What should the police have done to avoid a reversal of the conviction on appeal?

2. This case also took place before the landmark decision of *Kent v. U.S.* Should this youngster have the right to be heard in juvenile court and then given a transfer hearing? Were there characteristics of this youth that would seem to make him "amenable to treatment" in the juvenile corrections system? (Of course, this case occurred in the late 1940s and thus juvenile corrections was probably quite punitive at the time.)

3. Explain the relevance of the fourteenth amendment to this case. Exactly how did the U.S. Supreme Court apply the fourteenth amendment?

4. Critique the case disposition in light of the fact that the youth only served as a look-out while two other youngsters actually committed the robbery and murder.

C. Advising Juveniles of their Rights Under *Miranda v. Arizona*

In *Miranda v. Arizona*, the U.S. Supreme Court ruled that the in custody interrogation of criminal suspects can proceed only after they have been advised of their constitutional rights during interrogation, including: (1) the right to remain silent; (2) the right to consult legal counsel during interrogation; and, (3) the privilege against compelled self-incrimination. As discussed in the excerpt below, the *Gault* decision effectively extended the protections of the *Miranda* ruling to juvenile suspects.

Application of Paul L. GAULT and Marjorie Gault, Father and Mother of Gerald Francis Gault, a Minor, Appellants.

* * *

Mr. Justice Fortas delivered the opinion of the Court.

* * *

I.

On Monday, June 8, 1964, at about 10 a.m., Gerald Francis Gault and friend, Ronald Lewis, were taken into custody by the Sheriff of Gila County. Gerald was then still subject to a six months' probation order which had been entered on February 25, 1964, as a result of his having been in the company of another boy who had stolen a wallet from a lady's purse. The police action on June 8 was taken as the result of a verbal complaint by a neighbor of the boys, Mrs. Cook, about a telephone call made to her in which the caller or callers made lewd or indecent remarks. It will suffice for purposes of this opinion to say that the remarks or questions put to her were of the irritatingly offensive, adolescent, sex variety.

At the time Gerald was picked up, his mother and father were both at work. No notice that Gerald was being taken into custody was left at the home. No other steps were taken to advise them that their son had, in effect, been arrested. Gerald was taken to the Children's Detention Home. When his mother arrived home at about 6 o'clock, Gerald was not there. Gerald's older brother was sent to look for him at the trailer home of the Lewis family. He apparently learned then that Gerald was in custody. He so informed his mother. The two of them went to the Detention Home. The deputy probation officer, Flagg, who was also superintendent of the Detention Home, told Mrs. Gault "why Jerry was there" and said that a hearing would be held in Juvenile Court at 3 o'clock the following day, June 9.

Officer Flagg filed a petition with the court on the hearing day, June 9, 1964. It was not served on the Gaults. Indeed, none of them saw this petition until the habeas corpus hearing on August 17, 1964. The petition was entirely formal. It made no reference to any factual basis for the judicial action which it initiated. It recited only that "said minor is under the age of eighteen years, and is in need of the protection of this Honorable Court; [and that] said minor is a delinquent minor." It prayed for a hearing and an order regarding "the care and custody of said minor." Officer Flagg executed a formal affidavit in support of the petition.

On June 9, Gerald, his mother, his older brother, and Probation Officers Flagg and Henderson appeared before the Juvenile Judge in chambers. Gerald's father was not there. He was at work out of the city. Mrs. Cook, the complainant, was not there. No one was sworn at this hearing. No transcript or recording was made. No memorandum or record of the substance of the proceedings was prepared. Our information about the proceedings and the subsequent hearing on June 15, derives entirely from the testimony of the Juvenile Court Judge,[16] Mr. and Mrs. Gault and Officer Flagg at the habeas corpus proceeding conducted two months later. From this, it appears that at the June 9 hearing Gerald was questioned by the judge about the telephone call. There was conflict as to what he said. His mother recalled that Gerald said he only dialed Mrs. Cook's number and handed the telephone to his friend, Ronald. Officer Flagg recalled that Gerald had admitted making the lewd remarks. Judge McGhee testified that Gerald "admitted making one of these [lewd] statements." At the conclusion of the hearing, the judge said he would "think about it." Gerald was taken back to the Detention Home. He was not sent to his own home with his parents. On June 11 or 12, after having been detained since June 8, Gerald was released and

---

[16]Under Arizona law, juvenile hearings are conducted by a judge of the Superior Court, designated by his colleagues on the Superior Court to serve as Juvenile Court Judge. Arizona Const., Art. 6, § 15, A.R.S.; Arizona Revised Statutes (hereinafter ARS) §§ 8-201, 8-202.

driven home.[17] There is no explanation in the record as to why he was kept in the Detention Home or why he was released. At 5 p.m. on the day of Gerald's release, Mrs. Gault received a note signed by Officer Flagg. It was on plain paper, not letterhead. Its entire text was as follows:

> "Mrs. Gault:
>
> "Judge McGHEE has set Monday June 15, 1964 at 11:00 A.M. as the date and time for further Hearings on Gerald's delinquency
>
> "/s/Flagg"

At the appointed time on Monday, June 15, Gerald, his father and mother, Ronald Lewis and his father, and Officers Flagg and Henderson were present before Judge McGhee. Witnesses at the habeas corpus proceeding differed in their recollections of Gerald's testimony at the June 15 hearing. Mr. and Mrs. Gault recalled that Gerald again testified that he had only dialed the number and that the other boy had made the remarks. Officer Flagg agreed that at this hearing Gerald did not admit making the lewd remarks.[18] But Judge McGhee recalled that "there was some admission again of some of the lewd statements. He—he didn't admit any of the more serious lewd statements."[19] Again, the complainant, Mrs. Cook, was not present. Mrs. Gault asked that Mrs. Cook be present "so she could see which boy that done the talking, the dirty talking over the phone." The Juvenile Judge said "she didn't have to be present at that hearing." The judge did not speak to Mrs. Cook or communicate with her at any time. Probation Officer Flagg had talked to her once—over the telephone on June 9.

At this June 15 hearing a "referral report" made by the probation officers was filed with the court, although not disclosed to Gerald or his parents. This listed the charge as "Lewd Phone Calls." At the conclusion of the hearing, the judge committed Gerald as a juvenile delinquent to the State Industrial School "for the period of his minority [that is, until 21], unless sooner discharged by due process of law." An order to that effect was entered. It recites that "after a full hearing and due deliberation the Court finds that said minor is a delinquent child, and that said minor is of the age of 15 years."

No appeal is permitted by Arizona law in juvenile cases. On August 3, 1964, a petition for a writ of habeas corpus was filed with the Supreme Court of Arizona and referred by it to the Superior Court for hearing.

---

[17]There is a conflict between the recollection of Mrs. Gault and that of Officer Flagg. Mrs. Gault testified that Gerald was released on Friday, June 12, Officer Flagg that it had been on Thursday, June 11. This was from memory; he had no record, and the note hereafter referred to was undated.

[18]Officer Flagg also testified that Gerald had not, when questioned at the Detention Home, admitted having made any of the lewd statements, but that each boy had sought to put the blame on the other. There was conflicting testimony as to whether Ronald had accused Gerald of making the lewd statements during the June 15 hearing.

[19]Judge McGhee also testified that Gerald had not denied "certain statements" made to him at the hearing by Officer Henderson.

At the habeas corpus hearing on August 17, Judge McGhee was vigorously cross-examined as to the basis for his actions. He testified that he had taken into account the fact that Gerald was on probation. He was asked "under what section of * * * the code you found the boy delinquent?"

His answer is set forth in the margin.[20] In substance, he concluded that Gerald came within ARS § 8-201, subsec. 6(a), which specifies that a "delinquent child" includes one "who has violated a law of the state or an ordinance or regulation of a political subdivision thereof." The law which Gerald was found to have violated is ARS § 13-377. This section of the Arizona Criminal Code provides that a person who "in the presence of hearing of any woman or child * * * uses vulgar, abusive or obscene language, is guilty of a misdemeanor * * *." The penalty specified in the Criminal Code, which would apply to an adult, is $5 to $50, or imprisonment for not more than two months. The judge also testified that he acted under ARS § 8-201, subsec. 6(d) which includes in the definition of a "delinquent child" one who, as the judge phrased it, is "habitually involved in immoral matters."[21]

Asked about the basis for his conclusion that Gerald was "habitually involved in immoral matters," the judge testified, somewhat vaguely, that two years earlier, on July 2, 1962, a "referral" was made concerning Gerald, "where the boy had stolen a baseball glove from another boy and lied to the Police Department about it." The judge said there was "no hearing," and "no accusation" relating to this incident, "because of lack of material foundation." But it seems to have remained in his mind as a relevant factor. The judge also testified that Gerald had admitted making other nuisance phone calls in the past which, as the judge recalled the boy's testimony, were "silly calls, or funny calls, or something like that."

The Superior Court dismissed the writ, and appellants sought review in the Arizona Supreme Court.

* * *

[20]"Q. All right. Now, Judge, would you tell me under what section of the law or tell me under what section of—of the code you found the boy delinquent?

"A. Well, there is a—I think it amounts to disturbing the peace. I can't give you the section, but I can tell you the law, that when one person uses lewd language in the presence of another person, that it can amount to—and I consider that when a person makes it over the phone, that it is considered in the presence, I might be wrong, that is one section. The other section upon which I consider the boy delinquent is Section 8-201, Subsection (d), habitually involved in immoral matters."

[21]ARS § 8-201, subsec. 6, the section of the Arizona Juvenile Code which defines a delinquent child, reads:

"'Delinquent child' includes:

"(a) A child who has violated a law of the state or an ordinance or regulation of a political subdivision thereof.

"(b) A child who, by reason of being incorrigible, wayward or habitually disobedient, is uncontrolled by his parent, guardian or custodian.

"(c) A child who is habitually truant from school or home.

"(d) A child who habitually so deports himself as to injure or endanger the morals or health of himself or others."

The Supreme Court handed down an elaborate and wide-ranging opinion affirming dismissal of the writ and stating the court's conclusions as to the issues raised by appellants and other aspects of the juvenile process. See Chapter 3 for discussion of Gault from adjudication perspective.

* * *

FARE, ACTING CHIEF PROBATION OFFICER

V.

MICHAEL C.

CERTIORARI TO THE SUPREME COURT OF CALIFORNIA

* * *

MR. JUSTICE BLACKMUN delivered the opinion of the Court.

In *Miranda v. Arizona*, 384 U. S. 436 (1966), this Court established certain procedural safeguards designed to protect the rights of an accused, under the Fifth and Fourteenth Amendments, to be free from compelled self-incrimination during custodial interrogation. The Court specified, among other things, that if the accused indicates in any manner that he wishes to remain silent or to consult an attorney, interrogation must cease, and any statement obtained from him during interrogation thereafter may not be admitted against him at his trial. *Id.*, at 444–445, 473–474.

In this case, the State of California, in the person of its acting chief probation officer, attacks the conclusion of the Supreme Court of California that a juvenile's request, made while undergoing custodial interrogation, to see his *probation officer* is *per se* an invocation of the juvenile's Fifth Amendment rights as pronounced in *Miranda*.

I

Respondent Michael C. was implicated in the murder of Robert Yeager. The murder occurred during a robbery of the victim's home on January 19, 1976. A small truck registered in the name of respondent's mother was identified as having been near the Yeager home at the time of the killing, and a young man answering respondent's description was seen by witnesses near the truck and near the home shortly before Yeager was murdered.

* * *

On the basis of this information, Van Nuys, Cal., police took respondent into custody at approximately 6:30 p.m. on February 4. Respondent then was 16½ years old and on probation to the Juvenile Court. He had been on probation since the age of 12. Approximately one year earlier he had served a term in a youth corrections camp under the supervision of the Juvenile Court. He had a record of several previous offenses, including burglary of guns and purse snatching, stretching back over several years.

Upon respondent's arrival at Van Nuys station house two police officers began to interrogate him. The officers and respondent were the only persons in the room during the interrogation. The conversation was tape-recorded. One of the officers initiated the interview by informing respondent that he had been brought in for questioning in relation to a murder. The officer fully advised respondent of his *Miranda* rights. The following exchange then occurred, as set out in the opinion of the California Supreme Court, *In re Michael C.*, 21 Cal. 3d 471, 473–474, 579 P. 2d 7, 8 (1978) (emphasis added by that court):

"Q. ...Do you understand all of these rights as I have explained them to you?

"A. Yeah.

"Q. Okay, do you wish to give up your right to remain silent and talk to us about this murder?

"A. What murder? I don't know about no murder.

"Q. I'll explain to you which one it is if you want to talk to us about it.

"A. Yeah, I might talk to you.

"Q. Do you want to give up your right to have an attorney present here while we talk about it?

"A. *Can I have my probation officer here?*

"Q. Well I can't get a hold of your probation officer right now. You have the right to an attorney.

"A. How I know you guys won't pull no police officer in and tell me he's an attorney?

"Q. Huh?

"A. [How I know you guys won't pull no police officer in and tell me he's an attorney?]

"Q. Your probation officer is Mr. Christiansen.

"A. Yeah.

"Q. Well I'm not going to call Mr. Christiansen tonight. There's a good chance we can talk to him but I'm not going to call him right now. If you want to talk to us without an attorney present, you can. If you don't want to, you don't have to. But if you want to say something, you can, and if you don't want to say something you don't have to. That's your right. Do you understand that right?

"A. Yeah.

"Q. Okay, will you talk to us without an attorney present?

"A. Yeah I want to talk to you."

Respondent thereupon proceeded to answer questions put to him by the officers. He made statements and drew sketches that incriminated him in the Yeager murder.

Largely on the basis of respondent's incriminating statements, probation authorities filed a petition in Juvenile Court alleging that respondent had murdered Robert Yeager, in violation of Cal. Penal Code Ann. § 187 * * * and that respondent therefore should be adjudged a ward of the Juvenile Court, * * *.

App. 4–5. Respondent thereupon moved to suppress the statements and sketches he gave the police during the interrogation. He alleged that the statements had been obtained in violation of *Miranda* in his request to see his probation officer at the outset of the questioning constituted an invocation of his Fifth Amendment right to remain silent, just as if he had requested the assistance of an attorney. Accordingly, respondent argued that since the interrogation did not cease until he had a chance to confer with his probation officer, the statements and sketches could not be admitted against him in the Juvenile Court proceedings.

* * *

In support of his suppression motion, respondent called his probation officer, Charles P. Christiansen, as a witness. Christiansen testified that he had instructed respondent that if at any time he had "a concern with his family," or ever had "a police contact" App. 27, he should get in touch with his probation officer immediately. The witness stated that, on a previous occasion, when respondent had had a police contact and had failed to communicate with Christiansen, the probation officer had reprimanded him. *Id.*, at 28. This testimony, respondent argued, indicated that when he asked for his probation officer, he was in fact asserting his right to remain silent in the face of further questioning.

In a ruling from the bench, the court denied the motion to suppress. *Id.*, at 41–42. It held that the question whether respondent had waived his right to remain silent was one of fact to be determined on a case-by-case basis, and that the facts of this case showed a "clear waiver" by respondent of that right. *Id.*, at 42. The court observed that the transcript of the interrogation revealed that respondent specifically had told the officers that he would talk with them, and that this waiver had come at the outset of the interrogation and not after prolonged questioning. The court noted that respondent was a "16 and a half year old minor who has been through the court system before, has been to [probation] camp, has a probation officer, [and is not] a young naive minor with no experience with the courts." *Ibid.* Accordingly, it found that on the facts of the case respondent had waived his Fifth Amendment rights, notwithstanding the request to see his probation officer.[22]

* * *

[22]The California Court of Appeal, in an opinion reported and then vacated, affirmed. *In re Michael C.*, 135 Cal. Rptr. 762 (1977). That court noted that since the Juvenile Court's findings of fact resolved against respondent his contention that the confession had been coerced from him by threats and promises, it would have to "conclude that there was knowing and intelligent waiver of the minor's *Miranda* rights unless it can be said that the request to speak to a probation officer was in and of itself sufficient to invoke" respondent's Fifth Amendment privilege. *Id.*, at 765–766 (footnote omitted). It refused to extend the rule of *People* v. *Burton*, 6 Cal. 3d 375, 491 P. 2d 793 (1971), to include a request for a probation officer, finding it difficult to distinguish such a request from a request to see "one's football coach, music teacher or clergyman." 135 Cal. Rptr., at 766. Even if the *Burton* rule were applicable, the court held, there was sufficient evidence of an affirmative waiver of his rights by respondent to distinguish *Burton*, where the California Supreme Court had noted that there was "nothing in the way of affirmative proof that defendant did not intend to assert his privilege." 6 Cal. 3d, at 383, 491 P. 2d, at 798.

On appeal, the Supreme Court of California took the case by transfer from the California Court of Appeal and, by a divided vote, reversed. *In re Michael C.*, 21 Cal. 3d 471, 579 P. 2d 7 (1978). The court held that respondent's "request to see his probation officer at the commencement of interrogation negated any possible willingness on his part to discuss his case with the police [and] thereby invoked his Fifth Amendment privilege." *Id.*, at 474, 579 P. 2d, at 8. The court based this conclusion on its view that, because of the juvenile court system's emphasis on the relationship between a probation officer and the probationer, the officer was "a trusted guardian figure who exercises the authority of the state as *parens patriæ* and whose duty it is to implement the protective and rehabilitative powers of the juvenile court." *Id.*, at 476, 579 P. 2d, at 10. As a consequence, the court found that a minor's request for his probation officer was the same as a request to see his parents during interrogation, and thus under the rule of *Burton* constituted an invocation of the minor's Fifth Amendment rights.

The fact that the probation officer also served as a peace officer, and, whenever a proceeding against a juvenile was contemplated, was charged with a duty to file a petition alleging that the minor had committed an offense, did not alter, in the court's view, the fact that the officer in the eyes of the juvenile was a trusted guardian figure to whom the minor normally would turn for help when in trouble with the police. 21 Cal. 3d, at 476, 579 P.2d, at 10. Relying on *Burton*, the court ruled that it would unduly restrict *Miranda* to limit its reach in a case involving a minor to a request by the minor for an attorney, since it would be "'fatuous to assume that a minor in custody will be in a position to call an attorney for assistance and it is unrealistic to attribute no significance to his call for help from the only person to whom he normally looks—a parent or guardian.'" 21 Cal. 3d, at 475–476, 579 P. 2d, at 9, quoting *People v. Burton*, 6 Cal. 3d, at 382, 491 P. 2d, at 797–798. The court dismissed the concern expressed by the State that a request for a probation officer could not be distinguished from a request for one's football coach, music teacher, or clergyman on the ground that the probation officer, unlike those other figures in the juvenile's life, was charged by statute to represent the interests of the juvenile. 21 Cal. 3d, at 477, 579 P. 2d, at 10.

The court accordingly held that the probation officer would act to protect the minor's Fifth Amendment rights in precisely the way an attorney would act if called for by the accused. In so holding, the court found the request for a probation officer to be a *per se* invocation of Fifth Amendment rights in the same way the request for an attorney was found in *Miranda* to be, regardless of what the interrogation otherwise might reveal. In rejecting a totality-of-the-circumstances inquiry, the court stated:

> "Here, however, we face conduct which, regardless of considerations of capacity, coercion or voluntariness, per se invokes the privilege against self-incrimination. Thus our question turns not on whether the [respondent] has the ability, capacity or willingness to give a knowledgeable waiver, and hence whether he acted voluntarily, but whether, when he called for his probation officer, he exercised his Fifth Amendment privilege. We hold that in doing so he no less invoked the protection against self incrimination than if he asked for the presence of an attorney." *Ibid.*, 579 P. 2d, at 10–11.

See also *id.*, at 478 n. 4, 579 P. 2d, at 11 n. 4. The court went on to conclude that since the State had not met its "burden of proving that a minor who requests to see his probation officer does not intend to assert his Fifth Amendment privilege," *id.*, at 478, 579 P. 2d, at 11, the trial court should not have admitted the confessions obtained after respondent had requested his probation officer.[23]

The State of California petitioned this Court for a writ of certiorari. MR. JUSTICE REHNQUIST, as Circuit Justice, stayed the execution of the mandate of the Supreme Court of California. 439 U. S. 1310 (1978). Because the California judgment extending the *per se* aspects of *Miranda* presents an important question about the reach of that case, we thereafter issued the writ. 439 U. S. 925 (1978).

II

We note at the outset that it is clear that the judgement of the California Supreme Court rests firmly on that court's interpretation of federal law. This Court, however, has not heretofore extended the *per se* aspects of the *Miranda* safeguards beyond the scope of the holding in the *Miranda* case itself. We therefore must examine the California court's decision to determine whether that court's conclusion so to extend *Miranda* is in harmony with *Miranda's* underlying principles. For it is clear that "a State may not impose...greater restrictions as a matter of *federal constitutional law* when this Court specifically refrains from imposing them." *Oregon v. Hass*, 420 U.S. 714, 719 (1975) (emphasis in original). See *North Carolina v. Butler*, 441 U.S. 369 (1979).

The rule the Court established in *Miranda* is clear. In order to be able to use statements obtained during custodial interrogation of the accused, the State must warn the accused prior to such questioning of his right to remain silent and of his right to have counsel, retained or appointed, present during interrogation. 384 U.S., at 473. "Once [such] warnings have been given, the subsequent procedure is clear." *Ibid.*

> "If the individual indicates in any manner, at any time prior to or during questioning, that he wishes to remain silent, the interrogation must cease. At this point he has shown that he intends to exercise his Fifth Amendment privilege; any statement taken after the person invokes his privilege cannot be other than the product of compulsion, subtle or otherwise.... If the individual states that he wants an attorney, the interrogation must cease until an attorney is present. At that time, the individual must have an opportunity to confer with the attorney and to have him present during any subsequent questioning. If the individual cannot obtain an attorney and he indicates that he wants one before speaking to police, they must respect his decision to remain silent." *Id.*, at 473–474 (footnote omitted).

---

[23]Two justices concurred in the court's opinion and judgment. 21 Cal. 3d, at 478, 579 P. 2d, at 11. They expressed concern that a probation officer's public responsibilities would make it difficult for him to offer legal advice to a minor implicated in a crime, and that a minor advised to cooperate with the police, perhaps even to confess, justifiably could complain later "that he had been subjected to a variation of the Mutt-and-Jeff technique criticized in *Miranda*: initial interrogating by overbearing officers, then comforting by a presumably friendly and gentle peace officer in the guise of a probation officer." *Id.*, at 479, 579 P. 2d, at 12. * * *

Any statements obtained during custodial interrogation conducted in violation of these rules may not be admitted against the accused, at least during the State's case in chief. *Id.*, at 479. Cf. *Harris v. New York*, 401 U.S. 222, 224 (1971).

Whatever the defects, if any, of this relatively rigid requirement that interrogation must cease upon the accused's request for an attorney, *Miranda's* holding has the virtue of informing police and prosecutors with specificity as to what they may do in conducting custodial interrogation, and of informing courts under what circumstances statements obtained during such interrogation are not admissible. This gain in specificity, which benefits the accused and the State alike, has been thought to outweigh the burdens that the decision in *Miranda* imposes on law enforcement agencies and the courts by requiring the suppression of trustworthy and highly probative evidence even though the confession might be voluntary under traditional Fifth Amendment analysis. See *Michigan v. Tucker*, 417 U.S. 433, 443–446 (1974).

The California court in this case, however, significantly has extended this rule by providing that a request by a juvenile for his probation officer has the same effect as a request for an attorney. Based on the court's belief that the probation officer occupies a position as a trusted guardian figure in the minor's life that would make it normal for the minor to turn to the officer when apprehended by the police, and based as well on the state-law requirement that the officer represent the interest of the juvenile, the California decision found that consultation with a probation officer fulfilled the role for the juvenile that consultation with an attorney does in general, acting as a "'protective [device]...to dispel the compulsion inherent in custodial surroundings.'" 21 Cal. 3d, at 477, 57 P.2d, at 10, quoting *Miranda v. Arizona*, 384 U.S., at 458.

The rule in *Miranda*, however, was based on this Court's perception that the lawyer occupies a critical position in our legal system because of his unique ability to protect the Fifth Amendment rights of a client undergoing custodial interrogation. Because of this special ability of the lawyer to help the client preserve his Fifth Amendment rights once the client becomes enmeshed in the adversary process, the Court found that "the right to have counsel present at the interrogation is indispensable to the protection of the Fifth Amendment privilege under the system" established by the Court. *Id* at 469. Moreover, the lawyer's presence helps guard against overreaching by the police and ensures that any statements actually obtained are accurately transcribed for presentation into evidence. *Id.*, at 470.

The *per se* aspect of *Miranda* was thus based on the unique role the lawyer plays in the adversary system of criminal justice in this country. Whether it is a minor or an adult who stands accused, the lawyer is the one person to whom society as a whole looks as the protector of the legal rights of that person in his dealings with the police and the courts. For this reason, the Court fashioned in *Miranda* the rigid rule that an accused's request for an attorney is *per se* an invocation of his Fifth Amendment rights, requiring that all interrogation cease.

A probation officer is not in the same posture with regard to either the accused or the system of justice as a whole. Often he is not trained in the law, and so is not in a position to advise the accused as to his legal rights. Neither is he a trained advocate, skilled in the representation of the interests of his client before both police and courts. He does not assume the power to act on behalf of his client by virtue of his status as adviser, nor are the communications of the accused to the probation officer shielded by the lawyer-client privilege.

Moreover, the probation officer is the employee of the State which seeks to prosecute the alleged offender. He is a peace officer, and as such is allied, to a greater or lesser extent, with his fellow peace officers. He owes an obligation to the State, notwithstanding the obligation he may also owe the juvenile under his supervision. In most cases, the probation officer is duty bound to report wrongdoing by the juvenile when it comes to his attention, even if by communication from the juvenile himself. Indeed, when this case arose, the probation officer had the responsibility for filing the petition alleging wrongdoing by the juvenile and seeking to have him taken into the custody of the Juvenile Court. It was respondent's probation officer who filed the petition against him, and it is the acting chief of probation for the State of California, a probation officer, who is petitioner in this Court today.[24]

In these circumstances, it cannot be said that the probation officer is able to offer the type of independent advice that an accused would expect from a lawyer retained or assigned to assist him during questioning.

[T]he fact that the State has created a statutory duty on the part of the probation officer to protect the interests of the juvenile does not render the probation officer any more capable of rendering legal assistance to the juvenile or of protecting his legal rights, especially in light of the fact that the State has also legislated a duty on the part of the officer to report wrongdoing by the juvenile and serve the ends of the juvenile court system. The State cannot transmute the relationship between probation officer and juvenile offender into the type of relationship between attorney and client that was essential to the holding of *Miranda* simply by legislating an amorphous "duty to advise and care for the juvenile defendant." 21 Cal. 3d, at 477, 579 P. 2d, at 10. Though such a statutory duty might serve to distinguish to some degree the probation officer

---

[24]When this case arose, a California statute provided that a proceeding in juvenile court to declare a minor a ward of the court was to be commenced by the filing of a petition by a probation officer. Cal. Welf. & Inst. Code Ann. § 650 (West 1972). This provision since has been amended to provide that most such petitions are to be filed by the prosecuting attorney. 1976 Cal. Stats., ch. 1071, § 20. Respondent argues that, whatever the status of the probation officer as a peace officer at the time this case arose, the amendment of § 650 indicates that in the future a probation officer is not to be viewed as a legal adversary of the accursed juvenile. Consequently, respondent believes that any holding of this Court with regard to respondent's 1976 request for a probation officer will be mere dictum with regard to a juvenile's similar request today. Brief for Respondent 9–10, and n. 4.

We disagree. The fact that a California probation officer in 1976 was responsible for initiating a complaint is only one factor in our analysis. The fact remains that a probation officer does not fulfill the role in our system of criminal justice that an attorney does, regardless of whether he acts merely as a counselor or has significant law enforcement duties.

from the coach and the clergyman, it does not justify the extension of *Miranda* to requests to see probation officers. If it did, the State could expand the class of persons covered by the *Miranda per se* rule simply by creating a duty to care for the juvenile on the part of other persons, regardless of whether the logic of *Miranda* would justify that extension.

Nor do we believe that a request by a juvenile to speak with his probation officer constitutes a *per se* request to remain silent. As indicated, since a probation officer does not fulfill the important role in protecting the rights of the accused juvenile that an attorney plays, we decline to find that the request for the probation officer is tantamount to the request for an attorney.

We hold, therefore, that it was error to find that the request by respondent to speak with his probation officer *per se* constituted an invocation of respondent's Fifth Amendment right to be free from compelled self-incrimination. It therefore was also error to hold that because the police did not then cease interrogating respondent the statements he made during interrogation should have been suppressed.

III

Miranda further recognized that after the required warnings are given the accused, "[i]f the interrogation continues without the presence of an attorney and a statement is taken, a heavy burden rests on the government to demonstrate that the defendant knowingly and intelligently waived his privilege against self-incrimination and his right to retained or appointed counsel." 384 U.S., at 475. We noted in *North Carolina* v. *Butler*, 441 U.S., at 373, that the question whether the accused waived his rights "is not one of form, but rather whether the defendant in fact knowingly and voluntarily waived the rights delineated in the *Miranda* case." Thus, the determination whether statements obtained during custodial interrogation are admissible against the accused is to be made upon an inquiry into the totality of the circumstances surrounding the interrogation, to ascertain whether the accused in fact knowingly and voluntarily decided to forgo his right to remain silent and to have the assistance of counsel. *Miranda v. Arizona*, 384 U.S., at 475–477.

This totality-of-the-circumstances approach is adequate to determine whether there has been a waiver even where interrogation of juveniles is involved. We discern no persuasive reasons why any other approach is required where the question is whether a juvenile has waived his rights, as opposed to whether an adult has done so. The totality approach permits—indeed, it mandates—inquiry into all the circumstances surrounding the interrogation. This includes evaluation of the juvenile's age, experience, education, background, and intelligence, and into whether he has the capacity to understand the warnings given him, the nature of his Fifth Amendment rights, and the consequences of waiving those rights. See *North Carolina v Butler, supra*.

Courts repeatedly must deal with these issues of waiver with regard to a broad variety of constitutional rights. There is no reason to assume that such courts—especially juvenile courts, with their special expertise in this area—will be unable to apply the totality-of-the-circumstances analysis so as to take into account those special concerns that are present when young persons, often with limited experience and education and with immature judgment, are involved. Where the age and experience of a juvenile indicate that his request for his probation officer or his parents is, in fact, an invocation of his right to remain silent, the totality approach will allow the court the necessary flexibility to take this into account in making waiver determination. At the same time, that approach refrains from imposing rigid restraints on police and courts in dealing with an experienced older juvenile with an extensive prior record who knowingly and intelligently waives his Fifth Amendment rights and voluntarily consents to interrogation.

In this case, we conclude that the California Supreme Court should have determined the issue of waiver on the basis of all the circumstances surrounding the interrogation of respondent.

IV

We hold, in short, that the California Supreme Court erred in finding that a juvenile's request for his probation officer was a *per se* invocation of that juvenile's Fifth Amendment rights under *Miranda*. We conclude, rather, that whether the statements obtained during subsequent interrogation of a juvenile who has asked to see his probation officer, but who has not asked to consult an attorney or expressly asserted his right to remain silent, are admissible on the basis of waiver remains a question to be resolved on the totality of the circumstances surrounding the interrogation. On the basis of the record in this case, we hold that the Juvenile Court's findings that respondent voluntarily and knowingly waived his rights and consented to continued interrogation, and that the statements obtained from him were voluntary, were proper, and that the admission of those statements in the proceeding against respondent in Juvenile Court was correct.

The judgement of the Supreme Court of California is reversed, and the case is remanded for further proceedings not inconsistent with this opinion.

IT IS SO ORDERED.

MR. JUSTICE MARSHALL, with whom MR. JUSTICE BRENNAN and MR. JUSTICE STEVENS join, dissenting.

In *Miranda v. Arizona*, 384 U. S. 436 (1966), this Court sought to ensure that the inherently coercive pressures of custodial interrogation would not vitiate a suspect's privilege against self-incrimination.

* * *

It is * * * critical in the present context that we construe *Miranda*'s prophylactic requirements broadly to accomplish their intended purpose—"dispel[ling] the compulsion inherent in custodial surroundings." 384 U. S., at 458. To effectuate this purpose, the Court must ensure that the "protective device" of legal counsel, *id.*, at 465–466, 469, be readily available, and that any intimation of a desire to preclude questioning be scrupulously honored. Thus, I believe *Miranda* requires that interrogation cease whenever a juvenile requests an adult who is obligated to represent his interests. * * *

On my reading of *Miranda*, a California juvenile's request for his probation officer should be treated as a *per se* assertion of Fifth Amendment rights. The California Supreme Court determined that probation officers have a statutory duty to represent minor's interests and, indeed, are "trusted guardian figure[s]" to whom a juvenile would likely turn for assistance. 21 Cal. 3d, at 476, 579 P. 2d at 10. In addition, the court found, probation officers are particularly well suited to assist a juvenile "on such matters as to whether or not he should obtain an attorney" and "how to conduct himself with police." *Id.*, at 476, 477, 579 P. 2d, at 10. Hence, a juvenile's request for a probation officer may frequently be an attempt to secure protection from the coercive aspects of custodial questioning.

This Court concludes, however, that because a probation officer has law enforcement duties, juveniles generally would not call upon him to represent their interests, and if they did would not be well served. *Ante*, at 721-722. But that conclusion ignores the California Supreme Court's express determination that the officer's responsibility to initiate juvenile proceedings did not negate his function as personal advisor to his wards.[25]

* * *

MR. JUSTICE POWELL, dissenting.

Although I agree with the Court that the Supreme Court of California misconstrued *Miranda* v. *Arizona*, 384 U. S. 436 (1966),[26] I would not reverse the California court's judgment. This Court repeatedly has recognized that "the greatest care" must be taken to assure that an alleged confession of a juvenile was voluntary. See, *e.g., In re Gault*, 387 U. S. 1, 55 (1967); *Gallegos v. Colorado*, 370 U. S. 49, 54 (1962); *Haley* v. *Ohio*, 332 U. S. 596, 599–600 (1948) (plurality opinion Respondent was a young person, 16 years old at the time of arrest and the subsequent prolonged interrogation at the station house. Although respondent had had prior brushes with the law, and was under supervision by a probation officer, the taped transcript of his interrogation—as well as his testimony at the suppression hearing—demonstrates

---

[25]In filing the petition and performing the other functions enumerated *ante*, at 720–721, n. 5, the probation officer must act in the best interests of the minor. See *In re Steven C.*, 9 Cal. App. 3d 255, 264–265, 88 Cal. Rpt. 97, 101–102 (1970).

[26]The California Supreme Court, purporting to apply *Miranda* v. *Arizona*, stated:

"Here...we face conduct which, regardless of considerations of capacity, coercion or voluntariness, per se invokes the privilege against self-incrimination." 21 Cal. 3d 471, 477, 579 P. 2d 7, 10 (1978). I agree with the Court's opinion today that *Miranda* cannot be read as support for any such *per se* rule.

that he was immature, emotional,[27] and uneducated, and therefore was likely to be vulnerable to the skillful, two-on-one, repetitive style of interrogation to which he was subjected. App. 54-????.

When given *Miranda* warnings and asked whether he desired an attorney, respondent requested permission to "have my probation officer here," a request that was refused. App. at 55. That officer testified later that he had communicated frequently with respondent, that respondent had serious and "extensive" family problems, and that the officer had instructed respondent to call him immediately "at any time he has a police contact, even if they stop him and talk to him on the street." *Id.*, at 26-31.[28] The reasons given by the probation officer for having so instructed his charge were substantially the same reasons that prompt this Court to examine with special care the circumstances under which a minor alleged confession was obtained. After stating that respondent had been "going through problems," the officer observed that "many times the kids don't understand what is going on and what they are supposed to do relative to police...." *Id.*, at 29. This view of the limited understanding of the average 16-year-old was borne out by respondent's question when during interrogation, he was advised of his right to an attorney: "How I know you guys won't pull no police officer in and tell me he's an attorney?" *Id.*, at 55. It was during this part of the interrogation that the police had denied respondent's request to "have my probation officer here." *Ibid.*

The police then proceeded, despite respondent's repeated denial of any connection to the murder under investigation see *id.*, at 56-60, persistently to press interrogation until they extracted a confession. In *In re Gault*, in addressing police interrogation of detained juveniles, the Court stated:

> "If counsel was not present for some permissible reason when an admission was obtained [from a child], the greatest care must be taken to assure that the admission was voluntary, in the sense not only that it was not coerced or suggested, but also that it was not the product of ignorance of rights or of adolescent fantasy, fright or despair." 387 U. S., at 55.

It is clear that the interrogating police did not exercise "the greatest care" to assure that respondent's "admission was voluntary" In the absence of counsel, and having refused to call the probation officer, they nevertheless engaged in protracted interrogation.

Although I view the case as closed, I am not satisfied that this particular 16-year-old boy, in this particular situation, was subjected to a fair interrogation free from inherently coercive circumstances. For these reasons, I would affirm the judgment of the Supreme Court of California.

* * *

---

[27]The Juvenile Court Judge observed that he had "heard the tapes" the interrogation, and was "aware of the fact that Michael [respondent] was crying at the time he talked to the police officers." App. 53.

[28]The Supreme Court of California stated that a "probation officer [is] an official appointed pursuant to legislative enactment 'to represent the interests' of the juvenile [and]...has borne the duty to advise and care for the juvenile defendant." 21 Cal. 3d, at 477, 579 P. 2d, at 10.

FARE v. MICHAEL C.

1. Relate the majority opinion to the historical role of probation officers in juvenile courts. What conflict is inherent in the probation officer's job? How does the case of *In re Gault* relate to this case in terms of both the Fifth Amendment and the historical role of the probation officer in juvenile court?

2. How does the doctrine of "totality of circumstances" relate to this case?

3. What steps have state legislatures taken in the past thirty years to attempt to protect juvenile suspects from unfair police interrogation practices? What are the procedural statutory implications of the *Fare* case?

4. List the steps that the police interrogators took in *Fare* to assure that the interrogation was conducted within the confines of the Fifth Amendment? Were any steps missing? If so, which ones?

Following the U.S. Supreme Court's *Fare* decision, state courts have concluded that it leaves undisturbed the state requirement that a juvenile's parent or other interested adult be present during the interrogation. The opinion in *Commonwealth v. Henderson* is illustrative.

COMMONWEALTH OF PENNSYLVANIA

v.

ARNOLD T. HENDERSON, APPELLANT.

SUPREME COURT OF PENNSYLVANIA.

ARGUED SEPT. 14, 1981.

DECIDED NOV. 5, 1981.

* * *

ROBERTS, JUSTICE.

On June 5, 1979, our Superior Court entered an order setting aside the conviction of appellant Arnold Henderson, a juvenile, and remanding for a new trial because of the prosecution's use at trial of a statement obtained from appellant in violation of this Commonwealth's "interested adult" rule. 266 Pa.Super. 519, 405 A.2d 940. This Court denied the Commonwealth's petition for allowance of appeal. However, on April 21, 1980, over the dissent of Justices Brennan and Stevens, the Supreme Court of the United States granted the Commonwealth's petition for a writ of certiorari, vacated the Superior Court's determination, and remanded the matter to the Superior Court "for further consideration in light of *Fare v. Michael C.*, 442 U.S. 707 [99 S.Ct. 2560, 61 L.Ed.2d 197] (1979)." 446 U.S. 905, 100 S.Ct. 1829, 64 L.Ed.2d 256. The Superior Court has transferred the matter to this Court. Hence this opinion.

We conclude that, because *Fare v. Michael C.* addresses only the rights of the accused under the federal Constitution, it has no effect upon the Superior Court's application of our interested-adult rule, which is founded upon state law. Thus, the order of the Superior Court granting appellant a new trial is reinstated.

I

Our interested-adult rule is premised on this Court's belief that "the administering of *Miranda* warnings to a juvenile, without providing an opportunity to that juvenile to consult with a mature, informed individual concerned primarily with the interest of the juvenile, [is] inadequate to offset the disadvantage occasioned by his youth." *Commonwealth v. Smith*, 472 Pa. 492, 498, 372 A.2d 797, 800 (1977). Thus police seeking to subject a juvenile suspect to custodial interrogation are required first to provide the juvenile with the opportunity to consult with an adult interested in the juvenile's welfare. This rule

> "appreciates that the inexperience of the minor affects not only his or her ability to understand the full implication and consequences of the predicament but also renders the judgment inadequate to assess the spectrum of considerations encompassed in the waiver decision."

Commonwealth v. Smith, supra.

A number of other jurisdictions also recognize the need to provide special protestations to juveniles subjected to custodial interrogation. Our rule is also supported by respected scholarship, which recognizes that "[j]uveniles should not be permitted to waive constitutional rights on their own." Institute of Judicial Administration—American Bar Association Juvenile Justice Standards, Police Handling of Juvenile Problems § 3.2 (1980). See also, *e.g.*, Council of Judges of the National Council on Crime and Delinquency, Model Rules for Juvenile Courts, Rule 25 (1969).

II

The Commonwealth argues that the Supreme Court's mandate vacating the determination of the Superior Court poses an opportunity to consider the wisdom of our interested-adult rule afresh, and to adopt the test applied by the Supreme Court of California which had held, as a matter of federal constitutional law, that a statement of a juvenile should have been suppressed on the ground that the juvenile's request to see his probation officer constituted an invocation of his *Miranda* rights. In setting aside the determination, the Supreme Court enforced no federal rights of the State. Rather, the Court held only that the state court had erroneously imposed greater restriction on police conduct than are required by the federal Constitution.

The Supreme Court of the United States has expressly stated:

> "Our only power over state judgments is to correct them to the extent they incorrectly adjudge federal rights. And our power is to correct wrong judgments, not to revise opinions. We are not permitted to render an advisory opinion, and if the same judgment would be rendered by the state

court after we corrected its views of federal laws, our review could amount to nothing more than an advisory opinion."

Herb v. Pitcairn, 324 U.S. 117, 125–126, 65 S.Ct. 459, 463, 89 L.Ed. 789 (1945).

Thus the determination of the Supreme Court of the United States interpreting the federal Constitution does not and could not disturb the force of our interested-adult rule, a matter of Pennsylvania law. See *Commonwealth v. Ware*, 446 Pa. 52, 284 A.2d 700 (1971), cert. granted sub nom. *Pennsylvania v. Ware*, 405 U.S. 987, 92 S.Ct. 1254, 31 L.Ed.2d 453, subsequently vacated and denied, 406 U.S. 910, 92 S.Ct. 1606, 31 L.Ed.2d 821 (1972) ("it appearing that the judgment below rests upon an adequate state ground"). As this Court recently observed,

> "[I]t is well settled that a state may provide through its constitution a basis for the rights and liberties of its citizens independent from that provided by the Federal Constitution, and that the rights so guaranteed may be more expansive than their federal counterparts. *Prune-Yard Shopping Center v. Robins*, 447 U.S. 74, 80—82, 100 S.Ct. 2035, 2040–41, 64 L.Ed.2d 741 (1980); see *Oregon v. Hass*, 420 U.S. 714, 719, 95 S.Ct. 1215, 1219, 43 L.Ed.2d 570 (1975); *Cooper v. California*, 386 U.S. 58, 62, 87 S.Ct. 788, 791, 17 L.Ed.2d 730 (1967). * * *"

The decision of the Supreme Court of the United States in *Miranda v. Arizona*, 384 U.S. 436, 86 S.Ct. 1602, 16 L.Ed.2d 694 (1966), extended the federal fifth amendment privilege against self-incrimination to the setting of custodial interrogation, and applied the extension to the States by way of the fourteenth amendment. As early as 1969, three years after *Miranda*, this Court began to harmonize *Miranda's* interpretation of the federal privilege with this Court's interpretation of the Pennsylvania Constitution's prohibition against the compelling of an accused "to give evidence against himself." Pa.Const. art. I, § 9. In *Commonwealth v. Bruno*, 435 Pa. 200, 255 A.2d 519 (1969), this Court observed:

> "*Miranda v. Arizona*, extended the right against self-incrimination and the right to the assistance of counsel, from the formal 'criminal proceeding,' *i.e.*, the trial, to police interrogation. For similar reasons, we long ago indicated that the right against self-incrimination protects a person from being compelled to answer any question propounded to him by those making a mental examination 'for the purpose of testifying in regard thereto' at a criminal trial. *Commonwealth v. Musto*, 348 Pa. 300, 306, 35 A.2d 307, 311 (1944). Both *Miranda* and *Musto* simply recognize that the guilt determining process does not begin at trial."

Commonwealth v. Bruno, 435 Pa. at 207, 255 A.2d at 523.

Two years later, in *Commonwealth v. Ware*, 446 Pa. 52, 284 A.2d 700 (1971), this Court addressed the appropriate date on which to commence the application of *Miranda*. The Commonwealth contended that the rules of *Miranda* should be applied only to police conduct occurring after the date of the *Miranda* decision. Concluding that under the decision of the Supreme Court of the United States in *Johnson v. New Jersey*, 384 U.S. 719, 86 S.Ct. 1772, 16 L.Ed.2d 882 (1966), "the matter is no longer an open question," this Court rejected the Commonwealth's contention and held that "the *Miranda* standards must be applied to all post-*Miranda* trials...." 446 Pa. at 55, 284 A.2d at 702. The determination in *Ware* did not rest exclusively upon the decision of the Supreme Court in *Johnson*. Rather, this Court expressly added that "we adopt the *Johnson* position as a matter of state law." 446 Pa. at 56, 284 A.2d at 702. Because this Court could have reached the result in *Ware* by choosing to hold only that the matter was controlled by *Johnson*, *Ware's* reliance upon state law is significant. Indeed, the Supreme Court initially granted the Commonwealth's petition for a writ of certiorari, 405 U.S. 987, 92 S.Ct. 1254, 31 L.Ed.2d 453, but then vacated its order, "it appearing that the judgment below rests upon an adequate state ground." 406 U.S. 910, 92 S.Ct. 1606, 31 L.Ed.2d 821 (1972).

Subsequent case law demonstrates that *Ware's* deliberate reliance upon state law was a recognition that the principles embodied in *Miranda* are salutary and deserving of application as a matter not only of federal but also of state law. Following *Ware*, in *Commonwealth v. Triplett*, 462 Pa. 244, 341 A.2d 62 (1975), this Court considered the propriety of a prosecutor's use of an unconstitutionally obtained statement for impeachment purposes. In *Harris v. New York*, 401 U.S. 222, 91 S.Ct. 643, 28 L.Ed.2d 1 (1971), the Supreme Court of the United States held that a statement obtained in violation of *Miranda* could be used for impeachment purposes, provided that the statement was trustworthy. This Court rejected *Harris* and concluded that "any statement of a defendant declared inadmissible for any reason by a suppression court cannot be used for the purpose of impeaching the credibility of a defendant who elects to testify on his own behalf at trial." 462 Pa. at 248–49, 341 A.2d at 64. In harmony with the approach taken in *Ware*, this Court added: "[o]ur prohibition against the use of constitutionally infirm statements to impeach the credibility of a criminal defendant testifying in his own behalf is premised upon Pennsylvania Constitution Article I, Section 9...." 462 Pa. at 249, 341 A.2d at 64.[29]

Since *Ware* and *Triplett*, our cases have confirmed, in unanimous decisions, that this Court's approach to custodial interrogation claims is not controlled exclusively by decisions of the Supreme Court of the United States. In *Commonwealth v. Brown*, 473 Pa. 562, 375 A.2d 1260 (1977), as in *Ware* and *Triplett*, this Court reaffirmed the independent force of Pennsylvania law in determining the scope of rights to which a suspect subjected to custodial interrogation is entitled:

> "*Miranda v. Arizona*, [supra,] and the decisions of this Court, see *e.g.*, *Commonwealth v. Fisher*, 466 Pa. 216, 352 A.2d 26 (1976); *Commonwealth v. Romberger*, 464 Pa. 488, 347 A.2d 460 (1975), require that, before an individual is subjected to custodial interrogation, he must make a knowing

---

[29]As *Triplett* is reported at 462 Pa. 244, it would appear that only six members of the seven-member Court participated in the decision, and that *Triplett's* rejection of *Harris* on state constitutional grounds had the support of three members of the Court—Mr. Justice (now Chief Justice) O'Brien, Mr. Justice Nix, and Justice Manderino. However, at 341 A.2d 62, *Triplett* is reported as having been considered by a full seven-member Court, with the rejection of *Harris* as being shared by four members—the above-mentioned three as well as this writer. Court records confirm that this writer did indeed participate in the decision in *Triplett*, and shared the view expressed by Mr. Justice O'Brien.

Any uncertainty concerning the precedential value of *Triplett* is resolved by *Commonwealth v. Hannah*, 462 Pa. 256, 341 A.2d 68 (1975), where, on the basis of *Triplett*, five of this Court's seven members joined in an opinion reversing an order of the Superior Court and granting a new trial.

> and intelligent waiver of his privilege against self-incrimination and right to counsel, U.S.Const.Amend. V, VI, XIV; Pa.Const. Art. I, § 9, after adequate warning as to these rights."

473 Pa. at 569, 375 A.2d at 1264. Most recently, in *Commonwealth v. Meyer*, 488 Pa. 297, 412 A.2d 517 (1980), this Court confirmed the independence of this Court's test for "custody." Rejecting the Commonwealth's contention that this Court should follow the then-recent case of the Supreme Court, *Beckwith v. United States*, 425 U.S. 341, 96 S.Ct. 1612, 48 L.Ed.2d 1 (1976), this Court observed:

> "[T]he Commonwealth's exposition of what it views to be the guiding rule of law seriously understates the circumstances in which *Miranda* warnings must be given in Pennsylvania. The Commonwealth now, in supposed harmony with *Beckwith*, would have it that police must give warnings only if they interrogate one in actual custody or otherwise significantly deprived of freedom. But this jurisdiction's test of 'custodial interrogation' examines more than actual deprivation of freedom. * * * As this Court unanimously stated in *Brown*, supra,
>
> * * *
>
> 'the test of custodial interrogation is whether the individual being interrogated reasonably believes his freedom of action is being restricted.'"

488 Pa. at 306–307, 412 A.2d at 521.

Thus, beginning most notably with *Commonwealth v. Ware*, supra, our cases make clear that the core concepts originally articulated in *Miranda v. Arizona* not only have been followed pursuant to our obligation as a part of the federal system, but also have been recognized as separately compelled by the law of Pennsylvania. As a consequence, this Court has independently evaluated the proper approach to be followed to assure that this Commonwealth's privilege against self-incrimination is properly applied to custodial interrogation.

The rule of McCutchen is an additional instance in which this Court has sought to give proper meaning and independent force to this Commonwealth's privilege. Thus, whether the issue is the meaning of custody, *Commonwealth v. Meyer*, supra, the permissible use of an illegally-obtained statement, *Commonwealth v. Triplett*, supra, or the means of best assuring an effective waiver of rights by a juvenile suspect, *Commonwealth v. McCutchen*, supra, this Court is considering this Commonwealth's privilege apart from the privilege contained in the federal Constitution and recognizing the privilege as "an alternative and independent source of individual rights." *Commonwealth v. Tate*, supra.

Accordingly, the order of the Superior Court is reinstated.

LARSEN, Justice.

I dissent.

The question presented by this case is simply whether appellant Arnold T. Henderson knowingly, voluntarily and intelligently waived his constitutional rights before giving a statement to the police implicating himself in a homicide. The majority, although obfuscating the question to some degree, eventually concludes that he did not so waive his rights. The basis for this conclusion is the majority's "interested adult" rule which irrebuttably presumes that no one under the magic age of 18 years can make a statement to the police without the assistance of the indispensable "interested adult." *See, e.g., Commonwealth v. McCutchen*, 463 Pa. 90, 343 A.2d 669 (1975) and *Commonwealth v. Smith*, 472 Pa. 492, 372 A.2d 797 (1977). This rule supposedly rests upon a concern for the inexperience of youth. *Id.*

I do not share the majority's appreciation of this rule and believe that justice for all concerned can only be achieved by a flexible rule which considers all of the surrounding circumstances, including the experience possessed by many youthful participants in crime and other factors which indicate that a lack of chronological age has not disadvantaged the defendant or caused his will to be overborne.

FLAHERTY and KAUFFMAN, JJ., join in this dissenting opinion.

KAUFFMAN, Justice, dissenting.

I dissent from the majority opinion which imposes a rigid *per se* rule requiring consultation with an "interested adult" whenever a juvenile is interrogated by the police. The majority would exclude any incriminating statement made by an accused juvenile, *regardless of the circumstances*, where he has not consulted with an interested adult.

The federal Constitution clearly does not require this extreme result. *See Fare v. Michael C.*, 442 U.S. 707, 99 S.Ct. 2560, 61 L.Ed.2d 197 (1979). Without any concern for the particular circumstances of this case, however, the majority concludes that its rule is mandated by the law of this Commonwealth, and reinstates the Superior Court order vacating appellant's convictions of first degree murder, robbery, burglary, theft, criminal conspiracy and unauthorized use of an automobile. (at pgs. 388, 389–390, 392).[30] While I agree that state and federal constitutional protections are not necessarily coextensive, and that states may provide safeguards beyond those prescribed in the federal Constitution, nothing in the law of this Commonwealth dictates the inflexible rule fashioned by the majority.

I would, therefore, affirm the judgment of sentence.

LARSEN and FLAHERTY, JJ., join in this dissenting opinion.

COMMONWEALTH V. HENDERSON

1. The dissent mentioned a "bright line" between childhood and adulthood. How does this "bright line" relate to the "interested adult rule"?

2. Compare the "interested adult rule" with the "totality of circumstances rule" as they relate to police interrogations of juveniles.

---

[30]The trial court held that the written statement of appellant, a 15 year old, was properly admitted after a consideration of the totality of the circumstances.

3. Why did the majority in this case conclude that the appellant did not knowingly and intelligently waive his fifth amendment rights?

4. This case is an excellent research resource for fifth amendment applications. To what extent do such cases enlighten and inform with respect to the nature of youth and the disadvantages youths face in a custodial police interrogation situation?

THE ORDER MAINTENANCE TASK: LOW VISIBILITY INTERACTIONS BETWEEN POLICE AND JUVENILES

The bulk of police/juvenile encounters do not involve arrest. Thus, they fall outside the law enforcement function of Wilson's typology of the police role. More properly, one might characterize the task of policing juveniles as essentially an exercise in order maintenance— the use of police authority to prevent, defuse or resolve various types of interpersonal conflicts—often involving youth—which, left unchecked, might evolve into a more serious crime. This rather straightforward description of the police officer's order maintenance role—while intuitively reasonable—begs a host of important conceptual, legal, and practical questions. For example, the term "order maintenance" suggests that there is something called "order" which is presumably good, and its opposite, "disorder" which is presumably bad, and that police should act to increase the former, while preventing or reducing the latter. But, how are "order" and its opposite, "disorder" defined? More importantly, when we suggest, as we have above, that police are to use their authority to maintain order, what kind of "authority" is employed? Since order maintenance interactions do not seem to involve the exercise of arrest powers and reliance on the formal authority of the criminal law, on what grounds can police officers make their order maintenance decisions "stick"? How are we to determine if an officer's actions, or a departmental policy aimed at controlling some aspect of disorder is excessive or unreasonable? While complete answers to these questions is beyond the scope of this section of the chapter, we can perhaps draw some tentative conclusions as part of a brief analysis of order maintenance interactions between cops and kids.

A. Community Disorder and Crime

Although the notion that juvenile delinquency and adult crime breed in run down, seedy, disorganized and disordered areas in a city is not new,[31] recent works by Wilson and Kelling[32] and Skogan[33]

---

[31]See for example, Shaw et al., *Delinquency Areas*, (Chicago: University of Chicago Press, 1929); Shaw and McKay, *Juvenile Delinquency and Urban Areas* (revised ed.), (Chicago: University of Chicago Press, [1942] 1972).

[32]Wilson and Kelling, "Broken Windows" *The Atlantic Monthly*, March 1982: 29–38; Wilson and Kelling, "Making Neighborhoods Safe," *The Atlantic Monthly*, February 1989: 46–52.

[33]Skogan, *Disorder and Decline: Crime and the Spiral of Decay in American Neighborhoods*, (New York: The Free Press, 1990).

have redefined the concept of disorder somewhat, making it more measurable, and attempted to explore its relationship to crime.[34] Skogan's work is particularly helpful in clarifying the definition of disorder.

Using information from surveys of residents of 40 neighborhoods in six cities—Chicago, Philadelphia, San Francisco, Newark, Atlanta and Houston—supplemented with field observations, Skogan found that disorder in a neighborhood has both social and physical components. Social disorder is characterized public drinking in skid rows and public parks, groups of youths loitering on street corners who harass or threaten passersby, persons who engage in street level drug transactions, and noisy neighbors, and, in some locations, the presence of street prostitution and sexually oriented businesses.[35] Physical disorder related to the cleanliness of a neighborhood, and was typified by the presence of vandalized or abandoned autos or buildings, and excessive quantities of uncollected or scattered garbage. Chronically exposed to the "public displays of incivility"[36] and the noxious environment of an area in decline, high levels of disorder generate feelings of anger over the neighborhood's condition, demoralization that no one seems to care about the disorder, and increases the fear of victimization among community residents.[37] Elaborating on the relationship between disorder and demoralization, Skogan presents a model of the crime-disorder relationship in which disorder in a neighborhood reduces the level of trust people living in an area have for one another. Believing that no one will help them if attacked or victimized, people feel vulnerable in the face of crime. Also, disorder reduces the sense of ownership that people feel regarding the public spaces in their community. With people less willing to watch out for strangers and keep a protective eye on their neighbors, a curtain of social anonymity descends on an area, and opportunities to get away with crime increase.[38] Statistical analysis of the survey data, and systematic review of the field notes taken by observers sent to the neighborhoods in the study, provided substantial support for the model. For example, levels of disorder were negatively related to levels of neighborhood solidarity (-.59);[39] and positively related to robbery victimization (+.80).[40]

---

[34]For a critique of the crime-disorder relationship, see Taylor and Gottfredson, "Environmental Design, Crime and Prevention," in Reiss and Tonry (Eds.), *Communities and Crime*, 387 (Chicago: University of Chicago Press, 1986).

[35]Skogan, *supra*.

[36]*Id.*

[37]*Id.* The community resident's negative view of disorder and its detrimental consequences is not the only light in which one may view disorder. Skogan notes that some observers (who perhaps lived elsewhere) have suggested that a degree of disorder either enriches the lives of individuals, or promotes diversity and loosens the constricting bonds of society.

[38]*Id.*

[39]*Id.*

[40]*Id.*

B. Policing Disorder

A combination of technological, organizational, social and legal changes over the past 75 years or so have lowered the priority that law enforcement agencies assign to the problems of disorder. As several authors have noted, a large proportion of routine police activities in the early part of the twentieth century were devoted to order maintenance tasks consistent with the times.[41] However, these same authors go on to note that technological changes such as the widespread use of the telephone and the invention of the two way radio, while allowing faster police response in emergency situations, had the unintended consequences of reducing the need for decentralized police stations in individual communities (*i.e.*, the precinct house) and isolating officers on patrol from routine, non-emergency contact with community residents, thereby reducing both the officers' sensitivity to community norms regarding order, and their concern for the presence of disorder.

Organizationally, the trend toward the bureaucratic centralization of police operations (*i.e.*, the creation of detective bureaus, and vice units that operated out of single location that could be more easily supervised), undertaken in an effort to control corruption, also had the unintended consequence of separating police officers from routine contact with community residents.

Social changes, particularly the growing volume of serious crime, gradually forced a modification of police priorities toward law enforcement and away from order maintenance. The increased volume of serious crime also changed the nature of police citizen contacts: whereas in the past, daily, routine encounters with community residents permitted the identification, discussion and relatively amicable resolution of order maintenance problems, police citizen encounters in the present time occur in times of crisis and urgency, when both residents and police may be angry, upset or afraid. Such brief, emotion laden contacts between relative strangers do not foster congenial police community relations.

Finally, legal changes forced reduced concern for the problem of disorder and lowered the priority of police order maintenance activities. For example, judicial intolerance of the practice of making "sweep" arrests of disorderly persons and concern about the vagueness inherent in vagrancy and loitering statutes, made police reliance on these methods to control disorder untenable. Similarly the "medicalization" of

---

[41]Relying on several published works on the history of policing, such as Hartog, "Pigs and Positivism," *1985 Wisconsin Law Review* 899 (1985); Reiss, "Consequences of Compliance and Deterrence Models of Law Enforcement for the Exercise of Police Discretion" *47 Law and Contemporary Problems* 81 (1984); Monkkonen, *Police in Urban America, 1860–1920*, (Cambridge: Cambridge University Press, 1981) and Walker *A Critical History of Police Reform*, (Lexington, Massachusetts: Lexington Books, 1977), Skogan lists a wide variety of order maintenance activities routinely handled by police during the 1920s including, conducting health inspections, caring for lost children, licensing of street peddlers, rounding up stray animals, operating soup kitchens and shelters for the homeless, and providing aid to victims of health emergencies and accidents. He also describes in detail how the technological, organizational, social and legal changes briefly alluded to here changed the nature of policing. Necessarily, present discussion closely tracks his. Skogan, *id*.

some forms of deviance such as public drunkenness limited police ability to employ a traditional response—arrest—to a major component of social disorder.

There seem to be two likely effects of reduced police concern for order maintenance. First, order maintenance problems are designated "garbage calls" within the police bureaucracy (recall the characterization by Moore in the quotation above) and, absent a citizen complaint, are left to fester until they become law enforcement problems subject to resolution by a more traditional police response—arrest.

Second, where a citizen's complaint does force a police response to a problem involving disorderly, but not quite illegal behavior—for example a group of youths standing on a street corner making harassing comments to female passersby[42]—the authority on which the officer's intervention rests is largely symbolic rather than actual.[43] Thus, the enforcement of the rather amorphous "law" in such situations is apparently a source of discomfort for the police officers goaded into acting. As a result, intervening officers are likely to wind up resenting the complainant *and* the troublesome youth[44] while simultaneously fostering a belief among the juveniles that the police are unjustifiably harassing them. In her study of the dynamics of police juvenile interactions, Guarino-Ghezzi's interviews with a group of adjudicated delinquents in Boston revealed that aggressive efforts by police to control disorder tended to amplify it, corroding police-juvenile interactions.[45]

On the police side, then, a view of order maintenance tasks as "garbage calls," and a tendency to respond to disorder in a manner that gives rise to feelings of harassment in youth, gradually poisons the interactions between cops and neighborhood kids. But the attitudes and behaviors of youths contribute to the problem too. Guarino-Ghezzi found that youths feared police retaliation, and suggested that they "[felt] that police were indifferent to the chronic danger of their environment."

In addition to the fear of police retaliation feeling of vulnerability (leading to target aggression), the negative attitudes of juveniles toward the police may be reinforced indirectly by the presence of large numbers of ex-offenders among community residents.

---

[42]Such encounters have been labelled "little rapes." See Medea and Thompson, *Against Rape*, (New York: Farrar, Strauss and Geroux, 1974).

[43]Of course, as we have pointed out previously, one type of task may evolve into another. Thus, there could come a point in the police juvenile interaction where an arrest would become justifiable.

[44]Muir, *Police: Streetcorner Politicians*, (Chicago: University of Chicago Press, 1977).

[45]Guarino-Ghezzi, D. "Reintegrative Police Surveillance of Juvenile Offenders: Forging an Urban Model." 40 *Crime and Delinquency* 131 (1994).

IMPROVING POLICE-JUVENILE RELATIONS

Skogan[46] and Guarino-Ghezzi[47] suggest that police agencies may be able to increase their ability to control community disorder and improve relations with juvenile residents in an area by moving away from the centralized, bureaucratic and reactive methods of dealing with law enforcement problems, which have become the norm over the last 70 years or so. Instead, they recommend the use of an alternative approach that relies on the principles of a movement known as "community policing."

This new approach draws its principles from a wide variety of diverse efforts to overcome many different kinds of problems associated with more "traditional" policing doctrine, and has both supporters and critics.[48] For the purposes of the present chapter, it is sufficient to describe the community policing movement generally as one which emphasizes: (1) the transfer of at least some police operations out of a central headquarters into "community stations" located in neighborhoods in a jurisdiction; (2) the use of "citizen contact patrols" and other methods to facilitate regular, informal "two way communication" between police officers and local residents; (3) the "assum[ption] of a broadly focused, problem-oriented" view of the police role that actively seeks out and responds to citizen demands and needs that flow from the local community, rather than trying to identify community problems from the distance of central headquarters; and (4) the development of an active partnership between police and community residents wherein the police see their role as encompassing more than just law enforcement; instead, the goal is to help the community residents organize to prevent crime and solve local problems.[49] It should be emphasized however, that the "community policing" approach prescribes no "standard" model for implementing the four principles described above; tremendous variation in practices and policies can exist from one community policing program to another.

Using illustrations from a number of programs described by Guarino-Ghezzi, it is possible to briefly sketch some of the ways in which general principles of community policing have been adapted in an attempt to change the nature of police encounters with juveniles. For example, police in Aurora, Colorado have created decentralized gang-crime prevention units. Officers in these units "wear modified uniforms so that they are not perceived as traditional police officers," work altered shift patterns, and "make between 10 and 30 contacts with gang members on a daily patrol." The high frequency of informal contacts creates the impression that police surveillance of their activities and enforcement of the law are constant and consistent, and presumably reduces the juveniles' development of a view of the police as an incompetent, arbitrary army of occupation. The program also illustrates the community policing principle

---

[46]Skogan, *supra*.

[47]Guarino-Ghezzi, *supra*, at 46.

[48]For an overview of this approach or movement, see Moore, *supra*.

[49]These four characteristics are adapted from a discussion by Skogan, *supra*.

of two way communication, since frequent informal contacts with youths allows officers to develop information from the gang members themselves that can be used to prevent outbreaks of violence.

Finally, the third and fourth principles of community policing, which stress the formation of active partnerships between the police and community residents in order to identify and solve community problems, are illustrated by an innovative juvenile justice program in Carlesbad, California. Responding to community concerns about the local juvenile justice agencies' apparent inability to reduce youth crime, local police helped establish a citizen's tribunal which hears the cases of first time offenders and assigns punishments of community service or counseling.

THE SERVICE TASK: EMERGENCY SERVICE, EDUCATION/PREVENTION EFFORTS TARGETED AT JUVENILES

The final component of the police role is the provision of various types of service to members of the community. The specific activities that fall under the heading of service can vary tremendously, and therefore, it is not possible to provide anything approaching a complete description of this role. However, for illustrative purposes, two general types of services can be identified: (1) the provision of emergency aid on an *ad hoc* basis; and (2) the delivery of educational/crime prevention services to local youth.

A. Emergency Aid

Since police officers are available to respond to emergencies on a year-round, round-the-clock basis, they are frequently called upon to provide immediate aid to juveniles who are experiencing some sort of crisis, or who are in a life threatening situation. These services are provided on demand and frequently require officers to respond creatively in an *ad hoc* fashion to the dictates of a particular situation. Activities in this area can include such things as: transporting abused or neglected infants to a local shelter facility, the provision of emergency medical care, or providing on scene crisis counselling to a suicidal teenager.

B. Prevention Efforts

In many communities, police officers routinely visit local schools to conduct educational programs designed to prevent the development of delinquent behavior. One effort, the Drug Abuse Resistance Education (DARE) Program was developed in 1983 by the Los Angeles Police Department and Los Angeles School System. As part of the program, specially trained uniformed police officers visit elementary and secondary school classrooms and provide information of the dangers of drug abuse, and suggest ways that students can resisted the pressure of peers who may want them to try drugs. In the years since, similar programs have been developed in virtually all the states, and several foreign countries. It is estimated that DARE programs have been presented in more than 50,000 classrooms.[50] While popular with students,

[50]Statement of U.S. Representative Mel Levine, *Congressional Record—Daily ed.*, H6333–4, July 21, 1992.

school administrators, police and parents,[51] some have been critical of the long term impact of the program.[52] Despite the controversy, the DARE program stands as an excellent example of the kind of outreach efforts that police agencies can undertake to prevent the development of delinquent behavior in youth. In a more recent development, some jurisdictions are now assigning uniformed, armed officers on a full-time basis in some secondary schools. These School Resource Officers (SROs) respond in the event of an emergency, but also fulfill an educational and counselling role.[53]

CONCLUSION

As this chapter has shown, the widely varied nature of the police role can be organized into three general types of tasks: law enforcement, order maintenance and service. Although officers see their primary role as law enforcement, research has shown that the majority of contacts between the police and juveniles occur in order maintenance situations, where: (1) police officers and juveniles carry different perceptions of "orderly" or "civil" behavior; (2) the legal basis supporting police action is unclear; and (3) the necessary reliance on discretion can result in the appearance of inconsistent patterns of rule enforcement. These three factors contribute to the development of negative attitudes among cops and kids.

[51]Blasik and Belsito, *Drug Abuse Resistance Education Program (DARE): Evaluation Report*, (Florida: Broward County School Board, 1993).

[52]Becker, et al. "Impact Evaluation of Drug Abuse Resistance Education (DARE)," 22 *Journal of Drug Education* 283 (1992).

[53]Guarino-Ghezzi, *supra*, at 46.

CHAPTER 3

THE PRE-ADJUDICATORY PHASE OF THE JUVENILE JUSTICE PROCESS: DIVERSION, DETENTION AND TRANSFER OF JUVENILE OFFENDERS

THE PRE-ADJUDICATORY PHASE OF THE JUVENILE JUSTICE PROCESS: DIVERSION, DETENTION AND TRANSFER OF JUVENILE OFFENDERS

INTRODUCTION

Even a tiny pebble lodged firmly in a shoe causes discomfort out of all proportion to its size. No matter how much the wearer tries to ignore it, discomfort builds until it becomes impossible to notice anything else but the pain. Eventually, nothing matters but the pebble. By the 1960s, a small core of criminologists—known as "labelling" theorists—and a number of influential policymakers in the field of juvenile justice had come to the conclusion that the label "delinquent," once attached to youths, had much in common with a pebble in one's shoe: it focused people's attention on those who were labelled, and made it impossible to notice anything else about them. Eventually, it was thought, nothing mattered but the fact that they were delinquent. Moreover, labelling theorists suspected that the act of officially identifying young people as a delinquent could actually *produce* additional delinquent behavior by causing those who were labelled to reformulate their self concepts in accordance with the expectations of others. Concern with the stigmatizing effect of the delinquent label, then, combined with a number of other forces described below—created an intense pressure throughout the 1960s and 1970s to keep as many youths as possible *out* of the juvenile justice system. This strangely ironic policy,[1] known generally as *diversion*, will be one of the topics of this chapter.

Commentators point out that a number of due process problems can surface in the context of a diversion program. For example, the fact that diversion is meant to be a less stigmatizing and non-punitive alternative to adjudication and institutionalization, raises the possibility that prosecutors will use participation in a diversion program as an element of a plea bargain, contingent, of course, on the juvenile's admission of guilt, and thereby calling into question the voluntariness of the youth's participation.

---

[1]The policy is labelled ironic in recognition of the fact that, according to the traditional interpretation, the term "delinquency" and, the juvenile court itself was designed to spare children from the stigmatizing effects of the label, "criminal."

Additionally, issues of self-incrimination must be considered in relation to diversion programs. To the extent that a juvenile's suitability for a diversion program is made on the basis of an interview with a police officer, prosecutor or some other member of the juvenile court staff, the possibility that the juvenile will make an incriminating statement exists. The case *State v. Quiroz*, excerpted below, confronts just this issue:

STATE OF WASHINGTON, RESPONDENT,

v.

DAVID QUIROZ AND CLARK HAAS, APPELLANTS.

SUPREME COURT OF WASHINGTON,

EN BANC.

MARCH 5, 1987.

* * *

DORE, JUSTICE.

Two juvenile offenders challenge the use of a diversion agreement in their criminal history on the basis that the agreement violated their constitutional and statutory rights.

FACTS

This is a consolidated case dealing with two juvenile offenders. David Quiroz pleaded guilty to one count of taking a motor vehicle without permission and one count of second degree burglary. These offenses occurred in October 1985, and Quiroz was sentenced on November 26, 1985.

The Juvenile Justice Act of 1977, RCW 13.40, provides for very structured sentences, weighing both the severity of the offense as well as the juvenile's past criminal record. Quiroz' history consisted of two prior diverted misdemeanors, stemming from a single incident in September 1985. These misdemeanors effectively increased Quiroz' sentence from a maximum of 20 to 40 days. Similar increases also occurred in the amount of community supervision, community service, and fine which Quiroz received.

Quiroz challenged the use of the September 1985 diverted misdemeanors. Specifically, Quiroz asked the trial court to void the diversion agreement because at the time he was not informed of the nature of the charges against him. Furthermore, Quiroz alleged that his right to counsel and trial was denied. The trial court refused to grant Quiroz' motion and sentenced him using the two diverted misdemeanors. Quiroz appealed. Quiroz also raised an equal protection argument, claiming that he received a longer sentence for the second set of offenses because of his diversion agreement than he would have had he pleaded guilty to the first set of charges.

The companion case deals with a similar fact pattern. Clark Haas pleaded guilty to third degree theft for stealing two packs of cigarettes from a drug store. Haas' criminal history consisted of four misdemeanors, three of which had been diverted, and one felony. Haas challenged the use of one of the diverted offenses on constitutional grounds, as it had the effect of increasing his maximum detention sentence from 2 to 4 days as well as increasing the amount of community supervision and service. A different Yakima County judge also denied his motion to void his diversion agreement. Haas appealed, and Division Three consolidated the two cases for review before this court.

DIVERSION AGREEMENTS

A diversion agreement is "a contract between a juvenile accused of an offense and a diversionary unit whereby the juvenile agrees to fulfill certain conditions in lieu of prosecution." RCW 13.40.080(1). Typically, for minor offenses the county prosecutor often refers a juvenile to a probation officer who enters into a diversion agreement with the juvenile. A diversion agreement can require community service and supervision, as well as a fine, but the juvenile cannot be sentenced to detention unless after a hearing a judge decides the juvenile has violated the terms of the agreement. RCW 13.40.080(2); 13.40.080(6).

Diversion agreements benefit the State and the juvenile. The more informal diversion process is faster than court proceedings. The process also keeps juvenile offenders out of institutions and in the community where the resources to deal with their behavior are better suited to their age. *State v. Chatham*, 28 Wash.App.580, 624 P.2d 1180, *review denied*, 96 Wash.2d 1006 (1981), *State v. Tracy M.*, 43 Wash.App. 888, 720 P.2d 841 (1986). Finally, although the diversion agreement may for a time figure into a juvenile's criminal history and therefore affect a detention sentence for a future offense, the agreement is not the same as a conviction. Thus, the juvenile does not have the same stigma of having been convicted of a crime. Commen, *Diversion Agreements Under Washington's Juvenile Justice Act of 1977*, 14 Gonz.L.Rev. 423, 432 (1979).

RIGHT TO COUNSEL

Quiroz and Haas challenge the method the Yakima probation officers used during the diversion process. One of their chief objections is that they did not receive an adequate opportunity to consult with counsel.

In Quiroz' case, he arrived at the diversion unit prior to his appointment and was given a form entitled "Advice About Diversion." He read this form and then discussed it point by point with the probation officer who then entered into the diversion agreement with Quiroz. The advice agreement specifically stated:

> You have the right to talk to a lawyer to help you decide whether or not you should enter into a Diversion Agreement or go to court. If you cannot afford a lawyer, the Court will appoint one at no cost. If you do not believe you committed this offense, you should talk to a lawyer.

Brief of Respondent, app. 1. The probation officer further testified that had Quiroz wanted a lawyer or a more detailed explanation of the charges against him or his possible options, she would have referred him to a lawyer. Quiroz then signed the diversion agreement and a waiver of counsel form, which specifically stated:

> I know that a lawyer can look at my police reports, tell me about the law, help me understand my rights and help me decide whether I should enter into the diversion process or go to Juvenile Court. I have decided *not* to talk to a lawyer at this time.

Brief of Respondent, app. 1.

The facts surrounding Haas' interview are similar. Haas was in detention at the time of his interview. The probation officer assigned to the case, who had entered into a prior diversion agreement with Haas, gave Haas the same type of form Quiroz received about the diversion agreement and waiver of counsel. The probation officer then explained the forms to Haas, and Haas signed them.

Nevertheless, despite their signatures, the juveniles argue that they did not have an adequate opportunity to consult with counsel, and that any waiver of their rights could not be described as knowing, intelligent and voluntary. We agree that the short amount of time between the juveniles' receiving the forms and signing the diversion agreement, and the fact that the onus was placed on the juveniles to decide whether to ask for an attorney creates an issue of fact as to whether their waivers were completely voluntary. However, in hearings before two different judges, with testimony from both the juveniles and the probation officers, each court found that the juveniles made knowing and voluntary waivers of their right to counsel. Ample evidence supports the trial judge's conclusion, and we therefore will not overturn on appeal the lower court's determination that the juveniles waived their rights to counsel. *Thompson v. Grays Harbor Comm'ty Hosp.*, 36 Wash.App. 300, 675 P.2d 239 (1983).

ADEQUATE NOTICE OF CHARGES

The juveniles also argue that the diversion process did not adequately inform them of the nature of the charges against them. In both cases, the only notice the juveniles received about the nature of the charges was written at the top of the diversion agreement. In Quiroz' case, the agreement stated at the top: "Simple assault, Disorderly conduct, Resisting arrest." In Haas' case, the agreement stated "possession of a dangerous weapon." The probation officers gave no explanation as to what the legal description of the crimes were, nor what defenses or mitigating circumstances might apply. Nevertheless, the waiver of attorney form did state specifically that "a lawyer can...tell me about the law..."

The juveniles point to *In re Gault*, 387 U.S. 1, 87 S.Ct. 1428, 18 L.Ed.2d 527 (1967) for authority that this notice is inadequate. In *Gault*, notice to a juvenile was first given at the initial hearing, which was an adjudication on the merits. The charge against the child was for being a juvenile delinquent, and the juvenile never was informed of the underlying charges on which a delinquency finding was to be based.

The United States Supreme Court held that this notice was inadequate. The court stated that it is required "that the child and his parents or guardian be notified, in writing, of the specific charge of factual allegations to be considered at the hearing,...and in any event sufficiently in advance of the hearing to permit preparation." *Gault*, at 33, 87 S.Ct. at 1446.

Both juveniles were notified of the charges against them in writing at the top of the diversion forms. They could have received a detailed explanation of the factual and legal explanations of the charges from lawyers had they chosen to do so. Furthermore, while this notice would not have been sufficient to uphold a criminal conviction by a guilty plea, the less formal nature of the diversion process, coupled with the fact that such an agreement is not the same as a conviction, justifies a less formal notice process. As we said in *Sheppard v. Rhay*, 73 Was.2d 734, 737, 440 P.2d 422 (1968), in describing the due process requirements described in *Gault*,

> *In re Gault*, 387 U.S. 1, 18 L.Ed.2d 527, 87 Sup.Ct. 1428 (1967)...is not to be considered as a mandate to abandon the beneficial aspects of the juvenile court system so long as the essentials of due process and fair play are observed.

In this case, we believe the written notice given to the juveniles prior to their signing the diversion agreement which indicated that they could consult with counsel meets our conceptions of fair play. The juveniles had adequate notice of the charges.

RIGHTS SURROUNDING TRIAL

The juveniles also argue that the diversion process is tantamount to a conviction and does not safeguard basic constitutional rights such as: the right against self-incrimination, the right of confrontation and the right to trial. They also cite to *In re Keene*, 95 Wash.2d 203, 622 P.2d 360 (1980), which holds that a plea must have a factual basis in the record in order to be valid.

These arguments fail to recognize that a fundamental difference exists between a diversion agreement, which is essentially a contract between the juvenile and the diversion unit, and a guilty plea which results in a criminal conviction. A diversion agreement cannot result in a detention sentence, and requires at most that the juvenile pay a fine of $100 or less and attend community supervision and service activities for a short length of time. RCW 13.40.080(2). The procedure is designed to be informal, and as we held in a case determining the amount of procedural safeguards needed in a contempt proceeding, "the procedural safeguards afforded in each situation should be tailored to the specific function to be served by them." *Burlingame v. Consolidated Mines & Smelting Co., Ltd.*, 106 Wash.2d 328, 334, 722 P.2d 67 (1986). We believe the less formal procedure used in this diversion context need not guarantee that the juvenile be informed of the panoply of constitutional rights which the juvenile would have if he or she were pleading guilty. A diversion agreement is not equivalent to a conviction, and there is no necessity to formalize this procedure by a lengthy recitation of rights which attach during criminal proceedings.

FUTURE USE AS A BASE FOR INCREASING A SENTENCE

The juveniles point to this court's decision in *State v. Holsworth*, 93 Wash.2d 148, 607 P.2d 845 (1980) for the proposition that an unconstitutional conviction cannot be the basis for increasing a prison sentence. In *Holsworth*, this court refused to allow a conviction based on an unconstitutionally obtained guilty plea from being used in a habitual criminal sentencing hearing. This court reasoned that the use of the conviction to impose a habitual criminal finding renewed the constitutional violation which had occurred at the time of the earlier guilty plea.

To the extent the juveniles rely on the fact that an unconstitutionally obtained diversion agreement cannot be used to enhance a sentence, we dismiss the argument because we have ruled the process used in their cases was constitutional. However, the juveniles also claim that, because the diversion agreement can later be used to increase a detention sentence, additional constitutional rights associated with criminal adjudications apply. In essence, the juveniles attempt "to bootstrap" additional constitutional rights to the initial diversion agreement because the agreement can later have the effect of increasing a detention sentence.

This argument is without merit. In these cases the diversion agreement plainly indicated that it could serve to enhance a future crime's penalty. The agreement warned the juveniles of its effect on their criminal histories, and therefore, the juveniles cannot complain that they were unaware of its consequences. Therefore, because the agreement warned about the possibility of its future use, and because the agreement itself was not the same as a conviction, its future use did not violate their constitutional rights.

CONCLUSION

The diversion process which both juveniles completed was constitutional and did not violate the Juvenile Court Rules which we promulgated. The trial courts therefore did not err in denying their motions to void their diversion agreements. Furthermore, although it is not clear whether or not Quiroz' criminal history should have reflected two of his prior misdemeanors, he has specifically requested this court not to remand his case for resentencing.

The trial court's orders and sentences are affirmed.

STATE V. QUIROZ

1. Define the concept of "just deserts" and illustrate how this idea has been operationalized into sentencing guidelines in the federal government and in some states (including Washington State for juvenile justice).

2. Compare the sentencing goal of rehabilitation with the sentencing goal of just deserts.

3. Construct a pro-con debate with respect to Washington State's adoption of the just deserts sentencing model of their juvenile justice system. Be sure to address the traditional, historic mission of juvenile justice *vis-á-vis* adult criminal justice.

4. Should a juvenile's prior record that includes *diverted* misdemeanors be factored into the current sentencing formula thus increasing the severity of the sentence? To what degree should the variable of "prior record" including previously diverted offenses, be considered by sentencing judges in juvenile court?

5. Was the juvenile defendant adequately informed that signing a diversion agreement can later be used against him if he is formally sentenced for another offense in the future? Explain.

6. To what degree should diversion be an adversary proceeding?

WAIVER OR TRANSFER OF A CASE FROM CRIMINAL COURT FOR TRIAL AS AN ADULT: THROWING KIDS OUT OF THE SYSTEM

The motives underlying diversion are benevolent, at least in theory; they stem from a desire to prevent the negative labelling of youth that might occur as a consequence of official processing in the juvenile court. Essentially, diverted youths are "helped" out of the juvenile justice system into some alternative, less stigmatizing placement.

However, there is another group of youths who are removed from the juvenile justice system—via a process known as waiver, or transfer or certification—and sent to the criminal justice system for trial as adults. In contrast to the benevolent motives underlying diversion, the motives underlying waiver are explicitly punitive; they stem from a judgment that the youth is beyond the rehabilitative reach of the juvenile court, and perhaps beyond hope. Essentially, youths who are waived or transferred to criminal court are not so much helped out of the juvenile justice system, as thrown out of it.

While waiver mechanisms have existed in most jurisdictions for considerable periods of time, the public and legislative desire to "get tough" on juvenile crime has prompted an expansion of waiver provisions designed to make the criminal processing of juvenile offenders easier,[2] and, at least in some jurisdictions it seems, an increase in the use of waiver.[3]

---

[2]For example, statutes in some jurisdictions authorize the automatic waiver of juvenile offenders to criminal court under certain circumstances. See Champion and Mays, *Transferring Juveniles to Criminal Courts: Trends and Implications for Criminal Justice*, (New York: Praeger Publishers, 1991).

[3]Champion has documented a 104.3% increase (*i.e.*, 238 cases total) in waivers in the states of Virginia, Tennessee, Mississippi and Georgia between 1980 and 1988. See Champion, "Teenage Felons and Waiver Hearings: Some Recent Trends, 1980–1988," 35 *Crime and Delinquency* 577 (1989).

A. Transfer Mechanisms

1. Judicial Waiver

There are three basic types of waiver mechanisms. The most common is *judicial waiver*, where the judge, upon the prosecution's motion to try the case in adult court, must make a determination that transfer is appropriate. Until 1966, the dynamics of judicial waiver decisions were essentially uncontrolled, very much subject to the discretion of the individual judge. However, the U.S. Supreme Court decision in *Kent v. United States*, excerpted below, imposed strict guidelines for judges called upon to make waiver decisions.

MORRIS A. KENT, JR., PETITIONER,

v.

UNITED STATES.

DECIDED MARCH 21, 1966.

* * *

Mr. Justice FORTAS delivered the opinion of the Court.

Morris A. Kent, Jr., first came under the authority of the Juvenile Court of the District of Columbia in 1959. He was then aged 14. He was apprehended as a result of several housebreakings and an attempted purse snatching. He was placed on probation, in the custody of his mother who had been separated from her husband since Kent was two years old. Juvenile Court officials interviewed Kent from time to time during the probation period and accumulated a "Social Service" file.

On September 2, 1961, an intruder entered the apartment of a woman in the District of Columbia. He took her wallet. He raped her. The police found in the apartment latent fingerprints. They were developed and processed. They matched the fingerprints of Morris Kent, taken when he was 14 years old and under the jurisdiction of the Juvenile Court. At about 3 p.m. on September 5, 1961, Kent was taken into custody by the police. Kent was then 16 and therefore subject to the "exclusive jurisdiction" of the Juvenile Court. D.C.Code § 11-907 (1961), now § 11-1551 (Supp. IV, 1965). He was still on probation to that court as a result of the 1959 proceedings.

Upon being apprehended, Kent was taken to police headquarters where he was interrogated by police officers. It appears that he admitted his involvement in the offense which led to his apprehension and volunteered information as to similar offenses involving housebreaking, robbery, and rape. His interrogation proceeded from about 3 p.m. to 10 p.m. the same evening.[4]

---

[4]There is no indication in the file that the police complied with the requirement of the District Code that a child

(continued...)

Some time after 10 p.m. petitioner was taken to the Receiving Home for Children. The next morning he was released to the police for further interrogation at police headquarters, which lasted until 5 p.m.[5]

The record does not show when his mother became aware that the boy was in custody but shortly after 2 p.m. on September 6, 1961, the day following petitioner's apprehension, she retained counsel.

Counsel, together with petitioner's mother, promptly conferred with the Social Service Director of the Juvenile Court. In a brief interview, they discussed the possibility that the Juvenile Court might waive jurisdiction under D.C.Code § 11-914 (1961), now § 11-1553 (Supp. IV, 1965) and remit Kent to trial by the District Court. Counsel made known his intention to oppose waiver.

* * *

The Juvenile Court judge * * * held no hearing. He did not confer with petitioner or petitioner's parents or petitioner's counsel. He entered an order reciting that after "full investigation, I do hereby waive" jurisdiction of petitioner and directing that he be "held for trial for [the alleged] offenses under the regular procedure of the U.S. District Court for the District of Columbia." He made no findings. He did not recite any reason for the waiver. He made no reference to the motions filed by petitioner's counsel. We must assume that he denied, *sub silentio,* the motions for a hearing, the recommendation for hospitalization for psychiatric observation, the request for access to the Social Service file, and the offer to prove that petitioner was a fit subject for rehabilitation under the Juvenile Court's jurisdiction.[6]

Presumably, prior to entry of his order, the Juvenile Court judge received and considered recommendations of the Juvenile Court staff, the Social Service file relating to petitioner, and a report dated September 8, 1961, (three days following petitioner's apprehension), submitted to him by the

---

[4](...continued)
taken into custody, unless released to his parent, guardian or custodian, "shall be placed in the custody of a probation officer or other person designated by the court, or taken immediately to the court or to a place of detention provided by the Board of Public Welfare, and the officer taking him shall immediately notify the court and shall file a petition when directed to do so by the court." D.C.Code § 11-912 (1961), now § 16-2306 (Supp. IV, 1965).

[5]The elicited statements were not used in the subsequent trial before the United States District Court. Since the statements were made while petitioner was subject to the jurisdiction of the Juvenile Court, they were inadmissible in a subsequent criminal prosecution under the rule of Harling v. United States, 111 U.S.App.D.C. 174, 295 F.2d 161 (1961).

[6]It should be noted that at this time the statute provided for only one Juvenile Court judge. Congressional hearings and reports attest the impossibility of the burden which he was supposed to carry. See Amending the Juvenile Court Act of the District of Columbia, Hearing before Subcommittee No. 3 of the House Committee on the District of Columbia, 87th Cong., 1st Sess. (1961); Juvenile Delinquency, Hearings before the Subcommittee to Investigate Juvenile Delinquency of the Senate Committee on the Judiciary, 86th Cong., 1st Sess. (1959-1960); Additional Judges for Juvenile Court, hearing before the House Committee on the District of Columbia, 86th Cong., 1st Sess. (1959); H.R.Rep.No.1041, 87th Cong., 1st Sess. (1961); S.Rep.No.841, 87th Cong., 1st Sess. (1961); S.Rep.No.116, 86th Cong., 1st Sess. (1959). The statute was amended in 1962 to provide for three judged for the court. 76 Stat. 21; D.C.Code § 11-1502 (Supp. IV, 1965).

Juvenile Probation Section. The Social Service file and the September 8 report were later sent to the District Court and it appears that both of them referred to petitioner's mental condition. The September 8 report spoke of "a rapid deterioration of [petitioner's] personality structure and the possibility of mental illness." As stated, neither this report not the Social Service file was made available to petitioner's counsel.

The provision of the Juvenile Court Act governing waiver expressly provides only for "full investigation." It states the circumstances in which jurisdiction may be waived and the child held for trial under adult procedures, but it does not state standards to govern the Juvenile Court's decision as to waiver. The provision reads as follows:

> "If a child sixteen years of age or older is charged with an offense which would amount to a felony in the case of an adult, or any child charged with an offense which if committed by an adult is punishable by death or life imprisonment, the judge may, after full investigation, waive jurisdiction and order such child held for trial under the regular procedure of the court which would have jurisdiction of such offense if committed by an adult; or such other court may exercise the powers conferred upon the juvenile court in this subchapter in conducting and disposing of such cases."[7]

Petitioner appealed from the Juvenile Court's waiver order to the Municipal Court of appeals, which affirmed, and also applied to the United States district Court for a writ of habeas corpus, which was denied. On appeal from these judgments, the United States Court of Appeals held on January 22, 1963, that neither appeal to the Municipal Court of Appeals nor habeas corpus was available. In the Court of Appeals' view, the exclusive method of reviewing the Juvenile Court's waiver order was a motion to dismiss the indictment in the District Court. Kent v. Reid, 114 U.S.App.D.C. 330, 316 F.2d 331 (1963).

Meanwhile, on September 25, 1961, shortly after the Juvenile Court order waiving its jurisdiction, petitioner was indicted by a grand jury of the United States District Court for the District of Columbia. The indictment contained eight alleging two instances of housebreaking, robbery, and rape, and one of housebreaking and robbery.

* * *

At trial, petitioner's defense was wholly directed toward proving that he was not criminally responsible because "his unlawful act was the product of mental disease or mental defect." Durham v. United States, 94 U.S.App.D.C. 228, 241, 214 F.2d 862, 875, 45 A.L.R.2d 1430 (1954). Extensive evidence, including expert testimony, was presented to support this defense. The jury found as to the courts alleging rape that petitioner was "not guilty by reason of insanity." Under District of Columbia law, this made it mandatory that petitioner be transferred to St. Elizabeths Hospital, a mental institution, until his

[7]D.C.Code § 11-914 (1961), now § 11-1553 (Supp. IV, 1965).

sanity is restored.[8] On the six counts of housebreaking and robbery, the jury found that petitioner was guilty.[9]

Kent was sentenced to serve five to 15 years on each count as to which he was found guilty, or a total of 30 to 90 years in prison. The District Court ordered that the time to be spent at St. Elizabeths on the mandatory commitment after the insanity acquittal be counted as part of the 30- to 90-year sentence.

It is to petitioner's arguments as to the infirmity of the proceedings by which the Juvenile Court waived its otherwise exclusive jurisdiction that we address our attention. Petitioner attacks the waiver of jurisdiction on a number of statutory and constitutional grounds. He contends that the waiver is defective because no hearing was held; because no findings were made by the Juvenile Court; because the Juvenile Court stated no reasons for waiver; and because counsel was denied access to the Social Service file which presumably was considered by the Juvenile Court in determining to waive jurisdiction.

We agree that the order of the Juvenile Court waiving its jurisdiction and transferring petitioner for trial in the United States District Court for the District of Columbia was invalid. * * * The issue is the standards to be applied upon such review.

We agree with the Court of Appeals that the statute contemplates that the Juvenile Court should have considerable latitude within which to determine whether it should retain jurisdiction over a child or—subject to the statutory delimitation[10]—should waive jurisdiction. But this latitude is not complete. At the outset, it assumes procedural regularity sufficient in the particular circumstances to satisfy the basic requirements of due process and fairness, as well as compliance with the statutory requirement of a "full investigation." Green v. United States, 113 U.S.App.D.C. 348, 308 F.2d. 303 (1962).[11] The statute gives the Juvenile Court a substantial degree of discretion as to the factual considerations to be evaluated, the weight to be given them and the conclusion to be reached. It does not confer upon the Juvenile Court a license for arbitrary procedure. The statute does not permit the Juvenile Court to determine in isolation

---

[8]D.C.Code § 24-301 (1961).

[9]The basis for this distinction—that petitioner was "sane" for purposes of the housebreaking and robbery but "insane" for the purposes of the rape—apparently was they hypothesis, for which there is some support in the record, that the jury might find that the robberies had anteceded the rapes, and in that event, it might conclude that the housebreakings and robberies were not the products of his mental disease or defect, which the rapes were produced thereby.

[10]The statute is set out at p. 321, supra.

[11]"What is required before a waiver is, as we have said, 'full investigation.' * * * It prevents the waiver of jurisdiction as a matter of routine for the purpose of easing the docket. It prevents routine waiver in certain classes of alleged crimes. It requires a judgment in each case based on 'an inquiry not only into the fact of the alleged offense but also into the question whether the *parens patriæ* plan of procedure is desirable and proper in the particular case.' Pee v. United States, 107 U.S.App.D.C. 47, 50, 274 F.2d 556, 559 (1959)." Green v. United States, supra, at 350, 308 F.2d, at 305.

and without the participation or any representation of the child the "critically important" question whether a child will be deprived of the special protections and provisions of the Juvenile Court Act.[12] It does not authorize the Juvenile Court, in total disregard of a motion for hearing filed by counsel, and without any hearing or statement or reasons, to decide—as in this case—that the child will be taken from the Receiving Home for Children and transferred to jail along with adults, and that he will be exposed to the possibility of a death sentence[13] instead of treatment for a maximum, in Kent's case, of five years, until he is 21.[14]

* * *

1. The theory of the District's Juvenile Court Act, like that of other jurisdictions,[15] is rooted in social welfare philosophy rather than in the *corpus juris*. Its proceedings are designated as civil rather than criminal. The Juvenile Court is theoretically engaged in determining the needs of the child and of society rather than adjudicating criminal conduct. The objectives are to provide measures of guidance and rehabilitation for the child and protection for society, not to fix criminal responsibility, guilt and punishment. The State is *parens patriæ* rather than prosecuting attorney and judge.[16] But the admonition to function in a "parental" relationship is not an invitation to procedural arbitrariness.

* * *

3. It is clear beyond dispute that the waiver of jurisdiction is a "critically important" action determining vitally important statutory rights of the juvenile. The Court of Appeals for the District of Columbia Circuit has so held. See Black v. United States, supra; Watkins v. United States, 119 U.S.App.D.C. 409, 343 F.2d. 278 (1964). The statutory scheme makes this plain. The Juvenile Court is vested with "original and exclusive jurisdiction" of the child. This jurisdiction confers special rights and immunities. He is, as specified by the statute, shielded from publicity. He may be confined, but with rare exceptions he may not be jailed along with adults. He may be detained, but only until he is 21 years of age. The court is admonished by the statute to give preference to retaining the child in the custody of his parents

[12]See Watkins v. United States, 119 U.S.App.D.C. 409, 413, 343 F.2d 278, 282 (1964); Black v. United States, 122 U.S.App.D.C. 393, 355 F.2d 104 (1965).

[13]D.C.Code § 22-2801 (1961) fixes the punishment for rape at 30 years, or death if the jury so provides in its verdict. The maximum punishment for housebreaking is 15 years, D.C.Code § 22-1801 (1961); for robbery it is also 15 years, D.C.Code § 22-2901 (1961).

[14]The jurisdiction of the Juvenile Court over a child ceases when he becomes 21. D.C.Code § 11-907 (1961), now § 11-1551 (Supp. IV, 1965).

[15]All States have juvenile court systems. A study of the actual operation of these systems is contained in Note, *Juvenile Delinquents: The Police, State Courts, and Individualized Justice*, 79 Harv.L.Rev. 775 (1966).

[16]See Handler, *The Juvenile Court and the Adversary System: Problems of Function and Form*, 1965 Wis.L.Rev. 7.

"unless his welfare and the safety and protection of the public can not be adequately safeguarded without * * * removal." The child is protected against consequences of adult conviction such as the loss of civil rights, the use of adjudication against him in subsequent proceedings, and disqualification for public employment. D.C.Code §§ 11-907, 11-915, 11-927, 11-929 (1961).[17]

The net, therefore, is that petitioner—then a boy of 16—was by statute entitled to certain procedures and benefits as a consequence of his statutory right to the "exclusive" jurisdiction of the Juvenile Court. In these circumstances, considering particularly that decision as to waiver of jurisdiction and transfer of the matter to the District Court was potentially as important to petitioner as the difference between five years' confinement and a death sentence, we conclude that, as a condition to a valid waiver order, petitioner was entitled to a hearing, including access by his counsel to the social records and probation or similar reports which presumably are considered by the court, and to a statement of reasons for the Juvenile Court's decision. We believe that this result is required by the statute read in the context of constitutional principles relating to due process and the assistance of counsel.[18]

We are of the opinion that the Court of Appeals misconceived the basic issue and the underlying values in this case. It did note, * * * that the determination of whether to transfer a child from the statutory structure of the Juvenile Court to the criminal processes of the District Court is "critically important." We hold that it is, indeed, a "critically important" proceeding. The Juvenile Court Act confers upon the child a right to avail himself of that court's "exclusive" jurisdiction. * * *

Meaningful review requires that the reviewing court should review. It should not be remitted to assumptions. It must have before it a statement of the reasons motivating the waiver including, of course, a statement of the relevant facts. It may not "assume" that there are adequate reasons, nor may it merely assume that "full investigation" has been make. Accordingly, we hold that it is incumbent upon the Juvenile Court to accompany its waiver order with a statement of the reasons or considerations therefor. We do not read the statute as requiring that this statement must be formal or that it should necessarily include conventional findings of fact. But the statement should be sufficient to demonstrate that the statutory requirement of "full investigation" has been met; and that the question has received the careful consideration of the Juvenile Court; and it must set forth the basis for the order with sufficient specificity to permit meaningful review.

---

[17]These are now, without substantial changes, §§ 11-1551, 16-2307, 16-2308, 16-2313, 11-1586 (Supp. IV, 1965).

[18]While we "will not ordinarily review decisions of the United States Court of Appeals [for the District of Columbia Circuit], which are based upon statutes * * * limited [to the District]* * *," Del Vecchio v. Bowers, 296 U.S. 280, 285, 56 S.Ct. 190, 192, 80 L.Ed. 229, the position of that court, as we discuss *infra*, is self-contradictory. Nor have we deferred to decisions on local law where to do so would require adjudication of difficult constitutional questions. See District of Columbia v. Little, 339 U.S. 1, 70 S.Ct. 468, 94 L.Ed. 599.

Correspondingly, we conclude that an opportunity for a hearing which may be informal, must be given the child prior to entry of a waiver order. Under Black, the child is entitled to counsel in connection with a waiver proceeding, and under Watkins, counsel is entitled to see the child's social records. These rights are meaningless—an illusion, a mockery—unless counsel is given an opportunity to function.

The right to representation by counsel is not a formality. It is not a grudging gesture to a ritualistic requirement. It is of the essence of justice. Appointment of counsel without affording an opportunity for hearing on a "critically important" decision is tantamount to denial of counsel. There is no justification for the failure of the Juvenile Court to rule on the motion for hearing filed by petitioner's counsel, and it was error to fail to grant a hearing.

We do not mean by this to indicate that the hearing to be held must conform with all of the requirements of a criminal trial or even of the usual administrative hearing; but we do hold that the hearing must measure up to the essentials of due process and fair treatment. Pee v. United States, 107 U.S.App.D.C. 47, 50, 274 F.2d 556, 559 (1959).

With respect to access by the child's counsel to the social records of the child, we deem it obvious that since these are to be considered by the Juvenile court in making its decision to waive, they must be made available to the child's counsel. This is what the Court of Appeals itself held in Watkins. There is no doubt as to the statutory basis for this conclusion, as the Court of Appeals pointed out in Watkins. We cannot agree with the Court of Appeals in the present case that the statute is "ambiguous." The statute expressly provides that the record shall be withheld from "indiscriminate" public inspection, "except that such records or parts thereof *shall* be made available by rule of court or special order of court to such persons * * * as have a *legitimate interest* in the protection * * * of the child * * *." D.C.Code § 11-929 (b) (Supp. IV, 1965). * * * The Court of Appeals has held in Black, and we agree, that counsel must be afforded to the child in waiver proceedings. Counsel, therefore, have a "legitimate interest" in the protection of the child, and must be afforded access to these records.

We do not agree with the Court of Appeals' statement, attempting to justify denial of access to these records, that counsel's role is limited to presenting "to the court anything on behalf of the child which might help the court in arriving at a decision; it is not to denigrate the staff's submissions and recommendations." On the contrary, if the staff's submissions include materials which are susceptible to challenge or impeachment, it is precisely the role of counsel to "denigrate" such matter. There is no irrebuttable presumption of accuracy attached to staff reports. If a decision on waiver is "critically important" that the material submitted to the judge—which is protected by the statute only against "indiscriminate: inspection—be subjected, within reasonable limits having regard to the theory of the Juvenile Court Act, to examination, criticism and refutation. While the Juvenile Court judge may, of course, receive *ex parte* analyses and recommendations from his staff, he may not, for purposes of decision on waiver, receive and rely upon secret information, whether emanating from his staff or otherwise. The

Juvenile Court is governed in this respect by the established principles which control courts and quasijudicial agencies of the Government.

For the reasons stated, we conclude that the Court of Appeals and the District Court erred in sustaining the validity of the waiver by the Juvenile Court. The Government urges that any error committed by the Juvenile Court was cured by the proceeding before the District Court. It is true that the District Court considered and denied a moment to dismiss on the grounds of the invalidity of the waiver order of the Juvenile Court, and that it considered and denied a motion that it should itself, as authorized by statute, proceed in this case to "exercise the powers conferred upon the juvenile court." D.C.Code § 11-914 (1961), now § 11-1553 (Supp. IV, 1965). But we agree with the Court of Appeals in Black, that "the waiver question was primarily and initially one for the Juvenile Court to decide and its failure to do so in a valid manner cannot be said to be harmless error. It is the Juvenile Court, not the District Court, which has the facilities, personnel and expertise for a proper determination of the waiver issue." 122 U.S.App.D.C., at 396, 355 F.2d, at 107.

* * *

Reversed and remanded.

* * *

Mr. Justice STEWART, with whom Mr. Justice BLACK, Mr. Justice HARLAN and Mr. Justice WHITE join, dissenting.

This case involves the construction of a statute applicable only to the District of Columbia. Our general practice is to leave undisturbed decisions of the Court of Appeals for the district of Columbia Circuit concerning the import of legislation governing the affairs of the District. General Motors Corp. v. District of Columbia, 380 U.S. 553, 556, 85 S.Ct. 1156, 14 L.Ed.2d 68. It appears, however, that two cases decided by the Court of Appeals subsequent to its decision in the present case may have considerably modified the court's construction of the statute. Therefore, I would vacate this judgment and remand the case to the Court of Appeals for reconsideration in the light of its subsequent decisions, Watkins v. United States, 119 U.S.App.D.C. 409, 343 F.2d 278, and Black v. United States, 122 U.S.App.D.C. 393, 355 F.2d 104.

KENT V. U.S.

1. What is the logic for transferring a juvenile to the adult criminal justice system?

2. It should be noted that the *Kent* case represents the U.S. Supreme Court's first significant constitutional analysis of the juvenile justice system. It is also a case that contains ideological and doctrinal conflicts, such as *parens patriæ* versus police power, informal procedures versus due process, and rehabilitation versus punishment. Apply each conflict to the *Kent* case.

3. The *Kent* case formalized the transfer process in the judiciary, but various state legislatures have promulgated laws to process serious juvenile offenders in the adult criminal justice system *without* a due process hearing in juvenile court. What might be the specific contents of such laws?

2. Legislative Waiver

The second type of waiver provision is known as *legislative waiver*. Legislative waiver provisions work by excluding juveniles charged with certain crimes from the jurisdiction of the juvenile court. Under legislative waiver provisions, certain categories of young offenders are "defined out" of the juvenile court jurisdiction, and statutorily declared adults. The next case, *United States v. Bland* treats several issues raised in connection with a legislative waiver statute.

UNITED STATES OF AMERICA,

APPELLANT,

V.

JEROME T. BLAND.

NO. 71-1761.

UNITED STATES COURT OF APPEALS,

DISTRICT OF COLUMBIA CIRCUIT.

ARGUED APRIL 12, 1972.

DECIDED SEPT. 6, 1972.

REHEARING DENIED DEC. 20, 1972.

AS AMENDED JUNE 18, 19, 1973.

* * *

WILKEY, CIRCUIT JUDGE:

The United States as statutory appellant seeks review of a memorandum opinion and order of the United States District Court for the District of Columbia, holding 16 D.C.Code § 2301(3)(A) unconstitutional as (1) an arbitrary legislative classification and (2) a negation of the presumption of innocence.[19] Section 2301(3)(A) provides:

> The term "child" means an individual who is under 18 years of age, except that the term "child" does not include an individual who is sixteen years of age or older and—

[19] United States v. Bland, 330 F.Supp. 34 (D.D.C.1971).

(A) charged by the United states Attorney with (i) murder, forcible rape, burglary in the first degree, robbery while armed, or assault with intent to commit any such offense, or (ii) an offense listed in clause (i) and any other offense properly joinable with such an offense....[20]

The appellee, born 30 July 1954, had been indicated pursuant to Section 2301(3)(A) as an adult (he was sixteen at the time of his arrest and indictment) on charges of armed robbery of a post office and related offenses on 8 February 1971. Appellee moved below to dismiss the indictment for lack of jurisdiction, asserting that the statutory basis for prosecuting him as an adult was constitutionally deficient in that it failed to provide him with procedural due process. The District Court dismissed the indictment.[21]

I. *The Legislative Background*

Congress, pursuant to its constitutional authority to exercise exclusive jurisdiction over the District of Columbia,[22] created the Family Division of the Superior Court of the District of Columbia.[23]

The legislative history accompanying 16 D.C.Code § 2301 reveals Congress' intent in enacting this legislation: To improve the operation of the juvenile justice system in the District of Columbia by removing from its jurisdiction certain individuals between the ages of 16 and 18 whom Congress concluded (1) were beyond rehabilitation in the juvenile justice system, and (2) whose presence in that system served as a negative influence on other juveniles. This represents a policy judgment of Congress, after gathering extensive appropriate evidence, as to how persons should be classified as "adult" and "child" for the purposes of rehabilitation following the commission of a criminal offense. We note that the policy judgment was both negative and positive: some previously classified as juveniles were beyond rehabilitation; others of the same chronological age were susceptible to special juvenile treatment, and for any chance of success these latter should be protected against the hard-core repeat offenders of the same chronological age.

* * *

---

[20]16 D.C.Code § 2301(3)(A) (Supp. IV, 1971).

[21]Subsequent to the District Court's opinion and order in the case at bar, other judges of the United States District Court for the District of Columbia have ruled on the same issue, the first six to the contrary: (1) United States v. Tatum (Crim. No. 1145-71; order entered 29 September 1971; Judge Jones); (2) United States v. Riley (Crim. No. 1510-71; order entered 4 October 1971; Judge Smith); (3) United States v. Alexander, 333 F.Supp. 1213 (D.C.D.C.1971) (Judge Gesell); (4) United States v. Dickey, et al. (Crim. No. 1448-71; order entered June 14, 1972; Judge Gasch); (5) United States v. Steele (Crim. No. 1085-71; order entered 27 Oct. 1971; Judge Corcoran); (6) United States v. Reginald Barden (Crim. No. 271-72; order entered 16 March 1972; Judge Flannery); (7) United States v. McIlwain (Crim. No. 1178-71; order entered 10 May 1972; Judge Bryant); (8) United States v. Maurice L. Johnson (Crim. No. 2198-71; order entered May 10, 1972; Judge Bryant); and (9) United States v. Andrew E. Morgan (Crim. No. 850-71; order entered May 10, 1972; Judge Bryant).

[22]U.S.Const. art. I, § 8, cl. 17.

[23]11 D.C.Code § 1101(13) (Supp. IV, 1971).

The District Court found Section 2301(3)(A) invalid as violative of due process of law:

> The determination that a child should be tried as an adult cannot be made without the safeguard of basic due process. Without a provision in the new statute that would require some determination, reached after a fair hearing, that an individual is beyond the help of the Family Division, that statute must fall as violative of due process.[24]

To the Government's objection below that the statute specially classifies those individuals who are at least 16 years of age and charged with certain enumerated crimes by the United States Attorney as exempt from the Family Division's jurisdiction, the District Court found no standards in the statute to guide the United States Attorney in making this determination, hence it held that the statute denies due process to those individuals so charged.

A.

In relation to this holding of the District Court, we note in the first place that legislative classifications are entitled to a strong presumption of validity and may be "set aside only if no grounds can be conceived to justify them."[25] As the Supreme Court has long held:

> It is a salutary principle of judicial decision, long emphasized and followed by this Court, that the burden of establishing the unconstitutionality of a statute rests on him assails it, and the courts may not declare a legislative discrimination invalid unless, viewed in the light of facts made known or generally assumed, it is of such a character as to preclude the assumption that the classification rests upon some rational basis within the knowledge and experience of the legislators.[26]

As the discussion on the legislative background of Section 2301(3)(A), *supra*, indicates, Congress was well acquainted with the problems confronting the juvenile justice system in the District of Columbia; logically its definition of the Family Division's jurisdiction reflects its particular concern with the rise in the number of serious crimes committed by those 16 years of age and over coupled with the growing recidivist rate among this group.

Secondly, legislative exclusion of individuals charged with certain specified crimes from the jurisdiction of the juvenile justice system is not unusual. The Federal Juvenile Delinquency Act excludes offenses which are punishable by death or life imprisonment. Several states have similarly excluded certain

---

[24]See note 1, *supra*.

[25]McDonald v. Board of Election Com'rs, 394 U.S. 802, 809, 89 S.Ct. 1404, 1408, 22 L.Ed.2d 739 (1969), and cases cited.

[26]Metropolitan Casualty Insurance Co. v. Brownell, 294 U.S. 580, 584, 55 S.Ct. 538, 540, 79 L.Ed. 1070 (1935) (footnote omitted).

crimes in defining the jurisdiction of their respective systems of juvenile justice,[27] while others vest concurrent jurisdiction over enumerated crimes in both their adult and juvenile courts.[28] Finally, the United States District Court for the District of Maryland, upheld by the Fourth Circuit, while it did find a geographic age distinction in the jurisdiction of the Maryland Juvenile Court violative of due process, found no difficulties with the exclusion of those 14 years of age and over charged with capital crimes from juvenile jurisdiction.[29]

* * *

C.

The District Court's finding in the case at bar, and appellee's assertion to the same effect—that the exercise of the discretion vested by Section 2301(3)(A) in the United States Attorney to charge a person 16 years of age or older with certain enumerated offenses, thereby initiating that person's prosecution as an adult, violates due process—ignores the long and widely accepted concept of prosecutorial discretion, which derives from the constitutional principle of separation of powers. The Fifth Circuit, in holding that a court had no power to compel a United States Attorney to sign an indictment, stated:

> Although as a member of the bar, the attorney for the United States is an officer of the court, he is nevertheless an executive official of the Government, and it is as an officer of the executive department that he exercises a discretion as to whether or not there shall be prosecution in a particular case. It follows, as an incident of the constitutional separation of powers, that the courts are not to interfere with the free exercise of the discretionary powers of the attorneys of the United States in their control over criminal prosecutions.

While there may be circumstances in which courts would be entitled to review the exercise of prosecutorial discretion, these circumstances would necessarily include the deliberate presence of such

---

[27]Colo.Rev.Stat., §§ 22-1-3(17)(b), 22-1-4(4)(b); 10 Del.Code Ann. § 957, 11 Del.Code Ann. §§ 360(b), 363(d), 468A; Burns' Ind. Stat. §§ 9-3204(1), 9-3213, IC 1971, 31-5-7-4, 31-5-7-13; Iowa Code Ann. § 232.64; La. Const., art. 7, § 52; Md. Code Ann., art. 26, § 70-2(d) (1); Miss. Code Ann. § 7185-15; Nev.Rev.Stat. § 62.050; S.C. Const., art. 5, § 1; and Tenn. Code Ann. § 37-265.

Challenges to these provisions as violative of due process and equal protection of the law have not prevailed. *See* State v. Ayers, Del., 260 A.2d 162 (1969), in which the court rejected a Fourteenth Amendment challenge to 11 Del. Code Ann § 363(d) (an anti-riot statute), which provided that those over sixteen years of age and charged with violating this statute were to be tried as adults. *See also*, to the same effect, Prevatte v. Director, 5 Md.App. 406, 248 A.2d 170 (1968), and Davis v. State, Miss., 204 So.2d 270, rev'd on other grounds, 394 U.S. 721, 89 S.Ct. 1394, 22 L.Ed.2d 676 (1969).

[28]37 Ill.Ann.Stat. § 702-7(3), upheld in People v. Carlson, 108 Ill.App.2d 463, 247 N.E.2d 919 (1969). *See also* DeBacker v. Sigler, 185 Neb. 352, 175 N.W.2d 912 (1970), and Mayne v. Turner, 24 Utah 2d 195, 468 P.2d 369 (1970), sustaining concurrent jurisdiction in their respective adult and juvenile courts over certain enumerated offenses.

[29]Long v. Robinson, 316 F.Supp. 22 (D.Md.), aff'd 436 F.2d 1116 (4th Cir. 1971).

factors as "race, religion, or other arbitrary classification," not found in the case at bar.[30] For example, in the absence of such factors, this court has held that the exercise of prosecutorial discretion, even when it results in different treatment of codefendants originally charged in the same case with the same offense, does not violate due process or equal protection of the law.

The District Court and appellee in the case at bar point to the acknowledged significant effect of the United States Attorney's decision whether to charge an individual 16 years of age or older with certain enumerated offenses, and conclude that, in the absence of a hearing, due process is violated when such a decision is made. This, however, overlooks the significance of a variety of other common prosecutorial decisions, *e.g.*, whether to charge one person but not another possible codefendant; whether to charge an individual with a misdemeanor or a felony; *etc.*[31] Furthermore, the decision whether to charge an individual with a misdemeanor or a felony has long determined the court in which that person will be tried.[32] We cannot accept the hitherto unaccepted argument that due process requires in adversary hearing before the prosecutor can exercise his age-old function of deciding what charge to bring against whom. Grave consequences have always flowed from this, but never has a hearing been required.

* * *

[30]As the Supreme Court suggested in Oyler v. Boles, 368 U.S. 448, 82 S.Ct. 501, 7 L.Ed.2d 446 (1962):

Moreover, the conscious exercise of some selectivity in enforcement is not in itself a federal constitutional violation. Even though the statistics in this case might imply a policy of selective enforcement, it is not stated that the selection was deliberately based upon an unjustifiable standard such as race, religion or other arbitrary classification. Therefore grounds supporting a finding of a denial of equal protection were not alleged. 368 U.S., at 456, 82 S.Ct. at 506.

See also Washington v. United States, 130 U.S.App.D.C. 374, 401 F.2d 915 (1968), and United States v. CCO, 428 F.2d 264 (9th Cir.), cert. denied, 400 U.S. 903, 91 S.Ct. 141, 27 L.Ed.2d 140 (1970).

[31]Appellee's attempt to equate the United States Attorney's decision in the case at bar with the transfer of an individual from the jurisdiction of the juvenile court to that of adult court is unavailing. In contrast to such a situation, the case at bar involves *no* initial juvenile court jurisdiction; the United States Attorney's decision to charge an individual sixteen years of age or older with certain enumerated offenses operates automatically to exclude that individual from the jurisdiction of the Family Division. The cases cited by the appellee are equally inapposite: In re Gault, 387 U.S. 1, 87 S.Ct. 1428, 18 L.Ed.2d 527 (1967), did not involve the question of adult court jurisdiction over persons sixteen years of age or over; Kent v. United States, 383 U.S. 541, 86 S.Ct. 1045, 16 L.Ed.2d 84 (1966), Haziel v. United States, 131 U.S.App.D.C.298, 404 F.2d 1275 (1968), and Black v. United States, 122 U.S.App.D.C.393, 355 F.2d 104 (1965), all involved the "full investigation" requirement of 11 D.C. Code § 1553 (1967), the former local juvenile statute. Under former Section 1553, individual judgments were to be made by the Juvenile Court as to whether a particular youth should be "waived" for trial as an adult. The comparable transfer provision of the revised juvenile statute, 16 D.C. Code § 2307 (Supp. IV, 1971), is not an issue in the case at bar, which involves determination of which jurisdiction—adult or juvenile—attaches to appellee in the first instance. As such it cannot involve a transfer from a nonexistent juvenile jurisdiction to adult court.

[32]Also, since 1 February 1971 in the District of Columbia, the decision of *which* felony to charge has similarly determined the court having jurisdiction. 11 D.C. Code §§ 502, 923 (Supp. IV, 1971).

As such, judicial consideration of the legitimate scope of prosecutorial discretion clearly encompasses the exercise of such discretion where it has the effect of determining whether a person will be charged as a juvenile or as an adult. In the absence of such "suspect" factors as "race, religion, or other arbitrary classification," the exercise of discretion by the United States Attorney in the case at bar involves no violation of due process or equal protection of the law.

III. *The Presumption of Innocence Issue*

The District Court and appellee assert that the exercise of discretion by the United States Attorney under Section 2301(3)(A) violates due process in that it denies the individual charged the presumption of innocence.

This, however, mistakes the nature of the United States Attorney's decision in the case at bar to charge appellee with an offense enumerated in Section 2301(3)(A). While the decision does have the effect of determining whether appellee is to be tried as an adult or a juvenile, it is not a judgment of guilt or an imposition of penalty. On the contrary, it is simply the result of a determination by the United States Attorney that there is sufficient evidence to warrant prosecution of the appellee for the offense charged and that adult prosecution is appropriate. It in no manner relieves the Government of its obligation to prove appellee's guilt beyond a reasonable doubt.[33] Nor does it remove appellee's right to a jury trial. As the subsequent opinion of District Judge Gesell, ruling on this same issue under this statute, recognized:

> It should be noted that all the traditional protections of grand jury presentment, preliminary hearing and jury trial are afforded this group of [alleged] offenders and that in the event of convictions the extraordinarily flexible provisions of the Federal Youth Correction Act designed to create programs for limited incarceration and effective rehabilitation are completely available.[34]

The presumption of innocence, as the Supreme Court has long held, applies to the prosecution at trial and "...is a conclusion drawn by the law in favor of the citizen, by virtue whereof, *when brought to trial* upon a criminal charge, he must be acquitted, unless he is proven [beyond a reasonable doubt] to be guilty."[35] As such, the District Court's opinion below and appellee's reliance on, *inter alia*, Goldberg v. Kelly[36] and Jones v. Robinson[37] is mistaken; in contrast to the summary adjudications found wanting in

---

[33]Holt v. United States, 218 U.S. 245, 253, 31 S.Ct. 2, 54 L.Ed. 1021 (1910).

[34]See note 3, *supra*, United States v. Alexander, 333 F.Supp., at 1217.

[35]Coffin v. United States, 156 U.S. 432, 458, 15 S.Ct. 394, 404, 39 L.Ed. 481 (1895).

[36]397 U.S. 254, 90 S.Ct. 1011, 25 L.Ed.2d 287 (1970), which involved the cutting off of welfare funds without adequate notice and a prior hearing at which the welfare recipient could have the assistance of counsel and where the decision-maker did not state his reasons or the evidence upon which he based his decision.

[37]142 U.S.App.D.C. 221, 440 F.2d 249 (1971), applying the requirement of, *inter alia*, a hearing enunciated by Goldberg v. Kelly, note 36, *supra*, to the decision to transfer a patient accused of a crime to the maximum security (continued...)

those cases, the United States Attorney's decision in the case at bar marks only the beginning of the process of adjudication of appellee's guilt, a process marked by the presence of all the traditional protections or procedural due process, followed by the extraordinarily liberal rehabilitation provisions of the Federal Youth Corrections Act.

IV. *Conclusion*

For these reasons, the order of the District Court dismissing appellee's indictment, on the basis of its opinion holding 16 D.C. Code § 2301(3)(A) unconstitutional as an arbitrary legislative classification and as a negation of the presumption of innocence, is accordingly reversed and the case remanded for trial.

Reversed and remanded.

U.S. v. BLAND

1. The complications in this case stem largely from the fact that there is no family or juvenile court in the District of Columbia. Thus, there can be no waiver of jurisdiction *per se* in juvenile transfer cases. The prosecutor then, has discretion in such instances. Explain the role of prosecutorial discretion in the *Bland* case.

2. Does this case represent an exception to the hearing rule in *Kent*? Elaborate.

3. Can a legislature constitutionally allow prosecutors to exercise discretion in determining whether to prosecute a juvenile as an adult as long as this discretion has clear limits? Explain.

4. To what extent would a *Kent*-like waiver or transfer hearing place limits on prosecutorial discretion in juvenile transfer cases?

5. Describe the "equal protection claim" made in this case. How has the U.S. Supreme Court ruled in cases where "some selectivity in enforcement" has been exercised?

6. Bland was adjudicated for committing a crime that is both a local and federal offense in District of Columbia jurisdiction. Why did this further complicate the case and how did the U.S. Circuit Court of Appeals sort it out?

3. Prosecutorial Waiver

The third type of waiver mechanism, *prosecutorial waiver* vests the authority to transfer cases from juvenile to adult court with the prosecutor, who can bypass the juvenile court completely simply by filing the case directly in criminal court. This type of waiver statute is perhaps the most controversial, since it effectively makes the waiver decision part of the prosecutor's decision to charge, and therefore, unlike

[37](...continued)
section of St. Elizabeths Hospital.

judicial waiver decisions, not subject to appellate court review.[38] Also, because many county prosecutors are elected officials, the use of prosecutorial waiver can politicize the charging decision, since a prosecutor may occasionally come under intense public pressure to try certain youths as adults, or face the voters' wrath in the next election.[39] The following case, *People v. Thorpe*, focuses on the prosecutorial waiver mechanism.

THE PEOPLE OF THE STATE OF COLORADO,

PLAINTIFF–APPELLEE,

V.

GARY THORPE, DEFENDANT–APPELLANT.

NO. 80SA337.

SUPREME COURT OF COLORADO,

EN BANC.

FEB. 8, 1982.

RE-HEARING DENIED MARCH 15, 1982.

* * *

LEE, JUSTICE.

The defendant-appellant, Gary Thorpe, was convicted by jury of murder in the first degree, aggravated robbery, and conspiracy to commit aggravated robbery. We affirm the convictions.

On October 12, 1978, William Sather, proprietor of Sather Jewelry in Denver, was shot to death during an aggravated robbery of his store. An information was filed against the defendant and Richard Banks on November 14, 1978 charging them with first degree murder. The defendant, who was 16 years of age at the time, was charged in the district court pursuant to section 19-1-104(4)(b)(I), C.R.S.1973 (1978 Repl. Vol. 8).[40] Separate trials were granted on motion of the defendant.

* * *

---

[38]Champion and Mays, *supra*.

[39]Champion, *supra*, *citing* Bortner, "Traditional Rhetoric, Organizational Realities: Remand of Juveniles to Adult Court," 32 *Crime and Delinquency* 53 (1986).

[40]Section 19-1-104(4)(b)(I) provides in relevant part:

"(b) A child may be charged with the commission of a felony...when the child is: "(I) Alleged to have committed a crime of violence defined by section 18-1-105, C.R.S. 1973, as a class 1 felony, and is fourteen years of age or older..."

The defendant raises the following arguments for reversal of his conviction. First, he contends that section 19-1-104(4)(b)(I) is unconstitutional and its application to him denied him due process and equal protection of the law.

* * *

I.

Defendant's constitutional argument is based on his contention that section 19-1-104(4)(b)(I), C.R.S.1973 (1978 Repl. Vol. 8), is invalid because it allows a district attorney to charge a child 14 years of age or older alleged to have committed a crime of violence defined as a class 1 felony, with the commission of a felony and to prosecute the child in a criminal proceeding in the district court rather than as a juvenile in the juvenile court. The defendant reasons that the decision of the prosecutor to charge a juvenile as an adult when there are no statutory guidelines and without a prior hearing cannot be constitutionally justified as a valid exercise of prosecutorial discretion. Since there is no hearing prior to the charging process at which the juvenile may be present and heard, and be presented by counsel, the argument goes, he is denied due process. Furthermore, since the prosecutor may choose to prosecute one 14-year-old violent offender as an adult and another 14-year-old violent offender as a juvenile, and since there are no statutory criteria to guide him in making that decision, the statute denies one in the defendant's position equal protection of law.

The defendant recognizes that the proposition he urges us to adopt is contrary to this court's decision in *Myers v. District Court*, 184 Colo. 81, 518 P.2d 836 (1974), which considered a predecessor section of the Juvenile Code, now codified as section 19-1-104(4)(b)(II), C.R.S.1973 (1978 Repl. Vol. 8).[41] In *Myers* we held:

> "Petitioners' final argument is that the broad discretion granted to the district attorney by C.R.S.1963, 22-1-4(b)(iii) denies them due process and equal protection of the laws.
>
> "It is well settled that a prosecutor has constitutional power to exercise his discretion in deciding which of several possible charges to press in a prosecution. *See People v. Couch*, 179 Colo. 324, 500 P.2d 967 (1972); *People v. James*, 178 Colo. 401, 497 P.2d 1256 (1972); *People v. McKenzie*, 169 Colo. 521, 458 P.2d 232 (1969). It follows that the district attorney may properly invoke the concurrent jurisdiction of the district court under C.R.S.1963, 22-1-4(b)(iii) and C.R.S.1963, 22-1-3(17)(b)(iii) in deciding to proceed against a person between the ages of sixteen and eighteen

---

[41]Section 19-1-104(4)(b)(II) provides in relevant part:

"(b) A child may be charged with the commission of a felony...when the child is:

"(II) Alleged to have committed a crime defined by section 18-1-105, C.R.S.1973, as a class 2 or a class 3 felony or a nonclassified felony punishable by a maximum punishment of life imprisonment or death, except those felonies defined by section 18-3-403(1)(e), C.R.S.1973, and is sixteen years of age or older, and the child has been adjudicated a delinquent child within the previous two years and the act for which the child was adjudicated a delinquent would have constituted a felony if committed by an adult...."

> in district rather than juvenile court. *United States v. Cox*, 473 F.2d 334 (4th Cir.1973); *United States v. Bland*, 472 F.2d 1329 (D.C.Cir.1972)." (Footnote omitted.)

In *People v. District Court*, 191 Colo. 28, 549 P.2d 1317 (1976), we again upheld the exercise of prosecutorial discretion. In a juvenile proceeding the district attorney elected to amend the petition in delinquency to include a more serious felony, thus causing the case to be transferred for trial as a criminal case. We there stated:

> "It is clear that the design of the statute is to permit the juvenile court, in case of a less serious felony, to determine in a transfer hearing whether, in the best interests of the accused juvenile, the case should be transferred to the criminal side of the court, section 19-1-104(4)(a); but in those circumstances where a more serious felony is charged, as set forth in subsections (4)(b)(I), (II), and (III), no such discretion lies in the court to retain the case in the juvenile side of the court when the district attorney elects to have the case transferred for trial as a criminal action." *People v. District Court, supra.*

The prohibition against judicial intervention in or control of the exercise of prosecutorial discretion flows from the doctrine of separation of powers, expressly set out in Article III of the Colorado Constitution and inherent in the enumerated powers of the United States Constitution. The defendant acknowledges this firmly established principle and recognizes our many decisions upholding the exercise of discretion by a prosecutor in determining what charges shall be brought. *See, e.g., People v. District Court*, 186 Colo. 335, 527 P.2d 50 (1974) (prosecutor's election not to consent to deferred prosecution); *People v. Couch*, 179 Colo. 324, 500 P.2d 967 (1972) (election to proceed under a felony statute rather than misdemeanor statute); *People v. James*, 178 Colo. 401, 497 P.2d 1256 (1972) (determination by prosecutor under which statute to prosecute); *People v. McKenzie*, 169 Colo. 521, 458 P.2d 232 (1969) (election to charge defendant as a felonious possessor of marijuana rather than as a misdemeanant user).

The defendant, however, would have us overrule *Myers, supra*, and *People v. District Court, supra*, and adopt an exception to the principle of prosecutorial discretion in juvenile cases. He urges that we adopt the view espoused by the dissent in the case of *United States v. Bland*, 472 F.2d 1329 (D.C.Cir.1972), that since the consequences to the child from his prosecution in a criminal case vary so significantly from those flowing from a juvenile proceeding, the child should be afforded the same protections as he would have were the case filed in the juvenile court and transfer to the criminal division sought. *See*, sections 19-1-104(4)(a), 19-1-107, and 19-3-108, C.R.S.1973 (1978 Repl. Vol. 8).

The defendant cites *Kent v. United States*, 383 U.S. 541, 86 S.Ct. 1045, 16 L.Ed.2d 84 (1966), in support of his argument that a hearing with the assistance of counsel is required before the "critically important" decision is made to put the child through the criminal court process. This case, though instructive, lends no support to his position. There, the Federal Juvenile Court Act required a waiver of jurisdiction by the juvenile court before criminal proceedings could be brought by the United States

Attorney.[42] The Federal Juvenile Code vested original and exclusive jurisdiction of a child in the juvenile court and contained no provisions for a direct filing in a criminal proceeding, as does our statute, section 19-1-104(4)(b)(I).

We decline to require that a quasi-judicial hearing be held by the district attorney as a precondition to his determination that a child 14 years of age or older alleged to have committed a crime of violence defined as a class 1 felony shall be prosecuted in a criminal proceeding. The majority opinion in *Bland, supra,* which is consistent with our view, holds that, even though a prosecutor is an officer of the court, he is nevertheless a member of the executive department and acting as such when exercising his discretion in choosing what charges to file and in what court they should be filed. Therefore, while there may be circumstances in which courts would be entitled to review the prosecutorial discretion function, "in the absence of such 'suspect' factors as 'race, religion, or other arbitrary classification,' the exercise of discretion by the United States Attorney [in deciding whether a person shall be charged as a juvenile or an adult] in the case at bar involves no violation of due process or equal protection of the law."[43] *United States v. Bland, supra,* at 1337. * * * The statutory scheme prescribed by the legislature is clear and vests that determination solely in the discretion of the district attorney. If change in the procedures is deemed desirable, that is a matter for the judgment of the General Assembly.

Accordingly, we reject the defendant's argument that he was denied equal protection of the law because the district attorney chose to file a criminal action against him whereas another in his same circumstance could be treated as a juvenile and charged with delinquency. We reiterate that the conscious exercise of selectivity in the enforcement of laws is not in itself a constitutional violation of equal protection of the law, absent a showing that a prosecutor has exercised a policy of selectivity based upon an

---

[42]If a child sixteen years of age or older is charged with an offense which would amount to a felony in the case of an adult, or any child charged with an offense which if committed by an adult is punishable by death or life imprisonment, the judge may, after full investigation, waive jurisdiction and order such child held for trial under the regular procedure of the court which would have jurisdiction of such offense if committed by an adult; or such other court may exercise the powers conferred upon the juvenile court in this subchapter in conducting and disposing of such cases." D.C.Code § 11-914 (1961). The decision in *United States v. Bland, supra,* concerned D.C.Code 16-2301(3)(A), which allowed a direct filing in the U.S. District Court by the United States Attorney without juvenile court intervention against persons over 16 charged with certain violent crimes.

[43]There is no issue here, and the defendant does not contend that the district attorney constitutionally abused his discretion in this case by considering any suspect factors such as race, religion, or other arbitrary classification in determining that the defendant should be tried in a criminal proceeding rather than a juvenile proceeding.

We also note that even when a district attorney elects to file criminal charges against a juvenile in district court the court retains the power "to make any disposition of the case that any juvenile court would have and shall have the power to remand the case to the juvenile court for disposition at its discretion." Section 19-1-104(4)(c), C.R.S.1973 (1978 Repl. Vol. 8).

unjustifiable standard such as "race, religion, or any other arbitrary classification," which was not shown here. *People v. MacFarland*, 189 Colo. 363, 540 P.2d 1073 (1975).[44]

We also reject the defendant's challenge to the facial constitutionality of this statute. As we stated in *People v. McKenzie, supra,* "[We] must recognize that the legislature is free to adopt any classification it deems appropriate to promote the general welfare, so long as the classification bears a reasonable relation to a proper legislative purpose and is neither arbitrary nor discriminatory and operates equally on all persons within the classification." It is clear the General Assembly intended to exclude certain offenders from the juvenile court system by defining certain serious offenses as per se criminal and properly within the constitutional jurisdiction of the district court even if committed by a juvenile over the age of 14. This is not unreasonable in light of the apparent legislative decision that certain repeat offenders, or those who have committed serious offenses, should be separated from those juveniles who perpetrate relatively less serious or less violent crimes and who, in the view of the legislature, are more likely candidates for rehabilitation.

We are not persuaded by defendant's arguments that section 19-1-104(4)(b)(I), C.R.S.1973 (1978 Repl. Vol. 8), is invalid and we hold it to be constitutional on its face and as applied to the defendant.

* * *

Accordingly, the judgment of the trial court is affirmed.

PEOPLE V. THORPE

1. Why were the facts in this case not in conflict with *Kent v. U.S.*?
2. Why was the "equal protection" argument made by the defense unsuccessful on appeal? Relate the intent of the Colorado legislature with respect to prosecutorial discretion to your answer.

PRE-ADJUDICATORY DETENTION OF JUVENILES

Juveniles taken into custody by police can be temporarily detained in some type of secure facility while awaiting adjudication or other processing. And while the preadjudicatory detention of youths occurs frequently enough that it can be accurately viewed as a common, perhaps even routine, event within the juvenile justice system, it stands as one of the most controversial aspects of the entire juvenile justice

---

[44]This is not to say that the district attorney has no guidelines for the exercise of his discretion. The criteria specified in section 19-3-108(2)(b)(I) through (VI), C.R.S.1973 (1978 Repl. Vol. 8), for transfer from the juvenile court, as well as the legislative declaration of the purpose of the Juvenile Code, are available and should guide him in his decision to by-pass the juvenile court and proceed directly in the district court. Additionally, he should be governed by the standards implicit in the constitutional and statutory duties of his office.

process. In fact, one observer, with a bluntness uncharacteristic of most academic commentary has labelled preadjudicatory detention, "one of the areas of greatest abuse in the juvenile justice system."[45]

Preadjudicatory detention is controversial, first, because of the large number of youths held in the early stages of processing. In the early to mid-1980s, it was estimated that nearly half a million were young people were being "detained" in secure detention,[46] with perhaps an equal or greater number "held" in adult jails or lockups, also awaiting further processing.[47] According to Bookin-Weiner, whose research on juvenile detention appeared during the same time period, the number of juveniles held in preadjudicatory detention was *ten times* the number of youths institutionalized following adjudication.[48] More recent data that the volume of admissions to detention facilities has apparently remained steady. In 1990, there were 522,120 admissions to detention centers, with an additional 11,957 admissions to detention units housed within long term institutional facilities.[49] Of course, admissions data must be interpreted cautiously, since multiple admissions of the same individual during the same year are counted separately. The prevalence of detention is also reflected in court caseload statistics. In 1992, 296,100 of the juvenile court cases processed nationwide involved some period of detention between arrest and disposition.[50]

Second, the fact that so many youths are being detained *despite* longstanding and repeated recommendations by juvenile justice advisory groups, and federal legislation mandating significant reductions in the prevalence of detention only adds to the controversy. More than thirty five years ago, for example, the National Probation and Parole Association "recommended that the number of children detained in a detention facility should not be greater than 20 percent of all those offenders referred to the

---

[45]Bookin-Weiner, "Assuming Responsibility: Legalizing Preadjudicatory Juvenile Detention," 30 *Crime and Delinquency* 39 (1984).

[46]Commen, "The Supreme Court and Pretrial Detention of Juveniles: A Principled Solution to a Due Process Dilemma," 132 *University of Pennsylvania Law Review* 95 (1983) and Rubin, *Juvenile Justice: Policy, Practice and Law* (2d ed), (New York: Random House, 1985) *as cited in* Fraizer, "Preadjudicatory Detention" 144 in Roberts (ed.) *Juvenile Justice: Policies, Programs and Services*, (Chicago: Dorsey Press, 1989). The word "detained" appears in quotation marks in the text to reflect Fraizer's use of the term. Presumably the number reflects admissions to detention centers, rather than the number of individuals held.

[47]*Id.*, *citing* Community Research Center, *Removing Children from Adult Jails*, (Illinois: University of Illinois, 1980). The word "held" is in quotes to reflect Fraizer's use of the term; once again, the number probably reflects admissions rather than individuals held.

[48]Bookin-Weiner, *supra*.

[49]Bureau of Justice Statistics, *Children in Custody, 1990 Census of Public and Private Juvenile Detention, Correctional and Shelter Facilities*, (Washington, D.C.: 1991).

[50]Butts, et al. *Juvenile Court Statistics—1992*, (U.S. Department of Justice, Office of Juvenile Justice and Delinquency Prevention). Washingtion, D.C., in press.

court."[51] Later, in 1961, the National Council on Crime and Delinquency recommended that the proportion of juveniles detained be held at no more than ten percent of the offenders processed by the court.[52] Subsequent to these recommendations, the 1974 Juvenile Justice and Delinquency Prevention Act required states to reduce the number of status offenders held in detention and to separate juveniles from adult offenders in jail facilities. Later amendments to that legislation required states to remove juveniles from adult jails and other holding facilities by 1985.[53]

Unfortunately, compliance with these recommendations and legislative mandates fell far short of expectations:

> By the mid-1970s, a study of thirty eight states showed that only seven had detention rates below 20 percent and only one had a rate below 10 percent. The overall rate of detention, or the average for all thirty eight states, was 46 percent [citation omitted]. [Comparing] rates of detention over a ten-year period form 1966 through 1975 [the researchers] found remarkable stability....[T]he states that had the highest detention rates in 1966 also had the highest detention rates in 1975.[54]

Compliance with the jail removal mandates continued to be problematic through the 1980s and into the 1990s. For example, under a 1980 Amendment to the original legislation, the goal of "total removal" of juveniles by 1985 was abandoned. The amended legislation extended the deadline for total removal to 1988, provided that states had "achieved a 'substantial compliance' of 75% removal...and...made an 'unequivocal committment' to achieve full compliance."[55]

Further, a number of administrative regulations were created to provide exemptions to the removal mandates. Under these regulations, juveniles charged with felonies can be held for up to six hours in adult facilities "for the purposes of identification, processing or transfer to other facilities."[56] A 24 hour detention in an adult facility is permissible if:

> "(1) [t]he juvenile must be accused of a criminal-type offense; (2) the juvenile is awaiting an initial court appearance; (3) the state in which the juvenile is detained has an enforceable law requiring initial court appearance within 24 hours after being taken into custody, excluding Saturdays, Sundays

---

[51]Fraizer, *supra*.

[52]*Id.*

[53]This legislation was enacted into law as 42 U.S.C. § 5633 (a)(12)-(13) Subsequent amendment required the complete removal of juveniles from jails, 42 U.S.C. § 5633 (a)(14) *See also*, Swanger, "Hendrickson v. Griggs: A Review of Legal and Policy Implications for Juvenile Justice Policymakers," 34 *Crime and Delinquency* 209 (1988).

[54]Fraizer, *supra*, *citing* Poulin, et al., *Juveniles in Detention Centers and Jails: An Analysis of State Variations During the Mid-1970s*, (Washington, D.C.: U.S. Department of Justice, 1980).

[55]Fraizer and Bishop, "Jailing Juveniles in Florida: The Dynamics of Compliance With a Sluggish Federal Reform Initiative," 36 *Crime and Delinquency* 427 (1990) at 428.

[56]*Id.*

> and holidays; (4) the area is outside a Metropolitan Statistical Area...(5) no existing acceptable alternative is available and (6) the jail or lockup provides sight and sound separation between juvenile and adult offenders."[57]

Finally, juveniles charged with felonies and waived to adult court for trial were exempted from the removal mandate and could be held in adult facilites.[58]

One consequence of all this bureaucratic tinkering was a developing perception among state officials that the federal government was not really serious about enforcing the removal mandate, which translated into a general failure to comply with the removal mandate.[59] Others have argued that full compliance with the removal mandate was impossible, because states lacked the fiscal and administrative resources to do so.[60] Finally, additional research by Fraizer and Bishop suggests that factors such as the volume of juveniles processed, ignorance of the specific provisions of federal law mandating removal, conflicts between federal provisions and state laws governing juvenile detention, as well as "a general lack of resolve...or deliberate defiance of federal requirements" contributed to the problematic implementation the removal mandate.[61]

Finally, concern about the overuse of detention arises because the broad statutory language which typically governs the detention decision offers little in the way of meaningful guidelines that can be used to structure and check the discretion of a decisionmaker charged with determining if detention is warranted in individual cases. For example, in Arizona, youths can be detained:

> only if there is probable cause to believe that the child committed the acts alleged in the petition, and there is reasonable cause to believe: (1) That otherwise he will not be present at any hearing; or (2) That he is likely to commit an offense injurious to himself or others; or (3) That he must be held for another jurisdiction or (4) That the interests of the child or the public require custodial protection.[62]

Although these criteria seem reasonable at first glance, upon reflection it becomes clear that formulations like "interests of the child or public" are sufficiently elastic to allow detention in a wide variety of cases.

---

[57]*Id. citing* the *Federal Register*, June 20, 1985, at 25, 551.

[58]*Id.*

[59]*Id.*

[60]*Id. citing* "Removing Children From Adult Jails: A Guide To Action," *supra*; Steinhart and Krisberg, "Children in Jail," *State Legislatures* 12-16 (March, 1987); Schwartz, et al., "The Jailing of Juveniles in Minnesota: A Case Study," 34 *Crime and Delinquency* 133 (1988).

[61]*Id.*

[62]Szymanski, *Juvenile Detention Hearings: Time Requirements, Hearing Purpose, Criteria for Detaining (1993 Update)*, 2, (National Center for Juvenile Justice, 1994).

To be fair, it must be noted that states have implemented a number of strategies in an attempt to reduce the prevalence of detention and prevent abuses. These methods include affording juveniles a statutory right to bail or release on personal recognizance, or requiring that the initial detention decision be reviewed by a judicial officer at a detention hearing within 24 to 72 hours to determine if continued custody of the youth is warranted. Despite these safeguards, the detention of youth prior to adjudication remains a complex problem within the system. The cases below illustrate some of the controversies that can arise at this stage of the process.

The first case, *Application of Roberts*, deals with the issue of probable cause as it relates to the preadjudicatory detention of youth.

IN THE MATTER OF THE APPLICATION OF
DONOVAN ROBERTS FOR A WRIT OF
HABEAS CORPUS.
DONOVAN ROBERTS, BY AND THROUGH HIS
GUARDIAN AD LITEM ROBERT NAGLER,
PLAINTIFF-RELATOR,
V.
FRANK L. MILLS, JR., SUPERINTENDENT OF
THE SKIPWORTH DETENTION HOME,
DEFENDANT.
SC 27462.

SUPREME COURT OF OREGON,
IN BANC.
HEARD JAN. 20, 1981.
DECIDED JAN. 22, 1981.

* * *

LENT, JUSTICE.

This case arises out of proceedings in the Circuit Court of Lane County, Juvenile Department. Plaintiff is a child, 14 years of age, and defendant is the superintendent of Skipworth Juvenile Home in that county. A petition was filed in the circuit court alleging that the child was within the jurisdiction of the juvenile court under ORS 419.476(1)(a), which provides:

"(1) The juvenile court has exclusive jurisdiction in any case involving a person who is under 18 years of age and:

"(a) Who has committed an act which is a violation, or which if done by an adult would constitute a violation, of a law or ordinance of the United States or a state, county or city;"

* * *

The issue is whether the child may be detained by order of a court under ORS 419.577 without a judicial determination that there is probable cause to believe the child committed the acts alleged in the petition pursuant to ORS 419.476(1)(a).

* * *

The particular statute with which we are concerned is ORS 419.577. When a child is taken into custody, subsection (3) authorizes the juvenile court to release the child to the custody of a parent or other responsible person, or to order that the child remain in detention or shelter care for a brief period of time until a detention hearing is held.[63] Subsection (5) is as follows:

> "(5) Prior to an adjudication of the merits, the court may order that the child be held or placed in detention only when a petition has been filed alleging that the child is within the jurisdiction of the court by reason of paragraph (a) or (f) of subsection (1) of ORS 419.476 or when the court makes a written finding that the behavior of the child immediately endangers the physical welfare of the child or of another. No child shall be detained as a runaway or because the behavior of the child immediately endangers the physical welfare of the child or another under this subsection for more than 72 hours."

Insofar as this case is concerned, subsection (5), on its face, permits the juvenile court, without any probable cause hearing, to order indefinite detention of the child who is charged with being within the jurisdiction of the court under ORS 419.476(1)(a). Obviously, that procedure would not pass constitutional muster.

Defendant appears to contend that subsection (5) is saved, however, by reading it in conjunction with ORS 419.575(1), which provides:

> "(1) The juvenile court of each county shall designate the place or places in the county or at a reasonably short distance outside the county in which children are to be placed in detention or shelter care when taken into temporary custody. A child taken into temporary custody shall be placed in

[63]ORS 419.577(3) provides:

"(3) Pending further disposition of the case, the court may release the child to the custody of his parent or other responsible person or may order that the child remain in detention or shelter care subject to further order. No child shall be held in detention more than 24 hours, excluding Saturdays, Sundays and judicial holidays, except on order of the court nor for more than 48 hours, excluding Saturdays, Sundays and judicial holidays, except on order of the court made pursuant to a hearing on the matter of detention. No child shall be held or placed in detention on order of the court, except pursuant to subsection (5), (6) or (7) of this section."

> shelter care rather than detention unless the person placing the child in detention has reason to believe that the child will be found to be within the jurisdiction of the court by reason of paragraph (a) or (f) of subsection (1) of ORS 419.476 or the behavior of the child immediately endangers the physical welfare of the child or of another."

We doubt that that statute has any application to this case because of that part of ORS 419.577(3) quoted, supra, in n. 4, which provides:

> "No child shall be placed or held in detention on order of the court, except pursuant to subsection, (5), (6) or (7) of this section."

Assuming for the sake of argument, however, that ORS 419.575(1) and 419.577(5) are to be read together, the statutory requirement is only that the person placing the child in detention "has reason to believe" that the child has committed the acts alleged to meet the requirements of ORS 419.476(1)(a).[64]

Legislative history of the words "has reason to believe" indicates that the legislative committee which chose those words did so with the purpose of requiring something less than a finding of probable cause. Argument previously made to us by defendant shows that the statutes in question came form Senate Bill 703 introduced in 1975. As introduced, the bill proposed that a child be placed in shelter care rather than detention unless the court had "reasonable cause to believe" that the child would be found to be within the jurisdiction of the court under ORS 419.476(1)(a). The bill was amended, however, to provide the present wording of "reason to believe." The change was made after the Senate Committee on Judiciary heard testimony that the original wording might be interpreted to require "probable cause hearings or preliminary hearings" of the kind afforded adults charged with crimes. See the Minutes of the Senate Committee on Judiciary, March 31, 1975, and the Minutes of the House Judiciary Committee, June 2, 1975.

Defendant has argued to us that a finding of "probable cause" is not necessary to ensure that a juvenile's detention is reasonable, and that it is sufficient if the court finds that it is reasonably likely that the juvenile has committed the acts charged in the petition as meeting the requirements of ORS 419.476(1)(a). Defendant has acknowledged in oral argument on this case that if it is necessary to thwart the constitutional attack on the statutes, we should construe the words to require a finding of probable cause.

This court is committed to the proposition that statutes are to be construed so as to satisfy the constitution unless no other construction is possible. In *State v. Smyth*, 286 Or. 293, 296, 593 P.2d 1166 (1979), we said:

> "It is, of course, a commonplace that statutes will not be construed to violate constitutional prohibitions unless no other construction is possible. *State v. Harmon*, 225 Or. 571, 358 P.2d 1048

---

[64]The words "has reason to believe" present obvious ambiguities which do not require resolution in the case at bar. For example, is the test meant to be objective or subjective? Since the legislature is in session at this writing, perhaps those most concerned with the operation of ORS ch. 419 may wish to seek some clarifying amendments.

(1961) and cases there cited. Courts do not readily ascribe to legislators an intention to deprive persons of a right that the constitution guarantees."

Application of that rule here constrains us to hold that ORS 419.575(1) and 419.577(5), assuming they are to be read together, require a judicial finding that there is probable cause to believe that a child has committed the acts alleged to satisfy ORS 419.476(1)(a) prior to ordering detention of the child pending an adjudicatory hearing on the merits of the petition.

We do not hold that such judicial finding be the product of a full adversarial hearing, complete with the right to cross examination and confrontation as occurs upon a trial. See, for example, *Gerstein v. Pugh, supra; Moss v. Weaver*, 525 F.2d 1258 (5th Cir. 1976); and *Bell v. Superior Court in and for Cty. of Pima*, 117 Ariz. 551, 574 P.2d 39 (1977), for various descriptions of the kind of hearing that is required.

As noted above, defendant contends that a probable cause hearing was held in this case. For that contention, he first points to the order of December 30, 1980, which we have quoted in full near the outset of this opinion. We cannot agree that that order suffices to show a judicial finding of probable cause, or even a "reason to believe," that the child committed the alleged acts. The court specifically set forth a finding that "it is in the best interests of the child and the community" that the child be detained by defendant. That is the only stated finding. Had the referee perceived that his function was to inquire as to probable cause of the truth of the allegations, we believe that his order would have reflected this. We think the only fair conclusion to be drawn from his order is that he envisioned that he was only to satisfy himself, as referee, as to what the best interests of the child and community required.

Since judges and referees of the juvenile departments of the various courts of the state must make a probable cause determination in proceedings under ORS 419.577, they would be well advised to memorialize that determination in the order for detention.

Finally, we turn to the defendant's contention that there was indeed a probable cause hearing on December 30, 1980, prior to the making of the referee's order. We have nothing before us in that respect except a stipulated statement of facts by counsel as to what occurred at that detention hearing. We find that statement insufficient to show that there was a probable cause hearing by the referee. Moreover, we conclude there was no sufficient basis for a finding of probable cause.

It follows that the child must be discharged from defendant's custody insofar as that custody is dependent upon the validity of the court order of December 30, 1980.[65]

It is so ordered.[66]

---

[65]The stipulated facts show that perhaps this child is not entitled to complete liberty. We do not concern ourselves with any claims other than the defendant's claim of the right to detain him under the order of December 30, 1980.

[66]The child, in these proceedings, seeks certain other relief. He moves to intervene in other proceedings pending (continued...)

Plaintiff-relator discharged from custody.

APPLICATION OF ROBERTS

1. What is the primary purpose of a detention hearing in juvenile justice?
2. From the perspective of *parens patriæ*, critique the argument that "placing a juvenile in detention solely for his/her own good is insufficient pursuant to due process.
3. If detention is supposed to be for the child's own benefit, why should a probable cause hearing be required?
4. Why did the Supreme Court of Oregon conclude that no probable cause hearing was held, despite the fact that the state held a hearing?

The case below, *Schall v. Martin*, involves a due process challenge to the preventive detention of delinquents.

ELLEN SCHALL, COMMISSIONER OF NEW YORK CITY DEPARTMENT OF JUVENILE JUSTICE

V.

GREGORY MARTIN ET AL.

ROBERT ABRAMS, ATTORNEY GENERAL OF NEW YORK

V.

GREGORY MARTIN ET AL.

NOS. 82–1248, 82–1278.

* * *

Section 320.5(3)(b) of the New York Family Court Act authorizes pretrial detention of an accused juvenile delinquent based on a finding that there is a "serious risk" that the juvenile "may before the return date commit an act which if committed by an adult would constitute a crime." Appellees, juveniles who

[66](...continued)
before the court of a nature similar to this and to be declared a member of a certain class. We deny his motion to intervene and his request to be recognized as a member of the asserted class.

We reserve, for ancilary consideration, his petition for attorney fees as asserted in his petition for a writ of habeas corpus.

had been detained under § 320.5(3)(b), brought a habeas corpus class action in Federal District Court, seeking a declaratory judgment that § 320.5(3)(b) violates, *inter alia*, the Due Process Clause of the Fourteenth Amendment. The District Court struck down the statute as permitting detention without due process and ordered the release of all class members. The Court of Appeals affirmed, holding that since the vast majority of juveniles detained under the statute either have their cases dismissed before an adjudication of delinquency or are released after adjudication, the statute is administered, not for preventive purposes, but to impose punishment for unadjudicated criminal acts, and that therefore the statute is unconstitutional as to all juveniles.

Held: Section 320.5(3)(b) is not invalid under the Due Process Clause of the Fourteenth Amendment. Pp. 2409–2419.

* * *

JUSTICE RHENQUIST delivered the opinion:

I

Appellee Gregory Martin was arrested on December 13, 1977, and charged with first-degree robbery, second-degree assault, and criminal possession of a weapon based on an incident in which he, with two others, allegedly hit a youth on the head with a loaded gun and stole his jacket and sneakers. See petitioners' Exhibit 1b. Martin had possession of the gun when he was arrested. He was 14 years old at the time and, therefore, came within the jurisdiction of New York's Family Court.[67] The incident occurred at 11:30 at night, and Martin lied to the police about where and with whom he lived. He was consequently detained overnight.[68]

---

[67]In New York, a child over the age of 7 but less than 16 is not considered criminally responsible for his conduct. FCA § 301.2(1). If he commits an act that would constitute a crime if committed by an adult, he comes under the exclusive jurisdiction of the Family Court. § 302.1(1). That court is charged not with finding guilt and affixing punishment, *in re Bogart*, 45 Misc.2d 1075, 259 N.Y.S.2d 351 (1963), but rather with determining and pursuing the needs and best interests of the child insofar as those are consistent with the need for the protection of the community. FCA § 301.1. See *In re Craig S.*, 57 App.Div.2d 761, 394 N.Y.S.2sd 200 (1977). Juvenile proceedings are, thus, civil rather than criminal, although because of the restrictions that may be placed on a juvenile adjudged delinquent, some of the same protections afforded accused adult criminals are also applicable in this context. CF. FCA § 303.1.

[68]When a juvenile is arrested, the arresting officer must immediately notify the parent or other person legally responsible for the child's care. FCA § 305.2(3). Ordinarily, the child will be released into the custody of his parent or guardian after being issued an "appearance ticket" requiring him to meet with the probation service on a specified day. § 307.1(1). See n. 9, *infra*. If, however, he is charged with a serious crime, one of several designated felonies, see § 301.2(8), or if his parent or guardian cannot be reached, the juvenile may be taken directly before the Family Court. § 305.2. The Family Court judge will make a preliminary determination as to the jurisdiction of the court, appoint a law guardian for the child, and advise the child of his or her rights, including the right to counsel and the right to remain silent.

Only if, as in Martin's case, the Family Court is not in session and special circumstances exist, such as an (continued...)

A petition of delinquency was filed,[69] and Martin made his "initial appearance" in Family Court on December 14th, accompanied by his grandmother.[70] The Family Court Judge, citing the possession of the loaded weapon, the false address given to the police, and the lateness of the hour, as evidencing a lack of supervision, ordered Martin detained under § 320.5(3)(b) (at that time § 739(a)(ii); see n. 2, *supra*). A probable cause hearing was held five days later, on December 19th, and probable cause was found to exist for all the crimes charged. At the fact-finding hearing held December 27-29, Martin was found guilty on the robbery and criminal possession charges. He was adjudicated a delinquent and placed on two years' probation.[71] He had been detained pursuant to § 320.5(3)(b), between the initial appearance and the completion of the fact-finding hearing, for a total of 15 days.

* * *

---

[68](...continued)
inability to notify the parents, will the child be taken directly by the arresting officer to a juvenile detention facility. § 305.2(4)(c). If the juvenile is so detained, he must be brought before the Family Court within 72 hours or the next day the court is in session, whichever is sooner. § 307.3(4). The propriety of such detention, prior to a juvenile's initial appearance in Family Court, is not at issue in this case. Appellees challenged only judicially ordered detention pursuant to § 320.5(3)(b).

[69]A delinquency petition, prepared by the "presentment agency," originates delinquency proceedings. FCA § 310.1. The petition must contain, *inter alia*, a precise statement of each crime charged and factual allegations which "clearly apprise" the juvenile of the conduct which is the subject of the accusation. § 311.1. A petition is not deemed sufficient unless the allegations of the factual part of the petition, together with those of any supporting depositions which may accompany it, provide reasonable cause to believe that the juvenile committed the crime or crimes charged. § 311.2(2). Also, nonhearsay allegations in the petition and supporting deposition must establish, if true, every element of each crime charged and the juvenile's commission thereof. § 311.2(3). The sufficiency of a petition may be tested by filing a motion to dismiss under § 315.1.

[70]The first proceeding in Family Court following the filing of the petition is known as the initial appearance even if the juvenile has already been brought before the court immediately following his arrest. FCA § 320.2.

[71]The "fact-finding" is the juvenile's analogue of a trial. As in the earlier proceedings, the juvenile has a right to counsel at this hearing. § 341.2. See *In re Gault*, 387 U.S. 1, 87 S.Ct. 1428, 18 L.Ed.2d 527 (1967). Evidence may be suppressed on the same grounds as in criminal cases, FCA § 330.2, and proof of guilt, based on the record evidence, must be beyond a reasonable doubt, § 342.2. See *In re Winship*, 397 U.S. 358, 90 S.Ct. 1068, 25 L.Ed.2d (1970). If guilt is established, the court enters an appropriate order and schedules a dispositional hearing. § 345.1.

The dispositional hearing is the final and most important proceeding in the Family Court. If the juvenile has committed a designated felony, the court must order a probation investigation and a diagnostic assessment. § 351.1. Any other material and relevant evidence may be offered by the probation agency or the juvenile. Both sides may call and cross-examine witnesses and recommend specific dispositional alternatives. § 350.4. The court must find, based on a preponderance of the evidence, § 350.3(2), that the juvenile is delinquent and requires supervision, treatment, or confinement. § 352.1. Otherwise, the petition is dismissed. *Ibid.*

If the juvenile is found to be delinquent, then the court enters an order of disposition. Possible alternatives include a conditional discharge; probation for up to two years; nonsecure placement with, perhaps, a relative or the Division for Youth; transfer to the Commissioner of Mental Health; or secure placement. §§ 353.1-353.5. Unless the juvenile committed one of the designated felonies, the court must order the least restrictive available alternative consistent with the needs and best interests of the juvenile and the need for protection of the community. § 352.2(2).

The statutory provision at issue in these cases, § 320.5(3)(b), permits a brief pretrial detention based on a finding of a "serious risk" that an arrested juvenile may commit a crime before his return date. The question before us is whether preventive detention of juveniles pursuant to § 320.5(3)(b) is compatible with the "fundamental fairness" required by due process. Two separate inquiries are necessary to answer this question. First, does preventive detention under the New York statute serve a legitimate state objective? See *Bell v. Wolfish,* 441 U.S. 520, 534, n. 15, 99 S.Ct. 1861, 1871 n. 15, 60 L.Ed.2d 447 (1979); *Kennedy v. Mendoza-Martinez,* 372 U.S. 144, 168–169, 83 S.Ct. 554, 567–568, 9 L.Ed.2d 644 (1963). And, second, are the procedural safeguards contained in the FCA adequate to authorize the pretrial detention of at least some juveniles charged with crimes? See *Mathews v. Eldridge,* 424 U.S. 319, 335, 96 S.Ct. 893, 903 47 L.Ed.2d 18 (1976); *Gerstein v. Pugh,* 420 U.S. 103, 114, 95 S.Ct. 854, 863, 43 L.Ed.2d 54 (1975).

A

Preventive detention under the FCA is purportedly designed to protect the child and society from the potential consequences of his criminal acts. *People ex rel. Wayburn v. Schupf,* 39 N.Y.2d at 689–690, 385 N.Y.S.2d, at 521–522, 350 N.E.2d, at 910. When making any detention decision, the Family Court judge is specifically directed to consider the needs and best interests of the juvenile as well as the need for the protection of the community. FCA § 301.1; *In re Craig S.*, 57 App.Div.2d 761, 394 N.Y.S.2d 200 (1977). In *Bell v. Wolfish, supra,* at 534, n. 15, 99 S.Ct., at 1871 n. 15, we left open the question whether any governmental objective other than ensuring a detainee's presence at trial may constitutionally justify pretrial detention. As an initial matter, therefore, we must decide whether, in the context of the juvenile system, the combined interest in protecting both the community and the juvenile himself from the consequences of future criminal conduct is sufficient to justify such detention.

* * *

"The fact that a practice is followed by a large number of states is not conclusive in a decision as to whether that practice accords with due process, but it is plainly worth considering in determining whether the practice 'offends some principle of justice so rooted in the traditions and conscience of our people as to be ranked as fundamental.' *Snyder v. Massachusetts,* 291 U.S.97, 105 [54S.Ct. 330, 332, 78 L.Ed. 674] (1934)." *Leland v. Oregon,* 343 U.S. 790, 798, 72 S.Ct. 1002, 1007, 96 L.Ed. 1302 (1952). In light of the uniform legislative judgment that pretrial detention of juveniles properly promotes the interests both of society and the juvenile, we conclude that the practice serves a legitimate regulatory purpose compatible with the "fundamental fairness" demanded by the Due Process Clause in juvenile proceedings. *Cf. McKeiver v. Pennsylvania,* 403 U.S., at 548, 91 S.Ct., at 1987 (plurality opinion).[72]

---

[72]Appellees argue that some limit must be placed on the categories of crimes that detained juveniles must be accused of having committed or being likely to commit. But the discretion to delimit the categories of crimes justifying (continued...)

Of course, the mere invocation of a legitimate purpose will not justify particular restrictions and conditions of confinement amounting to punishment. It is axiomatic that "[d]ue process requires that a pretrial detainee not be punished." *Bell v. Wolfish*, 441 U.S., at 535, n. 16, 99 S.Ct., at 1872, n. 16. Even given, therefore, that pretrial detention may serve legitimate regulatory purposes, it is still necessary to determine whether the terms and conditions of confinement under § 320.5(3)(b) are in fact compatible with those purposes. *Kennedy v. Mendoza-Martinez*, 372 U.S., at 168–169, 83 S.Ct., at 567–568. "A court must decide whether the disability is imposed for the purpose of punishment or whether it is but an incident of some other legitimate governmental purpose." *Bell v. Wolfish, supra*, 441 U.S., at 538, 99 S.Ct., at 1873. Absent a showing of an express intent to punish on the part of the State, that determination generally will turn on "whether an alternative purpose to which [the restriction] may rationally be connected is assignable for it, and whether it appears excessive in relation to the alternative purpose assigned [to it]." *Kennedy v. Mendoza-Martinez, supra*, 372 U.S., at 168–189, 83 S.Ct., at 567–578. See *Bell v. Wolfish, supra*, 441 U.S., at 538, 99 S.Ct., at 1874; *Flemming v. Nestor*, 363 U.S. 603, 613–614, 80 S.Ct. 1367, 1373–1375, 4 L.Ed.2d 1435 (1960).

There is no indication in the statute itself that preventive detention is used or intended as a punishment. First of all, the detention is strictly limited in time. If a juvenile is detained at his initial appearance and has denied the charges against him, he is entitled to a probable-cause hearing to be held not more than three days after the conclusion of the initial appearance or four days after the filing of the petition, whichever is sooner. FCA § 325.1(2).[73] If the Family Court judge finds probable cause, he must also determine whether continued detention is necessary pursuant to § 320.5(3)(b). § 325.3(3).

Detained juveniles are also entitled to an expedited fact-finding hearing. If the juvenile is charged with one of a limited number of designated felonies, the fact-finding hearing must be scheduled to commence not more than 14 days after the conclusion of the initial appearance. § 340.1. If the juvenile is charged with a lesser offense, then the fact-finding hearing must be held not more than three days after the

---

[72](...continued)
detention, like the discretion to define criminal offenses and prescribe punishments, resides wholly with the state legislatures. *Whalen v. United States*, 445 U.S. 684, 689, 100 S.Ct. 1432, 1436, 63 L.Ed.2d 715 (1980); *Rochin v. California*, 342 U.S. 165, 168, 72 S.Ct. 205, 207, 96, L.Ed. 183 (1952). See also *Rummel v. Estelle*, 445 U.S. 263, 275, 100 S.Ct. 1133, 1139, 63 L.Ed.2d 382 (1980) ("the presence or absence of violence does not affect the strength of society's interest in deterring a particular crime").

More fundamentally, this sort of attack on a criminal statute must be made on a case-by-case basis. *United States v. Raines*, 362 U.S. 17, 21, 80 S.Ct. 519, 522, 4 L.Ed.2d 524 (1960). The Court will not sift through the entire class to determine whether the statute was constitutionally applied in each case. And, outside the limited First Amendment context, a criminal statute may not be attacked as overbroad. See *New York v. Ferber*, 458 U.S. 747, 102 S.Ct. 3348, 73 L.Ed.2d 1113 (1982).

[73]For good cause shown, the court may adjourn the hearing, but for no more than three additional court days. FCA § 325.1(3).

initial appearance.[74] In the latter case, since the times for the probable-cause hearing and the fact-finding hearing concide, the two hearings are merged.

Thus, the maximum possible detention under § 320.5(3)(b) of a youth accused of a serious crime, assuming a 3-day extension of the fact-finding hearing for good cause shown, is 17 days. The maximum detention for less serious crimes, again assuming a 3-day extension for good cause shown, is six days. These time frames seem suited to the limited purpose of providing the youth with a controlled environment and separating him from imporper influences pending the speedy dispositon of his case.

The conditions of confinement also appear to reflect the regulatory purposes relied upon by the State. When a juvenile is remanded after his initial appearance, he cannot, absent exceptional circumstances, be sent to a prison or lockup where he would be exposed to adult criminals. FCA § 304.1(2). Instead, the child is screened by an "assessment unit" of the Department of Juvenile Justice. Testimony of Mr. Kelly (Deputy Commissioner of Operations, New York City Department of Juvenile Justice), App. 286–287. The assessment unit places the child in either nonsecure or secure detention. Nonsecure detention involves an open facility in the community, a sort of "halfway house," without locks, bars, or security officers where the child receives schooling and counseling and has access to recreational facilities. *Id.*. at 285; Testimony of Mr. Benjamin, *id,* at 149–150.

Secure detention is more restrictive, but it is still consistent with the regulatory and *parens patriæ* objectives relied upon by the State. Children are assigned to separate dorms based on age, size, and behavior. They wear street clothes provided by the institution and partake in educational and recreational programs and counseling sessions run by trained social workers. Misbehavior is punished by confinement to one's room. See Testimony of Mr. Kelly, *id.*, at 292–297. We cannot conclude from this record that the controlled environment briefly imposed by the State on juveniles in secure pretrial detention "is imposed for the purpose of punishment" rather than as "an incident of some other legitimate governmental purpose." *Bell v. Wolfish*, 441 U.S., at 538, 99 S.Ct., at 1873.

* * *

Pretrial detention need not be considered punitive merely because a juvenile is subsequently discharged subject to conditions or put on probation. In fact, such actions reinforce the original finding that close supervision of the juvenile is required. Lenient but supervised disposition is in keeping with the Act's purpose to promote the welfare and development of the child.[75] As the New York Court of Appeals noted:

---

[74]In either case, the court may adjourn the hearing for not more than three days for good cause shown. FCA § 340.1(3). The court must state on the record the reason for any adjournment. § 340.1(4).

[75]Judge Quinones testified that detention at disposition is considered a "harsh solution." At the dispositional hearing, the Family Court judge usually has "a much more complete picture of the youngster" and tries to tailor the least restrictive dispositional order compatible with that picture. Testimony of Judge Quinones, App. at 279–281.

> "It should surprise no one that caution and concern for both the juvenile and society may indicate the more conservative decision to detain at the very outset, whereas the later development of very much more relevant information may prove that while a finding of delinquency was warranted, placement may not be indicated." *People ex rel. Wayburn v. Schupf*, 39 N.Y.2d, at 690, 385 N.Y.S.2d, at 522, 350 N.E.2d, at 910.

Even when a case is terminated prior to fact-finding, it does not follow that the decision to detain the juvenile pursuant to § 320.5(3)(b) amounted to a due process violation. A delinquency petition may be dismissed for any number of reasons collateral to its merits, such as the failure of a witness to testify. The Family Court judge cannot be expected to anticipate such developments at the initial hearing. He makes his decision based on the information available to him at that time, and the propriety of the decision must be judged in that light. Consequently, the final disposition of a case is "largely irrelevant" to the legality of a pretrial detention. *Baker v. McCollan*, 443 U.S. 137, 145, 99 S.Ct. 2689, 2695, 61 L.Ed.2d 433 (1979).

It may be, of course, that in some circumstances detention of a juvenile would not pass constitutional muster. But the validity of those detentions must be determined on a case-by-case basis. Section 320.5(3)(b) is not invalid "on its face" by reason of the ambiguous statistics and case histories relied upon by the court below.[76] We find no justification for the conclusion that, contrary to the express language of the statute and the judgment of the highest state court, § 320.5(3)(b) is a punitive rather than a regulatory measure. Preventive detention under the FCA serves the legitimate state objective, held in common with every state in the country, of protecting both the juvenile and society from the hazards of pretrial crime.

B

Given the legitimacy of the State's interest in preventive detention, and the nonpunitive nature of that detention, the remaining question is whether the procedures afforded juveniles detained prior to fact-finding provide sufficient protection against erroneous and unnecessary deprivations of liberty. See *Matthews v. Eldridge*, 424 U.S., at 335, 96 S.Ct., at 903, 47 L.Ed.2d 18.[77] In *Gerstein v. Pugh*, 420 U.S., at 114, 95

---

[76]Several *amici* argue that similar statistics obtain throughout the country. See, *e.g.*, Brief for American Bar Association as *Amicus Curiae* 23; Brief for Association for Children of New Jersey as *Amicus Curiae* 8, 11; Brief for Youth Law Center et al. as *Amicus Curiae* 13–14. But even if New York's experience were duplicated on a national scale, that fact would not lead us, as *amici* urge, to conclude that every State and the United States are illicitly punishing juveniles prior to their trial. On the contrary, if such statistics obtain nationwide, our conclusion is strengthened that the existence of the statistics in these cases is not a sufficient ground for striking down New York's statute. As already noted: "The fact that a practice is followed by a large number of states is not conclusive in a decision as to whether that practice accords with due process, but it is plainly worth considering in determining whether the practice 'offends some principle of justice so rooted in the traditions and conscience of our people as to be ranked as fundamental.' *Snyder v. Massachusetts*, 291 U.S. 97, 105 [54 S.Ct. 330, 332, 78 L.Ed. 674] (1934)." *Leland v. Oregon*, 343 U.S. 790, 798, 72 S.Ct. 1002, 1007, 96 L.Ed. 1302 (1952).

[77]Appellees urge the alleged lack of procedural safeguards as an alternative ground for upholding the judgment (continued...)

S.Ct., at 863, 43 L.Ed.2d 54, we held that a judicial determination of probable cause is a prerequisite to any extended restraint on the liberty of an adult accused of crime. We did not, however, mandate a specific time-table. Nor did we require the "full panoply of adversary safeguards—counsel, confrontation, cross-examination, and compulsory process for witnesses." *Id.* at 119, 95 S.Ct., at 866. Instead, we recognized "the desirability of flexibility and experimentation by the States." *Id.*, at 123 95 S.Ct. at 868. *Gerstein* arose under the Fourth Amendment, but the same concern with "flexibility" and "informality," while yet ensuring adequate predetention procedures, is present in this context. *In re Winship*, 397 U.S., at 366, 90 S.Ct., at 1074 25 L.Ed.2d 368; *Kent v. United States*, 383 U.S. 541, 554, 86 S.Ct. 1045, 1054, 16 L.Ed.2d 84 (1966).

In many respects, the FCA provides far more predetention protection for juveniles than we found to be constitutionally required for a probable-cause determination for adults in *Gerstein*. The initial appearance is informal, but the accused juvenile is given full notice of the charges against him and a complete stenographic record is kept of the hearing. See 513 F.Supp., at 702. The juvenile appears accompanied by his parent or guardian.[78] He is first informed of his rights, including the right to remain silent and the right to be represented by counsel chosen by him or by a law guardian assigned by the court. FCA § 320.3. The initial appearance may be adjourned for no longer than 72 hours or until the next court day, whichever is sooner, to enable an appointed law guardian or other counsel to appear before the court. § 320.2(3). When his counsel is presnet, the juvenile is informed of the charges against him and furnished with a copy of the delinquency petition. § 320.4(1). A representative from the presentment agency appears in support of the petition.

The nonhearsay allegations in the delinquency petition and supporting despositions must establish probable cause to believe the juvenile committed the offense. Although the Family Court judge is not required to make a finding of probable cause at the initial appearance, the youth may challenge the sufficiency of the petition on that ground. FCA § 315.1. Thus, the juvenile may oppose any recommended detention by arguing that there is not probable cause to believe he committed the offense or offenses with which he is charged. If the petition is not dismissed, the juvenile is given an opportunity to admit or deny the charges. § 321.1.[79]

---

[77](...continued)
of the Court of Appeals. Brief for Appellees 62-75. The court itself intimated that it would reach the same result on that ground, 689 F.2d, at 373-374, and Judge Newman, in his concurrence, relied expressly on perceived procedural flaws in the statute. Accordingly, we deem it necessary to consider the question.

[78]If the juveniles' parent or guardian fails to appear after reasonable and substantial efforts have been made to notify such person, the court must appoint a law guardian for the child. FCA § 320.3.

[79]If the child chooses to remain silent, he is assumed to deny the cahrges. FCA § 321.1. With the consent of the court and of the presentment agency, the child may admit to a lesser charge. If he wishes to admit to the charges or to a lesser charge, the court must, before accepting the admission, advise the child of his right to a fact-finding hearing
(continued...)

At the conclusion of the initial appearance, the presentment agency makes a recommendation regarding detention. A probation officer reports on the juvenile's record, including other prior and current Family Court and probation contacts, as well as relevant information concerning home life, school attendance, and any special medical or developmental problems. He concludes by offering his agency's recommendation on detention. Opposing counsel, the juvenile's parents, and the juvenile himself may all speak on his behalf and challenge any information or recommendation. If the judge does decide to detain the juvenile under § 320.5(3)(b), he must state on the record the facts and reasons for the detention.[80]

As noted, a detained juvenile is entitled to a formal, adversarial probable-cause hearing within three days of his initial appearance, with one 3-day extension possible for good cause shown.[81] The burden at this hearing is on the presentment agency to call witnesses and offer evidence in support of the charges. § 325.2. Testimony is under oath and subject to cross-examination. *Ibid.* The accused juvenile may call witnesses and offer evidence in his own behalf. If the court finds probable cause, the court must again decide whether continued detention is necessary under § 320.5(3)(b). Again, the facts and reasons for the detention must be stated on the record.

In sum, notice, a hearing, and a statement of facts and reasons are given prior to any detention under § 320.5(3)(b). A formal probable-cause hearing is then held within a short while thereafter, if the fact-finding hearing is not itself scheduled within three days. These flexible procedures have been found constitutionally adequate under the Fourth Amendment, see *Gerstein v. Pugh*, under the Due Process Clause, see *Kent v. United States, supra,* 557, 86 S.Ct., at 1055, 16 L.Ed.2d 84. Appellees have failed to note any additional procedures that would significantly improve the accuracy of the determination without unduly impinging on the achievement of legitimate state purposes.[82]

---

[79](...continued)
and of the possible specific dispositional orders that may result from the admission. *Ibid.* The court must also satisfy itself that the child actually did commit the acts to which he admits. *Ibid.*

With the consent of the victim or complainant and the juvenile, the court may also refer a case to the probation service for adjustment. If the case is subsequently adjusted, the petition is then dismissed. § 320.6.

[80]Given that under *Gerstein,* 420 U.S., at 119-123, 95 S.Ct., at 865-868, a probable-cause hearing may be informal and nonadversarial, a Family Court judge could make a finding of probable cause at the initial appearance. That he is not required to do so does not, under the circumstances, amount to a deprivation of due process. Appellees fail to point to a single example where probable cause was not found after a decision was made to detain the child.

[81]The Court in *Gerstein* indicated approval of pretrial detention procedures that supplied a probable-cause hearing within five days of the initial detention. *Id.*, at 124, n. 25, 95 S.Ct., at 868, n. 25. The brief delay in the probable-cause hearing may actually work to the advantage of the juvenile since it gives his counsel, usually appointed at the initial appearance pursuant to FCA § 320.2(2), time to prepare.

[82]Judge Newman, in his concurrence below, offered a list of statutory improvements. These suggested changes included: limitations on the crimes for which the juvenile has been arrested or which he is likely to commit if released; a determination of the likelihood that the juvenile's background; and a more specific standard of proof. The first and (continued...)

Appellees argue, however, that the risk of erroneous and unnecessary detentions is too high despite these procedures because the standard for detention if fatally vague. Detention under § 320.5(3)(b) is based on a finding that there is a "serious risk" that the juvenile, if released, would commit a crime prior to his next court appearance. We have already seen that detention of juveniles on that ground serves legitimate regulatory purposes. But appellees claim, and the District Court agreed, that it is virtually impossible to predict future criminal conduct with any degree of accuracy. Moreover, they say, the statutory standard fails to channel the discretion of the Family Court judge by specifying the factors on which he should rely in making that prediction. The procedural protections noted above are thus, in their view, unavailing because the ultimate decision is intrinsically arbitrary and uncontrolled.

Our cases indicate, however, that from a legal point of veiw there is nothing inherently unattainable about a prediction of future criminal conduct. Such a judgment forms an important element in many decisions,[83] and we have specifically rejected the contention, based on the same sort of sociological data relied upon by appellees and the District Court, "that it is impossible to predict future behavior and that the question is so vague as to be meaningless." *Jurek v. Texas,* 428 U.S. 262, 274, 96 S.Ct. 2950, 2957, 49 L.Ed.2d 929 (1976) (opinion of Stewart, POWELL and STEVENS, JJ.); *id.*, at 279, 96 S.Ct., at 2959 (WHITE, J., concurring in judgment).

We have also recognized that a prediction of future criminal conduct is "an experienced prediction based on a host of variables" which cannot be readily codified. *Greenholtz v. Nebraska Penal Inmates,* 442, U.S. 1, 16, 99 S.Ct. 2100, 2108, 60 L.Ed.2d 668 (1979). Judge Quinones of the Family Court testified at trial that he and his colleagues make a determination under § 320.5(3)(b) based on numerous factors including the nature and seriousness of the charges; whether the charges are likely to be proved at

---

[82](...continued)
second of these suggestions have already been considered. See n. 18 and 27, *supra*. We need only add to the discussion in n. 18 that there is no indication that delimiting the category of crimes justifying detention would improve the accuracy of the § 320.5(3)(b) determination in any respect. The third and fourth suggestions are discussed in text, *infra*.

[83]See *Jurek v. Texas*, 428 U.S. 262, 274–275, 96 S.Ct. 2950, 2957–2958, 49 L.Ed.2d 929 (1976) (death sentence imposed by jury); *Greenholtz v. Nebraska Penal Inmates*, 442 U.S. 1, 9–10, 99 S.Ct. 2100, 2104–2105, 60 L.Ed.2d 668 (1979) (grant of parole); *Morrissey v. Brewer*, 408 U.S. 471, 480, 92 S.Ct. 2593, 2599, 33 L.Ed.2d 484 (1972) (parole revocation).

A prediction of future criminal conduct may also form the basis for an increased sentence under the "dangerous special offender" statute, 18 U.S.C. § 3575. Under § 3575(f), a "dangerous" offender is defined as an individual for whom "a period of confinement longer than that provided for such [underlying] felony is required for the protection of the public from further criminal conduct by the defendant." The statute has been challenged numerous times on the grounds that the standard is unconstitutionally vague. Every Court of Appeals considering the question has rejected that claim. *United States v. Davis,* 710 F.2d 104, 108–109 (CA3), cert. denied, 464 U.S. 1001, 104 S.Ct. 505 78 L.Ed.2d 695 (1983); *United States v. Schell,* 692 F.2d 672, 675–676 (CA10 1982); *United States v. Williamson,* 567 F.2d 610, 613 (CA4 1977); *United States v. Bowdach,* 561 F.2d 1160, 1175 (CA5 1977); *United States v. Neary,* 552 F.2d 1184, 1194 (CA7), cert. denied, 434 U.S. 864, 98 S.Ct. 197, 54 L.Ed.2d 139 (1977); *United States v. Stewart,* 531 F.2d 326, 336–337 (CA6), cert. denied, 426 U.S. 922, 96 S.Ct. 2629, 49 L.Ed.2d 376 (1976).

trial; the juvenile's prior record; the adequacy and effectiveness of his home supervision; his school situation, if known; the time of day of the alleged crime as evidence of its seriousness and a possible lack of parental control; and any special circumstances that might be brought to his attention by the probation officer, the child's attorney, or any parents, relatives, or other responsible persons accompanying the child. Testimony of Judge Quinones, App. 254–267. The decision is based on as much information as can reasonably be obtained at the initial appearance. *Ibid.*

Given the right to a hearing, to counsel, and to a statement of reasons, there is no reason that the specific factors upon which the Family Court judge might rely must be specified in the statute. As the New York Court of Appeals concluded, *People ex rel. Wayburn v. Schupf,* 39 N.Y.2d, at 690, 385 N.Y.S.2d, at 522, 350 N.E.2d, at 910, "to a very real extent Family Court must exercise a substitute parental control for which there can be no particularized criteria." There is also no reason, we should add, for a federal court to assume that a state court judge will not strive to apply state law as conscientiously as possible. *Sumner v. Mata,* 449 U.S. 539, 549, 101 S.Ct. 764, 770, 66 L.Ed.2d 722 (1981).

It is worth adding that the Court of Appeals for the Second Circuit was mistaken in its conclusion that "[i]ndividual litigation...is a practical impossibility because the periods of detention are so short that the litigation is mooted before the merits are determined." 689 F.2d, at 373. In fact, one of the juveniles in the very case histories upon which the court relied was released from pretrial detention on a writ of habeas corpus issued by the State Supreme Court. New York courts also have adopted a liberal view of the doctrine of "capable of repetition, yet evading review" precisely in order to ensure that pretrial detention orders are not unreviewable. In *Peopleex rel. Wayburn v. Schupf, supra,* at 686, 385 N.Y.S.2d, at 520, 350 N.E.2d, at 908, the court declined to dismiss an appeal from the grant of a writ of habeas corpus despite the technical mootness of the case.

> "Because the situation is likely to recur...and the substantial issue may otherwise never be reached (in view of the predictably recurring happenstance that, however expeditiously an appeal might be prosecuted, fact-finding and dispositional hearings normally will have been held and a disposition made before the appeal could reach us),...we decline to dismiss [the appeal] on the ground of mootness."

The required statement of facts and reasons justifying the detention and the stenographic record of the initial appearance will provide a basis for the review of individual cases. Pretrial detention orders in New York may be reviewed by writ of habeas corpus brought in State Supreme Court. And the judgment of that court is appealable as of right and may be taken directly to the Court of Appeals if a constitutional question is presented. N.Y.Civ.Prac. Law § 5601(b)(2) (McKinney 1978). Permissive appeal from a Family Court order may also be had to the Appellate Division. FCA § 365.2. Or a motion for reconsideration may be directed to the Family Court judge. § 355.1(1)(b). These postdetention procedures provide a sufficient mechanism for correcting on a case-by-case basis any erroneous detentions ordered under § 320.5(3). Such procedures may well flesh out the standards specified in the statute.

III

The dissent would apparently have us strike down New York's preventive detention statute on two grounds: first, because the preventive detention of juveniles constitutes poor public policy, with the balance of harms outweighing any positive benefits either to society or to the juveniles themselves, *post,* at 2423–2425, 2433, and, second, because the statute could have been better drafted to improve the quality of the decisionmaking process, *post,* at 2431–2432. But it is worth recalling that we are neither a legislature charged with formulating public policy nor an American Bar Association committee charged with drafting a model statute. The question before us today is solely whether the preventive detention system chosen by the State of New York and applied by the New York Family Court comports with constitutional standards. Given the regulatory purpose for the detention and the procedural protections that precede its imposition, we conclude that § 320.5(3)(b) of the New York FCA is not invalid under the Due Process Clause of the Fourteenth Amendment.

The judgment of the Court of Appeals is *Reversed.*

* * *

SCHALL V. MARTIN

1. Is there a right to bail in the adult criminal justice system? Explain.
2. Critique § 320.5(3)(b) of the New York Family Court Act from a "least restrictive alternative" perspective. How could the law be revised to curtail judicial discretion?
3. Explain the issue of "predicting dangerousness" as it is relevant to *Schall.* What criteria were used by the family court judge in this case? Could this type of decision making be improved upon? See, for example, John Monahan, *Predicting Violent Behavior.* Beverly Hills, CA: Sage, 1981; Stephen Pfohl, "Predicting Dangerousness: A Social Deconstruction of Psychiatric Reality" in Linda Teplin, ed. *Mental Health in Criminal Justice.* Beverly Hills, CA: Sage, 1984.
4. Does §320.5(3)(b) punish the juvenile before adjudication? Explain.

THE INTAKE DECISION

A. The Dynamics of the Intake Decision

As indicated in the sections above, the preadjudicatory phases of the juvenile justice process involve a series of decisions about whether to divert or detain a juvenile or refer the case for adjudication. In the final section of this chapter we will briefly examine the factors that influence the various decisions made at intake.

1. Offense Seriousness and Prior Record of the Offender

As in the adult criminal justice system, intake decisions in the juvenile justice system are affected to a great degree by the serious of the current offense and the prior record of the offender. Obviously, the more serious the offense, or the more extensive the prior record of the offender, the greater the likelihood of that the case will be referred to the court for formal adjudication.

Ironically, the U.S. Supreme Court decision in *In re Gault*,[84] while designed to inject greater due process protections at the adjudicatory stages of the juvenile justice system by granting juveniles the right to counsel, also had a profound, if ancilary impact on the intake phase of the process. In the aftermath of *Gault*, prosecutors began to exert a greater degree of control over the intake decision. Initially, the prosecutor's role was limited to reviewing petitions prepared by intake staff for legal sufficiency. Over time however, their role has become much more active, to the point where, in some jurisidictions, prosecutors have the power to review, and even overrule decisions made at intake.[85]

2. The Impact of Extralegal Variables on the Intake Decision

The impact of a variety of extralegal variables, such as gender, race and age on the intake decision have been examined by a number of researchers; the results of some of the more significant studies have been summarized by Lettessa et al.[86] In regard to gender, they note that while females tend to be less likely to be involved in delinquent activity overall, and less likely to participate in serious delinquent behavior in particular, they frequently receive *more* severe dispositions for offenses of lesser seriousness, and *less* severe dispositions for offenses of greater seriousnss compared to males. Moreover, in their study of the operation of a juvenile diversion program in a large midwestern county, they found the treatment of females to be generally consistent with this previous research: the females in their sample "were diverted for significantly less serious offenses than males, render[ing] this [finding] consistent with prior research that indicates females will receive more state intervention then their male counterparts for the same offense."[87]

Latessa et al. also note the inconsistency of previous findings regarding the effects of race on juvenile court processing, with some studies suggesting that it does influence processing decisions, and others

---

[84]*In re Gault*, *supra*, Chapter 2 and *infra*, Chapter 4.

[85]See Rubin, *Juvenile Justice: Policy Practice and Law* (2d. ed.), 165–171 (New York: Random House, 1985).

[86]Lettessa, et al. *Juvenile Diversion: Factors Related to Decision Making and Outcome*, in Decker (ed.) *Juvenile Justice Policy: Analyzing Trends and Outcomes*, (Beverly Hills: Sage Publications, 1984) at 150–153.

[87]*Id*.

finding no influence.[88] In their study of the midwestern diversion program, race did seem to influence outcome, with minority youth entering the diversion program for less serious offenses, and having a higher likelihood of referral to a treatment program than others.[89]

Like race, the impact of age on processing decisions open to question because of the inconsistent findings of previous research.[90] However, Latessa et al. found that both younger and older offenders had a lower likelihood of referral to treatment compared to youth 13–15 years of age.[91]

B. Due Process Concerns at Intake

Intake officers must weigh a complex constellation of legal and social factors when making the intake decision. Given the nature of the intake determination, therefore, there is always the possibility that, during the course of intake officer's interview, incriminating statements may made by the juvenile. The last case in this chapter, therefore deals with admissions made by a juvenile during a preadjudicatory hearing.

CONCLUSION

This chapter began by focusing on two major procedures used to remove juveniles from the system prior to adjudication: diversion to some type of treatment program or service agency outside of the juvenile court, and transfer or waiver, a procedure in which a small proportion of juvenile offenders are tried as adults in criminal court. Turning next to those juveniles who are not removed from the system via diversion or transfer, we considered the issues and problems surrounding the use of preadjudicatory detention. The chapter then closed with a brief description of the dynamics of the intake decision, considering how it may be influenced by the extralegal factors of gender, race and age.

The next chapter focuses of the adjudicatory stages of the juvenile court process, the phase where the actual determination of delinquency is made.

---

[88] *Id.*

[89] *Id.*

[90] *Id.*

[91] *Id.*

CHAPTER 4

THE ADJUDICATORY STAGES OF THE JUVENILE JUSTICE PROCESS

THE ADJUDICATORY STAGES OF THE JUVENILE JUSTICE PROCESS

INTRODUCTION

A. *In re Gault* and the Beginnings of Due Process in the Juvenile Court

In retrospect, it was an odd beginning to a revolution. When 15-year-old Gerald Gault made an obscene phone call to a woman named Cook on June 8, 1964, he set in motion a series of events that would eventually work radical alterations in the structure, the operations, and, indeed even the guiding philosophy of the juvenile court. Gerald couldn't have known it at the time, of course, but on that Monday morning in June, his adolescent prank would be the beginning of three-year legal battle that would, in the end, be decided by the United States Supreme Court. And, like all revolutions, the one Gerald triggered on that morning would have profound repercussions for years afterward.

Gerald Gault's case was an altogether routine—even minor—matter, handled with all the informality that the *parens patriæ* doctrine underlying the juvenile court allowed. Following Mrs. Cook's receipt of the call and her complaint to the Gila County Sheriff, Gerald was picked up later that day and taken to the Children's Detention Home.[1] Both parents were at work, but no attempt was made to notify them of their son's arrest; Gerald's mother learned about it from Gerald's brother that evening when she came home. When she and the brother went to the Detention Home, a deputy probation officer named Flagg told them that a hearing in Juvenile Court would be held the next afternoon.

A delinquency petition was filed with the juvenile court the next morning. Justice Fortas, the author of the U.S. Supreme Court decision in the case referred to the petition as an "entirely formal"[2] document, which stated only that Gerald was a minor, a delinquent, and "in need of the protection of [the c]ourt."[3] Nothing in the document described what Gerald had allegedly done, nor was a copy of the document served on Gerald's parents.

---

[1]The statement of the facts of *Gault* presented here is intended as a brief summary, for the purposes of introducing the material in the chapter. A more detailed description of the facts relied on by the Court accompanies our excerpt of the *Gault* case.

[2]*In re Gault*, 387 U.S. 1 (1967) at 4.

[3]*Id.*

Later that afternoon, Gerald, his mother, his brother and two probation officers, Flagg and Henderson, appeared in chambers before a judge named McGhee. Once again, Justice Fortas's opinion clearly captures the informal atmosphere of the proceedings:

> Gerald's father was not there....Mrs. Cook, the complainant was not there. No one was sworn at the hearing. No transcript or recording was made. No memorandum or record of the substance of the proceedings was prepared. Our information about the proceedings and the subsequent hearing on June 15, derives entirely from the testimony of the Juvenile Court Judge [footnote omitted], Mr. and Mrs. Gault and Officer Flagg at the habeas corpus proceeding conducted two months later.[4]

Apparently, Gerald was questioned briefly by the judge. However, the participants differed as to whether Gerald admitted making the phone call. In any event, the judge concluded the hearing, saying only that he would "think about it."[5] Gerald was returned to the detention home, and released a day or two later, at which time Mrs. Gault received a handwritten note telling her that the next hearing in Gerald's case was scheduled for June 15, 1964.

At the June 15 hearing, Gerald testified again, but apparently, no transcript or record was made of the hearing. Once again, witnesses differed about whether Gerald admitted making the call or not. Once again, Mrs Cook, the complainant, was absent. The judge also received a "referral report" from the probation officers; no copy was furnished to Gerald's parents. At the conclusion of the hearing the judge found Gerald delinquent and committed him to the State Industrial School, "for the period of his minority, unless sooner discharged by due process of law."[6] In other words, Gerald was facing institutionalization for up to five years, for making an obscene phone call. In contrast, an adult convicted of a similar offense under the laws in force at the time, could receive a maximum fine of fifty dollars or a maximum jail term of two months.

Ultimately, in *Gault*, the Supreme Court concluded that the promise of special treatment and the benefits of rehabilitation under the umbrella of *parens patriæ* did not adequately compensate for the absence of procedural due process during an adjudicatory hearing in juvenile court. *Gault* mandated that juveniles facing confinement for delinquent acts be provided with some basic procedural protections during an adjudicatory hearing, including notice of charges, the provision of a formal hearing, the opportunity to confront and cross examine witnesses, the protection against self incrimination, and, most importantly, the right to be represented by counsel. The Supreme Court's extension of these basic procedural rights to juveniles in *Gault* is generally regarded as the beginning of a period of "constitutionalist revision"[7] or

---

[4]*Id.*

[5]*Id.*

[6]*Id.* at 8.

[7]The phrase is taken from the title of Part 5 of Faust and Brantingham (eds.), *Juvenile Justice Philosophy:*
(continued...)

"constitutional domestication"[8] in juvenile court history; it is from this that *Gault* derives its "revolutionary" status.[9]

Despite its unquestionable importance, however, the *Gault* decision is fairly narrowly written. While it is important to remember *Gault* for what it did do, it is just as important to remember what it *did not* do. By itself, it did not question the need for the juvenile court; nor did it view the court's rehabilitative orientation, or its grounding in *parens patriæ* as fundamentally wrong. By itself, it offered limited due process protections only to those delinquents whose acts exposed them to the possibility of confinement; presumably, these same protections were not available to juveniles brought before the court for status offenses such as running away or truancy, or to delinquents whose cases could be disposed of through less severe interventions. And, by itself, the due process requirements of *Gault* were applicable only at the adjudicatory phase of the juvenile justice process; what other procedural safeguards (if any) were necessary at other points in the system had yet to be determined.

The *Gault* decision fundamentally and forever changed the juvenile justice system, and served as the basis for the subsequent consideration (but not always the extension) of additional due process rights for juveniles in cases such as *In re Winship*, 397 U.S. 358 (1970), *McKeiver v. Pennsylvania*, 403 U.S. 528 (1970), and *Breed v. Jones*, 421 U.S. 519 (1975), among others. However, *Gault* also triggered a debate over the meaning, the effectiveness, and the consequences of the "due process revolution" that persists to this day. The cases that follow highlight some of the major due process questions that have been addressed as part of the revolution inspired by *Gault* and its progeny.

ESTABLISHING THE CORE DUE PROCESS RIGHTS

A. The Basic Rights at Adjudication: Notice of Charges, Right to Counsel, Right to Confront and Cross Examine Witnesses, Protection Against Self-Incrimination

APPLICATION OF PAUL L. GAULT AND MARJORIE GAULT, FATHER AND MOTHER OF GERALD FRANCIS GAULT, A MINOR, APPELLANTS.

---

[7](...continued)
Readings, Cases Comments, 361 (Minnesota: West Publishing Co., 1974).

[8]Feld, "Juvenile (In)Justice and the Criminal Court Alternative," 39 *Crime and Delinquency* 405 (1993).

[9]There is, of course, a bit of historical slight-of-hand in attributing the advent of due process in the juvenile justice system to the *Gault* decision, since another important juvenile rights case, *Kent v. United States* (*see infra*) was decided in 1966, shortly before *Gault*. Because *Kent* dealt with narrow procedural questions regarding the process for transferring or "waiving" a juvenile's case to criminal court for trial as an adult, it was never quite accorded the same revolutionary status as the more generally applicable *Gault* decision.

No. 116.

ARGUED DEC. 6, 1966.

DECIDED MAY 15, 1967.

* * *

(The first section of the Gault case is included in Chapter 2.)

II.

The Supreme court of Arizona held that due process of law is requisite to the constitutional validity of proceedings in which a court reaches the conclusion that a juvenile has been at fault, has engaged in conduct prohibited by law, or has otherwise misbehaved with the consequence that he is committed to an institution in which his freedom is curtailed. This conclusion is in accord with the decisions of a number of courts under both federal and state constitutions.

* * *

Failure to observe the fundamental requirements of due process has resulted in instances, which might have been avoided, of unfairness to individuals and inadequate or inaccurate findings of fact and unfortunate prescriptions of remedy. Due process of law is the primary and indispensable foundation of individual freedom. It is the basic and essential term in the social compact which defines the rights of the individual and delimits the powers which the state may exercise. As Mr. Justice Frankfurter has said: "The history of American freedom is, in no small measure, the history of procedure." But, in addition, the procedural rules which have been fashioned from the generality of due process are our best instruments for the distillation and evaluation of essential facts from the conflicting welter of data that life and our adversary methods present. It is these instruments of due process which enhance the possibility that truth will emerge from the confrontation of opposing versions and conflicting data. "Procedure is to law what 'scientific method' is to science."

It is claimed that juveniles obtain benefits from the special procedures applicable to them which more than offset the disadvantages of denial of the substance of normal due process. As we shall discuss, the observance of due process standards, intelligently and not ruthlessly administered, will not compel the States to abandon or displace any of the substantive benefits of the juvenile process. But it is important, e think, that the claimed benefits of the juvenile process should be candidly appraised.

* * *

Ultimately, however, we confront the reality of that portion of the Juvenile Court process with which we deal in this case. A boy is charged with misconduct. The boy is committed to an institution where he may be restrained of liberty for years. It is of no constitutional consequence—and of limited practical meaning—that the institution to which he is committed is called an Industrial School. The fact of the matter is that, however euphemistic the title, a "receiving home" or an "industrial school" for juveniles is an institution of confinement in which the child is incarcerated for a greater or lesser time. His world becomes "a building with whitewashed walls, regimented routine and institutional hours * * *." Instead of mother and father and sisters and brothers and friends and classmates, his world is peopled by guards, custodians, state employees, and "delinquents" confined with him for anything from waywardness to rape and homicide.

In view of this, it would be extraordinary if our Constitution did not require the procedural regularity and the exercise of care implied in the phrase "due process." Under our Constitution, the condition of being a boy does not justify a kangaroo court. The traditional ideas of Juvenile Court procedure, indeed, contemplated that time would be available and care would be used to establish precisely what the juvenile did and why he did it—was it a prank of adolescence or a brutal act threatening serious consequences to himself or society unless corrected?[10] Under traditional notions, one would assume that in a case like that of Gerald Gault, where the juvenile appears to have a home, a working mother and father, and an older brother, the Juvenile Judge would have made a careful inquiry and judgment as to the possibility that the boy could be disciplined and dealt with at home, despite his previous transgressions.[11] Indeed, so far as appears in the record before us, except for some conversation with Gerald about his school work and his "wanting to go to * * * Grand Canyon with his father," the points to which the judge directed his attention were little different from those that would be involved in determining any charge of a penal statute.[12] The essential difference between Gerald's case and a normal criminal case is that safeguards available to adults were discarded in Gerald's case. The summary procedure as well as the long commitment was possible because Gerald was 15 years of age instead of over 18.

If Gerald had been over 18, he would not have been subject to Juvenile Court proceedings.[13] For the particular offense immediately involved, the maximum punishment would have been a fine of $5 to $50,

---

[10]Cf., however, the conclusions of the D.C. Crime Comm'n Report, pp. 692–693, concerning the inadequacy of the "social study records"upon which the Juvenile Court Judge must make this determination and decide on appropriate treatment.

[11]The Juvenile Judge's testimony at the habeas corpus proceeding is devoid of any meaningful discussion of this. He appears to have centered his attention upon whether Gerald made the phone call and used lewd words. He was impressed by the fact that Gerald was on six months' probation because he was with another boy who allegedly stole a purse—a different sort of offense, sharing the feature that Gerald was "along." And he even referred to a report which he said was not investigated because "there was no accusation" "because of lack of material foundation."

With respect to the possible duty of a trial court to explore alternatives to involuntary commitment in a civil proceeding, cf. Lake v. Cameron, 124 U.S. App.D.C. 264, 364 F.2d 657 (1966), which arose under statutes relating to treatment of the mentally ill.

[12]While appellee's brief suggests that the probation officer made some investigation of Gerald's home life, etc., there is not even a claim that the judge went beyond the point stated in the text.

[13]ARS §§ 8-201, 8-202.

or imprisonment in jail for not more than two months. Instead, he was committed to custody for a maximum of six years. If he had been over 18 and had committed an offense to which such a sentence might apply, he would have been entitled to substantial rights under the Constitution of the United States as well as under Arizona's laws and constitution. The United States Constitution would guarantee him rights and protections with respect to arrest, search, and seizure, and pretrial interrogation. It would assure him of specific notice of the charges and adequate time to decide his course of action and to prepare his defense. He would be entitled to clear advice that he could be represented by counsel, and, at least if a felony were involved, the State would be required to provide counsel if his parents were unable to afford it. If the court acted on the basis of his confession, careful procedures would be required to assure its voluntariness. If the case went to trial, confrontation and opportunity for cross-examination would be guaranteed. So wide a gulf between the State's treatment of the adult and of the child requires a bridge sturdier than mere verbiage, and reasons more persuasive than cliché can provide. As Wheeler and Cottrell have put it, "The rhetoric of the juvenile court movement has developed without any necessarily close correspondence to the realities of court and institutional routines."[14]

In Kent v. United States, supra, we stated that the Juvenile Court Judge's exercise of the power of the state as *parens patriæ* was not unlimited. We said that "the admonition to function in a 'parental' relationship is not an invitation to procedural arbitrariness."[15] With respect to the waiver by the Juvenile Court to the adult court of jurisdiction over an offense committed by a youth, we said that "there is no place in our system of law for reaching a result of such tremendous consequences without ceremony—without hearing, without effective assistance of counsel, without a statement of reasons."[16] We announced with respect to such waiver proceedings that while "We do not mean * * * to indicate that the hearing to be held must conform with all of the requirements of a criminal trial or even of the usual administrative hearing; but we do hold that the hearing must measure up to the essentials of due process and fair treatment."[17] We reiterate this view, here in connection with a juvenile court adjudication of "delinquency," as a requirement which is part of the Due Process Clause of the Fourteenth Amendment of our Constitution.

We now turn to the specific issues which are presented to us in the present case.

---

[14]*Juvenile Delinquency—Its Prevention and Control*, (Russell Sage Foundation, 1966), p. 35. The gap between rhetoric and reality is also emphasized in the Nat'l Crime Comm'n Report, pp. 80–81.

[15]383 U.S., at 555, 86 S.Ct., at 1054.

[16]383 U.S., at 554, 86 S.Ct., at 1053. The Chief Justice stated in a recent speech to a conference of the National Council of Juvenile Court Judges, that a juvenile court "must function within the framework of law and * * * in the attainment of its objectives it cannot act with unbridled caprice." "Equal Justice for Juveniles," 15 *Juvenile Court Judges Journal*, No. 3, pp. 14, 15 (1964).

[17]383 U.S., at 562, 86 S.Ct., at 1057.

III.

NOTICE OF CHARGES.

Appellants allege that the Arizona Juvenile Code is unconstitutional or alternatively that the proceedings before the Juvenile Court were constitutionally defective because of failure to provide adequate notice of the hearings. No notice was given to Gerald's parents when he was taken into custody on Monday, June 8. On that night, when Mrs. Gault went to the Detention Home, she was orally informed that there would be a hearing the next afternoon and was told the reason why Gerald was in custody. The only written notice Geralds' parents received at any time was a note on plain paper from Officer Flagg delivered on Thursday or Friday, June 11 or 12, to the effect that the judge had set Monday, June 15, "for further Hearings on Gerald's delinquency."

A "petition" was filed with the court on June 9 by Officer Flagg, reciting only that he was informed and believed that "said minor is a delinquent minor and that it is necessary that some order be made by the Honorable Court for said minor's welfare." The applicable Arizona statute provides for a petition to be filed in Juvenile Court, alleging in general terms that the child is "neglected, dependent or delinquent." The statute explicitly states that such a general allegation is sufficient, "without alleging the facts."[18] There is no requirement that the petition be served and it was not served upon, given to, or shown to Gerald or his parents.[19]

The Supreme Court of Arizona rejected appellants' claim that due process was denied because of inadequate notice. it stated that "Mrs. Gault knew the exact nature of the charge against Gerald from the day he was taken to the detention home." The court also pointed out that the Gaults appeared at the two hearings "without objection." The court held that because "the policy of the juvenile law is to hide youthful errors from the full gaze of the public and bury them in the graveyard of the forgotten past," advance notice of the specific charges or basis for taking the juvenile into custody and for the hearing is not necessary. It held that the appropriate rule is that "the infant and his parents or guardian will receive a petition only reciting a conclusion of delinquency.[20] But no later than the initial hearing by the judge, they

---

[18]ARS § 8-222, subsec. B.

[19]Arizona's Juvenile Code does not provide for notice of any sort to be given at the commencement of the proceedings to the child or his parents. Its only notice provision is to the effect that if a person other than the parent or guardian is cited to appear, the parent or guardian shall be notified "by personal service" of the time an place of hearing. ARS § 8-224. The procedure for initiating a proceeding, as specified by the statute, seems to require that after a preliminary inquiry by the court, a determination may be made "that formal jurisdiction should be acquired." Thereupon the court may authorize a petition to be filed. ARS § 8-222. It does not appear that this procedure was followed in the present case.

[20]No such petition was served or supplied in the present case.

must be advised of the facts involved in the case. If the charges are denied, they must be given a reasonable period of time to prepare."

We cannot agree with the court's conclusion that adequate notice was given in this case. Notice, to comply with due process requirements, must be given sufficiently in advance of scheduled court proceedings so that reasonable opportunity to prepare will be afforded, and it must "set forth the alleged misconduct with particularity." It is obvious, as we have discussed above, that no purpose of shielding the child from the public stigma of knowledge of his having been taken into custody and scheduled for hearing is served by the procedure approved by the court below. The "initial hearing" in the present case was a hearing on the merits. Notice at that time is not timely; and even if there were a conceivable purpose served by the deferral proposed by the court below, it would have to yield to the requirements that the child and his parents or guardian be notified, in writing, of the specific charge or factual allegations to be considered at the hearing, and that such written notice be given at the earliest practicable time, and in any event sufficiently in advance of the hearing to permit preparation. Due process of law requires notice of the sort we have described—that is, notice which would be deemed constitutionally adequate in a civil or criminal proceeding. It does not allow a hearing to be held in which a youth's freedom and his parents' right to his custody are at stake without giving them timely notice, in advance of the hearing, of the specific issues that they must meet. Nor, in the circumstances of this case, can it reasonably be said that the requirement of notice was waived.[21]

IV.

RIGHT TO COUNSEL

Appellants charge that the Juvenile Court proceedings were fatally defective because the court did not advise Gerald or his parents of their right to counsel, and proceeded with the hearing, the adjudication of delinquency and the order of commitment in the absence of counsel for the child and his parents or an express waiver of the right thereto. The Supreme Court of Arizona pointed out that "[t]here is disagreement [among the various jurisdictions] as to whether the court must advise the infant that he has a right to counsel."[22] It noted its own decision in Arizona State Dept. of Public Welfare v. Barlow, 80 Ariz. 249,

---

[21]Mrs. Gault's "knowledge" of the charge against Gerald, and/or the asserted failure to object, does not excuse the lack of adequate notice. Indeed, one of the purposes of notice is to clarify the issues to be considered, and as our discussion of the facts, supra, shows, even the Juvenile Court Judge was uncertain as to the precise issues determined at the two "hearings." Since the Gaults had no counsel and were not told of their right to counsel, we cannot consider their failure to object to the lack of constitutionally adequate notice as a waiver of their rights. Because of our conclusion that notice given only at the first hearing is inadequate, we need not reach the question whether the Gaults even received adequately specific notice even at the June 9 hearing, in light of the fact they were never apprised of the charge of being habitually involved in immoral matters.

[22]For recent cases [recent to *Gault*] in the District of Columbia holding that there must be advice of the right to (continued...)

296 P.2d 298 (1956), to the effect "that *the parents* of an infant in a juvenile proceeding cannot be denied representation by counsel of their choosing." (Emphasis added.) It referred to a provision of the Juvenile Code which it characterized as requiring "that the probation officer shall look after the interests of neglected, delinquent and dependent children," including representing their interests in court.[23] The court argued that "The parent and the probation officer may be relied upon to protect the infant's interests." Accordingly it rejected the proposition that "due process requires that an infant have a right to counsel." It said that juvenile courts have the discretion, but not the duty, to allow such representation; it referred specifically to the situation in which the Juvenile Court discerns conflict between the child and his parents as an instance in which this discretion might be exercised. We do not agree. Probation officers, in the Arizona scheme, are also arresting officers. They initiate proceedings and file petitions which they verify, as here, alleging the delinquency of the child; and they testify, as here, against the child. And here the probation officer was also superintendent of the Detention Home. The probation officer cannot act as counsel for the child. His role in the adjudicatory hearing, by statute and in fact, is as arresting officer and witness against the child. Nor can the judge represent the child. There is no material difference in this respect between adult and juvenile proceedings of the sort here involved. In adult proceedings, this contention has been foreclosed by decisions of this Court.[24] A proceeding where the issue is whether the child will be found to be "delinquent" and subjected to the loss of his liberty for years is comparable in seriousness to a felony prosecution. The juvenile needs the assistance of counsel to cope with problems of law,[25] to make skilled inquiry into the facts, to insist upon regularity of the proceedings, and to ascertain

---

[22](...continued)
counsel, and to have counsel appointed if necessary, see, *e.g.*, Shioutakon v. District of Columbia, 98 U.S.App.D.C. 371, 236 F.2d 666, 60 A.L.R.2d 686 (1956); Black v. United States, 122 U.S.App.D.C. 393, 355 F.2d 104 (1965); In re Poff, 135 F.Supp. 224 (D.C.D.C.1955). Cf. also In re Long, 184 So.2d 861, 862 (Sup.Ct.Miss., 1966); People v. Dotson, 46 Cal.2d 891, 299 P.2d 875 (1956).

[23]The section cited by the court, ARS § 8-204, subsec. C, reads as follows:

"The probation officer shall have the authority of a peace officer. He shall:

"1. Look after the interests of neglected, delinquent and dependent children of the county.

"2. Make investigations and file petitions.

"3. Be present in court when cases are heard concerning children and represent their interests.

"4. Furnish the court information and assistance as it may require.

"5. Assist in the collection of sums ordered paid for the support of children.

"6. Perform other acts ordered by the court."

[24]Powell v. State of Alabama, 287 U.S. 45, 61, 53 S.Ct. 55, 61, 77 L.Ed. 158 (1932); Gideon v. Wainwright, 372 U.S. 335, 83 S.Ct. 792, 9 L.Ed.2d 799 (1963).

[25]In the present proceedings, for example, although the Juvenile Judge believed that Gerald's telephone conversation was within the condemnation of ARS § 13-377, he suggested some uncertainty because the statute prohibits the use of vulgar language "in the presence or hearing of" a woman or child.

whether he has a defense and to prepare and submit it. The child "requires the guiding hand of counsel at every step in the proceedings against him."[26] Just as in Kent v. United States, supra, 383 U.S., at 561–562, 86 S.Ct., at 1057–1058, we indicated our agreement with the United States Court of Appeals for the District of Columbia Circuit that the assistance of counsel is essential for purposes of waiver proceedings, so we hold now that it is equally essential for the determination of delinquency, carrying with it the awesome prospect of incarceration in a state institution until the juvenile reaches the age of 21.[27]

During the last decade, court decisions, experts, and legislatures have demonstrated increasing recognition of this view. In at least one-third of the States, statutes now provide for the right of representation by retained counsel in juvenile delinquency proceedings, notice of the right, or assignment of counsel, or a combination of these. In other States, court rules have similar provisions.

We conclude that the Due Process Clause of the Fourteenth Amendment requires that in respect of proceedings to determine delinquency which may result in commitment to an institution in which the juvenile's freedom is curtailed, the child and his parents must be notified of the child's right to be represented by counsel retained by them, or if they are unable to afford counsel, that counsel will be appointed to represent the child.

V.

CONFRONTATION, SELF-INCRIMINATION, CROSS-EXAMINATION

Appellants urge that the writ of habeas corpus should have been granted because of the denial of the rights of confrontation and cross-examination in the Juvenile Court hearings, and because the privilege against self-incrimination was not observed. The Juvenile Court Judge testified at the habeas corpus hearing that he had proceeded on the basis of Gerald's admissions at the two hearings. Appellants attack this on the ground that the admissions were obtained in disregard of the privilege against self-incrimination. If the confession is disregarded, appellants argue that the delinquency conclusion, since it was fundamentally based on a finding that Gerald had made lewd remarks during the phone call to Mrs. Cook, is fatally defective for failure to accord the rights of confrontation and cross-examination which the Due Process Clause of the Fourteenth Amendment of the Federal Constitution guarantees in state proceedings generally.

Our first question, then, is whether Gerald's admission was improperly obtained and relied on as the basis of decision, in conflict with the Federal Constitution. For his purpose, it is necessary briefly to recall the relevant facts.

---

[26]Powell v. State of Alabama, 287 U.S. 45, 69, 53 S.Ct. 55, 64 (1932).

[27]This means that the commitment, in virtually all cases, is for a minimum of three years since jurisdiction of juvenile courts is usually limited to age 18 and under.

Mrs. Cook, the complainant, and the recipient of the alleged telephone call, was not called as a witness. Gerald's mother asked the Juvenile Court judge why Mrs. Cook was not present and the judge replied that "she didn't have to be present." So far as appears, Mrs. Cook was spoken to only once, by Officer Flagg, and this was by telephone. The judge did not speak with her on any occasion. Gerald had been questioned by the probation officer after having been taken into custody. The exact circumstances of this questioning do not appear but any admissions Gerald may have made at this time do not appear in the record.[28] Gerald was also questioned by the Juvenile Court Judge at each of the two hearings. The judge testified in the habeas corpus proceeding that Gerald admitted making "some of the lewd statements * * * [but not] any of the more serious lewd statements." There was conflict and uncertainty among the witnesses at the habeas corpus proceeding—the Juvenile Court Judge, Mr. and Mrs. Gault, and the probation officer—as to what Gerald did or did not admit.

We shall assume that Gerald made admissions of the sort described by the Juvenile Court Judge, as quoted above. Neither Gerald nor his parents were advised that he did not have to testify or make a statement, or that an incriminating statement might result in his commitment as a "delinquent."

The Arizona Supreme Court rejected appellants' contention that Gerald had a right to be advised that he need not incriminate himself. It said: "We think the necessary flexibility for individualized treatment will be enhanced by a rule which does not require the judge to advise the infant of a privilege against self-incrimination."

In reviewing this conclusion of Arizona's Supreme Court, we emphasize again that we are here concerned only with a proceeding to determine whether a minor is a "delinquent" and which may result in commitment to a state institution. Specifically, the question is whether, in such a proceeding, an admission by the juvenile may be used against him in the absence of clear and unequivocal evidence that the admission was made with knowledge that he was not obliged to speak and would not be penalized for remaining silent. In light of Miranda v. State of Arizona, 384 U.S. 436, 86 S.Ct. 1602, 16 L.Ed.2d 694 (1966), we must also consider whether, if the privilege against self-incrimination is available, it can effectively be waived unless counsel is present or the right to counsel has been waived.

It has long been recognized that the eliciting and use of confessions or admissions require careful scrutiny. * * *

The privilege against self-incrimination is, of course, related to the question of the safeguards necessary to assure that admissions or confessions are reasonably trustworthy, that they are not the mere fruits of fear or coercion, but are reliable expressions of the truth. The roots of the privilege are, however, far deeper. They tap the basic stream of religious and political principle because the privilege reflects the

---

[28]For this reason, we cannot consider the status of Gerald's alleged admissions to the probation officers. Cf., however, Comment, Miranda Guarantees in the California Juvenile Court, 7 Santa Clara Lawyer 114 (1966).

limits of the individuals' attornment to the state and—in a philosophical sense—insists upon the equality of the individual and the state. In other words, the privilege has a broader and deeper thrust than the rule which prevents the use of confessions which are the product of coercion because coercion is thought to carry with it the danger of unreliability. One of its purposes is to prevent the state, whether by force or by psychological domination, from overcoming the mind and will of the person under investigation and depriving him of the freedom to decide whether to assist the state in securing his conviction.

It would indeed be surprising if the privilege against self-incrimination were available to hardened criminals but not to children. The language of the Fifth Amendment, applicable to the States by operation of the Fourteenth Amendment, is unequivocal and without exception.

With respect to juveniles, both common observation and expert opinion emphasize that the "distrust of confessions made in certain situations" is imperative in the case of children from an early age through adolescence. In New York, for example, the recently enacted Family Court Act provides that the juvenile and his parents must be advised at the start of the hearing of his right to remain silent. The New York statute also provides that the police must attempt to communicate with the juvenile's parents before questioning him, and that absent "special circumstances" a confession may not be obtained from a child prior to notifying his parents or relatives and releasing the child either to them or to the Family Court. In In Matters of W. and S., referred to above, the New York Court of Appeals held that the privilege against self-incrimination applies in juvenile delinquency cases and requires the exclusion of involuntary confessions, and that People v. Lewis, 260 N.Y. 171, 183 N.E. 353, 86 A.L.R. 1001 (1932), holding the contrary, had been specifically overruled by statute.

Against the application to juveniles of the right to silence, it is argued that juvenile proceedings are "civil" and not "criminal," and therefore the privilege should not apply. It is true that the statement of the privilege in the Fifth Amendment, which is applicable to the States by reason of the Fourteenth Amendment, is that no person "shall be compelled in any *criminal case* to be a witness against himself." However, it is also clear that the availability of the privilege does not turn upon the type of proceeding in which its protection is invoked, but upon the nature of the statement or admission and the exposure which it invites. The privilege may, for example, be claimed in a civil or administrative proceeding, if the statement is or may be inculpatory.

It would be entirely unrealistic to carve out of the Fifth Amendment all statements by juveniles on the ground that these cannot lead to "criminal" involvement. In the first place, juvenile proceedings to determine "delinquency," which may lead to commitment to a state institution, must be regarded as "criminal" for purposes of the privilege against self-incrimination. To hold otherwise would be to disregard substance because of the feeble enticement of the "civil" label-of-convenience which has been attached to juvenile proceedings. Indeed, in over half of the States, there is not even assurance that the juvenile will be kept in separate institutions, apart from adult "criminals." In those States juveniles may be placed in or transferred to adult penal institutions after having been found "delinquent" by a juvenile court. For this purpose, at least, commitment is a deprivation of liberty. It is incarceration against one's will, whether it is called "criminal" or "civil." And our Constitution guarantees that no person shall be "compelled" to be a witness against himself when he is threatened with deprivation of his liberty—a command which this Court has broadly applied and generously implemented in accordance with the teaching of the history of the privilege and its great office in mankind's battle for freedom.

In addition, apart from the equivalence for this purpose of exposure to commitment as a juvenile delinquent and exposure to imprisonment as an adult offender, the fact of the matter is that there is little or no assurance in Arizona, as in most if not all of the States, that a juvenile apprehended and interrogated by the police or even by the Juvenile Court itself will remain outside of the reach of adult courts as a consequence of the offense for which he has been taken into custody. In Arizona, as in other States, provision is made for Juvenile Courts to relinquish or waive jurisdiction to the ordinary criminal courts. In the present case, when Gerald Gault was interrogated concerning violation of a section of the Arizona Criminal Code, it could not be certain that the Juvenile Court Judge would decide to "suspend" criminal proceedings to an adjudication in Juvenile Court.

It is also urged, as the Supreme Court of Arizona here asserted, that the juvenile and presumably his parents should not be advised of the juvenile's right to silence because confession is good for the child as the commencement of the assumed therapy of the juvenile court process, and he should be encouraged to assume an attitude of trust and confidence toward the officials of the juvenile process. This proposition has been subjected to widespread challenge on the basis of current reappraisals of the rhetoric and realities of the handling of juvenile offenders.

Further, authoritative opinion has cast formidable doubt upon the reliability and trustworthiness of "confessions" by children. * * * The recent decision of the New York Court of Appeals referred to above, In Matters of W. and S. deals with a dramatic and, it is to be hoped, extreme example. Two 12-year-old Negro boys were taken into custody for the brutal assault and rape of two aged domestics, one of whom died as the result of the attack. One of the boys was schizophrenic and had been locked in the security ward of a mental institution at the time of the attacks. By a process that may best be described as bizarre, his confession was obtained by the police. A psychiatrist testified that the boy would admit "whatever he thought was expected so that he could get out of the immediate situation." The other 12-year-old also "confessed." Both confessions were in specific detail, albeit they contained various inconsistencies. The Court of Appeals, in an opinion by Keating, J., concluded that the confessions were products of the will of the police instead of the boys. The confessions were therefore held involuntary and the order of the Appellate Division affirming the order of the Family Court adjudging the defendants to be juvenile delinquents was reversed.

We conclude that the constitutional privilege against self-incrimination is applicable in the case of juveniles as it is with respect to adults. * * * If counsel was not present for some permissible reason when an admission was obtained, the greatest care must be taken to assure that the admission was voluntary, in the sense not only that it was not coerced or suggested, but also that it was not the product of ignorance of rights or of adolescent fantasy, fright or despair.

The "confession" of Gerald Gault was first obtained by Officer Flagg, out of the presence of Gerald's parents, without counsel and without advising him of his right to silence, as far as appears. The judgement of the Juvenile Court was stated by the judge to be based on Gerald's admissions in court. Neither "admission" was reduced to writing, and, to say the least, the process by which the "admissions," were obtained and received must be characterized as lacking the certainty and order which are required of proceedings of such formidable consequences. Apart from the "admission," there was nothing upon which a judgment or finding might be based. There was no sworn testimony. Mrs. Cook, the complainant, was not present. The Arizona Supreme Court held that "sworn testimony must be required of all witnesses including police officers, probation officers and others who are part of or officially related not the juvenile court structure." We hold that this is not enough. No reason is suggested or appears for a different rule in respect of sworn testimony in juvenile courts than in adult tribunals. Absent a valid confession adequate to support the determination of the Juvenile Court, confrontation and sworn testimony by witnesses available for cross-examination were essential for a finding of "delinquency" and an order committing Gerald to a state institution for a maximum of six years.

As we said in Kent v. United States, 383 U.S. 541, 554, 86 S.Ct. 1045, 1053, 16 L.Ed.2d 84 (1966), with respect to waiver proceedings, "there is no place in our system of law for reaching a result of such tremendous consequences without ceremony * * *." We now hold that, absent a valid confession, a determination of delinquency and an order of commitment to a state institution cannot be sustained in the absence of sworn testimony subjected to the opportunity for cross-examination in accordance with our law and constitutional requirements.

Judgment reversed and cause remanded with directions.

APPLICATION OF GAULT

1. Use the *Gault* case to argue that the juvenile justice system may become extinct early in the next century.

2. Explain the roles of defense attorneys pursuant to the *Gault* case. What roles do prosecutors now have in juvenile court because of *Gault* and how do the roles of probation officers differ from those of prosecutors?

3. Is the mission of rehabilitation (based on *parens patriæ*) consistent with procedural due process in juvenile court adjudications? Explain.

4. Assess Judge McGhee's knowledge of juvenile training schools and the effects of secure institutionalization upon children. How could a training school decrease Gerald Gault's future proclivity to make obscene phone calls? Examine Judge McGhee's sentencing logic.

B. The Burden of Proof at the Adjudicatory Hearing

IN THE MATTER OF SAMUEL WINSHIP,

ARGUED JAN. 20, 1970.

DECIDED MARCH 31, 1970.

* * *

MR. JUSTICE BRENNAN delivered the opinion of the Court.

This case presents the single, narrow question whether proof beyond a reasonable doubt is among the "essentials of due process and fair treatment" required during the adjudicatory stage when a juvenile is charged with an act which would constitute a crime if committed by an adult.[29]

During a 1967 adjudicatory hearing, conducted pursuant to § 742 of the Act, a judge in New York Family Court found that appellant, then a 12-year-old boy, had entered a locker and stolen $112 from a woman's pocketbook. The petition which charged appellant with delinquency alleged that his act, "if done by an adult, would constitute the crime or crimes of Larceny." The judge acknowledged that the proof might not establish guilt beyond a reasonable doubt, but rejected appellant's contention that such proof was required by the Fourteenth Amendment. The judge relied instead on § 744(b) of the New York Family Court Act which provides that "[a]ny determination at the conclusion of [an adjudicatory] hearing that a [juvenile] did an act or acts must be based on a preponderance of the evidence."[30] During a subsequent dispositional hearing, appellant was ordered placed in a training school for an initial period of 18 months, subject to annual extensions of his commitment until his 18th birthday—six years in appellant's case. We reverse.

---

[29]Thus, we do not see how it can be said in dissent that this opinion "rests entirely on the assumption that all juvenile proceedings are 'criminal prosecutions,' hence subject to constitutional limitations." As in *Gault*, "we are not here concerned with * * * the pre-judicial stages of the juvenile process, nor do we direct our attention to the post-adjudicative or dispositional process." 387 U.S., at 13, 87 S.Ct., at 1436. In New York, the adjudicatory stage of a delinquency proceeding is clearly distinct from both the preliminary phase of the juvenile process and from its dispositional stage. See N.Y. Family Court Act §§ 731-749. Similarly, we intimate no view concerning the constitutionality of the New York procedures governing children "in need of supervision." See *id.*, at §§ 711, 712, 742-745. Nor do we consider whether there are other "essentials of due process and fair treatment" required during the adjudicatory hearing of a delinquency proceeding. Finally, we have no occasion to consider appellant's argument that § 744(b) is a violation of the Equal Protection Clause, as well as a denial of due process.

[30]The ruling appears in the following portion of the hearing transcript:

Counsel: "Your Honor is making a finding by the preponderance of the evidence."

Court: "Well, it convinces me."

Counsel: "It's not beyond a reasonable doubt, Your Honor."

Court: "That is true * * * Our statute says a preponderance and a preponderance it is."

I

The requirement that guilt of a criminal charge be established by proof beyond a reasonable doubt dates at least from our early years as a Nation. * * * It is now accepted in common law jurisdictions as the measure of persuasion by which the prosecution must convince the trier of all the essential elements of guilt." C. McCormick, Evidence § 321, pp. 681–682 (1954); see also 9 J. Wigmore, Evidence, § 2497 (3d ed. 1940).

* * *

The reasonable-doubt standard plays a vital role in the American scheme of criminal procedure. It is a prime instrument for reducing the risk of convictions resting on factual error. The standard provides concrete substance for the presumption of innocence—that bedrock "axiomatic and elementary" principle whose "enforcement lies at the foundation of the administration of our criminal law." * * * As the dissenters in the New York Court of Appeals observed, and we agree, "a person accused of a crime * * * would be at a severe disadvantage, a disadvantage amounting to a lack of fundamental fairness, if he could be adjudged guilty and imprisoned for years on the strength of the same evidence as would suffice in a civil case." * * *

Moreover, use of the reasonable-doubt standard is indispensable to command the respect and confidence of the community in applications of the criminal law. It is critical that the moral force of the criminal law not be diluted by a standard of proof that leaves people in doubt whether innocent men are being condemned. It is also important in our free society that every individual going about his ordinary affairs have confidence that his government cannot adjudge him guilty of a criminal offense without convincing a proper factfinder of his guild with utmost certainty.

Lest there remain any doubt about the constitutional stature of the reasonable-doubt standard, we explicitly hold that the Due Process Clause protects the accused against conviction except upon proof beyond a reasonable doubt of every fact necessary to constitute the crime with which he is charged.

II

We turn to the question whether juveniles, like adults, are constitutionally entitled to proof beyond a reasonable doubt when they are charged with violation of a criminal law. The same considerations that demand extreme caution in factfinding to protect the innocent adult apply as well to the innocent child. We do not find convincing the contrary arguments of the New York Court of Appeals, *Gault* rendered untenable much of the reasoning relied upon by that court to sustain the constitutionality of § 744(b). The Court of Appeals indicated that a delinquency adjudication "is not a 'conviction' (§ 781); that it affects no right or privilege, including the right to hold public office or to obtain a license (§ 782); and a cloak of protective confidentiality is thrown around all the proceedings (§§ 783–784)." 24 N.Y.2d, at 200, 299 N.Y.S.2d, at 417–418, 247 N.E.2d, at 255–256. The court said further: "The delinquency status is not made a crime; and the proceedings are not criminal. There is, hence, no deprivation of due process in the statutory provision [challenged by appellant] * * *." 24 N.Y.2d, at 203, 299 N.Y. S.2d, at 420, 247 N.E.2d, at 257. In effect the Court of Appeals distinguished the proceedings in question here from a criminal prosecution by use of what *Gault* called the 'civil' label-of-convenience which has been attached to juvenile proceedings." 387 U.S., at 50, 87 S.Ct., at 1455. But *Gault* expressly rejected that distinction as a reason for holding the Due Process Clause inapplicable to a juvenile proceeding. 387 U.S., at 50–51, 87 S.Ct., at 1455, 1456. The Court of Appeals also attempted to justify the preponderance standard on the related ground that juvenile proceedings are designed "not to punish, but to save the child." 24 N.Y.2d, at 197 299 N.Y.S.2d, at 254. Again, however, *Gault* expressly rejected this justification. 387 U.S., at 27, 87 S.Ct., at 1443. We made clear in that decision that civil labels and good intentions do not themselves obviate the need for criminal due process safeguards in juvenile courts, for "[a] proceeding where the issue is whether the child will be found to be 'delinquent' and subjected to the loss of his liberty for years is comparable in seriousness to a felony prosecution." *Id.*, at 36, 87 S.Ct., at 1448.

Nor do we perceive any merit in the argument that to afford juveniles the protection of proof beyond a reasonable doubt would risk destruction of beneficial aspects of the juvenile process. Use of the reasonable-doubt standard during the adjudicatory hearing will not disturb New York's policies that a finding that a child has violated a criminal law does not constitute a criminal conviction, that such a finding does not deprive the child of his civil rights, and that juvenile proceedings are confidential. Nor will there be any effect on the informality, flexibility, or speed of the hearing at which the factfinding takes place. And the opportunity during the post-adjudicatory or dispositional hearing for a wide-ranging review of the child's social history and for his individualized treatment will remain unimpaired. Similarly, there will be no effect on the procedures distinctive to juvenile proceedings that are employed prior to the adjudicatory hearing.

The Court of Appeals observed that "a child's best interest is not necessarily, or even probably, promoted if he wins in the particular inquiry which may bring him to the juvenile court." 24 N.Y.2d, at 199, 299 N.Y.S.2d, at 417, 247 N.E.2d, at 255. It is true, of course, that the juvenile may be engaging in a general course of conduct inimical to his welfare that calls for judicial intervention. But that intervention cannot take the form of subjecting the child to the stigma of a finding that he violated a criminal law and to the possibility of institutional confinement on proof insufficient to convict him were he an adult.

We conclude, as we concluded regarding the essential due process safeguards applied in *Gault*, that the observance of the standard of proof beyond a reasonable doubt "will not compel the States to abandon or displace any of the substantive benefits of the juvenile process." *Gault, supra,* at 21, 87 S.Ct., at 1440.

Finally, we reject the Court of Appeals' suggestion that there is, in any event, only a "tenuous difference" between the reasonable-doubt and preponderance standards. The suggestion is singularly unpersuasive. In this very case, the trial judge's ability to distinguish between the two standards enabled him to make a finding of guilt that he conceded he might not have made under the standard of proof beyond a reasonable doubt. Indeed, the trial judge's action evidences the accuracy of the observation of commentators that "the preponderance test is susceptible to the misinterpretation that it calls on the trier of fact merely to perform an abstract weighing of the evidence in order to determine which side has produced the greater quantum, without regard to its effect in convincing his mind of the truth of the proposition asserted." * * *

III

In sum, the constitutional safeguard of proof beyond a reasonable doubt is as much required during the adjudicatory stage of a delinquency proceeding as are those constitutional safeguards applied in *Gault*—notice of charges, right to counsel, the rights of confrontation and examination, and the privilege against self-incrimination. We therefore hold, in agreement with Chief Judge Fuld in dissent in the Court of Appeals, "that, where a 12-year-old child is charged with an act of stealing which renders him liable to confinement for as long as six years, then, as a matter of due process * * * the case against him must be proved beyond a reasonable doubt." * * *

REVERSED.

IN RE WINSHIP

1. Prior to the *Winship* case, why was the stringent standard of "proof beyond a reasonable doubt" solely limited to adult criminal adjudications? Why did this standard not apply to civil psychiatric commitment proceedings, child custody conflicts, and court disputes related to state dispensation of welfare benefits?

2. Winship was originally adjudicated on the basis of "preponderance of evidence." While the U.S. Supreme Court deemed this to be unconstitutional, could the High Court have invoked the more stringent *civil* standard of "clear and convincing" evidence instead of the non-civil "proof beyond a reasonable doubt?" Explain.

3. Why is the civil law—criminal law distinction important in this case?

4. Why is the disposition initially received by Winship noteworthy here (18 months of incarceration subject to extensions until his 18th birthday)? Recall that Winship was 12 years old at the time of the offense.

GUILTY PLEAS AND PLEA BARGAINS IN JUVENILE COURT

A. Formalizing the Guilty Plea Process

One of the most significant consequences of the *Gault's* introduction of defense counsel into the adjudicatory phase of the juvenile justice process. This, in turn, led to an increased role for prosecutors at this point as well.[31] Gradually, heightened concern for due process and the presence of attorneys, combined with growing public and legislative acceptance of harsher penalties for juvenile offenders has effectively transformed the adjudicatory hearing from a clinical process designed to diagnose "what's wrong" with delinquents, to a fact-finding process designed to determine something closer to the traditional notions of guilt or innocence, as would be found in the criminal trial of an adult.[32]

This transformation of the adjudicatory phase has also brought with it a growing reliance on plea bargaining within the juvenile court. Unfortunately, though the extent, nature, and impact of plea negotiations in juvenile courts have not been studied with the same intensity as plea negotiation in adult court,[33] recent work by Sanborn[34] does provide some insight into the process.

Sanborn interviewed a total of 100 juvenile court officials (judges, prosecutors and defense attorneys, and probation officers) selected from an urban, a suburban, and a rural juvenile court within an unnamed jurisdiction. His interview data revealed that all of the major participants in the process had strong incentives for engaging in plea negotiation. For example, since the youth's involvement in the offense was often readily apparent, defense attorneys attempted to serve the interests of their juvenile clients by getting the number of charges reduced, or by advocating for a less severe disposition in the case, so as to "keep the youth's record as innocuous as possible."[35] Respondents also suggested that defense attorneys engaged in negotiation to conserve resources in crowded urban courts, or less charitably, because they "wanted to get rid of a case due to laziness or a desire to collect a quick fee."[36]

Sanborn's respondents regarded prosecutors as "record oriented," attuned primarily to racking up convictions, or in this case, adjudications. Thus, prosecutorial incentives to plea bargain were more administrative in nature: they stemmed from the desire to reduce a backlog of cases, or to obtain an adjudication for a lesser charge, when the case was weak (due, for example, to a missing witness), or to achieve the certainty of an adjudication on a lesser charge when it was uncertain what the juvenile court judge would decide in the case. Somewhat paradoxically, there was also a sense in which delinquency cases seemed to be viewed as "set piece" battles, in which the outcome (*i.e.*, adjudication) was known in

---

[31]Sanborn, "Philosophical, Legal and Systemic Aspects of Juvenile Court Plea Bargaining," 39 *Crime and Delinquency* 509 (1993). An excellent discussion of the increasingly strong presence of the prosecutor at the intake and adjudicatory phases of the criminal justice process can also be found in Rubin, *Juvenile Justice: Policy, Practice and Law* (2d ed.), 164–171 (New York: Random House, 1985).

[32]Sanborn, *id.*

[33]For a review of the existing literature, see Sanborn, *id.*

[34]*Id.*

[35]*Id.*

[36]*Id.*

advance, since probation officers routinely prepared disposition reports prior to the court hearing; consequently, plea bargaining in these instances was viewed as a way of saving time. Plea bargaining was also justified as a way of "spar[ing] witnesses the ordeal of...testif[ing] at trial" and as a method for compensating for a prosecutor's tendency to overcharge the youth.[37]

Finally, plea bargaining was viewed as beneficial to the court itself because it helped reduce case backlogs, especially by allowing the rapid disposition of cases where both the state and the defense agreed on the appropriate disposition. In addition, plea negotiations permitted the more timely (and guaranteed) delivery of treatment and services to youths, and, in the opinion of some, laid the foundation for rehabilitation by giving delinquent youths the opportunity to admit their responsibility for the offense. Finally, plea agreements were seen as a useful mechanism for allowing the development of compromise dispositions, satisfactory to both the prosecution and the defense, while avoiding the extreme outcomes (presumably acquittal or harsh punishments) occasionally produced by the adversarial process of trial.[38]

When asked about factors that served as obstacles to plea negotiation, slightly more that half of Sanborn's respondents (most of whom worked in the urban court) indicated that prosecutorial intrasingence sometimes stood in the way of reaching an agreement.[39] Other factors that were occasionally seen as complicating the negotiation process included: the interference of victims and parents, personality conflicts between judges or counsel, and the seriousness of the case.[40] On the whole, the vast majority of the respondents (92%) believed that plea negotiation, particularly charge bargaining, served a positive function within the juvenile court.[41] The case that follows considers the question of the appropriate role of the juvenile court judge in the plea negotiation process.

JURY TRIAL ISSUES IN JUVENILE COURT

A. Availability of the Right to a Jury Trial

JOSEPH MCKEIVER AND EDWARD TERRY,

APPELLANTS,

V.

STATE OF PENNSYLVANIA

[37]The prosecutorial incentives to plea bargain summarized here are discussed more fully *id.*

[38]*Id.*

[39]*Id.*

[40]*Id.*

[41]*Id.*

IN RE BARBARA BURBUS ET AL.,

ARGUED DEC. 9 AND 10, 1970.

DECIDED JUNE 21, 1971.

* * *

MR. JUSTICE BLACKMUN announced the judgments of the Court and an opinion in which THE CHIEF JUSTICE, MR. JUSTICE STEWART, and MR. JUSTICE WHITE join.

These cases present the narrow but precise issue whether the Due Process Clause of the Fourteenth Amendment assures the right to trial by jury in the adjudicative phase of a state juvenile court delinquency proceeding.

I

The issue arises understandably, for the Court in a series of cases already has emphasized due process factors protective of the juvenile.

* * *

From these six cases—*Haley, Gallegos, Kent, Gault, DeBacker, and Winship*—it is apparent that:

1. Some of the constitutional requirements attendant upon the state criminal trial have equal application to that part of the state juvenile proceeding that is adjudicative in nature. Among these are the rights to appropriate notice, to counsel, to confrontation and to cross-examination, and the privilege against self-incrimination. Included, also, is the standard of proof beyond a reasonable doubt.

2. The Court, however, has not yet said that all rights constitutionally assured to an adult accused of crime also are to be enforced or made available to the juvenile in his delinquency proceeding. Indeed, the Court specifically has refrained from going that far:

> "We do not mean by this to indicate that the hearing to be held must conform with all of the requirements of a criminal trial or even of the usual administrative hearing; but we do hold that the hearing must measure up to the essentials of due process and fair treatment." *Kent*, 383 U.S., at 562, 86 S.Ct., at 1057; *Gault*, 387 U.S., at 30, 87 S.Ct., at 1445.

3. The Court, although recognizing the high hopes and aspirations of Judge Julian Mack the leaders of the Jane Adams School[42] and the other supporters of the juvenile court concept, has also noted the disappointments of the system's performance and experience and the resulting widespread disaffection. *Kent*, 383 U.S., at 555–556, 86 S.Ct., at 1054–1055; *Gault*, 387 U.S., at 17–19, 87 S.Ct., at 1438–1439. There have been, at one and the same time, both an appreciation for the juvenile court judge who is

[42]See Mr. Justice Fortas' article, "Equal Rights—For Whom?" 42 N.Y.U.L.Rev. 401, 406 (1967).

devoted, sympathetic, and conscientious, and a disturbed concern about the judge who is untrained and less than fully imbued with an understanding approach to the complex problems of childhood and adolescence. There has been praise for the system and its purposes, and there has been alarm over its defects.

4. The Court has insisted that these successive decisions do not spell the doom of the juvenile court system or even deprive it of its "informality, flexibility, or speed." *Winship*, 397 U.S., at 366, 90 S.Ct., at 1074. On the other hand, a concern precisely to the opposite effect was expressed by two dissenters in *Winship*. *Id.*, at 375–376, 90 S.Ct., at 1078–1079.

II

With this substantial background already developed, we turn to the facts of the present cases:

No. 322. Joseph McKeiver, then age 16, in May 1968 was charged with robbery, larceny, and receiving stolen goods (felonies under Pennsylvania law, Pa. Stat.Ann., Tit. 18 §§ 4704, 4807, and 4817 (1963)) as acts of juvenile delinquency. At the time of the adjudication hearing he was represented by counsel.[43] His request for a jury trial was denied and his case was heard by Judge Theodore S. Gothics of the Court of Common Pleas, Family Division, Juvenile Branch, of Philadelphia County, Pennsylvania. McKeiver was adjudged a delinquent * * *.

Edward Terry, then age 15, in January 1969 was charged with assault and battery on a police officer and conspiracy (misdemeanors under Pennsylvania law, Pa.Stat.Ann, Tit. 18 §§ 4708 and 4302 (1963)) as acts of juvenile delinquency. His counsel's request for a jury trial was denied and his case was heard by Judge Joseph C. Bruno of the same Juvenile Branch of the Court of Common Pleas of Philadelphia County. Terry was adjudged a delinquent on the charges. * * *.

The Supreme Court of Pennsylvania granted leave to appeal in both cases and consolidated them. The single question considered, as phrased by the court, was "whether there is a constitutional right to a jury trial in juvenile court."

IV

The right to an impartial jury "[i]n all criminal prosecutions" under federal law is guaranteed by the Sixth Amendment. Through the Fourteenth Amendment that requirement has now been imposed upon the States "in all criminal cases which—were they to be tried in a federal court—would come within the Sixth Amendment's guarantee." This is because the Court has said it believes "that trial by jury in criminal cases is fundamental to the American scheme of justice." Duncan v. Louisiana, 391 U.S. 145, 149, 88 S.Ct.

[43]At McKeiver's hearing his counsel advised the court that he had never seen McKeiver before and "was just in the middle of interviewing" him. The court allowed him five minutes for the interview. Counsel's office, Community Legal Services, however, had been appointed to represent McKeiver five months earlier. App.2.

1444, 1447, 20 L.Ed.2d 491 (1968); Bloom v. Illinois, 391 U.S. 194, 210–211, 88 S.Ct. 1477, 1486–1487, 20 L.Ed.2d 522 (1968).

This, of course, does not automatically provide the answer to the present jury trial issue, if for no other reason than that the juvenile court proceeding has not yet been held to be a "criminal prosecution," within the meaning and reach of the Sixth Amendment, and also has not yet been regarded as devoid of criminal aspects merely because it usually has been given the civil label. *Kent*, 383 U.S. at 554, 86 S.Ct., at 1054; *Gault*, 387 U.S., at 17, 49–50, 87 S.Ct., at 1438, 1455–1456; *Winship*, 397 U.S., at 365–366, 90 S.Ct., at 1073–1074.

* * *

Thus, accepting "the proposition that the Due Process Clause has a role to play," *Gault*, 387 U.S., at 13, 87 S.Ct., at 1436, our task here with respect to trial by jury, as it was in *Gault* with respect to other claimed rights, "is to ascertain the precise impact of the due process requirement." *Id.*, at 13–14, 87 S.Ct., at 1436.

V

The * * * juveniles' basic argument is that they were tried in proceedings "substantially similar to a criminal trial." They say that a delinquency proceeding in their State is initiated by a petition charging a penal code violation in the conclusory language of an indictment; that a juvenile detained prior to trial is held in a building substantially similar to an adult prison; that in Philadelphia juveniles over 16 are, in fact, held in the cells of a prison; that counsel and the prosecution engage in plea bargaining; that motions to suppress are routinely heard and decided; that the usual rules of evidence are applied; that the customary common-law defenses are available; that the press is generally admitted in the Philadelphia juvenile courtrooms; that members of the public enter the room; that arrest and prior record may be reported by the press (from police sources, however, rather than from the juvenile court records); that, once adjudged delinquent, a juvenile may be confined until his majority in what amounts to a prison (see In re Bethea, 215 Pa.Super. 75, 76, 257 A.2d 368, 369 (1969), describing the state correctional institution at Camp Hill has a "maximum security prison for adjudged delinquents and youthful criminal offenders"); and that the stigma attached upon delinquency adjudication approximates that resulting from conviction in an adult criminal proceeding.

VI

All the litigants here agree that the applicable due process standard in juvenile proceedings, as developed by *Gault and Winship*, is fundamental fairness. As that standard was applied in those two cases, we have an emphasis on factfinding procedures. The requirements of notice, counsel, confrontation, cross-examination, and standard of proof naturally flowed from this emphasis. But one cannot say that in our legal system the jury is a necessary component of accurate factfinding. There is much to be said for it, to be sure, but we have been content to pursue other ways for determining facts. Juries are not required, and have not been, for example, in equity cases, in workmen's compensation, in probate, or in deportation cases. Neither have they been generally used in military trials. In *Duncan* the Court stated, "We would not assert, however, that every criminal trial—or any particular trial—held before a judge alone is unfair or that a defendant may never be as fairly treated by a judge as he would be by a jury." 391 U.S., at 158, 88 S.Ct., at 1452. In *DeStefano*, for this reason and others, the Court refrained from retrospective application of *Duncan,* an action it surely would have not taken had it felt that the integrity of the result was seriously at issue. And in Williams v. Florida, 399 U.S. 78, 90 S.Ct. 1893, 26 L.Ed.2d 446 (1970), the Court saw no particular magic in a 12-man jury for a criminal case, thus revealing that even jury concepts themselves are not inflexible.

Despite all these disappointments, all these failures, and all these shortcomings, we conclude that trial by jury in the juvenile court's adjudicative stage is not a constitutional requirement. We so conclude for a number of reasons:

1. The Court has refrained, in the cases heretofore decided, from taking the easy way with a flat holding that all rights constitutionally assured for the adult accused are to be imposed upon the state juvenile proceeding. What was done in *Gault* and in *Winship* is aptly described in Commonwealth v. Johnson, 211 Pa.Super. 62, 74, 234 A.2d 9, 15 (1967):

> "It is clear to us that the Supreme Court has properly attempted to strike a judicious balance by injecting procedural orderliness into the juvenile court system. It is seeking to reverse the trend [pointed out in *Kent*, 383 U.S., at 556, 86 S.Ct. 1045] whereby 'the child receives the worst of both worlds: * * *.'"

2. There is a possibility, at least, that the jury trial, if required as a matter of constitutional precept, will remake the juvenile proceeding into a fully adversary process and will put an effective end to what has been the idealistic prospect of an intimate, informal protective proceeding.

3. The President's Commission on Law Enforcement and Administration of Justice, Task Force Report: Juvenile Delinquency and Youth Crime (1967), although concededly pre-*Gault,* is notable for its not making any recommendation that the jury trial be imposed upon the juvenile court system. This is so despite its vivid description of the system's deficiencies and disappointments. Had the Commission deemed this vital to the integrity of the juvenile process, or to the handling of juveniles, surely a recommendation or suggestion to this effect would have appeared. The intimations, instead, are quite the other way. Task Force Report 38. Further, it expressly recommends against abandonment of the system and against the return of the juvenile to the criminal courts.[44]

---

[44]"Nevertheless, study of the juvenile courts does not necessarily lead to the conclusion that the time has come to jettison the experiment and remand the disposition of children charged with crime to the criminal courts of the country. As trying as are the problems of the juvenile courts, the problems of the criminal courts, particularly those (continued...)

4. The Court specifically has recognized by dictum that a jury is not a necessary part even of every criminal process that is fair and equitable. Duncan v. Louisiana, 391 U.S., at 149–150, n. 14, and 158, 88 S.Ct., at 1447, and 1452.

5. The imposition of the jury trial on the juvenile court system would not strengthen greatly if at all the factfinding function, and would, contrarily, provide an attrition of the juvenile court's assumed ability to function in a unique manner. It would not remedy the defects of the system. Meager as has been the hoped-for advance in the juvenile field, the alternative would be regressive, would lose what has been gained, and would tend once again to place the juvenile squarely in the routine of the criminal process.

6. The juvenile concept held high promise. We are reluctant to say that, despite disappointments of grave dimensions, it still does not hold promise, and we are particularly reluctant to say, as do the Pennsylvania appellants here, that the system cannot accomplish its rehabilitative goals. So much depends on the availability of resources, on the interest and commitment of the public, on willingness to learn, and on understanding as to cause and effect and cure. In this field, as in so many others, one perhaps learns best by doing. We are reluctant to disallow the States to experiment further and to seek in new and different ways the elusive answers to the problems of the young, and we feel that we would be impeding that experimentation by imposing the jury trial. The States, indeed, must go forward. If, in its wisdom, any State feels the jury trial is desirable in all cases, or in certain kinds, there appears to be no impediment to its installing a system embracing that feature. That, however, is the State's privilege and not its obligation.

7. Of course there have been abuses. The Task Force Report has noted them. We refrain from saying at this point that those abuses are of constitutional dimension. They relate to the lack of resources and of dedication rather than to inherent unfairness.

8. There is, of course, nothing to prevent a juvenile court judge, in a particular case where he feels the need, or when the need is demonstrated, from using an advisory jury.

---

[44](...continued)
of the lower courts, which would fall heir to much of the juvenile court jurisdiction, are even graver; and the ideal of separate treatment of children is still worth pursuing. What is required is rather a revised philosophy of the juvenile court based on the recognition that in the past our reach exceeded our grasp. The spirit that animated the juvenile court movement was fed in part by a humanitarian compassion for offenders who were children. That willingness to understand and treat people who threaten public safety and security should be nurtured, not turned aside as hopeless sentimentality, both because it is civilized and because social protection itself demands constant search for alternatives to the crude and limited expedient of condemnation and punishment. But neither should it be allowed to outrun reality. The juvenile court is a court of law, charged like other agencies of criminal justice with protecting the community against threatening conduct. Rehabilitating offenders through individualized handing is one way of providing protection, and appropriately the primary way in dealing with children. But the guiding consideration for a court of law that deals with threatening conduct is nonetheless protection of the community. The juvenile court, like other courts, is therefore obliged to employ all the means at hand, not excluding incapacitation, for achieving that protection. What should distinguish the juvenile from the criminal courts is greater emphasis on rehabilitation, not exclusive preoccupation with it." Task Force Report 9.

9. "The fact that a practice is followed by a large number of states is not conclusive in a decision as to whether that practice accords with due process, but it is plainly worth considering in determining whether the practice 'offends some principle of justice so rooted in the traditions and conscience of our people as to be ranked as fundamental.' Snyder v. Massachusetts, 291 U.S. 97, 105, 54 S.Ct. 330, 332, 78 L.Ed. 674 (1934)." Leland v. Oregon, 343 U.S. 790, 798, 72 S.Ct. 1002, 1007, 96 L.Ed. 1302 (1952). It therefore is of more than passing interest that at least 28 States and the District of Columbia by statute deny the juvenile a right to a jury trial in cases such as these. The same result is achieved in other States by judicial decision. In 10 States statutes provide for a jury trial under certain circumstances.

10. Since *Gault* and since *Duncan* the great majority of States, in addition to Pennsylvania and North Carolina, that have faced the issue have concluded that the considerations that led to the result in those two cases do not compel trial by jury in the juvenile court. * * *

11. Stopping short of proposing the jury trial for juvenile proceedings are the Uniform Juvenile Court Act, § 24(a), approved in July 1968 by the National Conference of Commissioners on Uniform State Laws; the Standard Juvenile Court Act, Art. V, § 19, proposed by the National Council on Crime and Delinquency (see W. Sheridan, Standards for Juvenile and Family Courts 73 Dept. of H. E. W., Children's Bureau Pub. No. 437-1966); and the Legislative Guide for Drafting Family and Juvenile Court Acts § 29(a) (Dept. of H. E. W., Children's Bureau Pub. No. 472-1969).

12. If the jury trial were to be injected into the juvenile court system as a matter of right, it would bring with it into that system the traditional delay, the formality, and the clamor of the adversary system and, possibly, the public trial. It is of interest that these very factors were stressed by the District Committee of the Senate when, through Senator Tydings, it recommended, and Congress then approved, as a provision in the District of Columbia Crime Bill, the abolition of the jury trial in the juvenile court. S.Rep. No. 91-620, pp. 13-14 (1969).

13. Finally, the arguments advanced by the juveniles here are, of course, the identical arguments that underlie the demand for the jury trial for criminal proceedings. The arguments necessarily equate the juvenile proceeding—or at least the adjudicative phase of it—with the criminal trial. Whether they should be so equated is our issue. Concern about the inapplicability of exclusionary and other rules of evidence, about the juvenile court judge's possible awareness of the juvenile's prior record and of the contents of the social file; about repeated appearances of the same familiar witnesses in the persons of juvenile and probation officers and social workers—all to the effect that this will create the likelihood of pre-judgment—chooses to ignore it seems to us, every aspect of fairness, of concern, of sympathy, and of paternal attention that the juvenile court system contemplates.

If the formalities of the criminal adjudicative process are to be superimposed upon the juvenile court system, there is little need for its separate existence. Perhaps that ultimate disillusionment will come one day, but for the moment we are disinclined to give impetus to it.

Affirmed.

McKEIVER V. PENNSYLVANIA

1. The *McKeiver* case slowed the historical momentum towards the "constitutionalization" of the juvenile court. The cases of *Kent*, *Gault*, and *Winship* were rendering the informal, socialized juvenile court extinct, but this process came to a halt with McKeiver. Is it possible that the majority viewed the *McKeiver* case as a "final threat" to the historical endurance of the benevolent juvenile court? After all, the very existence of procedural due process insinuates that the state (and its training schools) may not be very benevolent towards those offenders under its custody.

2. The majority stated that a jury trial is not necessary for accurate fact-finding in the adjudication process. Why then, do adult defendants not have a right to bench trials?

3. The majority was clearly concerned that providing a right to jury trials in juvenile court could turn adjudications into fully adversarial proceedings? Did the *Gault* case already accomplish this adversarial orientation. Explain.

4. According to the majority, jury trials would not remedy the problem of questionable rehabilitative practices in juvenile court. Critique this statement.

B. Time to Overrule *McKeiver*?

In another article,[45] Sanborn has argued that the underlying philosophy and the practices of the contemporary of the juvenile court have changed so much since *McKeiver* was decided that it should now be overruled. Sanborn raises several arguments in support of this position. To begin with, the alteration of juvenile court aims to include retribution, coupled with the increasingly punitive orientation of juvenile court dispositions necessitates the extension of the right to jury trials to juvenile offenders. To Sanborn, the renewed concern for retribution is amply demonstrated by the fact that at the time the article was written, forty three jurisdictions have modified the purpose clauses of their juvenile court legislation to allow consideration of the welfare of the community alongside the welfare of the juvenile when deciding cases, while two others (Minnesota and Washington) appear to give community interests *preference* over the interests of youth.[46]

According to Sanborn, such trends work to erase the unique character of the juvenile court as a helping institution that the court recognized in *McKeiver*, and have effectively transformed it into a rough

---

[45]Sanborn, "The Right to a Public Jury Trial: A Need for Today's Juvenile Court," 76 *Judicature* 230 (February-March, 1993).

[46]*Id.* at 234.

analog of the criminal court. Thus, the extension of a Sixth Amendment right to a jury trial to juveniles is well justified.

Also significant, according to Sanborn, is the subsequent decision in *Breed v. Jones*, where the Court explicitly acknowledged that the stigma and deprivation of liberty that occur following an adjudication of delinquency are virtually no different than the stigmatizing effect of a criminal conviction or the loss of liberty experienced by adult offenders who are imprisoned.[47] Equating juvenile court adjudications and criminal trials in these terms, the Court was compelled, in *Breed*, to extend the Fifth Amendment's ban on double jeopardy to young people as well as adults. More fundamentally, however, *Breed's* placement of delinquency adjudications and criminal trials on equal footing once more makes it harder to view the juvenile court as a unique institution, and harder to remain true to *McKeiver's* holding that jury trials are inappropriate for juveniles.

Next, Sanborn notes that the Supreme Court's reluctance to extend jury trial rights to juveniles stemmed, in part, from a desire to facilitate the rehabilitative efforts of the court by preserving some remnant of the procedural informality that had existed prior to the *Gault* decision, as well as the atmosphere of confidentiality that traditionally accompanied adjudicatory hearings.[48] Sanborn takes issue with this position, suggesting that greater procedural formality—not less—is more likely to effect rehabilitation, since public jury trials may act to enhance the juvenile's perception that he or she was being treated fairly and by sending a clear and unambiguous signal that society regards juvenile crime as a serious matter. Consequently, juveniles who are given a jury trial may more readily accept responsibility for their actions.

Sanborn is similarly skeptical of the notion that confidential proceedings do much to promote rehabilitation. First, he notes that juvenile court's promise of confidentiality has long been recognized (even by the Court in *Gault*) as more of an illusion than reality, and that access to someone's juvenile record is readily obtainable. Second, he points out that many states now allow increased media (and, in some cases, public) access to adjudicatory hearings, which "nullifies the position that the public does not belong in juvenile court...[and] in turn undermines the stand that jury trials are inappropriate there."[49] Third, he notes that the Supreme Court's decision in the 1979 case, *Smith v. Daily Mail Publishing Company*, which upheld the right of a newspaper to publish the name of an alleged juvenile delinquent, as long as the juveniles name was obtained legally, seems to undercut *McKeiver's* pro-confidentiality position.

As a final argument for extending a Sixth Amendment right to jury trials to juveniles, Sanborn suggests that the use of jurors to decide delinquency cases would reduce the possibility of bias at the adjudicatory phase. Prior research suggests that juvenile court judges' may be unduly influenced in their

---

[47]Sanborn, *supra*.

[48]*Id.* at 236.

[49]Sanborn, *supra*.

determinations of delinquency by factors such as prior contact with the offender in court, the youth's detention status, the presence of strong prosecutorial or public pressure favoring adjudication, or the casual application evidentiary standards to the facts of the case. Sanborn suggests that the presence of members of the public, sitting as jurors would act to reduce the possible influence of these extra-legal factors on case outcomes.

It is important to mention here that currently, many states do permit jury trials in juvenile court by authority of state statute. Defendants in juvenile courts, however, are not entitled to jury trials on national constitutional grounds.

THE BAN AGAINST DOUBLE JEOPARDY

A. Does the Double Jeopardy Ban Apply to Juveniles?

Breed v. Jones discusses various aspects of the ban on double jeopardy as it applies to juvenile offenders. It is particularly helpful to consider the indirect impact that *Breed* has on the *McKeiver* decision.

ALLEN F. BREED, ETC., PETITIONER,

V.

GARY STEVEN JONES.

* * *

MR. CHIEF JUSTICE BURGER delivered the opinion of the Court.

We granted certiorari to decide whether the prosecution of respondent as an adult, after Juvenile Court proceedings which resulted in a finding that respondent had violated a criminal statute and a subsequent finding that he was unfit for treatment as a juvenile, violated the Fifth and Fourteenth Amendments to the United States Constitution.

On February 9, 1971, a petition was filed in the Superior Court of California, County of Los Angeles, Juvenile Court, alleging that respondent, then 17 years of age, was a person described by Cal.Welf. & Inst'ns Code § 602 (1966), in that, on or about February 8, while armed with a deadly weapon, he had committed acts which, if committed by an adult, would constitute the crime of robbery in violation of Cal.Penal Code § 211 (1970). The following day, a detention hearing was held, at the conclusion of which respondent was ordered detained pending a hearing on the petition.

At a hearing conducted on March 15, the Juvenile Court indicated its intention to find respondent "not...amenable to the care, treatment and training program available through the facilities of the juvenile court" under Cal.Welf. & Inst'ns Code § 707 (Supp.1967). Respondent's counsel orally moved "to continue the matter on the ground of surprise," contending that respondent "was not informed that it was going to be a fitness hearing." The court continued the matter for one week, at which time, having considered the report of the probation officer assigned to the case and having heard her testimony, it declared respondent "unfit for treatment as a juvenile," and ordered that he be prosecuted as an adult.

After a preliminary hearing respondent was ordered held for trial in Superior Court, where an information was subsequently filed accusing him of having committed robbery, in violation of Cal.Penal Code § 211 (1970), while armed with a deadly weapon, on or about February 8, 1971. Respondent entered a plea of not guilty, and he also pleaded that he had "already been placed once in jeopardy and convicted of the offense charged, by the judgment of the Superior Court of the County of Los Angeles, Juvenile Court, rendered...on the 1st day of March, 1971." The court found respondent guilty of robbery in the first degree under Cal.Penal Code § 211a (1970) and ordered that he be committed to the California Youth Authority.

* * *

We granted certiorari because of a conflict between Courts of Appeals and the highest courts of a number of States on the issue presented in this case and similar issues and because of the importance of final resolution of the issue to the administration of the juvenile-court system.

* * *

II

Jeopardy denotes risk. In the constitutional sense, jeopardy describes the risk that is traditionally associated with a criminal prosecution. See Price v. Georgia, 398 U.S. 323, 326, 329, 90 S.Ct. 1757, 1759, 26 L.Ed.2d 300 (1970); Serfass v. United States, 420 U.S. 377, 387–389, 95 S.Ct. 1055, 1062–1063, 43 L.Ed.2d 265 (1975). Although the constitutional language, "jeopardy of life or limb," suggests proceedings in which only the most serious penalties can be imposed, the Clause has long been construed to mean something far broader than its literal language. See Ex parte Lange, 18 Wall. 163, 170–173, 21 L.Ed. 872 (1874).[50] At the same time, however, we have held that the risk to which the Clause refers is not present in proceedings that are not "essentially criminal." Helvering v. Mitchell, 303 U.S. 391, 398, 58 S.Ct. 630, 632, 82 L.Ed. 917 (1938). See United States ex rel. Marcus v. Hess, 317 U.S. 537, 63 S.Ct. 379, 87 L.Ed. 443 (1943); One Lot Emerald Cut Stones v. United States, 409 U.S. 232, 93 S.Ct. 489, 34 L.Ed.2d 438 (1972). See also J. Sigler, Double Jeopardy 60–62 (1969).

[50]Distinctions which in other contexts have proved determinative of the constitutional rights of those charged with offenses against public order have not similarly confined the protection of the Double Jeopardy Clause. Compare Robinson v. Neil, 409 U.S. 505, 93 S.Ct. 876, 35 L.Ed.2d 29 (1973), with Baldwin v. New York, 399 U.S. 66, 90 S.Ct. 1886, 26 L.Ed.2d 437 (1970), and Argersinger v. Hamlin, 407 U.S. 25, 92 S.Ct. 2006, 32 L.Ed.2d 530 (1972). For the details of Robinson's trial for violating a city ordinance, See Robinson v. Henderson, 268 F.Supp. 349 (E.D.Tenn.1967), aff'd, 391 F.2d 933 (CA6 1968).

Although the juvenile-court system had its genesis in the desire to provide a distinctive procedure and setting to deal with the problems of youth, including those manifested by antisocial conduct, our decisions in recent years have recognized that there is a gap between the originally benign conception of the system and its realities. With the exception of McKeiver v. Pennsylvania, 403 U.S. 528, 91 S.Ct. 1976, 29 L.Ed.2d 647 (1971), the Court's response to that perception has been to make applicable in juvenile proceedings constitutional guarantees associated with traditional criminal prosecutions. In re Gault, 387 U.S. 1, 87 S.Ct. 1428, 18 L.Ed.2d 527 (1967); In re Winship, 397 U.S. 358, 90 S.Ct. 1068, 25 L.Ed.2d 368 (1970). In so doing the Court has evinced awareness of the threat which such a process represents to the efforts of the juvenile-court system, functioning in a unique manner, to ameliorate the harshness of criminal justice when applied to youthful offenders. That the system has fallen short of the high expectations of its sponsors in no way detracts from the broad social benefits sought or from those benefits that can survive constitutional scrutiny.

We believe it is simply too late in the day to conclude, as did the District Court in this case, that a juvenile is not put in jeopardy at a proceeding whose object is to determine whether he has committed acts that violate a criminal law and whose potential consequences include both the stigma inherent in such a determination and the deprivation of liberty for many years.[51] For it is clear under our cases that determining the relevance of constitutional policies, like determining the applicability of constitutional rights, in juvenile proceedings, requires that courts eschew "the 'civil' label-of-convenience which has been attached to juvenile proceedings," In re Gault, *supra*, 387 U.S. at 50, 87 S.Ct. at 1455, and that "the juvenile process...be candidly appraised." 387 U.S. at 21, 87 S.Ct. at 1440. See In re Winship, *supra*, 397 U.S. at 365–366, 90 S.Ct. at 1073.

As we have observed, the risk to which the term jeopardy refers is that traditionally associated with "actions intended to authorize criminal punishment to vindicate public justice." United States ex rel. Marcus v. Hess, *Supra*, 317 U.S. at 548–549, 63 S.Ct. at 388. Because of its purpose and potential consequences, and the nature and resources of the State, such a proceeding imposes heavy pressures and burdens—psychological, physical, and financial—on a person charged. The purpose of the Double Jeopardy Clause is to require that he be subject to the experience only once "for the same offense." See Green v. United States, 355 U.S. 184, 187, 78 S.Ct. 221, 223, 2 L.Ed.2d 199 (1957); Price v. Georgia, 398 U.S., at 331, 90 S.Ct. at 1762; United States v. Jorn, 400 U.S. 470, 479, 91 S.Ct. 547, 554, 27 L.Ed.2d 543 (1971) (opinion of Harlan, J.).

In In re Gault, *supra*, 387 U.S. at 36, 87 S.Ct. at 1448, this Court concluded that, for purposes of the right to counsel, a "proceeding where the issue is whether the child will be found to be 'delinquent' and subjected to the loss of his liberty for years is comparable in seriousness to a felony prosecution." See

[51]At the time of respondent's dispositional hearing, permissible dispositions included commitment to the California Youth Authority until he reached the age of 21 years. See Cal.Welf. & Inst'ns Code §§ 607, 731 (1966). Petitioner has conceded that the "adjudicatory hearing is, in every sense, a court trial." Tr. of Oral Arg. 4.

In re Winship, *supra*, 397 U.S. at 366, 90 S.Ct. at 1073. The Court stated that the term "delinquent" had "come to involve only slightly less stigma than the term 'criminal' applied to adults," In re Gault, *supra*, 387 U.S. at 24, 87 S.Ct. at 1441; see In re Winship, *supra*, 397 U.S. at 367, 90 S.Ct. at 1074, and that, for purposes of the privilege against self-incrimination, "commitment is a deprivation of liberty. It is incarceration against one's will, whether it is called 'criminal' or 'civil,'" In re Gault, *supra*, 387 U.S. at 50, 87 S.Ct. at 1455. See 387 U.S., at 27, 87 S.Ct. at 1443; In re Winship, *supra*, 397 U.S. at 367,[52] 90 S.Ct. at 1074.

Thus, in terms of potential consequences, there is little to distinguish an adjudicatory hearing such as was held in this case from a traditional criminal prosecution. For that reason, it engenders elements of "anxiety and insecurity" in a juvenile, and imposes a "heavy personal strain." * * * And we can expect that, since our decisions implementing fundamental fairness in the juvenile-court system, hearings have been prolonged, and some of the burdens incident to a juvenile's defense increased, as the system has assimilated the process thereby imposed. * * *

We deal here, not with "the formalities of the criminal adjudicative process," McKeiver v. Pennsylvania, 403 U.S., at 551, 91 S.Ct. at 1989 (opinion of Blackmun, J.), but with an analysis of an aspect of the juvenile-court system in terms of the kind of risk to which jeopardy refers. Under our decisions we can find no persuasive distinction in that regard between the proceeding conducted in this case pursuant to Cal.Welf. & Inst'ns Code § 701 (1966) and a criminal prosecution, each of which is designed "to vindicate [the] very vital interest in enforcement of criminal laws." United States v. Jorn, *supra*, 400 U.S. at 479, 91 S.Ct. at 554. We therefore conclude that respondent was put in jeopardy at the adjudicatory hearing. Jeopardy attached when respondent was "put to trial before the trier of the facts," 400 U.S., at 479, 91 S.Ct., at 554, that is, when the Juvenile Court, as the trier of the facts, began to hear evidence. See Serfass v. United States, 420 U.S. at 388, 95 S.Ct., at 1062.[53]

III

Petitioner argues that, even assuming jeopardy attached at respondent's adjudicatory hearing, the procedure by which he was transferred from Juvenile Court and tried on a felony information in Superior Court did not violate the Double Jeopardy Clause. The argument is supported by two distinct, but in this case overlapping, lines of analysis. First, petitioner reasons that the procedure violated none of the policies

---

[52]Nor does the fact "that the purpose of the commitment is rehabilitative and not punitive...change its nature.... Regardless of the purposes for which the incarceration is imposed, the fact remains that it is incarceration. The rehabilitative goals of the system are admirable, but they do not change the drastic nature of the action taken. Incarceration of adults is also intended to produce rehabilitation." Fain v. Duff, 488 F.2d, at 225. See *President's Commission on Law Enforcement and Administration of Justice, Task Force Report: Juvenile Delinquency and Youth Crime* 8-9 (1967).

[53]The same conclusion was reached by the California Court of Appeal in denying respondent's petition for a writ of habeas corpus. In re Gary J., 17 Cal.App.3d 704, 710, 95 Cal.Rptr. 185, 189 (1971).

of the Double Jeopardy Clause or that, alternatively, it should be upheld by analogy to those cases which permit retrial of an accused who has obtained reversal of a conviction on appeal. Second, pointing to this Court's concern for "the juvenile court's assumed ability to function in a unique manner," McKeiver v. Pennsylvania, *supra*, 403 U.S., at 547, 91 S.Ct., at 1987, petitioner urges that, should we conclude traditional principles "would otherwise bar a transfer to adult court after a delinquency adjudication," we should avoid that result here because it "would diminish the flexibility and informality of juvenile court proceedings without conferring any additional due process benefits upon juveniles charged with delinquent acts."

A

We cannot agree with petitioner that the trial of respondent in Superior Court on an information charging the same offense as that for which he had been tried in Juvenile Court violated none of the policies of the Double Jeopardy Clause. For, even accepting petitioner's premise that respondent "never faced the risk of more than one punishment," we have pointed out that "the Double Jeopardy Clause...is written in terms of potential or risk of *trial* and conviction, not punishment." Price v. Georgia, 398 U.S. at 329, 90 S.Ct. at 1761. (Emphasis added.) And we have recently noted:

> "The policy of avoiding multiple trials has been regarded as so important that exceptions to the principle have been only grudgingly allowed. Initially, a new trial was thought to be unavailable after appeal, whether requested by the prosecution or the defendant.... It was not until 1896 that it was made clear that a defendant could seek a new trial after conviction, even though the Government enjoyed no similar right.... Following the same policy, the Court has granted the Government the right to retry a defendant after a mistrial only where 'there is a manifest necessity for the act, or the ends of public justice would otherwise be defeated.' United States v. Perez, 9 Wheat 579, 580, 6 L.Ed. 165 (1824)." United States v. Wilson, 420 U.S. 332, 343, 344, 95 S.Ct. 1013, 1022, 43 L.Ed.2d 232 (1975). (Footnote omitted.)

Respondent was subjected to the burden of two trials for the same offense; he was twice put to the task of marshaling his resources against those of the State, twice subjected to the "heavy personal strain" which such an experience represents. United States v. Jorn, 400 U.S., at 479, 91 S.CT., at 554. We turn, therefore, to inquire whether either traditional principles or "the juvenile court's assumed ability to function in a unique manner," McKeiver v. Pennsylvania, *supra*, 403 U.S. at 547, 91 S.Ct. at 1987, supports an exception to the "constitutional policy of finality" to which respondent would otherwise be entitled. United States v. Jorn, supra, at 479, 91 S.Ct., at 554.

* * *

C

The possibility of transfer from juvenile court to a court of general criminal jurisdiction is a matter of great significance to the juvenile. See Kent v. United States, 383 U.S. 541, 86 S.Ct. 1045, 16 L.Ed.2d 84 (1966). At the same time, there appears to be widely shared agreement that not all juveniles can benefit from the special features and programs of the juvenile-court system and that a procedure for transfer to an adult court should be available. See, *e.g.*, National Advisory Commission on Criminal Justice Standards and Goals, Courts, Commentary to Standard 14.3, pp. 300–301 (1973). This general agreement is reflected in the fact that an overwhelming majority of jurisdictions permits transfer in certain circumstances.[54] As might be expected, the statutory provisions differ in numerous details. Whatever their differences, however, such transfer provisions represent an attempt to impart to the juvenile-court system the flexibility needed to deal with youthful offenders who cannot benefit from the specialized guidance and treatment contemplated by the system.

* * *

IV

We hold that the prosecution of respondent in Superior Court, after an adjudicatory proceeding in Juvenile Court, violated the Double Jeopardy Clause of the Fifth Amendment, as applied to the States through the Fourteenth Amendment. The mandate of the Court of Appeals, which was stayed by that court pending our decision, directs the District Court "to issue a writ of habeas corpus directing the state court, within 60 days, to vacate the adult conviction of Jones and either set him free or remand him to the juvenile court for disposition." Since respondent is no longer subject to the jurisdiction of the California Juvenile Court, we vacate the judgment and remand the case to the Court of Appeals for such further proceedings consistent with this opinion as may be appropriate in the circumstances.

So ordered.

Judgment vacated and case remanded.

BREED V. JONES

1. The state of California argued that in this case the youth's double jeopardy protections were not violated. They claimed that the youth was "only punished once." Explain and critique this argument.
2. In terms of due process, what do transfer hearings have in common with regular juvenile court adjudications? How are they procedurally different? Be sure to address the standards of proof in both situations.
3. Jeopardy denotes "risk." Elaborate on the U.S. Supreme Court's contention that despite the fact that, juvenile adjudication is supposed to be predicated on *parens patriæ* or rehabilitation, it also places a juvenile defendant "at risk" as "risk" appears in the fifth amendment.

---

[54]See generally Task Force Report, *supra*, n. 12, at 24–25. See also Rudstein, *Double Jeopardy in Juvenile Proceedings*, 14 Wm. & Mary L.Rev. 266, 297–300 (1972); Carr, *The Effect of the Double Jeopardy Clause on Juvenile Proceedings*, 6 U.Tol.L.Rev. 1, 21–22 (1974).

CONCLUSION

Our attempt in this chapter was to outline some of the basic legal issues surrounding the adjudicatory phase of the juvenile justice process. It is important to remember that the issues discussed in this chapter are meant to be illustrative rather than exhaustive of those which can arise when judges are called upon to decide whether or not someone is delinquent.

The next chapter deals with the dispositional hearing, a separate proceeding in which juvenile court judges decide what to do with those who have been found delinquent. We also address issues relating to various dispositional options that are commonly imposed by juvenile courts.

CHAPTER 5

THE DISPOSITION AND TREATMENT OF ADJUDICATED OFFENDERS

THE DISPOSITION AND TREATMENT OF ADJUDICATED OFFENDERS

INTRODUCTION

The previous chapter described the adjudicatory phase of the juvenile justice process, where the primary question before the court was whether or not a particular youth was delinquent. In this chapter, the focus is on the dispositional stage, where the juvenile court judge, working in concert with a number of other actors in the system, must decide what to do with a youth who has been adjudicated delinquent. The decision is an exceedingly complex one, for at least five reasons. First, because it involves making a complicated judgment about the kind of person the offender is. For example, is the youth an otherwise responsible person whose delinquent act is an isolated incident, an aberation really, that resulted from a single, foolish choice? Or, is the delinquent behavior symptomatic of a more serious problem affecting the offender or his or her family? Or, is the person a hard core, serious offender who is committed to the criminal lifestyle, and shows little inclination to change? Does this person represent a threat to the community? The judge might also take into account the offender's age and his/her record of prior contacts with the court, and the outcomes of any previous adjudications. Of course, these are not the only possibilities, but they illustrate the kinds questions judges might ask themselves about the offender in the process of deciding his or her fate.

Second, a dispositional decision reflects a complex judgment about the nature of the offense involved. Was it serious or minor? A first offense, or simply the most current of a long string of prior offenses that have gradually escalated in seriousness? How much harm was caused by the offense? Was the harm done to a particular person or their property, or was this an offense involving some type of harm to the community at large?

Third, a judge may also consider the general purposes of punishment when crafting a disposition as indicated in the case that follows.

Fourth, a dispositional decision can be affected by a variety of external or systemic factors, that are independent of the specific characteristics of the case. For example, even though a judge might consider a youth an appropriate candidate for placement in a secure facility, overcrowding at the institution might preclude the choice of this disposition, forcing the judge to select some alternative placement.

Fifth, and perhaps most importantly, the dispositional decision is complex because it frequently requires the judge to reconcile conflicting views about the nature of the offender, the nature of the offense and what constitues the appropriate disposition in the case. For example, in some jurisdictions, both juvenile probation officers and defense attorneys are permitted to submit disposition recommendations for a particular case to the judge. As research has shown, the reports containing these recommmendations quite frequently paint contrasting pictures of the offender and his or her offense, perhaps with the probation department arguing that the youth is a hard core, serious delinquent who deserves institutionalization, and the defense attorney adopting a "softer" view of the delinquent and advocating for a less severe placement, perhaps in some community treatment program.[1] Frequently, the juvenile court judges' dispositional decision reflects either a choice between, or something of an accommodation of, these contrasting views and recommendations.

In recognition of the importance of this last point, the analysis of the dispositional stages of the juvenile justice process presented in this chapter will begin with a brief description of how probation officers and defense attorneys can influence dispositional decisions.

LAYING THE FOUNDATION FOR THE DISPOSITIONAL DECISION: DISPOSITION RECOMMENDATIONS OF PROBATION OFFICERS AND DEFENSE ATTORNEYS

A. The Probation Officer's Social Investigation

In the period between the adjuducatory hearing and the dispositional hearing, a probation officer attached to the juvenile court typically conducts a "social investigation" of the newly adjudicated delinquent. This investigation consists primarily of one or more interviews with the offender and his or her parents, which are designed to explore the circumstances surrounding the offense and identify any type of underlying physical, psychological, or social pathology that may have contributed to it. In many instances, probation officers may gather additional information about the youth by conducting supplemental interviews with teachers and school officials, employers, psychologists, caseworkers from other social service agencies who may also be working with the family, police officers who may be familiar with the offender from previous informal contacts, or others.[2] The results of the social investigation are then used as the basis for a written report to the juvenile court judge, which contains a set of recommendations for the disposition

---

[1]For a description of the impact of these "defense based" disposition recommendations on the outcomes of dispositional hearings, see Macallair, "Disposition Case Advocacy in San Francisco's Juvenile Justice System: A New Approach to Deinstitutionalization," 40 *Crime and Delinquency* 84 (1995).

[2]Jacobs, *Screwing the System and Making It Work: Juvenile Justice in a No-Fault Society*, at 108, 136, (Chicago: University of Chicago Press, 1990). At a later point in his book (pp. 137–144), Jacobs notes that a great deal of the information that probation officers receive from these "supplemental" sources occurs on an informal basis, through the exchange of personal favors, since agency policies regarding the confidentiality of client case records and federal laws governing the privacy of various types of welfare and educational records (*e.g.*, the Privacy Act of 1974) frequently preclude the timely, open, and above board exchange of such information through official channels.

of the case, and perhaps a detailed "treatment plan" outlining the types of theraputic, educational or social services that will be provided to the youth or his family in an effort to effect the youth's rehabilitation. In many ways, the contents of social investigation reports strongly resemble the presentence investigation reports that probation officers compile to assist criminal court judges in the sentencing of adult offenders.

B. The Disposition Debate: The Juvenile Court Judge and The Probation Officer's Recommendations

Juvenile court judges, of course, have the ultimate authority (and bear the ultimate responsibility) for the selection of an appropriate disposition in a particular case; the probation officers' social investigation reports, recommendations and treatment plans are designed as a guide for making those determinations. Consequently, judges are not obligated to abide by the recommendations in the social investigation; they may modify them, add to them or ignore them altogther and select an entirely different dispositional alternative. Anecdotal data suggest, however, that probation officers' recommendations are accorded considerable weight by judges. For example, one judge interviewed by Jacobs "estimate[d] that he accepts 80 percent of recommendations, at least in general outline," an estimate which apparently was confirmed by many of the probation officers Jacobs observed as well.[3]

For their part, probation officers also seem well aware of their power to shape dispositions, and, as Jacobs describes, exert this influence in a variety of ways. One veteran officer he interviewed noted that judges were more likely to accept recommendations when they were backed up by a carefully drafted and seemingly feasible plans for the treatment of the offender.[4]

However, as Jacob's work illustrates, the formalization of juvenile court *procedures* in the post-*Gault* world, gradually formalized the *relationships* between members of the juvenile courtroom "work group."[5] Ironically, just as the formalization of probation officer-judge work roles was increasing the distance between them, judges were becoming more dependent on probation officers to manage the burgeoning court caseloads caused by increasing levels of juvenile crime. But by the same token, probation officers are dependent upon judges to do their work: judicial approval is necessary before the officer's treatment plan can be implemented, and judical authority to impose more stringent sanctions may be needed latter on, should a youth fail to comply with the probation officer's initial set of recommendations.

Moreover, because the relationship between the judge and probation officer is symbiotic, each party is in a position to informally sanction inappropriate behavior on the part of the other. Conversely, probation

---

[3]See Jacobs, *supra*.

[4]Jacobs, *supra*.

[5]For more on courtroom work groups, see Eisenstein and Jacob, *Felony Justice: An Organizational Analysis of Criminal Courts*, 10 (Boston: Little, Brown and Co., 1977); Rossett and Cressey, *Justice By Consent: Plea Bargaining in the American Courthouse*, 91 (Philadelphia: J.B. Lippencott Co., 1976)

officers can impose their own set of informal sanctions on judges, "by intentionally bringing in recommendations significantly different than the judge is prepared to affirm," thus "undermin[ing] the presumption of institutional fairness and competence" of the court, and straining the judge's relationships with offenders and their parents, or worse by actively encouraging offenders to appeal the judge's rulings.[6] Of course, the reckless or profligate use of the tactics described above, by either side, is an invitation to disaster; used sparingly, however, they exist as an informal but complementary set of checks and balances on the exercise of judicial and administrative discretion.

C. The Formulation of Disposition Recommendations By Defense Attorneys: The Rise of "Disposition Case Advocacy" in Juvenile Court

In San Francisco, defense attorneys working in juvenile court have begun to draft and present their own disposition recommendations at the dispositional hearings for their clients. The goal of this so-called "disposition case advocacy" (DCA) is twofold: (1) to counterbalance the perceived dominance of the juvenile probation department at this stage of the juvenile justice process; and (2) to reduce the number of institutionalized youths.[7]

DCA gives defense attorneys an opportunity develop and submit for consideration less restrictive treatment programs in community based facilities, and thus counter the bureaucratic inertia of the probation department.

Both anecdotal and empirical evidence indicates that DCA may in fact be effective in reducing the number of institutional commitments. Macallair reports that judges who are informed of the harsh conditions of confinement in CYA facilities and the high recidivism rates seem more willing to consider alternative dispositions.[8] Moreover, the data from a controlled study conducted by the RAND corporation indicates that the use of dispostion advocacy by defense attorneys led to a significant reduction in the use of secure confinement. In the study, 243 adjudicated youths were randomly assigned to either an experimental or a control group. Members of the experimental group receiving disposition reports prepared by the defense; members of the control group, while represented by counsel, did not have the benefit of these reports. At the conclusion of the study, researchers found the two groups differed significantly in terms of disposition: 72 percent of those in the experimental group were diverted from the system compared to 49 percent of the control group.[9]

---

[6]*Id.*

[7]Macallair, *supra.*

[8]*Id.*

[9]*Id., citing* Greenwood and Turner, *Implementing and Managing Innovative Correctional Programs: Lessons from OJJDP's Private Sector Initiative*, (Santa Monica, CA: RAND Corporation, 1991).

THE JUDGE'S DISPOSITIONAL DECISION

A. Findings of Fact as Part of the Dispositional Order

After reviewing the dispositional recommendations submitted by the probation department (and perhaps others) at a dispositional hearing, the judge's choice of a dispositional option is formalized when he or she enters a document known as a *dispositional order* into the court record. The cases below raise several issues regarding the factors that a judge may consider when reaching a dispositional decision or the content of a dispositional order.

DISPOSITIONAL ALTERNATIVES IN JUVENILE COURT

A. The Dispositional Continuum

As discussed in Chapter 1, the traditional view of juvenile court history holds that the Progressive-era reformers envisioned the juvenile court as a social institution committed to rehabilitation rather than punishment, where justice would be tailored to meet the needs of each individual offender. We also saw that, in this view, the reformers' desire to craft a special justice system for juvenile offenders arose out of their concern that punishment in the adult criminal justice system was too harsh for those of tender years.

Implicit in these principles of individualized justice and rehabiltative treatment, at least in theory, is the notion that agents of the juvenile justice system should have at their command, a wide variety of dispositional alternatives, so that they effectively carry out the court's traditional mandate to provide youthful offenders with personalized care and correction to youthful offenders. This range of dispositional alternatives would begin with some minor sanction (recall how the early juvenile court judges asserted that they could effect the rehabilitation of a youth with a friendly but firm talk) and end with institutionaliztion as a last resort.

Of course, in light of the historical material presented in Chapter 1 and the U.S. Supreme Court's *Gault* decision presented in Chapter 4, the court never quite achieved its lofty goal of the benevolent correction of youths; institutionalization—albeit in "special" facilties such as reformatories and training schools—quickly became the dispositional alternative of choice. And, given modern American society's increasing fear of, growing intolerance of, and ever harsher response to juvenile crime, the punitive institutionalization of youth is likely to continue; the only difference is that in today's society people are less euphemistic and more enthusiastic when they talk about punishing juvenile delinquents and "giving them what they deserve."

However, even if the juvenile justice system has, in practice, overutilized institutionalization at the expense of other less restrictive and more creative dispositions, it still makes sense, from an analytical standpoint, to think about the dispositional alternatives available to the juvenile court judge as if they were arrayed along a rough continuum of severity. Using this framework, Emerson,[10] for example, classifies short term detention as the juvenile justice system's "first resort" and institutionalization in a secure facility as its "last resort" when responding to troubled youth, with a variety of community based placements falling somewhere in between these two anchor points. Our discussion of the dispositional alternatives used in the juvenile justice system is organized around a similar framework: the alternatives explored below are arrayed along a rough continuum of least to most severe. Once again, however, we note that our presentation is designed to be illustrative rather than exhaustive, and specific jurisdictions may differ as to the availability of the various options discussed below.

LOW SEVERITY SANCTIONS

A. Conditional Discharges or Adjournments

Although their use is somewhat difficult to document, many jurisdictions offer first time or minor juvenile offenders a disposition that is analogous to a "suspended sentence" or a "conditional discharge" or an "adjournment in contemplation of dismissal" in the adult criminal justice system.[11] This type of disposition operates in juvenile court in much the same way as it does in the adult system: a formal finding of delinquency is suspendend provided offenders acknowledge their responsibility for an offense (usually via a written confession), and avoid any additional police contacts for a specified period of time in the future. Jacobs also notes that dispositions of this type are typically accompanied by a warning from the judge to the effect that more serious consequences will result from future offending.[12]

B. Group Home Treatment

For first time offenders or in cases where a juvenile's misconduct is relatively minor, group home treatment has historically been the disposition of choice. Group homes are typically small community-based residential treatment facilities where case workers and counselors function as house parents who attempt to recreate "a family type atmosphere."[13] Research examining the efficacy of group home treatment programs in reducing subsequent delinquent behavior has produced mixed results, however. For example,

---

[10]Emerson, "On Last Resorts," 89 *American Journal of Sociology* 1 (1981).

[11]See Inciardi, *Criminal Justice*, 698 (Florida: Academic Press, 1984).

[12]Jacobs, *supra*.

[13]Haghighi and Lopez, "Success/Failure of Group Home Treatment Programs for Juveniles," 57 *Federal Probation* 53 (September, 1993).

work by Stewart et al.[14] and Gaier and Sarnacki[15] have concluded that group home treatment can be effective in "interrupting" delinquent behavior since it is designed to alter the delinquent's environment and provide a meaningful family-type setting. In contrast, Murray and Dox[16] report that group homes are not as effective as institutions in reducing juvenile recidivism. The popularity of group home treatment has also declined in recent years, since it is perceived to be a rehabilitative, "soft" approach to the delinquency problem, inconsistent with the currently popular punitive response to juvenile crime.[17]

C. Electronic Monitoring

A number of jurisdictions have experimented with the electronic monitoring of juvenile offenders, either as an adjunct to a disposition of probation, or in lieu of commitment to a more secure facility. At present, this dispositional alternative seems to be growing rapidly in popularity, inasmuch as it represents a low cost alternative to secure placement in already overcrowded facilities. In electronic monitoring programs, offenders wear a small device, called an encoder on their wrist or ankle. Another device, known as a verifier, is attached to the offender's telephone. Once the devices are activated, a computer at the probation department periodically places a telephone call to the verifier, at random times during the day or evening (appropriate allowances are made in the verification schedule so that the offender can attend school or work). When a call is received, the offender must insert the encoder into the verifier box. If the youth fails to respond to the call by inserting the encoder into the verifier, the computer is programed to document the violation and automatically notify the youth's probation officer via an electronic pager.

D. Fines

Although the use of fines is a common punishment in the adult criminal justice system, they are not a typical dispositional alternative in juvenile court, as discussed in the case presented below.

IN RE DAVID K.

NO. 1287

COURT OF SPECIAL APPEALS OF MARYLAND.

MAY 13, 1981.

* * *

---

[14]Stewart, et al. "Decreasing Court Appearances of Juvenile Status Offenders," 67 *Social Casework: The Journal of Contemporary Social Work* 74 (1986), *cited in* Haghighi and Lopez, *id*.

[15]Gaier and Sarnacki, "Shifts in Delinquent Behavior," 27 *Juvenile and Family Court Journal* 15 (1976) *cited in* Haghighi and Lopez, *supra* n. 13.

[16]Murray and Dox, *Beyond Probation*, (California: Sage Publications, 1979) *cited in* Haghighi and Lopez, *supra*, n. 13.

[17]Haghighi and Lopez, *supra*, n. 13.

WILNER, JUDGE.

The seventeen-year-old appellant was found to be a delinquent child by reason of his having committed certain traffic offenses. He makes no complaint about that finding. What he does complain of is the dispositional order entered by the court. Specifically, he asks in this appeal whether the juvenile court had the authority to (1) require him to pay a $500 fine, and (2) suspend his driving privileges for an indefinite period.

The relevant facts are not in dispute. We shall adopt the statement of them set forth in appellant's brief:

> "On May 24, 1980, at approximately 4:00 p.m. Maryland State Police Trooper S.A. McGee was operating a stationary radar speed gun at U.S. Route 50 and Bell Road in Worcester County. At that the time, a 1966 Buick automobile, operated by the Appellant, was observed in the fast lane of eastbound U.S. Route 50 at a high rate of speed. The radar speed gun indicated the vehicle was travelling at 101 miles per hour in the 55 mile per hour speed zone at that location....The vehicle was stopped at U.S. Route 50 east of Maryland Route 610, and at that time the police officer could detect a moderate to strong odor of alcohol on the operator. The Appellant's manner was that of an intoxicated person in the opinion of the officer, in that his face was flushed and he staggered when attempting to walk. Also in the motor vehicle...was a passenger who also smelled of the odor of alcohol. In plain view in the rear seat of the motor vehicle were ten 16 ounce Colt 45 Malt Liquor cans which were unopened. The beer was in an ice filled cooler with no top. A blood sample was obtained from the Appellant which was tested for the presence of alcohol. The said sample was found to contain 0.15% ethel [sic] alcohol by weight."

As a result of this occurrence, a juvenile petition was filed in Circuit Court for Worcester County charging appellant with being delinquent by (1) possessing an alcoholic beverage in violation of Md.Ann. Code Art. 27 § 406A, (2) operating a motor vehicle while intoxicated, in violation of Transportation article, § 21-902(a), (3) driving while impaired by the consumption of alcohol, in violation of Transportation article, § 21-902(b), and (4) speeding, in violation of Transportation article, § 21-801.1. At or before the adjudicatory hearing, the State dismissed charges (1) and (3), but proceeding on an agreed statement of facts, the court found charges (2) and (4) to be sustained, and, accordingly, entered a finding of delinquency.

Pursuant to Courts article § 3-809, and apparently without objection, the proceeding was then transferred for purposes of disposition to Montgomery County, where appellant and his family lived. After holding a disposition hearing, the District Court for that county, Juvenile Division, entered an order: (1) committing appellant to the Maryland Training School; (2) suspending that commitment and placing appellant in the care of his parents under a program of probation to be provided by the Juvenile Services Administration; (3) directing the Appellant to receive "a tour" of the Maryland Training School and referring him to "the DWI School"; (4) suspending appellant's privilege to operate a motor vehicle; (5) fining appellant $500, to be paid at the rate of $100 a month; and (6) continuing the court's jurisdiction over appellant.

In the Stipulation of Facts entered by the parties, we are told that appellant objected to parts (4) and (5) of the order—the suspension of driving privileges and the fine. It does not appear in the stipulation, although it does on the record, that the court had before it a "social history" indicating that appellant had previously been charged with vandalism, which charge had been informally adjusted, based upon agreement to pay restitution of $1,400, that he had two previous speeding violations, that he consumes a six-pack of beer twice a week (and has been drinking beer since ninth grade), that he occasionally uses marijuana, and that, in the social worker's view, he did not seem to be taking this episode very seriously.

Appellant's attack on the...fine is based on overlapping, yet distinct theories.

By way of introduction, he correctly states that the primal focus of the Juvenile Causes Act is rehabilitation and not punishment. This is clear from § 3-802 of the Courts article, in which the Legislature set forth the purposes of the juvenile law, from § 3-824, which states that an adjudication of delinquency is not a "criminal conviction for any purpose and does not impose any of the civil disabilities ordinarily imposed by a criminal conviction," from most of the other operative provisions of that law, and from the interpretations given to the law by the appellate courts of this State.* * *

In accord with this philosophy is Courts article, § 3-820, which lays out the dispositional options available to a juvenile court following a finding of delinquency. Section 3-820(b) provides:

> "The overriding consideration in making a disposition is a program of treatment, training and rehabilitation best suited to the physical, mental and moral welfare of the child consistent with the public interest [footnote omitted]. The court may:
>
> (1) Place the child on probation or under supervision in his own home or in the custody or under the guardianship of a relative or other fit person, upon terms the court deems appropriate;
>
> (2) Commit the child to the custody or under the guardianship of the Juvenile Services Administration, a local department of social services, the Department of Health and Mental Hygiene or a public or licensed private agency; or
>
> (3) Order the child, parent, guardian or custodian of the child to participate in rehabilitative services that are in the best interest of the child and the family."

It is important also, at the outset, to make clear what the court did. As we have noted, it committed appellant to the training school and then suspended that commitment in lieu of a program of probation to be provided by the Juvenile Services Administration. The succeeding obligations imposed upon appellant by the rest of the order were not expressed as conditions of probation, but rather as independent requirements.[18]

---

[18]We note this simply as a fact and not to suggest that, if stated as a condition of probation, these impositions would necessarily be viewed any differently. *See, for example, State v. Rugon*, 355 So.2d 876, 878 (La.1977): "Formulating the sentence so as to make the exaction a condition of probation does not change its essential nature nor bar its classification as a fine." Compare *People v Labarbera*, 89 Cal. App.2d 639, 201 P.2d 584 (1949); *Shore v Edmisten*, 290 N.C. 628, 277 S.E.2d 553 (1976); and *Brown v. State*, 559 P.2d 107 (Alaska 1977).

(1) Power to Fine

The penultimate paragraph, at issue here, said:

> "ORDERED that the minor child...be fined by the Court the sum of $500.00, said sum is payable in payments of $100.00 per month with the first payment due on or before the 30th day of September, 1980, and subsequent monthly payments due each and every month thereafter until the amount has been paid in full and satisfied...."

That, without question is a *fine*—not an order of restitution to an injured party (*see* Courts article § 3-829) but a fine payable to the State; and it is clear to us that it was beyond the power of the court to impose.

A fine is a penal exaction; it may be imposed only "if there is a 'conviction' which necessarily requires an finding of guilt." *Commissioner of Motor Vehicles v. Lee*, 254 Md. 279, 286, 255 A.2d 44 (1969). It has consistently and universally been defined and considered in the context of a criminal proceeding, as a punishment imposed upon a conviction of a crime. *See, for example,* 36A C.J.S. *Fines* § 1, quoted in *Lee, supra*; *also People ex rel. Doss v. Doss,* 35 Ill. App.3d 365, 342 N.E.2d 60, 63 (1975): "Generally, a fine is a pecuniary punishment for a violation of a law and relates to a criminal offense"; *Bergman v. State,* 187 Wash.622, 60 P.2d 699, 700 (1936): "A fine is a sum of money exacted, as a pecuniary punishment, from a person guilty of an offense..."; *State v. Pitts*, 26 Ariz.App. 390, 548 P.2d 1202, 1203 (1976): "A fine is a criminal penalty...and clearly constitutes a 'sentence'...." * * *

As appellant points out, some state juvenile codes expressly permit the imposition of a fine in juvenile cases [citations omitted]. The Maryland Code, however, makes no such provision. It permits the court to fine or imprison an *adult* upon conviction of contributing to a child's status as delinquent, in need of supervision, or in need of assistance (Courts article § 3-831); but nowhere in the range of dispositional options set forth in § 3-820(b) is there any mention of or allusion to the imposition of a fine. Indeed, as is clear by the very nature of the fine, such an option would be entirely inconsistent with the current non-criminal thrust of our juvenile code. It is for that reason that we conclude that the court had no authority to impose the fine.

* * *

ORDERS IMPOSING $500 FINE...VACATED.

IN RE DAVID K.

1. Define the concept of "restitution" and distinguish it from "a fine."

2. Why are juvenile courts in some jurisdictions generally prohibited from imposing a fine on juveniles found to be delinquent?

3. Reiterate Judge Wilner's rationale for affording juvenile court judges wide discretion in the sentencing/dispositional process.

MEDIUM SEVERITY SANCTIONS

A. Post Adjudicatory Detention

Although the manifest purpose of detention is to confine juveniles who are a threat to themselves or others, or a danger to the community, or prevent flight to avoid adjudication, it is widely recognized that a short period of detention—a "taste of the bars"—is frequently used following adjudication to shock an otherwise recalcitrant youth into complying with the probation officer's rehabilitative efforts.

Apart from an attention getting device, short term detention is also employed as *sanction* for minor misbehavior that occurs following adjudication, but is not worth dealing with by other more extreme means:

No matter how common its occurence, the use of post-adjudicatory detention as a sanction or as "wake up call" to convince reluctant offenders to "get with the program" is problematic for several reasons. First, it represents a violation of the spirit, if not the letter of most detention statutes. Second, its use is also likely to be self limiting since logically offenders can quickly become inured to the shock of incarceration the more often they experience it. Finally, the use of detention for these purposes can be grounds for litigation, as the case below demonstrates.

EDWARD AND DARLENE BAKER, WITH, AND IN BEHALF OF THEIR MINOR CHILD, GLENN ANTHONY BAKER, AND ALL OTHER PERSONS SIMILARLY SITUATED, PLAINTIFFS,

V.

ALLEN HAMILTON, SHERIFF AND JAILOR OF JEFFERSON COUNTY, KENTUCKY, ET AL., DEFENDANTS.

CIV. A. NO. 7148.

UNITED STATES DISTRICT COURT,

W.D. KENTUCKY,

LOUISVILLE DIVISION.

APRIL 25, 1972.

* * *

ALLEN, DISTRICT JUDGE.

* * *

The pleadings allege in substance that...juveniles are being unconstitutionally placed by the Juvenile Court in the Jefferson County Jail. It is alleged that imprisonment and detention of such juveniles in the Jail violates the rights of juveniles to due process of law under the Fourteenth Amendment in that they are not provided rehabilitative care and treatment and punishment [sic] without having been committed and found guilty of a criminal offense under the laws of Kentucky.

It is also alleged that subjecting juveniles to imprisonment with adults in the Jail constitutes cruel and unusual punishment in violation of the Eighth Amendment of the Constitution both because of the physical inadequacy and undesirable conditions in the Jail and because the juveniles have not been charged as being criminals under the laws of Kentucky.

* * *

The Court, with consent of counsel, visited the Jefferson County Jail in late January, 1972. From the Court's observation and the testimony of the witnesses, the following is found to be the condition of the Jail.

It is an old structure built in 1907. One of the defendants referred to it as a "decrepit" structure and one admitted that a characterization of it by a grand jury as a disgrace was true. The jail is drafty and is subject to the influence of extreme heat and cold on the outside. Some of the windows were broken out and many lightbulbs needed replacing. To the credit of the defendant Hamilton, he has asked for an appropriation for indirect lighting and for the replacement of the windows. Many of the locks on the cell doors have been inoperable and here again Sheriff Hamilton has asked for appropriations to remedy this situation. The cells themselves are 5' × 9' and have two bunks in them, a sink, and a toilet. They also have one overhead bulb as illumination....The materials used in the Jail are practically all of steel [which] has deteriorated to such an extent that prisoners have often been able to fabricate...weapons from the deteriorated metal.

* * *

When juveniles enter the Jail, some effort is made to place them with lesser offenders....The Jail contains about 400 inmates on the average. The variety of prisoners held there range from persons who have been convicted of the most serious felonies to those who are awaiting trial for misdemeanors and other minor offenses. Federal prisoners are held there...while awaiting trial...

There has been one major disturbance at the Jail during 1971 when tear gas was used to quell the disorder. There has been one suicide in the Jail during the last year and three prisoners have died there. There are fights on occasions between inmates of the Jail, and there was one occasion were an act of perversion was performed upon a juvenile, although apparently by five other juveniles. Many alcoholics are confined in the Jail for periods of as much as ten days and often go through their withdrawal symptoms while there and add to the confusion and noise of the jail by their shouts in manifestation of withdrawal symptoms.

* * *

The Jail employs a psychiatrist who is there for two and one-half hours a week. His primary duty is to confer with prisoners...in order to see if they are capable of standing trial...

Defendant Hamilton has recently employed a physician who will be on duty for two hours a day each day of the week. In addition there are two nurses who are on the Jail workforce. Also the Jail has six social workers who act as liaison between the prisoners and the outside world. As stated by defendant Hamilton, they do not hold degrees in social work and they do not pretend to give in-depth treatment or assistance to the prisoners.

* * *

Judge Thompson places juveniles in an adult jail for detention purposes because of his belief that such juveniles are so tough and mature physically that they cannot be controlled by the detention center or have created a disturbance at the center or have interfered with its functioning. As to the others he has placed in the Jail as part of [their] disposition[,] this is done for shock value and is not based on any psychological or psychiatric advice given to the Judge but purely because of his belief that juveniles who are hardened physically and sophisticated in their outlook should observe the realities that confront them when they reach adulthood if they do not change their ways.

Judge Thompson is of the opinion that confinement of juveniles in the County Jail does not have any adverse effect on them because of the relatively short period of confinement. It is established that Glenn Anthony Baker and Perry Ford [another plaintiff] apparently suffered no physical or mental harm as a result of their confinement in the Jail.

* * *

The next question to be decided is whether or not the confinement of forty-five juveniles for detention purposes to the Jefferson County Jail and fifteen juveniles for dispositional purposes to the same institution...constituted a violation of the Fourteenth Amendment rights of those sixty juveniles. In this case it is to be noted that Judge Thompson intends, if allowed to do so by this Court to continue the practice followed in 1971 into the future,...

* * *

KRS 208.120 provides specifically that no child under sixteen shall at any time be detained in any police station, lockup, jail or prison except that, on the basis of a hearing for that purpose, by the Juvenile

Court judge, a child whose conduct or condition is such as to endanger the safety or welfare of others in the detention facility for children, may be placed in a jail or other place of detention for adults, *but in a room or ward entirely separate from adult prisoners.* (Emphasis ours).

As to the disposition of juveniles who are not charged with a felony, KRS 208.140 and KRS 208.200 contemplate that...the court may place the child either in his own home, a suitable family home or boarding home or a public or private institution other than the Child Welfare Department or commit the child to the Child Welfare Department for an indeterminate period not to exceed the age of twenty-one.

An examination of Chapter 208 reveals that the primary concern of the legislature was that children under the age of eighteen should be treated differently from adults who have committed crimes....Throughout the statutes are found references to the welfare of the child. See for example, KRS 208.200(a), KRS 208.120, KRS 208.330(3), pertaining to rehabilitation and, more specifically, KRS 208.440 which provides that the Department of Child Welfare shall be responsible for the development of such additional facilities as are necessary and provide an adequate and modern program for the care, treatment and rehabilitation of children. See also, KRS 208.520 which is to the same effect emphasizing the rehabilitation, training and education of juvenile delinquents.

* * *

In reaching its decision on this phase of the case, the Court takes note of the fact that Jefferson County Jail does not provide separate rooms or wards for juveniles. It takes note of the fact that it is a penal institution designed primarily for punishment rather than rehabilitation. It takes note of the fact that the Juvenile Court Judge does not hold a hearing contemplated by KRS 208.120 before sending pre-dispositional juvenile offenders to the county jail, and that the hearings are without counsel [when they are held].

The Court is of the opinion that the present system used by the Juvenile Court Judge and his Trial Commissioners of selective placement of forty five juveniles in the Jefferson County Jail in pre-dispositional matters and of fifteen juveniles as a dispositional matter, even though these commitments be for limited periods of time, constitute a violation of the Fourteenth Amendment in that it is treating for punitive purposes the juveniles as adults and yet not according them for due process purposes the right [sic] accorded to adults. No matter how well intentioned the Juvenile Court Judge's acts are in this respect, they cannot be upheld where they constitute a violation of the Fourteenth Amendment.

We come now to the question of whether or not the commitment of the sixty juveniles...constituted a violation of the Eighth Amendment of the United States Constitution. The Court reaches the conclusion that such confinement does violate the Eighth Amendment and relies upon the case of Jones v Wittenberg [323 F.Supp. 93 (D.C.N.D. Ohio, 1971]. In *Jones*, Judge Young referred to the conditions of the Lucas County Jail as follows:

> "We may suppose that the constitutional provision against cruel and unusual punishment was directed against such activities. In any event when the total picture of confinement in the Lucas County Jail is examined, what appears is confinement in cramped and overcrowded quarters, lightless, airless, damp and filthy with leaking water and human wastes, slow starvation, deprivation of most human contacts, except with others in the same sub-human state, no exercise or recreation, little if any medical attention, no attempt at rehabilitation, and for those who in despair or frustration lash out at their surroundings, confinement, stripped of clothing and every last vestige of humanity, in a sort of oubliette."

Jones held that confinement in the Lucas County Jail as to adults violated the Eighth Amendment. This Court realizes that conditions in the Jefferson County Jail are not as bad as the Lucas County Jail and that officials of Jefferson County are making substantial efforts to improve conditions, but is of the opinion that there are sufficient elements present in the Jefferson County Jail to hold that confinement therein, as to juveniles constitutes cruel and unusual punishment. Specifically, these elements are as follows—cramped quarters, poor illumination, bad circulation of air, broken locks, no outdoor exercise, or recreation and no attempt at rehabilitation, in addition to the condition of the "hole" [*i.e.*, solitary confinement], which Judge Thompson described as horrible.

BAKER V. HAMILTON

1. Critique "deterrence theory" as it applies to this case.

2. Unlike pretrial detention cases, the *Baker* case involves a juvenile who was *sentenced* to an adult jail. How does this case differ from cases where children are merely detained (prior to adjudication) in adult jails? Address issues such as harm to the child, correctional goals, right to treatment, and the Eighth Amendment.

3. While the trend across the 1970s and 1980s has been to avoid placing juveniles in adult jails, the 1990s has experienced a widespread public fear of juvenile crime. Is it possible that this fear could result in an increase of juvenile placements in adult jails? Explain.

B. Probation Supervision

1. "Regular" Probation

Like adult offenders, juveniles can be placed on probation for a period of time following adjudication. And, like adult probationers, they are subject to the surveillance of a probation officer. They can also be required to participate in rehabilitation programs, and abide by specified conditions of probation. However, as the cases below demonstrate, the specific conditions of probation, imposed by the juvenile court judge can become the subject of subsequent litigation.

IN THE INTEREST OF TOMMIE LEE GREEN,

A CHILD.

No. 44549

SUPREME COURT OF MISSISSIPPI.

OCT. 16, 1967.

MOTION FOR STAY OF JUDGMENT DENIED

NOV. 6, 1967.

* * *

ETHRIDGE, CHIEF JUSTICE:

This is an appeal by Tommie Lee Green, a child under the age of eighteen years, from an order of the Youth Court of Grenada County transferring his custody from his parents to the Superintendent of the Oakley Training School. That order was grounded upon the Youth Court's finding that Green had violated the conditional probation that he was under as a result of an earlier proceeding in that court wherein Green had been adjudicated a delinquent child. We affirm.

The County Attorney of Grenada County filed a petition with the Youth Court alleging that Green, a...boy then of the age of fifteen years and one month, was a delinquent child because he had stolen an automobile. Process was had on the youth, his father and stepmother. After a hearing, the court concluded that Green was a delinquent or neglected child, continued the matter until next term, and held:

> The Court is of the opinion that it would be for the best interest of said minor child that he be placed in the care and custody of his parents with the following restrictions: 1) That he be in the house from 7:00 P.M. to 7:00 A.M. unless in the immediate custody of both parents; 2) That he stay out of all trouble; 3) That he and both parents report to the Sheriff once a month; 4) That he be in Youth Court at 9:00 A.M. on the first Monday of May; and that his father is put on probation pending his being at the next Youth Court hearing.
>
> And the Sheriff of Grenada County, Mississippi, is hereby directed to deliver the said minor child to the natural parents and there to be and remain until the further order of this court. The Court hereby retains jurisdiction of this matter and reserves the right to change or modify this order at any time.

In October 1966 the county attorney filed another petition reciting the foregoing facts, and charging that Green had failed to comply with the second requirement of the court's order, "that he stay out of all trouble," in that he left his classroom at Grenada's John Rundle High School at 10 A.M. and went to the Carrie Dotson High School, urging other students to walk out of classes during the regular school period, and in other ways disrupting classes at both of the schools. The petition asked the court to adjudge that the youth had violated the conditions of his placement, and to show cause why he should not be committed to the state training school, or his custody otherwise be changed. On this petition there was process and a full hearing, with a transcript of the testimony.

The Youth Court again found that Green was a delinquent child. He had violated the conditions of his probation, and it would be for his best interest that he be placed in the Oakley Training School. An appeal was taken from this order * * *

Appellant contends that the condition of his probationary custody with his parents, that "he should stay out of trouble," is so vague as to violate the due process clause of the Fourteenth Amendment. The Youth Court Act gives the tribunal power to place a child under supervision in his own home or in that of a relative "under such terms as the court shall determine and direct." Miss.Code 1942 Ann. § 7185–09 (Supp.1966). Although criminal probation statutes are not pertinent to juveniles, they are relevant to the basic question of specificity of formulation of the conditions of probation. A standard condition which is frequently applied is that the probationer shall maintain "good behavior," or "violate no law." Such conditions have been almost universally upheld. They are no more vague or indefinite than the condition that the juvenile "stay out of all trouble." *E.g.*, Mason v. Cochran, 209 Miss. 163, 46 So.2d 106 (1950). Conditions of probation are frequently broadly phrased, since the many types of appropriate causes for revocation cannot be predicted. Note, Legal Aspects of Probation Revocation, 59 Colum.L.Rev. 311, 314–16 (1959). Appellant by his own admission committed acts for which he could be prosecuted criminally. The Youth Court was amply justified in finding that the condition was valid under the particular facts of this case, and that the appellant violated it.

In 1964 and 1966 the Youth Court Act was amended to provide certain exceptions to the jurisdiction of that court over delinquent or neglected or battered children, including such offenses as breach of the peace and disorderly conduct, disturbing the public peace and committing malicious mischief. Thus appellant argues that the Grenada County Youth Court never had jurisdiction over him, because his acts in the Grenada School were offenses of the excepted types, and not within its jurisdiction. Miss.Code 1942 Ann. § 7581–03 (Supp.1966). However, code section 7185–04 authorizes the Youth Court, once it has obtained jurisdiction in the case of any child, to retain such jurisdiction until he becomes twenty years of age. The court found Green to be a delinquent child over a year before the occurrence of the events upon which revocation of probation was based. In that order, the court specifically stated: "The court hereby retains jurisdiction of this matter and reserves the right to change or modify this order at any time." This retention of jurisdiction was restated in the subsequent regularly scheduled reopening of the hearings.

Thus the exceptions to the Youth Court's jurisdiction, set forth in section 7185–03, do not apply here. That court, already vested with jurisdiction over Green, having found him to be a delinquent child, imposed probationary conditions. Section 7185–03 did not have the effect of depriving the Youth Court of jurisdiction over minors already adjudicated to be delinquent, simply because the minor in question committed acts which might possibly be classified under one of the many exceptions in section 7185–03.

No legislative intent to that effect appears from the statute. Green was not charged with committing a crime or misdemeanor, but with violating the conditions of his probation in the custody of his parents.

* * *

AFFIRMED.

RODGERS, BRADY, PATTERSON, and SMITH, JJ., concur.

IN RE GREEN

1. Comment on the fact that the Court in *Green* placed the *father* of the juvenile on probation. What possible rationales might be advanced to justify such an action?

2. Are the concepts of "delinquency" and "status offense" muddled in this case? Explain.

IN RE MAXWELL C., JR. A PERSON COMING UNDER THE JUVENILE COURT LAW. THE PEOPLE, PETITIONER AND RESPONDENT, v. MAXWELL C., JR., A MINOR, APPELLANT.

B-002479.

COURT OF APPEAL, SECOND DISTRICT,

DIVISION 6

AUG. 1, 1984.

* * *

ABBE, ASSOCIATE JUSTICE.

Appellant minor was adjudged a ward of the court upon his admission of allegations of a petition filed pursuant to Welfare and Institutions Code section 602 [footnote omitted]. The petition alleged the minor received and concealed stolen property as proscribed by Penal Code section 496. We find merit in appellant's contention the court abused its discretion in ordering as a condition of probation that he pay restitution to the victim for all loses and damages suffered by the victim in the burglary of his auto wherein the goods were stolen.

During the disposition hearing the victim appeared and requested the full amount of his losses in the sum of $1,134.95. The losses included damage to the vehicle in securing entry thereto, vandalism and other damage done to the dash in removing the stereo. The stolen stereo unit, which appellant possessed had been restored to the victim by the appellant's father prior to the filing of the petition. The stereo unit was in damaged condition and required testing and repair, the costs of which were included in the total.

The information available to the court on disposition indicates appellant at all times denied responsibility for the burglary of the auto. He readily admitted knowingly receiving the stolen stereo. He refused to identify the person from whom he received the stereo. The court expressed doubts whether it had proper authority to impose full restitution for the burglary over appellant's objection, but did so because "...the Court believes the minor ripped off the property but did not plead to ripping off the property." It is therefore necessary to determine whether a court has discretion to order a probationer to pay restitution for losses due to criminal conduct which was neither charged and found to be true nor admitted. For the reasons set forth below, we conclude a court may not do so.

Restitution orders for juvenile offenders are specifically allowed by statute for minors adjudged wards of the court (§ 731) and have been upheld even where no statute specifically authorizes them (*Charles S. v. Superior Court* (1982) 32 Cal.3d 741, 187 Cal.Rptr. 144, 653 P.2d 648). Such orders, however, are appropriate only where they serve a rehabilitative function. (*Id.; cf., People v. Richards* (1976) 17 Cal.3d 614, 620, 131 Cal.Rptr. 537, 552 P.2d 97.)

Orders for restitution have been permitted in adult probation cases which were not limited to the losses actually caused by the conduct for which the person was convicted. (*People v. Lent* (1975) 15 Cal.3d 481, 486, 124 Cal.Rptr. 905, 541 P.2d 545.) However, the restitution must be directly related to the crime charged and must relate to acts by the accused which were committed with the same state of mind as the offense of which he was convicted in order that the statutory rehabilitative effect can take place. (*People v. Richards, supra,* 17 Cal.3d 614, 622, 131 Cal.Rptr. 537, 552 P.2d 97.) With minors as well as adults "[n]o rehabilitative purpose can be served by forcing a person to confront tendencies which differ from those which induced his crime...." (*Id.*) The state of mind with which burglary or vandalism are committed is different than that required for receiving stolen property.

We also note due process considerations have played an important role in determining whether a particular restitution order may exceed the actual losses from conduct which the accused has been found to have committed. Such orders have been found appropriate where evidence at trial or thereafter shows the requisite connection between the offense committed and all the losses for which restitution is ordered. (See *People v. Lent, supra,* 15 Cal.3d p. 481, 124 Cal.Rptr. 905, 541 P.2d 545.) The orders are invalidated where there is no evidence in the record from which the trial court could rationally conclude the probationer was responsible for other losses ordered paid. (See *People v. Richards, supra,* 17 Cal.3d pp. 614, 624, 131 Cal.Rptr. 537, 552 P.2d 97.)

In *Richards* (*Id.*) a restitution order was made at a sentencing procedure which, as in the instant case, did not include a hearing to determine facts related to the accused's conduct other than those already in the record. There the court ordered the probationer to pay restitution for losses to the victims of charged criminal conduct for which the probationer had been acquitted at trial. Here a minor was ordered to pay all damages from a burglary and vandalism of an auto for which appellant had not been charged. A minor cannot be found to have committed an offense neither specifically alleged nor necessarily included in the alleged offense without his consent, (see *In re Robert G.* (1982) 31 Cal.3d 437, 182 Cal.Rptr. 644, 644 P.2d 837.) The minor "...should not have the additional task of persuading the judge regarding the subsequent...disposition on other charges." (*People v. Richards, supra,* 17 Cal.3d p. 624, 131 Cal.Rptr. 537, 552 P.2d 97.)

Finally we note that section 729.6 at the time of the minor's offense and disposition required restitution as a condition of probation upon a section 602 finding when the court does not remove the minor from the physical custody of the parents. While minor here was temporarily removed from the parents' home, the probation conditions including restitution were imposed "upon release from residential treatment program" to his parents. Subdivision (b)(3) of former section 729.6 defined restitution for purposes of the section and limited the amount thereof to "...losses...caused by the defendant [sic] as a result of committing the crime for which he or she was convicted [sic]." This section therefore appears to limit restitution as a condition of probation only to those losses proximately caused by the criminal conduct which the accused has been found to have committed.

The order placing the appellant on probation on condition that he make restitution for all of the losses suffered by the victim is reversed. As the court has already determined that minor is a proper candidate for probation, the case is remanded with directions to grant probation on reasonable conditions, but not including that he pay restitution to the victim for all losses and damages suffered by the victim in the burglary of his automobile.

STONE, P.J. and GILBERT, J., concur.

Hearing denied; BROUSSARD and REYNOSO, JJ., dissenting.

IN RE MAXWELL

1. Elaborate on the legislative intent of restitution programs from the perspectives of retribution, restorative justice, and rehabilitation, and discuss the place of restitution in the juvenile justice system.

2. In *Maxwell C.* it is clear that the demands of the victim played a significant role in the juvenile court judge's dispositional decision. To what extent should the victim's view on disposition be allowed to influence the outcome of the case?

3. What type of restitution order would be reasonable in this case? Provide detailed justification.

2. Intensive Probation Supervision

In the mid- and late-1980s, a number of jurisdictions experimented with "intensive supervision" programs as an alternative to the secure confinement of youthful offenders. They are represented here as a "medium severity" sanction because they place strict controls on the offender (*e.g.*, frequent surveillance on evenings and weekends, stringent curfews, random drug screenings, *etc.*), yet also contain program components aimed at the rehabilitation and treatment of delinquents, such as therapeutic and life skills counseling, and community service.[19] A recent article by Weibush[20] describes and evaluates the effectiveness of one such intensive supervision program developed by the juvenile court in Lucas County (Toledo), Ohio.

For a period of 18 months, researchers documented the number and types of contacts between the offenders and their probation or parole officers, the frequency and types of service referrals made and subsequent criminal activity of the research subjects.[21] Members of the intensive supervision group had about twice as many contacts with probation officers than the members of the DYS group, or the probation group, indicating that the goal of intensive supervision was being met.[22] The three groups also differed significantly in the level of referrals for counseling or community service: 99 percent of the experimental group received counseling during the follow up period, while 92 percent of this group performed community service. In contrast, the proportion of subjects receiving similar referrals was smaller in the two comparison groups. Such a difference would be expected, since the intensive supervision program emphasized both treatment and control.[23]

As to the level of recidivism for the three groups, researchers found that 82 percent of the experimental group were charged with a new offense and 77 percent were adjudicated for a subsequent crime during the 18 month follow up period.

In evaluating these results, one is tempted to focus on the high recidivism rates of the experimental group, and the lack of a statistically significant difference between it and the two comparison groups and conclude that the intensive supervision program was a failure. But this is perhaps a premature conclusion when one considers the results in light of the relative costs of institutionalization versus intensive supervision. Researchers calculated that the annual cost of placing one offender on intensive supervision

---

[19]Wiebush, "Juvenile Intensive Supervision: The Impact on Felony Offenders Diverted From Institutional Placement," 39 *Crime and Delinquency* 68-69 (January, 1993).

[20]*Id.*

[21]*Id.*

[22]*Id.*

[23]*Id.*

was approximately $6,020, while the annual cost of institutionalizing one offender was $32,320.[24] The similarity of the recidivism rates in the three groups suggests that while levels of subsequent offending in the experimental group were no worse than re-offense levels of the comparison groups, these results could be obtained at a significantly lower economic cost, compared to institutionalization. Also, while intensive supervision is clearly no worse than institutionalization in preventing recidivism, it avoids the human costs of incarceration, such as the disruption of family and community ties, as well as the potentially damaging physical, psychological and criminogenic effects of incarceration.[25]

Looking at the types of subsequent offenses, less than ten percent of the members of *all three* groups were adjudicated for a major felony, such as rape, armed robbery or aggravated assault, and about 15 percent of the members of *all three* groups were adjudicated for a seious property crime, such as burglary or auto theft.[26] The similarity of these results also shows the effectiveness of intensive supervision, since one would expect the proportion of serious offenses to be much higher in the experimental group, given that their prior records were so much more serious than the prior records of those in the comparison groups.[27]

C. Wilderness Programs and Boot Camps

A number of jurisdictions operate "wilderness" or "adventure" programs and "boot camps" for youthful offenders. Wilderness programs are designed to help juveniles overcome these deficiencies by placing a group of them in a demanding and stressful outdoor environment (*e.g.*, a camp in the remote woods or an oceangoing sailboat) where they must learn how to cooperate, to solve problems, and to resolve conflicts in order to survive. "Boot camps" are designed to be even more stressful and challenging experiences, in which youthful offenders are compelled to undergo an intense form of training similar to the kind experienced by new military recruits. In boot camp programs, corrections officers take on the role of military "drill instructors" who attempt to rehabilitate offenders by employing a combination of rigorous physical training, manual labor, and outright intimidation.

---

[24] *Id.*

[25] *Id.*

[26] *Id.*

[27] *Id.*

MAKING THE PARENTS OF DELINQUENTS PAY: A NEW MEDIUM RANGE SANCTION?

A. Parental Liability for the Delinquent Acts of Their Children

Some states have recently enacted legislation making parents financially responsible for the damages caused by the delinquent acts of their children. The excerpt below is an example of a statute passed in Michigan.

PUBLIC ACTS 1993—NO. 344

CHAPTER XIIA

712A.18 Orders of disposition; reimbursement; hearing; guidelines and model schedule; restitution; condition of probation; community service; "juvenile offense" defined; fingerprints; report to state police; payment of assessment. [M.S.A. 27.3178(598.18)]

Sec. 18. (1) If the court finds that a child concerning whom a petition is filed is not within this chapter, the court shall enter an order dismissing the petition. Except as otherwise provided in subsection (10), if the court finds that a child is within this chapter, the court may enter any of the following orders of disposition that are appropriate for the welfare of the child and society in view of the facts proven and ascertained;

* * *

(17) If the court determines that the juvenile is or will be unable to pay all of the restitution ordered, after notice to the juvenile's parent and an opportunity for the parent to be heard, the court may order the parent or parents having supervisory responsibility for the juvenile at the time of the acts upon which an order of restitution is based to pay not more than $5,000.00 of the restitution ordered. As used in this subsection, "parent" does not include a foster parent.

(18) If the court orders a parent to pay restitution under subsection (17), the court shall take into account the financial resources of the parent and the burden that the payment of restitution will impose, with due regard to any other moral or legal financial obligations that the parent may have. If a parent is required to pay restitution under subsection (17), the court shall provide for payment to be made in specified installments and within a specified period of time.

(19) A parent who has been ordered to pay restitution under subsection (17) may petition the court for a modification of the amount of restitution owed or for a cancellation of any unpaid portion of the restitution. The court shall cancel all or part of the amount of restitution due, if it appears to the satisfaction of the court that payment of the amount due will impose a manifest hardship on the parent.

B. Parental Liability for the Costs of Incarcerating Their Delinquent Children

Some states have attempted to extend the concept of parental liability by making parents responsible for the costs of caring for an offender while he or she is in custody. In California, such a policy has been struck down on constitutional grounds, as discussed in the case below.

IN RE JERALD C., A PERSON COMING UNDER THE JUVENILE COURT LAW.

COUNTY OF SANTA CLARA, PLAINTIFF AND RESPONDENT,

v.

HIRAM G., DEFENDANT AND APPELLANT.

S.F. 24392.

SUPREME COURT OF CALIFORNIA,

IN BANK.

DEC. 10, 1982.

* * *

BROUSSARD, ASSOCIATE JUSTICE.

The father of Jerald C., a minor appeals from an order requiring reimbursement to the County of Santa Clara for the costs of the care and support of Jerald while in custody.

Jerald was declared a ward of the court pursuant to Welfare and Institutions Code section 602[28] and was placed in custody at juvenile hall and boys ranch. He was subsequently committed to the California Youth Authority. The county sought reimbursement under the provisions of section 903 at the rate of $265 per month for juvenile hall and boys ranch custody prior to September, 1980, at a rate of $33 per day for 33 days in juvenile hall in October and November, 1980, and at the rate of $25 per month for subsequent commitment to the California Youth Authority. After a hearing, appellant was ordered to pay the above amounts at the rate of $100 per month [footnote omitted].

Section 903 provides: "The father, mother, spouse or other person liable for the support of a minor person, the estates of such persons, and the estate of such minor person, shall be liable for the cost of his care, support, and maintenance in any county institution in which he is placed, detained or committed pursuant to the order of the juvenile court, or for the cost to the county in which the juvenile court making

---

[28]Unless otherwise indicated all section references are to the Welfare and Institutions Code.

the order is located, of his care, support, and maintenance in any other place in which he is placed, detained, or committed pursuant to the order of the juvenile court. The liability of such persons (in this article called relatives) and estates shall be a joint and several liability."[29]

Statutes requiring responsible relatives to reimburse governmental agencies for support have been sustained against claims of denial of equal protection. In *Swoap v. Superior Court* (1973) 10 Cal.3d 490, 111 Cal.Rptr. 136, 516 P.2d 840, this court upheld statutes requiring responsible adult children to support needy or poor elderly parents and providing that the children must reimburse the state for support provided by it to the parents. Pointing out that a long tradition of law and a measureless history of societal custom had established the duty of adult children to support their poor parents, the court concluded that the duty imposed by the statutes bears a rational relationship to the accomplishment of the state purpose of relieving the public treasury and that the statutes do not arbitrarily charge one class of society for the cost of public assistance. (10 Cal.3d at pp. 502–507, 111 Cal.Rptr. 136, 516 P.2d 840.)

* * *

However, relative responsibility statutes have been invalidated when the government charges were not for support which the relative refused or failed to provide but for the cost of maintaining public institutions for public benefit.

"A statute obviously violates the equal protection clause if it selects one particular class of persons for a species of taxation and no rational basis supports such classification. [Citations.] Such a concept for the state's taking of a free man's property manifestly denies him equal protection of the law [citations omitted]." Such limitation on the government's ability to raise money has been traced to the Magna Charta and the Petition of Right. (See tenBroek, *California's Dual System of Family Law: Its Origin, Development, and Present Status, Part III* (1965) 17 Stan.L.Rev. 614, 643) To charge the cost of operation of state functions conducted for public benefit to one class of society is arbitrary and violates the basic constitutional guarantee of equal protection of the law. (*Id.*, at p. 639).

In accordance with this fundamental principle, it has been recognized that parents may not be charged for costs when their children are incarcerated in prison or committed to state hospitals for the dangerous. Nor may adult children be charged for such incarceration or commitment of their parents. The cases have reasoned that when incarceration or commitment is for the protection of society, it is arbitrary to assess relatives for the expense [citations omitted].

In [*Dept. of Mental Hygiene v.*] *Kirchner* [(1964), 60 Cal 2d. 716, 36 Cal.Rptr. 488, 388 P.2d 720 (remanded, 380 U.S. 194, 85 S.Ct. 871, 13 L.Ed.2d 753; subsequent opn. 62 Cal.2d 586, 43 Cal.Rptr.

---

[29]Although the record is not clear, the $25 charge by the county while the child is committed to the Youth Authority is apparently an attempt by the county to recover the $25 it must pay to the state each month that the child is committed to the Youth Authority. (§ 912). If so, it would seem that the cost is a confinement cost rather than a support cost.

329, 400 P.2d 321);] the court explained: "Recently in *Department of Mental Hygiene v. Hawley* (1963) 59 Cal 2d. 247, [28 Cal.Rptr. 718, 379 P.2d 22], the department, relying on section 6650, attempted to collect from a father for the cost of care, support, and maintenance in a state hospital for the mentally ill or insane of his son who had been charged with crime, but before trial of the criminal issue (and obviously without adjudication of that issue) had been found by the court to be insane and committed to such state hospital. We there held (pp. 255–256 [6] [28 Cal.Rptr. 718, 379 P.2d 22]) that '[t]he enactment and administration of laws providing for sequestration and treatment of persons in appropriate state institutions—subject of course, to the constitutional guarantees—who would endanger themselves or others if at large is a proper state function; being so, it follows that the expense of providing, operating and maintaining such institutions should (subject to reasonable exceptions *against the inmate or his estate*) be borne by the state.' (Italics added.) We further held that recovery could not constitutionally be had against the father of the committed patient. This holding is dispositive of the issue before us. Whether the commitment is incidental to the alleged violation of penal statute, as in *Hawley*, or is essentially a civil commitment, as in the instant case, the purposes of confinement and treatment or care in either case encompass the protection of society from the confined person, and his own protection and possible reclamation as a productive member of the body politic. Hence, the cost of maintaining the state institution, including provision of adequate care for its inmates, cannot be arbitrarily charged to one class in society; such assessment violates the equal protection clause." (*Dept. of Mental Hygiene v. Kirchner supra*, 60 Cal 2d. at pp. 719, 36 Cal.Rptr. 488, 388 P.2d 720.)

Whatever the basis for other commitments by the juvenile court (see §§ 300, 601), the purposes of the confinement and treatment in commitments pursuant to section 602 include "the protection of society from the confined person." (*Dept. of Mental Hygiene v. Kirchner supra*, 60 Cal 2d. at pp. 720, 36 Cal.Rptr. 488, 388 P.2d 720.)

* * *

The purpose of juvenile commitment proceedings "to protect the public from criminal conduct by minors" (§ 202) rehabilitation and treatment [citations omitted] brings the commitment squarely within the rule of *Kirchner*. * * *

While it is true that section 602 proceedings are not technically criminal [footnote omitted] and commitment of a juvenile under the section is not for the purpose of punishment or a conviction (§ 203) [citations omitted], it is apparent from *Kirchner* and *Hawley* that these are not determinative factors. *Kirchner* involved commitment of a mentally ill person who was neither charged with nor convicted of a crime; although in *Hawley* the child was charged with crime, the criminal proceedings were suspended at the time of commitment, there was no conviction, and confinement was not for the purpose of punishment. As was true in *Kirchner* and *Hawley*, commitment under section 602 is not for the purpose of providing support and maintenance for the committed person but for the purpose of protecting society.

The county seeks to distinguish *Kirchner* and *Hawley* on the ground that the obligation to support a minor child is a common law obligation whereas the obligation to support an adult child or parent is a statutory obligation. However, the duty to reimburse for support and maintenance imposed by section 903 goes beyond the common law duty codified in Civil Code section 207. Under the latter code section the liability of parents to reimburse third parties who provide support applies only where a parent "neglects" to provide support, and there is no liability when the child abandons the parent without cause (Civ.Code, § 208). Section 602 commitments are not based on a refusal or failure to provide support. Ordinarily, the parents are willing to provide support, but the state, by taking custody has deprived them of the opportunity to provide ordinary support of their child.

In seeking reimbursement of expenses incurred in section 602 commitments, the county is not seeking recovery of expenditures for support of the minor, but expenses for confinement for the protection of society. Although parents of children committed under section 602 are thereby relieved of their ordinary burden of support, the reimbursement provision of section 903 is not based on such burden but upon the governmental cost of confinement. And it is apparent from the reimbursement sought in the instant case that the charges were not limited to the reasonable cost of support in a home but included confinement costs.

Moreover, common law and statutory origin furnish no basis for the urged distinction because the statutory duty to provide support for needy parents and adult children has existed for so long. As pointed out in *Swoap v. Superior Court, supra* 10 Cal.3d 490, 111 Cal.Rptr. 136, 516 P.2d 840, it "is abundantly clear that children have generally been subject to a duty to support poor parents for a very long time, indeed. It is true, as stated in *Kirchner* and *Boss*, that there was no such duty at common law. Nevertheless, the duty is deep rooted and of venerable ancestry; it can be traced back over almost four centuries to the year 1601 when it emerged as part and parcel of the Elizabethan Poor Law [citation omitted]. Professor tenBroek has clearly demonstrated that 'legal liability of relatives [imposed by Elizabethan Poor Law] was designed to indemnify the public and to minimize its cost in relieving the poor.'" (tenBroek, *supra*, 16 Stan.L.Rev.257, 283).

* * *

As in *Swoap*, the long tradition of law and history of societal custom of a duty to support poor adult children and parents must be deemed the substantial equivalent of the common law duty to support minor children. The duties may not be distinguished in terms of the state's right to reimbursement. On the one hand, the State, in accordance with *Swoap*, may obtain reimbursement for support allowances paid to or for minors. On the other hand, the common law duty to support minor children does not authorize the state to recover the costs of confinement imposed for the protection of society and the minor and his rehabilitation. Under *Kirchner*, those costs may not be recovered when an adult is confined for the protection of society, and they may not be recovered when minors are placed in custody for the protection of society.

It is urged that while the county may not recover the costs of confinement and treatment, it should be permitted to recover costs incurred in supporting and maintaining the juvenile based on the parental common law duty and cases upholding responsible relative statutes in other situations. Even assuming that it is economically feasible to segregate the types of costs borne by the institutions and to allocate in a reasonable manner a portion of the costs to each juvenile, we must reject the proposed allocation for the following reasons. The allocation would be equally possible in *Kirchner* and *Hawley* situations, but neither case permitted the allocation, and the allocation would involve a partial repudiation of well-settled principles of law. As pointed out above section 903 reimbursement goes beyond the parental duty of reimbursement imposed...because there is no reason to believe that absent commitment the parents would refuse or fail to provide support themselves. * * *

Our conclusion that the county may not recover its costs does not mean that the parents will be unjustly enriched. One of the greatest misfortunes a parent may suffer is the incarceration of an offspring for crime. To imply that the avoidance of support obligation balances or exceeds such misfortune would betray a misguided sense of values. Incarcerating the child, the state neither intends nor provides benefits to the parents. The state's purpose and the benefits provided are for society generally.

* * *

The order appealed from is reversed.

* * *

IN RE JERALD C.

1. Should parents be financially liable to the county when their children are incarcerated in juvenile facilities? State both sides of this issue, pro and con.

HIGH SEVERITY SANCTIONS

A. Secure Facilities and Training Schools: Prisons by Any Other Name?

As with adult offenders, the typical "end of the line" sanction for serious delinquent offenders is incarceration in a "secure facility" or a "training school." These euphemistic terms have been used in an effort disguise the similarity of such institutions to adult prisons and perhaps pay lip service to the traditional rehabilitative aims of the juvenile justice system. However, public intolerance of juvenile offenders and legislative desires to "get tough" on juvenile crime have made it easier for members of society to see these institutions for what they really are: prisons that punish kids. The cases below deal with various aspects surrounding the long term incarceration of children, and their care as inmates.

B. Determining the Length of Confinement

To regularize judicial decisions regarding the length of confinment for juvenile offenders and prevent sentencing disparity, some jurisdictions now employ sentencing guidelines similar to those used in adult criminal court. Like the guidelines used to sentence adults, the lengths of juvenile sentences are a function of the seriousness of the current offense and the youth's prior record. The case below discusses some of the issues surrounding the application of sentencing guidelines in specific cases.

UNITED STATES, PETITIONER

V.

R.L.C.

NO. 90–1577.

ARGUED DEC. 10, 1991

DECIDED MARCH 24, 1992.

* * *

JUSTICE SOUTER announced the judgment of the Court and delivered the opinion with respect to Parts I, II–A, and III, and an opinion with respect to Parts II–B and II–C, in which **THE CHIEF JUSTICE, JUSTICE WHITE**, and **JUSTICE STEVENS** join.

The provisions of the Juvenile Delinquency Act require the length of official detention in certain circumstances to be limited to "the maximum term of imprisonment that would be authorized if the juvenile had been tried and convicted as an adult." 18 U.S.C. § 5037(c)(1)(B). We hold that this limitation refers to the maximum sentence that could be imposed if the juvenile were being sentenced after the application of the United States Sentencing Guidelines.

I

Early in the morning of November 5, 1989, after a night of drinking, the then–16–year–old respondent R.L.C. and another juvenile stole a car with which they struck another automobile, fatally injuring one of its passengers 2–year–old La Tesha Mountain. R.L.C. is a member of the Red Lake Band of Chippewa Indians and these events took place on the Red Lake Indian Reservation...These circumstances provide federal jurisdiction in this case [citation omitted]....[and] the Government charged R.L.C. with an act of juvenile delinquency.

After a bench trial, the District Court found R.L.C....to have committed an act of juvenile delinquency within the meaning of § 5031, since his acts would have been the crime of involuntary manslaughter in violation of 18 U.S.C. §§ 1112(a) and 1153 if committed by an adult. The maximum sentence for involuntary manslaughter under 18 U.S.C. § 1112(b) is three years. At R.L.C.'s disposition hearing the District Court...accordingly committed him to official detention for three years.

...[T]he United States Court of Appeals for the Eighth Circuit, 915 F.2d 320 (1990), vacated R.L.C.'s sentence and remanded for resentencing, after concluding that 36 months exceeded the cap imposed by § 5037(c)(1)(B) upon the period of detention to which a juvenile delinquent may be sentenced. Although the statute merely provides that juvenile detention may not extend beyond "the maximum term of imprisonment that would be authorized if the juvenile had been tried and convicted as an adult" [footnote omitted], the Court of Appeals read this language to bar a juvenile term longer than the sentence a court could have imposed on a similarly situated adult after applying the United States Sentencing Guidelines...The court found, and the government agrees,...[that] the Guidelines would yield a sentencing range of 15–21 months for a similarly situated adult. The Court of Appeals therefore concluded that the maximum period of detention to which R.L.C. could be sentenced was 21 months....We granted the Government's petition for certiorari,...to resolve the conflict between the Eighth Circuit's holding in this case and the Ninth Circuit's position, adopted in *United States v. Marco L.*, 868 F.2d 1121, cert. denied, 493 U.S. 956, 110 S.Ct. 369, 107 L.Ed.2d 355 (1989), and endorsed by the Government.

II

A

The Government...argues that the word "authorized" [in § 5037(c)(1)(b), above] must mean the maximum term of imprisonment provided for by the statute defining the offense, since only Congress can "authorize" a term of imprisonment in punishment for a crime. As against the position that the Sentencing Guidelines now circumscribe a trial court's authority, the Government insists that our concern must be with the affirmative authority for imposing a sentence, which necessarily stems from statutory law. It maintains that in any event, the Sentencing Commission's congressional authorization to establish sentencing guidelines does not create affirmative authority to set punishments for crime, and that the Guidelines do not purport to authorize the punishments to which they relate.

But this is too easy. The answer to any suggestion that the statutory character of a specific penalty provision give it primacy over administrative sentencing guidelines is that the mandate to apply the Guidelines is itself statutory. See 18 U.S.C. § 3553(b). More significantly, the Government's argument that "authorization" refers only to what is affirmatively provided by penal statutes, without reference to the Sentencing Guidelines to be applied under statutory mandate, seems to us to beg the question. Of course it is true that no penalty would be "authorized" without a statute providing specifically for the penal consequences of defined criminal activity. The question, however, is whether Congress intended the courts to treat the upper limit of such a penalty as "authorized" even when proper application of a statutorily mandated guideline in an adult case would bar imposition up to the limit, and an unwarranted upward departure from the proper guideline range would be reversible error. 18 U.S.C. § 3742. Here it suffices to say that the Government's construction is by no means plain. The text is at least equally consistent with treating "authorized" to refer to the result of applying all statutes with a required bearing on the sentencing decision, including not only those that empower the court to sentence but those that limit the legitimacy of its exercise of that power. This, indeed, is arguably the more natural construction.

* * *

B

On the assumption that ambiguity exists, we turn to examine the textual evolution of the limitation in question and the legislative history that may explain or elucidate it [footnote omitted]. * * *

With the Sentencing Reform Act of 1984 (chapter II of the Comprehensive Crime Control Act of 1984, Pub.L. 98–473, § 214(a), 98 Stat. 2013), § 5037 was rewritten. As § 5037(c)(1)(B), its relevant provision became "the maximum term of imprisonment that would be authorized *by section 3581(b)* if the juvenile had been tried and convicted as an adult." 18 U.S.C. §§ 5037(c)(1)(B), (c)(2)(B)(ii) (1982 Ed., Supp.II) (emphasis added). The emphasized language was quickly deleted however by the Criminal Law and Procedure Technical Amendments Act of 1986 [citation omitted], resulting in the present statutory text, "the maximum term of imprisonment that would have been authorized if the juvenile had been tried and convicted as an adult." It thus lost the reference to § 3581(b), which would have guided the sentencing court in identifying the "authorized" term of imprisonment.

R.L.C. argues that this loss is highly significant. Section 3581(b) [footnote omitted] was and still is part of a classification system adopted in 1984 for use in setting the incidents of punishment for federal offenses by reference to letter grades reflecting their relative seriousness...Section 3581(b) sets out the maximum term of imprisonment for each letter grade, providing, for instance, that the authorized term of imprisonment for a Class C felony is not more than 12 years, for a Class D, not more than 6, and for a Class E not more than 3.

The deletion of the reference to § 3581(b) with its specific catalog of statutory maximums would seem to go against the Government's position. Since, for example, a juvenile who had committed what would have been a Class E felony would apparently have been subject to three years of detention, because § 3581(b) "authorized" up to three years of imprisonment for an adult, the deletion of the reference to § 3581(b) would appear to indicate some congressional intent to broaden the range of inquiry when determining what was authorized [footnote omitted].

* * *

[Moreover, t]he Senate Report accompanying the 1986 Technical Amendments Act states that the amendment "makes clear that juvenile sentences are to be of equal length as those for adult offenders committing the same crime." S.Rep. No. 99-278, p. 3 (1986). This, in turn, reflects the statement in the Senate Report accompanying the Sentencing Reform Act, that changes in juvenile sentencing law were included "in order to conform it to changes made in adult sentencing laws." S.Rep. No. 98–225, p. 155 (1983), U.S.Code Cong. & Admin.News, 1984, pp, 3182, 3338. The most fundamental of the Sentencing Reform Act's changes, was, of course, the creation of the Sentencing Guidelines Commission, authorized to promulgate the guidelines for use by sentencing courts. It hardly seems likely that Congress adopted the current § 5037(c) with a purpose to conform juvenile and adult maximum sentences without intending the recently authorized Guidelines scheme to be considered for that purpose. The legislative history thus reinforces our initial conclusion that § 5037 is better understood to refer to the maximum sentence permitted under the statute requiring application of the Guidelines [footnote omitted].

C

We do not think any ambiguity survives. If any did, however, we would choose the construction yielding the shorter sentence, by resting on the venerable rule of lenity. See, *e.g.*, *United States v. Bass,* 404 U.S.336, 347–348, 92 S.Ct. 515, 522–523, 30 L.Ed.2d 488 (1971), rooted in "'the instinctive distaste against men languishing in prison unless the lawmaker has clearly said they should,'" (*id.*, at 348, 92 S.Ct., at 523 (quoting H. Friendly, Benchmarks 209 (1967)). While the rule has been applied not only to resolve issues about the substantive scope of criminal statutes, but to answer questions about the severity of sentencing, see *Bifulco v. United States*, 447 U.S. 381, 387, 100 S.Ct. 2247, 2252, 65 L.Ed.2d 205 (1980), its application is unnecessary in this case, since "we have always reserved lenity for those situations in which a reasonable doubt persists about a statute's intended scope even *after* resort to 'the language and structure, legislative history, and motivating policies' of the statute." *Moskal v. United States*, 498 U.S. —, —, 111 S.Ct. 461, 465, 112 L.Ed.2d 449 (1990) (citation omitted) [footnote omitted].

III

We hold, therefore, that application of the language in § 5037(c)(1)(B) permitting detention for a period not to exceed "the maximum term of imprisonment that would be authorized if the juvenile had been tried and convicted as an adult" refers to the maximum length of sentence to which a similarly situated adult would be subject if convicted of the adult counterpart of the offense and sentenced under the statute requiring application of the Guidelines, 18 U.S.C. § 3553(b). Although determining the maximum permissible sentence under § 5037(c)(1)(B) will therefore require sentencing and reviewing courts to determine an appropriate guideline range in juvenile–delinquency [sic] proceedings, we emphasize that it does not require plenary application of the Guidelines to juvenile delinquents.[30] Where that statutory provision applies, a sentencing court's concern with the Guidelines goes solely to the upper limit of the

[30]The Sentencing Guidelines, of course, do not directly apply to juvenile delinquency proceedings. We observe that 28 USC § 995(a)(19), also enacted as part of the Sentencing Reform Act of 1984, gives the Sentencing Commission power to "study the feasibility of developing guidelines for the disposition of juvenile delinquents." The Government reports that the Sentencing Commission has recently begun such study. See Brief for United States 11, n. 1.

proper guideline range as setting the maximum term for which a juvenile may be committed to official detention, absent circumstances that would warrant departure under § 3553(b).

The judgment of the Court of Appeals is

AFFIRMED.

* * *

U.S. v. R.L.C.

1. What was the legislative intent of the "United States Sentencing Guidelines"? Explain how these Guidelines function. Address the issue of judicial discretion as it relates to this sentencing method.
2. Why are the federal "Guidelines" historically inconsistent with the traditional goals of juvenile justice?
3. What is the "Technical Amendments Act"?
4. Explain the "rule of lenity" and its relevance to the *R.L.C.* case.
5. Examine the main issue in this case from an "equal protection" standpoint (comparing adults to juveniles). Then adopt a "substantive due process approach" and examine 18 U.S.C. § 5037(c); that is, should this law be found "void for vagueness"?

ANTOINETTE LOLLIS, ON HER OWN BEHALF, AND ON BEHALF OF ALL OTHERS SIMILARLY SITUATED, NAMELY THOSE CHILDREN CONFINED TO TRAINING SCHOOLS IN THE STATE OF NEW YORK, PLAINTIFFS,

v.

NEW YORK STATE DEPARTMENT OF SOCIAL SERVICES, GEORGE K. WYMAN, COMMISSIONER, STATE DEPARTMENT OF SOCIAL SERVICES, FRANK SHAUGHNESSEY, SUPERINTENDENT, BROOKWOOD ANNEX TO THE HUDSON STATE TRAINING SCHOOL FOR GIRLS, ET AL., DEFENDANTS.

JOE PENA, ON HIS OWN BEHALF, AND ON BEHALF OF ALL OTHERS SIMILARLY SITUATED, NAMELY THOSE CHILDREN CONFINED TO AND

PAROLED FROM TRAINING SCHOOLS IN THE

STATE OF NEW YORK, PLAINTIFFS,

V.

NEW YORK STATE DEPARTMENT OF SOCIAL SERVICES,

GEORGE K. WYMAN, COMMISSIONER, STATE DEPARTMENT OF SOCIAL

SERVICES ET. AL., DEFENDANTS.

NOS. 70 CIV. 4750, 70 CIV. 4868

UNITED STATES DISTRICT COURT,

S.D. NEW YORK.

DEC. 18, 1970.

* * *

LASKER, DISTRICT JUDGE.

Plaintiffs in these companion cases are children who claim that their treatment while in custody in New York State training schools has constituted cruel and unusual punishment under the Eighth Amendment or punishment imposed in violation of the Fourteenth Amendment * * *.

* * *

I.

Antoinette Lollis ("Lollis") is a fourteen-year-old inmate of the Brookwood Annex to the Hudson Training School for Girls ("Brookwood Annex") in Claverack, New York. She was committed first in September 1969 as a "Person in Need of Supervision" pursuant to § 711 ff of the New York Family Court Act. She was released on June 30, 1970, but on the complaint of her mother...was returned, without hearing, to the training school in mid-August, 1970.

Neither in the present case nor previously has the plaintiff been accused of any crime. Although in the present instance her mother claimed that Lollis threatened her with a knife, this Lollis denies.

Two or three days after her return to custody, plaintiff became involved in a fight with a matron and another inmate. The record indicates that the plaintiff was abusive and aggressive and bore the responsibility for the start of the fracas. Before peace returned it took several persons to subdue Lollis.

Immediately thereafter, without a hearing, plaintiff was confined to what is colloquially known within the training school system as a "strip room"—so called because it is stripped of all facilities normally available to inmates. Here she remained until September 4, 1970, being released at that time at the insistence of Family Court Judge Beatrice Burstein, who made an inspection of the School on September 2, 1970, and discovered Lollis confined to the strip room.

Judge Burstein's detailed report of the Lollis case, dated September 22, 1970, describes the following conditions:

> "She [Lollis] was kept in a room about 6′ × 9′ for 24 hours a day. The first seven or eight days of confinement she was visited by a social worker. Then the social worker went on vacation and one other staff member visited her once. She was completely unoccupied for 24 hours daily. Nonetheless, I inquired how she kept herself busy. She replied by saying 'I sleep all day and I cry all night.' She had, indeed, requested to see a psychiatrist, but was informed that she would not be able to see him until she was released from solitary. She had reported that she had been receiving tranquilizers for a long period of time and felt a need for them now but was unable to secure them since the psychiatrist was not available for a visit. It should be noted that Brookwood has the services of a psychiatrist one half-day every other week.
>
> "She wore pajamas all day, sat staring at the wall and did absolutely nothing.
>
> * * *
>
> "There was a wooden bench * * * There was a blanket on the bench and this was where the child rested for twenty-four hours."

Although the room contained a window it was blinded so that it "absolutely prevented the youngster from looking outside." In each of the four wings there was a strip room for isolation purposes. The room in which the plaintiff was confined was at the end of the hospital wing, completely removed from the balance of the population.

Judge Burstein questioned the Superintendent as to when Lollis might be released. He replied that, although the case was reviewed each day by the staff, he could not suggest a definite date, since release depended on Lollis' exhibiting some "movement" on her apology to the matron (the matron was by now on vacation). When removal from the strip room occurred, he informed her, it did not mean automatic return to the community, but the child would be locked in her own room for a transition period.

* * *

It is important to note that after her departure from the school Judge Burstein energetically attempted through administrative channels to secure relief for Lollis. * * * Finally, through efforts of the National Council on Crime and Delinquency, Judge Burstein was able to speak to the Deputy Commissioner in Charge of Institutions, who arranged for Lollis to be released on September 4, 1970, two weeks after she had been originally isolated.

In opposition to the Lollis motion, an equally detailed, undated, report of Superintendent Frank Shaughnessy states that the strip room (described...as a "security room") measures 9′4" × 7′8", that the bed is a "bunk bed built into one of the walls, attached to the walls and the floor," 7′8" long, 2′7" wide and 1′6 1/2" high. A mattress is made available at night. It is claimed that the top pane of the window was low enough to permit visibility, and that the lower panes were painted to prevent an inmate from distracting other inmates engaged in recreation outside the room. Girls in a "security room" are kept in pajamas to prevent absconding and the hiding of dangerous objects. Lollis was issued a bathrobe, but destroyed it; for this reason it was not replaced. The use of the bathroom and the shower is made available. It is stated that Lollis was visited on a number of occasions by child care workers to discuss her case and by nurses. She continued her aggressive and anti-social behavior. Her case was reviewed daily by the Adjustment Committee, and on September 4th, the Committee decided that, since Lollis "indicated a willingness to resume the program and maintain herself," she should be returned to her own room in preparation for later resumption of normal activities, which occurred on September 9th. The report further states that "every effort is made to return a youngster to the regular program as quickly as possible" and that the girls are allowed to write their family and to receive letters while confined in a "secure room."

* * *

III.

I come now to the merits of the Lollis case.

The Eighth Amendment's prohibition of cruel and unusual punishment is binding on the states through the Fourteenth Amendment. Robinson v. California, 370 U.S. 660, 82 S.Ct. 1417, 8 L.Ed.2d 758 (1962); Francis v. Resweber 329 U.S. 459, 67 S.Ct. 374, 91 L.Ed. 422 (1947).

The concept of cruel and unusual punishment has, of course, varied through the course of history, and as the court observed in Trop v. Dulles, 356 U.S. 86, 101 78 S.Ct. 590, 598, 2 L.Ed.2d 630 (1958):

> "The [Eighth] Amendment must draw its meaning from the evolving standards of decency that mark the progress of a maturing society."

Two tests have been applied to determine whether the amendment applies: first, whether the punishment is disproportionate to the offense, Weems v. United States 217 U.S. 349, 30 S.Ct. 544, 54 L.Ed. 793 (1909); second the severity or harshness of the sanction as measured by "broad and idealistic concepts of dignity, civilized standards, humanity and decency * * *" Jackson v. Bishop, 404 F.2d 571, 579 (8th Cir. 1968) Opinion of Judge (now Mr. Justice) Blackmum.

In support of Lollis motion there have been submitted the affidavits of seven psychiatrists, psychologists, and educators of delinquent juveniles. They are unanimous in their condemnation of extended isolation as imposed on children, finding it not only cruel and inhuman, but counterproductive to the development of the child. This group is made up of men and women of high standing and expertise [footnote omitted]. Most surprisingly, although the key to decision of the Eighth Amendment issue lies in a determination as to whether Lollis' two week isolation in a stripped room was disproportionate or inherently harsh, no affidavit on the subject has been submitted by the defendants. Indeed, the only contest, if it may be termed a contest, which defendants have made of the affidavits of experts supporting plaintiff's motion is to offer an unsworn statement of Superintendent Shaughnessy entitled, "Isolation Policies," which refers (1) to the writings of Dr. William Glasser whose qualifications are not set forth; (2) to certain experimental work of "Tyler and Brown" and "Burchard and Tyler" not identified in any way, however well known they may or may not be to the cognoscenti; and (3) to the views of Dr. Lewis Jarett, a consultant at the Brookwood Annex, who is director of Columbia County Mental Health Clinic (N.Y.), that the use of security rooms can be a "helpful experience." Even if Superintendent Shaughnessy's statement with its second-hand references to the views of others were to be accorded the quality of an affidavit, it is clearly outweighed by the affidavits in support of the plaintiff's motion, not because of their number, (though that is impressive), but because of the standing of the affiants, the wealth and diversity of their expertise, and the unconditional nature of their opinions.

* * *

Concern as to isolated or solitary confinement of children in New York State Training Schools is not of sudden origin. As a result of the primary urging of the Citizens' Committee for the Children of New York, Inc., an established private welfare organization which had studied state training schools in depth [citation omitted], the New York State Legislature at its 1970 session passed Assembly Bill 4658 intended to regulate the imposition of such confinement. The bill, which would have barred solitary confinement for children under 13 (except for medical reasons, and then only when authorized by medical personnel) and allowed such confinement for older children by administrative personnel only up to 24 hours, and thereafter upon certification of the State Commissioner of Social Services only up to 48 hours, was vetoed by the Governor on grounds urged by the highly respected Community Service Society (of New York City) that the regulation of such isolation should be administrative rather than legislative to allow some element of flexibility. In his veto message, the Governor expressed his concern as to the isolated confinement of children and "urged" the New York State Department of Social Services to enact regulations to control such confinement, which as noted earlier, the State Board of Social Welfare did in fact do during July, 1970 [citation omitted].

Measured by the standards of the Eighth Amendment cases cited above, the views of experts in the field of adolescent psychology, just quoted, and the legislative consensus expressed by the passage of Assembly Bill 4658, a two-week confinement of a fourteen-year-old girl in a stripped room in night clothes with no recreational facilities or even reading matter must be held to violate the Constitution's ban on cruel and unusual punishment [citation omitted].

In so holding, I do not mean to intimate that the isolation of children under any circumstances is unconstitutional, but merely that the treatment of Lollis in this case violated permissible bounds. I share the hesitancy of fellow judges in interfering with the administration of custodial institutions, and sympathize with the difficult problems which disciplinary matters present to administrative officials, especially when they may be "second guessed" by the courts. But the teaching of Wright v. McMann, *supra*, 387 F.2d 519, is that where a constitutional violation occurs the courts may not ignore it in favor of the integrity of administrative authority.

The determination that the Eighth Amendment has here been violated renders it unnecessary to determine whether the treatment of Lollis may also be vulnerable under other provisions of the Constitution.

* * *

Accordingly, defendant Shaughnessy and anyone subject to his direction will be enjoined, pending trial, from placing plaintiff in isolation for an extended period or without the enjoyment of reasonable facilities during any such isolation. For the purpose of implementing this injunction, there shall be included in the decree standards for the imposition of any isolation...Defendant Shaughnessy shall, within 10 days of the filing of this opinion, submit to the court and to the plaintiff's counsel proposed standards...* * *

Plaintiff's request for a preliminary injunction to restrain "defendants from imposing prolonged solitary confinement upon any child confined to a New York State Training School" is denied, without prejudice, except to the extent granted above. There is no showing that the action of other defendants is such as to warrant interference by the court, or that other children are in jeopardy [footnote omitted]. Indeed, the record establishes that isolation is never invoked at five of the twelve training schools, and rarely at two others. While the box score is not entirely satisfactory, it does demonstrate the inappropriateness of a statewide injunction...* * *

* * *

LOLLIS V. NEW YORK STATE DEPARTMENT OF SOCIAL SERVICES

1. Note that the *Lollis* case is dated 1970, three years prior to the development and dissemination of the report by the National Advisory Commission on Criminal Justice Standards and Goals. In the juvenile justice area, this report recommended the development of programs for neglected children, for increasing the use of diversion, and for using institutionalization as a last resort. These policies were adopted by many states, but not in a uniform way. Critique the placement of Antoinette Lollis in the Brookwood Annex from the perspective of the National Advisory Commission.

2. Assess the use of the "security room" in Brookwood. Be sure to apply an Eighth Amendment analysis.

3. Why did the U.S. District Court refuse to issue a state-wide injunction to halt solitary confinement practices in New York State training schools?

FLORA SANTANA, ET AL., PLAINTIFFS, APPELLANTS,

V.

JENARO COLLAZO COLLAZO, ET AL., DEFENDANTS, APPELLEES.

FLORA SANTANA, ET AL., PLAINTIFFS, APPELLEES,

AND

UNITED STATES OF AMERICA, PLAINTIFF-INTERVENOR, APPELLANT,

V.

JENARO COLLAZO, ET AL., DEFENDANTS, APPELLEES.

NO. 82–1345, 82–1418.

UNITED STATES COURT OF APPEALS, FIRST CIRCUIT.

ARGUED JUNE 8, 1983.

DECIDED AUG. 3, 1983.

REHEARING AND REHEARING EN BANC DENIED SEPT. 30, 1983.

* * *

COFFIN, CIRCUIT JUDGE.

In October, 1975 eight juvenile residents of the Mayaguez Industrial School (Mayaguez), in Mayaguez, Puerto Rico, filed a complaint under 42 U.S.C. § 1983, urging the court to declare conditions at Mayaguez unconstitutional. * * *

Between August 11, 1978, and June, 1979, the parties submitted three proposed consent decrees, all of which the district court rejected as "unduly and unnecessarily disruptive of the Commonwealth's juvenile justice system."

* * * On February 15, 1982, the court rendered its decision, reported at 533 F.Supp. 966 (D.P.R.1982). It analyzed the legal theories on which the plaintiffs relied and set out detailed factual findings regarding the conditions at the camps. The court rejected the plaintiffs' proposed "right to treatment," but agreed that conditions at the camp were reviewable under the Eighth Amendment and the due process clause [footnote omitted]. With five exceptions, relating primarily to the use of the intensive care or "isolation" unit at Mayaguez, see 533 F.Supp. at 992, the court found conditions at Mayaguez and Maricao constitutionally acceptable.

On appeal, plaintiff's challenge the court's refusal to enter the proposed consent decrees. They also renew their claim for a "right to treatment," and on that basis, challenge a number of conditions and deprivations which the court found constitutionally acceptable. Finally, they urge that certain conditions, particularly those relating to the use of the isolation unit as a disciplinary sanction, which use the district court did not enjoin or limit, violate their right not to be cruelly and unusually punished. * * *

II. CONDITIONS OF CONFINEMENT AT MAYAGUEZ AND MARICAO

On appeal, plaintiffs renew both their "right to treatment" claims and their Eighth Amendment challenge to the length of time a juvenile may be confined in isolation at Mayaguez and to the conditions under which the juveniles live while so isolated. We agree with the district court that the state has no constitutional obligation to provide rehabilitative treatment to the juveniles within its custody, simply because its professed purpose in taking custody of the juveniles is to help them. We are concerned, however, that the district court, in rejecting the right to treatment, may have passed too lightly over other substantive limitations on the conditions of involuntary confinement, particularly the extensive use of isolation at Mayaguez. Before addressing those concerns, we pause to explain why we agree with the district court's rejection of a broad right to rehabilitative treatment and training.

A. Right to Rehabilitative Treatment and Training

Plaintiffs challenge, as violative of their right to rehabilitative treatment, the inadequate intake assessment of each juvenile's psychiatric, medical, academic, vocational and social strengths, weaknesses and needs, coupled with the inadequate classification system (based on age and physical characteristics); the absence of adequate individualized treatment plans covering all aspects of each juvenile's care, education, growth and development; the absence of adequate educational, vocational and recreational programs; the deficient qualifications and training of the staff; and overreliance on the custodial staff. Basically, they claim that the juveniles are just being incarcerated, not rehabilitated, and that in light of the state's professed purpose in institutionalizing the juveniles—to treat them—the state has an obligation to provide the promised treatment.

A number of courts have found that juveniles involuntarily incarcerated have a right to rehabilitative treatment (*See, e.g., Morgan v. Sproat* 432 F.Supp. 1130 (S.D. Miss.1977); *Martarella v. Kelley*, 349 F.Supp. 575, 586, 600 (S.D.N.Y.1972); *Nelson v. Heyne*, 355 F.Supp. 451 (N.D.Ind.1972) *aff'd* 491 F.2d 352 (7th Cir.1974). The reasoning of these courts is two-fold. First, relying on the Supreme Court's insistence, in *Jackson v. Indiana*, 406 U.S.715, 738, 92 S.Ct. 1845, 1858, 32 L.Ed.2d 435 (1972), that "the nature and duration of commitment must bear some reasonable relation to the purpose for which the individual is committed," courts have reasoned that because the state's authority over delinquent juveniles derives from its parens patriæ interest in their welfare, see, *e.g.*, 34 L.P.R.A. § 2015, due process requires that juveniles confined under that authority be given treatment consistent with the beneficent purpose of their confinement. *See Morgan v. Sproat, supra*, 432 F.Supp. at 1135–36; *Martarella v. Kelley, supra*, 349 F.Supp. at 585. Second, courts have relied on the fact that the juvenile justice system denied certain due process safeguards, which denials have been found constitutionally acceptable because the purpose of incarceration is rehabilitation, not punishment [citation omitted]. Thus, the "quid pro quo" for the denied safeguards us the promised rehabilitation. *See Morgan v. Sproat, supra*, 432 F.Supp. at 1136 and the cases discussed therein.

As the district court in this case recognized, both of the theoretical bases for the claimed right to rehabilitative treatment are questionable. Although states have asserted their parens patriæ authority in exercising control over problem juveniles, they may legitimately confine individuals solely to protect society from them. *See, O'Conner v. Donaldson,* 422 U.S. 563, 583, 95 S.Ct. 2486, 2497, 45 L.Ed.2d 396 (1975) (Burger, C.J., concurring); *McKeiver v. Pennsylvania*,...403 U.S. at 546 n. 6, 91 S.Ct. at 1986 n. 6. In addition, even without treatment, simply removing a juvenile from a dangerous or unhealthy environment may be a legitimate exercise of the state's *parens patriæ* authority [footnote omitted]. *Cf. O'Conner v. Donaldson, supra*, 422 U.S. at 584, 95 S.Ct. 2498. *See also Morales v. Turman*, 562 F.2d 993, 998 (5th Cir.1977). In short, since rehabilitative treatment is not the only legitimate purpose of juvenile confinement, the Supreme Court's insistence that the nature of confinement must bear a rational relationship to the purpose of confinement gains plaintiffs little ground in their effort to establish a right to rehabilitative treatment.

The second aspect of the quid pro quo theory has even less merit. The procedural protections accorded juvenile offenders may differ from those accorded criminal defendants, because the demands of due process differ according to the interests of the individual and of society in the given situation. *See Morrissey v. Brewer*, 408 U.S. 471, 480–84, 92 S.Ct. 2593, 2599–01, 33 L.Ed.2d 484 (1972); *Morales v. Turman, supra*, 562 F.2d at 998. The Supreme Court has found certain distinctions between the protections accorded juveniles and those accorded criminal defendants constitutionally acceptable *See, e.g., McKeiver v. Pennsylvania*, 403 U.S. at 550–51, 91 S.Ct. at 1988–89. Were that not the case, no amount of treatment would make up for the denial of due process along the way. *Cf. O'Conner v. Donaldson, supra*, 422 U.S. at 585–88, 95 S.Ct. 2498-2500 (Burger, C.J., concurring.)

In short, there is no legally cognizable quo to trigger a compensatory quid. We therefore agree with the district court that although rehabilitative training is no doubt desirable and sound as a matter of policy, and perhaps, of state law [footnote omitted], plaintiffs have no constitutional right to that rehabilitative training. With that in mind, we turn to the plaintiffs' challenge to the practice of confining juveniles to the isolation unit at Mayaguez as punishment for disciplinary infractions.

B. Due Process and Eighth Amendment Limitations on the Confinement of Juveniles to Isolation.

The district court made a number of factual findings regarding the use of isolation at Mayaguez.[31] See 533 F.Supp. at 983, 989–90. The Court noted, for instance that:

[31]There is no isolation unit at Maricao.

"34. The intensive care complex at Mayaguez, which is also referred to as the 'isolation' or 'disciplinary' unit, is a separate concrete building located approximately fifty yards from the quadrangle where the regular dormitories are located. It...is surrounded by a ten foot high chain link fence, topped with barbed wire. The cells face inward and are approximately nine feet by nine feet square in size. They contain one bed, a toilet facility and a window facing the outside of the building. The window and the door are barred. The ceiling is ten to twelve feet high. The cells themselves are clean, but bare, except for a wood slab with a foam mattress covered by a sheet, and a wash basin and toilet. Cross ventilation offers adequate ventilation. Neither the door nor windows are screened.

"74. It is a regular practice in Mayaguez to separate juveniles individually from the rest of the inmate population for disciplinary reasons. Juveniles so sanctioned are placed in the individual cells....

"76. The average length of stay in the isolation cells, from September 18, 1979 to December 18, 1979 which is a representative period, was 13.3 days. There are, however, several known cases of juveniles having spent several months at one stretch in isolation.

"77. The sole activity of juveniles while in isolation is eating and sleeping. They do not attend the Mayaguez academic or vocational program and are not allowed any writing or reading material in their cells except the Bible. Furthermore, they are not allowed any physical exercise or recreation; the only time they are allowed out of their isolation cell is for a daily shower."

The court then enjoined certain uses of the isolation unit as unconstitutional. It forbade commitment of a juvenile to isolation because of "any illness, sickness, or physical or mental defect of disease"; commitment to isolation of any pre-trial juvenile detainee; and commitment to isolation of any juvenile without notice of the charges against him and an opportunity to contest them. It also instructed defendants to write and post disciplinary rules specifying proscribed conduct and resulting sanctions. *Id.*, at 992. * * *

A number of courts have found conditions of isolation similar to those at Mayaguez unconstitutional when imposed on juvenile offenders. *See e.g., Feliciano v. Barcelo*, 497 F.Supp. 14 (D.P.R.1979); *Morgan v. Sproat, supra*, 432 F.Supp. at 1138–40; *Pena v. New York State Division for Youth*, 419 F.Supp. 203, 210–211 (S.D.N.Y.1976); *Nelson v. Heyne, supra*, 355 F.Supp. at 456–57; *Inmates of Boys' Training School v. Affleck*, 346 F.Supp. 1354 (D.R.I.1972); *Lollis v. New York State Department of Social Services*, 322 F.Supp. 473, 482 (S.D.N.Y.1970),.... The reasoning of those courts however, has been closely tied to their determinations that conditions of juvenile detention must be rehabilitative [citations omitted].

The Supreme Court has not addressed the use of isolation in a juvenile detention center. While we are unwilling to say that isolation of juveniles is necessarily unconstitutional, we are satisfied that the conditions relevant to an assessment of isolation in a juvenile camp are somewhat different from those relevant to an assessment of the same treatment in a prison. In the first place, as the Supreme Court has noted, there is no simple test for determining whether conditions of confinement are cruel and unusual. The Eighth Amendment draws its meaning from "evolving standards of decency that mark the progress of a maturing society." *Trop v. Dulles*, 356 U.S. 86, 101, 78 S.Ct. 590, 598, 2 L.Ed.2d 630 (1958). It would not be unreasonable to assume that society's conscience might be shocked by the conditions of confinement imposed on a juvenile in an isolation cell, when it would be unwilling to label the same treatment, given to an adult, cruel and unusual. See, *e.g.*, *Lollis v. New York State Department of Social Services*, 328 F.Supp. at 1118.

Even more important than Eighth Amendment concerns, for our purposes, juveniles, like plaintiffs, who have not yet been convicted of crimes, have a due process interest in freedom from unnecessary bodily restraint which entitles them to closer scrutiny of their conditions of confinement than that accorded convicted criminals. In *Youngberg v. Romero*, 457 U.S. 307, 102 S.Ct. 2452, 73 L.Ed.2d 28 (U.S.1982), for instance, the Supreme Court required that restrictions on the liberty of an involuntarily confined mental patient be reasonably related to legitimate governmental interests imposing those restrictions. Although it noted that even convicted criminals retain a liberty interest in freedom from bodily restraint, the Court indicated that the interest is entitled to more careful protection when the individual asserting it has not been convicted of a crime. See 457 U.S. at 320, 102 S.Ct. at 2460.

* * *

The Supreme Court has recognized that the deprivation of liberty and conditions of confinement of both juvenile detainees and involuntary confinement of the mentally ill may be sufficiently analogous to criminal punishment to warrant the protection of the Eighth Amendment. *See Ingraham v. Wright*, 430 U.S. at 669 n. 37, 97 S.Ct. at 1411 n. 37. The possibility of Eighth Amendment protection, however, does not mean that the state may assert punishment as a legitimate goal of incarceration. Thus, because the state has no legitimate interest in punishment, the conditions of juvenile confinement, like those of confinement of the mentally ill, are subject to more exacting scrutiny than conditions imposed on convicted criminals. *See Youngberg*, 457 U.S. at 321, 102 S.Ct. at 2461 * * *

The distinction between conditions imposed for the legitimate purpose of maintaining institutional order and safety and those that amount to retribution is a fine one. See *Bell v. Wolfish*, 441 U.S. at 535–40, 99 S.Ct. at 1872–74. Certainly, administrators of a juvenile home must be free to discipline the home's residents. And, in doing so, the state, of course inflicts punishment for offending behavior. The distinction, however, is not an entirely meaningless one, *Cf. Ingraham v. Wright*, 430 U.S. at 671 & n. 40, 97 S.Ct. at 1412 & n. 40 (distinguishing between disciplinary punishment which requires no Eighth Amendment scrutiny, and retributive punishment, which requires criminal conviction). In a case such as this, it may simply be a matter of the closeness with which courts should be willing to scrutinize the state's asserted interest in imposing burdensome conditions of confinement. When conditions are imposed on convicted criminals, the Supreme Court has deferred to the judgment of prison administrators unless conditions are cruel and unusual, because "[t]o the extent that such conditions are restrictive and even harsh, they are part of the penalty that criminal offenders pay for their offenses against society." *Rhodes v. Chapman*, 452 U.S. at 347, 101 S.Ct. at 2399. For an individual not convicted of a crime, however, restrictions on his liberty beyond his initial incarceration must be reasonably related to some legitimate governmental objective—of rehabilitation, safety or internal order and security. *See Youngberg*, 457 U.S. at 320, 102 S.Ct. at 2460; *Bell v. Wolfish*, 441 U.S. at 539, 99 S.Ct. at 1874. * * *

The district court did not have the benefit of the Supreme Court's guidance in *Youngberg*, and made no findings regarding the legitimacy and weight of the state's interest in confining the juveniles in isolation. Were there nothing of concern in the record, we might be inclined to assume that the state's interest, presumably in protecting the juveniles from harm, in discouraging offending behavior and in preventing escapes, was sufficient to justify the deprivations imposed. A number of experts testified, however, that isolation for longer than a few hours serves no legitimate therapeutic or disciplinary purpose and is unnecessary to prevent harm unless a juvenile is severely emotionally disturbed. In addition, the experts testified [that] extended isolation can be psychologically damaging, and under the conditions at Mayaguez, may be physically harmful.[32] The district court recognized that "[i]solation as a disciplinary measure, under the circumstances present in this case, entails a substantial curtailment of a juvenile's freedom." 533 F.Supp. at 990. We agree and are satisfied that the curtailment is enough to warrant further examination of the necessity for and conditions of this confinement.

The Supreme Court has cautioned us against substituting our judgment for that of correctional officials charged with maintaining institutional order and security. *Bell v. Wolfish*, 441 U.S. at 547–48, 99 S.Ct. at 1878–79. It may be that certain juveniles at Mayaguez are so difficult to control [and] that extended isolation is a reasonable way to maintain order, prevent injury and deter escapes. In that case, regardless of the wisdom of such a practice as a matter of policy and of the fact that juveniles may suffer from the practice, we would be unwilling to say, on the record before us, that the practice was unconstitutional. On the other hand, when a juvenile is confined in isolation for an extended period of time—sometimes months—with little attention from camp administrators or counselors, no exercise, and no contact with other juveniles, it seems likely that the experience accomplishes nothing more than the unnecessary infliction of pain. Whatever the constitutional legitimacy of such practices in a prison, we consider ourselves charged by the Supreme Court's due process analysis in *Youngberg* and *Bell v. Wolfish* to ask whether the significant restriction of the juveniles' liberty interests is reasonably related to a legitimate governmental objective, or simply adds to the punishment already imposed by incarceration.

The district court made no findings regarding the therapeutic or damaging effects of extended isolation. It ordered defendants to post disciplinary rules specifying proscribed conduct and sanctions to be imposed for violations thereof, but set no limits on the length of time a juvenile may be put in isolation, the offenses that would warrant it, or the conditions that a juvenile may be subject to while in isolation. Rather than substitute our judgment for that of the district court, we think a remand is necessary for the court to consider, based on the testimony already presented to it and its own examination of conditions at

[32]Juveniles held in the isolation unit at Mayaguez apparently have suffered dehydration, numerous insect bites, severe depression and signs of sensory deprivation.

Mayaguez, whether and to what extent isolation as employed there is reasonably related to any legitimate governmental objectives. In doing so, the court should consider whether isolation should be limited to certain time periods and should require additional safeguards, such as close supervision by a qualified expert and periodic review of the continuing need for isolation. Finally, the court should consider whether minimal additional individual attention might reduce the need for isolation * * *

Several witnesses testified that a major source of the camp's inability to address its disciplinary and escape problems without the extensive use of isolation is the fact that it makes little effort to separate juveniles according to their particular problems, but only according to size and age. Thus, while one juvenile may be incorrigible, a number of others are simply retarded and could benefit from training in how to conform their behavior to acceptable patterns. Instead, they learn from their incorrigible peers, with whom they are cast. Similarly, dealing with emotionally disturbed juveniles as a group with common problems might significantly reduce the emotional outbursts leading to their confinement in isolation. * * *

...[I]f the state can avoid the current extensive use of isolation by minimal additional attention—to distinguish between and attempting to address the sources rather than the effects of the residents' behavior problems, it may well be unreasonable for the state not to do so [citation omitted]...If behavior problems at Mayaguez are attributable to a limited number of particularly difficult older juveniles, removal of those few might enable the administrators to maintain control of the situation and avoid the need for placing a number of juveniles in extended isolation. We profess no expertise in the administration of a camp for juveniles. Nor have we, like the district court, had the benefit of first hand knowledge of the evidence in the case and physical examination of the camps themselves. We are, however, troubled by the possibility that some juveniles at Mayaguez have been and will continue to be subjected to unpleasant and perhaps physically and psychologically damaging restrictions on their liberty that are not reasonably related to legitimate governmental interests in imposing those restrictions.

* * *

...On the remaining issues of the constitutionality of defendants' use of isolation as a disciplinary sanction at Mayaguez...the judgment is vacated and remanded for further proceedings consistent with this opinion....

SANTANA V. COLLAZO

1. What is the logic for the U.S. Court of Appeals' ruling that "the state has no constitutional obligation to provide rehabilitative treatment to the juveniles within its custody"? How does this square with the history of juvenile justice and its legislative intent (*i.e.*, socialized juvenile court history)?

2. Is incapacitation a legitimate legislative intent of juvenile incarceration? Explain.

3. Compare the holding in *Santana v. Collazo* with *Nelson v. Heyne*.

4. Explicate the *quid pro quo* doctrine as it applies to "right to treatment" cases in juvenile corrections.

C. Parole Revocation

Finally, like adult offenders, juveniles can be paroled from institutions. The case below considers what due process protections are necessary before a juvenile's parole can be revoked.

THE PEOPLE OF THE STATE OF NEW YORK EX REL. JAMES SILBERT, AS LAW GUARDIAN, ON BEHALF OF ANTHONY R., RESPONDENT,

V.

A. ALFRED COHEN, AS THE SUPERINTENDENT OF WARWICK STATE TRAINING SCHOOL FOR BOYS, APPELLANT.

THE PEOPLE OF THE STATE OF NEW YORK EX REL. JAMES SILBERT, AS LAW GUARDIAN, ON BEHALF OF RODERICK R., RESPONDENT,

V.

A. ALFRED COHEN, AS THE SUPERINTENDENT OF WARWICK STATE TRAINING SCHOOL FOR BOYS, APPELLANT.

COURT OF APPEALS OF NEW YORK.

JUNE 9, 1971.

* * *

FULD, CHIEF JUDGE.

In People ex rel Menechino v. Warden 27 N.Y.2d 376, 318 N.Y.S.2d 449, 267 N.E.2d 238, this court held that adult parolees are constitutionally entitled to the assistance of counsel on parole revocation hearings. (See also People ex rel. Maggio v. Casscles 28 N.Y.2d 415, 322 N.Y.S.2d 688, 271 N.E.2d 517.) [footnote omitted] On this appeal, we must decide whether juvenile delinquents have a similar right to a hearing and the aid of an attorney.

In November of 1966, Anthony R. and Roderick R. were adjudged juvenile delinquents and subsequently placed on probation. In July, 1967, their probation was revoked and they were later placed in Highland State Training School for a period of 18 months. Roderick was paroled in June, 1968 and Anthony in October, 1968. When they were paroled, neither they nor their parents were advised of the conditions of parole. In June, 1970, new delinquency petitions, alleging acts of assault and petit larceny, were filed against both boys. Although charges were dismissed, their parole was revoked, pursuant to section 437 of the Social Services Law (formerly the Social Welfare Law), without a hearing and they were returned to the training school. The boys' law guardian, who had urged the court to grant revocation hearings, thereupon sued out writs of habeas corpus on their behalf, claiming that the refusal to permit such hearings constituted a denial of due process. The court at Special Term denied the requested relief, but, on appeal, the Appellate Division reversed, sustained the writs and ordered both boys discharged from custody. It was the Appellate Division's conclusion that "[r]evocation of parole, whether of a juvenile or an adult, is a deprivation of liberty [and that] due process requires a fair hearing precede such deprivation." (36 A.D.2d 331, 332, 320 N.Y.S.2d 608, 609.)

As we indicated in Menechino 27 N.Y.2d at p. 382, 318 N.Y.S.2d at p. 453, 267 N.E.2d at p. 241), a parolee may not again be deprived of his liberty unless the parole board decides, after a hearing, that he has violated his parole. The hearing to be accorded him is, we declared, "an accusatory proceeding in which the outcome—liberty or imprisonment—is dependent upon the board's factual determination as to the truth of specific allegations of misconduct." This being so, the proceeding involves a deprivation of liberty just as much as did the original criminal action and, by that token, falls within the protective ambit of due process.

The right to be heard would be "of little avail if it did not comprehend the right to be heard by counsel" (Powell v. Alabama, 287 U.S. 45, 68–69, 53 S.Ct. 55, 64, 77 L.Ed. 158) and no tribunal, whether board or court should be allowed to base its determination on a possibly mistaken view of the facts owing to the parolee's inability, absent counsel, to make a proper factual presentation. It is for such a reason, among others, that the right to a lawyer, far from being limited to the narrow confines of criminal prosecutions, has been treated as "an essential element of due process, applicable to all proceedings, whether they be classified as civil, criminal or administrative, where individual liberty is at stake." (People ex rel Menechino v. Warden 27 N.Y.2d 376, 383, 318 N.Y.S.2d 449, 454, 267 N.E.2d 238, 242, *supra.*)

Since due process demands notice, a hearing and the aid of counsel, it is beside the point that there is no statute requiring that a juvenile be afforded a hearing in a parole revocation proceeding. As a matter of fact, section 437 of the Social Services Law actually authorizes the revocation of parole and the return of a juvenile to a training school without any hearing whatsoever. Indeed, in the two cases before us, neither of the boys, their father, nor their law guardian were ever informed as to what the conditions of parole were, much less the conditions which had been assertedly violated; even the Family Court judge who revoked parole was not sure of the reasons for such action.

The circumstance that we deal with a juvenile rather than an adult does not call for a different result. The Supreme Court expressly stated in In re Gault, 387 U.S. 1, 10, 87 S.Ct. 1428, 1435, 18 L.Ed.2d 527, that before a "juvenile is taken from the custody of his parents and committed to a state institution pursuant to proceedings in which the Juvenile Court has virtually unlimited discretion," fundamental fairness and due process require that "the following rights" be accorded him: "1. Notice of the charges; 2. Right to counsel; 3. Right to confrontation and cross-examination; 4. Privilege against self incrimination; 5. Right to a transcript of the proceedings; and 6. Right to appellate review." Insistence upon such procedural safeguards will not undercut or interfere with the Family Court's goal of rehabilitation.

The Attorney-General contends that the requisite hearing should be informal. As long as the juvenile has an opportunity to rebut the charge leveled against him and as long as his attorney is able to ask questions that test the testimony offered against him, due process is assured. It is, of course, difficult to mandate "informality." The type of hearing, its length, its character, must be left to the sound discretion of the Family Court judge and, in this connection the Supreme Court's language in *Gault* is instructive. "It is urged," the Court stated, "that the juvenile benefits from informal proceedings in the court. The early conception of the Juvenile Court proceeding was one in which a fatherly judge touched the heart and conscience of the erring youth by talking over his problems, by paternal advice and admonition, and in which, in extreme situations, benevolent and wise institutions of the State provided guidance and help 'to save him from a downward career.' Then, as now, goodwill and compassion were admirably prevalent. But recent studies have, with surprising unanimity, entered sharp dissent as to the validity of this gentle conception. They suggest that the appearance as well as the actuality of fairness, impartiality and orderliness—in short, the essentials of due process—may be a more impressive and more therapeutic attitude so far as the juvenile is concerned." (387 U.S. at pp. 25-26, 87 S.Ct. 1442).

* * *

There is no warrant for the fear that to give the juvenile a right to such basic procedural safeguards will provoke friction in the hopefully beneficent relationship between him and his social worker and, certainly, no justification for the belief that a hearing and the presence of an attorney will unduly prolong the parole revocation proceeding or transmute it into a full-blown trial. A lawyer's assistance is needed in order to marshal the facts and introduce evidence of mitigating circumstances, in short, to help the juvenile to present his case [citation omitted]. To paraphrase what we wrote in Menechino 27 N.Y.2d 376, 383 318 N.Y.S.2d 449, 454 267 N.E.2d 238, 242 *supra*) participation by counsel need be no greater than is required to assure, to the court as well as the parolee, that the court is accurately informed of the facts and the presentation of testimony need be no greater than is necessary for the same purpose.

* * *

The order appealed from should be affirmed, without costs.

People ex rel. Silbert v. Cohen

1. What rights do juvenile parolees have when the State is attempting to revoke their parole and reincarcerate them? Place this answer in the context of procedural due process.

2. Why did the New York Attorney General argue that the parole revocation proceeding should be informal?

3. What role should defense counsel play at juvenile parole revocation proceedings? Is there a "right to counsel" for indigent juveniles during parole revocation proceedings?

4. Compare and contrast the rights of adults and juveniles in parole revocation proceedings (see *Morrissey v. Brewer* 92 S.Ct. 2593, 1972).

CONCLUSION

This chapter has illustrated a variety of critical issues surrounding the various dispositional alternatives for adjudicated juvenile delinquents. In the chapter that follows, we explore a variety of issues pertaining to the death penalty for first degree murderers under the age of twenty-one.[33]

[33]Chapter 6 in our 1995 expanded edition of this text comprises a variety of recurring themes and emerging issues in juvenile justice in addition to the death penalty controversy.

CHAPTER 6

THE DEATH PENALTY AND JUVENILE MURDERERS

THE DEATH PENALTY AND JUVENILE MURDERERS

IMPOSING THE DEATH PENALTY ON JUVENILE MURDERERS: A CONSTITUTIONAL ASSESSMENT[1]

INTRODUCTION

For nearly a century, the juvenile court has existed to shield the majority of youthful offenders from the full weight of the criminal law (Ryerson, 1978; Mennel, 1973; Fox, 1970). As Justice Fortas noted in *Kent v. United States* (1966:1055), a juvenile placed under the court's protection is entitled to a variety of "special rights and immunities." For example:

> He is...shielded from publicity. He may be confined, but with rare exceptions, he may not be jailed along with adults. He may be detained, but only until he is 21 years of age. The court is admonished by the statute to give preference to retaining the child in the custody of his parents "unless his welfare and the safety and protection of the public cannot be adequately safeguarded without...removal." The child is protected against the consequences of adult conviction such as the loss of civil rights, the use of adjudication against him in subsequent proceedings and disqualification for public employment (*Kent v. United States*, 1966:1055).

In theory at least, the special procedures of the juvenile court "provide measures of guidance and rehabilitation for the child and protection for society..." (*Kent v. United States*, 1966:1054). And, despite intense criticism, confidence in the court's rehabilitative orientation—described in *Kent* and subsequent Supreme Court decisions (*e.g.*, *In re Gault*, 1967; *In re Winship*, 1970; *Breed v. Jones*, 1975), and discussed in detail by many others (*e.g.*, Ryerson, 1978; Mennel, 1973; Fox, 1970; Platt, 1972)—remains strong. For example, the National Coalition of State Juvenile Justice Advisory Groups has recently taken the position that "the vast majority of juvenile offenders can be successfully rehabilitated when provided with a treatment program that has a specific plan of care..." (Juvenile Justice Digest, *cited in* Whitehead and Lab, 1990:399).

Policy makers recognize, however, that there are some youths who are extremely dangerous, or not amendable to the treatment offered by the juvenile court. As a result, all the states and the District of

[1]The text in this section of the Chapter is taken from Gewerth and Dorne, "Imposing the Death Penalty on Juvenile Murderers: A Constitutional Assessment" 75 *Judicature* (June/July 1991) and appears with the permission of the American Judicature Society. The original citation format has been preserved; the references for this section can be found at the conclusion of the Chapter.

Columbia have established mechanisms for transferring or waiving juvenile court jurisdiction in these exceptional cases so that young offenders can be tried in a criminal court and punished as adults (for an overview of these provisions, see, Jamison and Flanagan, 1989:159-61 [Table 1.105]). Once a case is waived to adult court for trial, an accused youth loses the "special rights and immunities" offered by the juvenile court. In addition, the accused youth is subject to the full range of penalties for criminal behavior, including, at least in some jurisdictions, execution (*Thompson v. State*, 1986:784).

While the number of juvenile offenders on death row is extremely small,[2] several recent U.S. Supreme Court decisions (*Eddings v. Oklahoma*, 1982; *Thompson v. Oklahoma*, 1988; *Stanford v. Kentucky*, 1989) and the publicity generated in another involving an Indiana juvenile named Paula Cooper (Hackett, King and Stanger, 1987), has prompted legislators (Streib, 1986, 1987a), academics (Hamm, 1987, 1989; Skovron, Scott and Cullen, 1986; Streib, 1987b) and others (Southern Coalition on Jails and Prisons, 1986) to examine this difficult problem in some detail. The purpose of this paper is to review the constitutional issues surrounding the capital punishment of offenders whose crimes were committed as juveniles. To facilitate the analysis of this complex topic, we will begin with a description of the nature and extent of the protection afforded by the cruel and unusual punishment clause of the Eighth Amendment (U.S. Constitution, Amend. VIII), and a review of the standards and methods judges must employ to determine if a punishment violates this provision. In the course of this review we will focus primarily on how the U.S. Supreme Court has applied these standards and methods of review in capital cases. Then, we will focus on judicial interpretation and application of such standards to juvenile executions. The issue of "youth as a mitigating factor" is emphasized, but other concerns are addressed as well such as public opinion, laws of other nations, juvenile offender psychological responsibility, and whether or not executing juveniles satisfies the so-called social "objectives" of capital punishment. The conclusion brings these issues back to bear on the Eighth Amendment as they may guide future high court reviews of juvenile death penalty cases.

The Constitution, Punishment, and the Penalty of Death

A. Non-Controversial Issues Regarding the Scope of Eighth Amendment Protection

1. Only Acts are Punishable

Despite the intense debate surrounding the precise meaning of the cruel and unusual punishment clause and its relationship to capital punishment, there are a few aspects of the controversy that appear clear and well settled. One of these agreed upon principles concerns the substantive limitations that the Eighth Amendment places on the state's power to define criminal behavior. It is beyond dispute that the

---

[2]In 1986, there were 1,772 on U.S. death row, 37 of whom committed their capital crimes when they were 15, 16, or 17 years of age (Streib 1987:xi). More recently, the total U.S. death row inmate population rose to over 2250. Thirty-seven states currently have death penalty statutes on their books.

state can legitimately punish people only for what they do or fail to do; it cannot punish people for what they are. Thus, in *Robinson v. California* (1962), the U.S. Supreme Court declared that a state statute making the status of being a narcotic addict a crime violated the cruel and unusual punishment clause.

2. The Death Penalty is Not Unconstitutional *Per Se*

Regarding another well settled issue, both supporters (van den Haag, 1975:225; van den Haag and Conrad, 1983:157; Berger, 1982:43–50) and opponents (Bedau, 1977:14; van den Haag and Conrad, 1983:163; Amnesty International, 1979) of capital punishment acknowledge that the text of the Fifth Amendment of the United States Constitution ("No person shall be held to answer for a *capital*...crime, unless on a presentment or indictment," or "be twice put in jeopardy of *life*" for the same offense, or "be deprived of *life*...without due process of law."), when read together with the text of the Eighth Amendment ("excessive bail shall not be required, nor excessive fines imposed, nor cruel and unusual punishments inflected"), clearly indicates that the Framers of the Constitution considered the death penalty to be an acceptable punishment for criminal behavior. Also, since the same Congress that ratified the Bill of Rights made "murder, forgery of public securities, robbery and rape punishable by death" a short time later (Berger, 1982:47), one simply cannot argue that execution runs counter to the original intention of the "cruel and unusual punishment" clause. This brute fact of constitutional history has been repeatedly recognized by the Supreme Court (see, for example, *Wilkerson v. Utah*, 1879:347; *In re Kemmler*, 1890:933; *Louisiana ex rel. Francis v. Resweber*, 1947:376; *Trop v. Dulles*, 1958:597; Burger, 1982:2 n. 3). Indeed, in *Furman v. Georgia* (1972:2823 [dissenting opinion]) Justice Powell wrote of

> ...the unswerving position that this Court has taken in opinions spanning the last hundred years. On virtually every occasion that any opinion has touched on the question...it has been asserted affirmatively, or tacitly assumed, that the Constitution does not prohibit the penalty.

In the same decision, Justice Blackmun wrote, "The several concurring opinions acknowledge, as they must, that until today capital punishment was accepted and assumed as not unconstitutional *per se* under the Eighth Amendment or the Fourteenth Amendment" (*Furman v. Georgia*, 1972:2813 [dissenting opinion]; *Gregg v. Georgia*, 1976:2927; see also Berger, 1982:45 n. 74).

3. Barbaric Forms of Punishment Are Forbidden

Finally, as the Court established in *Wilkerson v. Utah* (1879) and *In re Kemmler* (1890), there is substantial agreement that the cruel and unusual punishment clause prohibits the physical torture of offenders and barbaric forms of execution such as crucifixion or burning at the stake (Bedau, *cited in* Berger, 1982:49; van den Haag, 1975:200; Knight and Early, Jr., 1986:59–60; Note [Petersen], 1989:119; *Wilkerson v. Utah*, 1879:348; *In re Kemmler*, 1890:933; *Louisiana ex rel. Francis v. Resweber*, 1947:376; *Ford v. Wainwright*, 1986:2599; *Solem v. Helm*, 1983:3006). Some argue that the boundaries of the Eighth Amendment should not extend beyond this narrow construction (*see generally*, *Weems v. United States*,

1910:558–68 [dissenting opinion]; *McGautha v. California*, 1971:1476–77 [dissenting opinion]; Berger, 1982:29–50; van den Haag, 1975:225–28).

B. The Expansion of the Eighth Amendment

1. *Weems v. United States* and Disproportionate Punishments

Generally, however, the U.S. Supreme Court has rejected the narrow construction of the Eighth Amendment described above (*Gregg v. Georgia*, 1976:2924). Beginning with the decision in *Weems v. United States* (1910), the Court held that the Eighth Amendment prohibited not only torture and punishments that were barbaric, but also sanctions that were grossly disproportionate to the offense. Weems, a disbursement officer working in the Philippine Islands, was convicted of making two false entries in the cash book at the port of Manilla. He was sentenced to fifteen years imprisonment (in chains, and at "hard and painful" labor) and fined. Upon release, he was to be permanently barred from holding public office, stripped forever of his right to vote, and placed on perpetual surveillance (*Weems v. United States*, 1910:545).

In his opinion, Justice McKenna argued that the expansion of the cruel and unusual punishment clause to cover disproportionate sentences was justified because:

> Time works changes, brings into existence new conditions and purposes. Therefore, a principle, to be vital, must be capable of wider application than the mischief which gave it birth...In the application of a constitution...our contemplation cannot be only of what has been, but of what may be (*Weems v. United States*, 1910:551).

According to the plurality, the Court's holding was also required by "a precept of justice that punishment for crime should be graduated and proportioned to the offense" (*Weems v. United States*, 1910:549). Finally, the Court pointed to statements in other cases which seemed to support the notion that a grossly disproportionate sentence could amount to cruel and unusual punishment. In particular, Justice McKenna cited a statement taken from a dissenting opinion by Justice Field "that the prohibition was directed...against all punishments which, by their excessive length or severity, are greatly disproportionate to the offense charged" (*O'Neil v. Vermont, cited in Weems v. United States*, 1910:551), as well as the view expressed in an early Massachusetts case that "punishment in a state prison for a long term of years might be so disproportionate to the offense as to constitute cruel and unusual punishment" (*McDonald v. Commonwealth, cited in Weems v. United States*, 1910:549).

2. *Trop v. Dulles* and the "Evolving Standards of Decency"

Five decades later, the *Weems* decision was extended still further in *Trop v. Dulles* (1958). In *Trop* (1958:591–92), a former U.S. Army private who was convicted, imprisoned, and dishonorably discharged for desertion during World War II, was denied a passport pursuant to Section 401(g) of the Nationality Act (8 U.S.C.A. 1481(a) (8)). Under this provision, deserters who were dismissed or dishonorably discharged were stripped of their citizenship. Trop appealed the denial of his passport application, and sought a declaratory judgment restoring his citizenship.

In deciding Trop's case, the Court concluded, as it had in *Weems*,

> that the words of the Amendment are not precise [citation omitted], and that their scope is not static. The Amendment must draw its meaning from the evolving standards of decency that mark the progress of a maturing society (*Trop v. Dulles*, 1958:598).

It then ruled that the "use of denationalization, as a punishment is barred by the Eighth Amendment" (*Trop v. Dulles*, 1958:598). However, the rationale used by Chief Justice Warren to reach this conclusion in *Trop* was substantially different than the reasoning in *Weems*. "Since wartime desertion is punishable by death," he writes,

> there can be no argument that the penalty of denationalization is excessive in relation to the gravity of the crime. *The question is whether this penalty subjects the individual to a fate forbidden by the principle of civilized treatment guaranteed by the Eighth Amendment.* (*Trop v. Dulles*, 1958:597 [emphasis added]).

And, at another point in the opinion he states:

> The basic concept underlying the Eighth Amendment is nothing less than the dignity of man. While the state has the power to punish, the Amendment stands to assure that this power will be exercised within the limits of civilized standards. (*Trop v. Dulles*, 1958:597–98).

Thus, under the standards developed in *Wilkerson*, *Kemmler*, *Weems* and *Trop*, the cruel and unusual punishment clause would appear to prohibit: (1) torture and barbaric forms of execution; (2) penalties that are disproportionate to the offense; (3) sanctions that are contrary to "evolving standards of decency" in a society; and (4) punishments that fall below a standard of "civilized treatment" or violate the "dignity of man."

C. The Eighth Amendment and the Administration of the Death Penalty

1. *Furman v. Georgia* and the Problem of Uncontrolled Discretion

Weems and the other cases described above reveal how the Supreme Court has gradually expanded the boundaries of the Eighth Amendment and, as a consequence, limited the types of punishment that may be imposed. But the Court has also relied on the cruel and unusual punishment clause to control *the process* by which punishments—specifically, the death penalty—may be imposed as well. In these cases, the issue is not so much whether the death penalty is barbaric, or disproportionate, or offensive to evolving standards of decency, but rather what methods the states may use to determine which offenders will die. The rules governing the process for imposing the death penalty began to take shape in *Furman v. Georgia* (1972). There, in nine separate opinions totalling more than 200 pages, five Justices (Douglas, Brennan, Stewart, White and Marshall) ruled that states may not leave the decision to impose the death penalty to the "uncontrolled discretion of judges or juries" (*Furman v. Georgia*, 1972:2734). *Furman* invalidated most death penalty statutes because they provided "no standards [to] govern the selection of the penalty [and] allowed [p]eople to live or die...on the whim of one man or of 12" (*Furman v. Georgia*, 1972:2734). Furman also struck down state statutes allowing automatic imposition of the death penalty upon the conviction of certain crimes such as first degree murder.

2. The Response to *Furman*: Mandatory Death Penalties and "Guided Discretion" Systems

The legislative response to *Furman* took two forms (*see generally*, Gillers, 1980; Paternoster and Kazyaka, 1988:116; Goodpaster, 1983:788–89). One group of jurisdictions tried to overcome the problem of uncontrolled discretion by making the death penalty mandatory for offenders convicted of first degree murder, and occasionally a few other serious crimes, such as treason or aggravated rape. For example, under the North Carolina statute enacted in 1974, execution was the sole punishment established for homicides committed by "poison, lying in wait, imprisonment, starving, torture," "any other kind of willful, deliberate and premeditated killing," and killings "committed in the course of any arson, rape, robbery, kidnapping, burglary, or other felony" (N.C. Gen. Stat. § 14–17 [Cum. Supp. 1975]). A similar statute was enacted in Louisiana that same year (La. Rev. Stat. Ann. § 14:30 [1974]).

Meanwhile, a second group of states adopted so-called "guided discretion" statutes. Under these provisions, the discretionary application of the death penalty was still permitted. However, before it could be imposed, the sentencing judge or jury was required to find (beyond a reasonable doubt), that one or more of the specific aggravating circumstances enumerated in the statute was present in the case.[3] For example, under Florida law, the death sentence is permitted if the jury finds, *inter alia*, that the capital felony was committed by a prisoner, or that the defendant had a prior capital or violent felony conviction, or that it was committed in an attempt to avoid arrest or escape custody (Fla. State. Ann. § 921.141(5) [Supp. 1976–1977]). Additionally, these statutes frequently imposed other requirements designed to control sentencing discretion. For example, Florida law also required the jury to consider specified mitigating circumstances before it could impose a death sentence (Fla. Stat. Ann. § 921.141(6) [Supp. 1976–1977]).[4]

---

[3]Texas used a slightly different method for guiding discretion in capital cases. Rather than enumerating a list of aggravating and mitigating circumstances, the Texas capital punishment statute required the jury to answer a series of three questions:

(1) whether the conduct of the defendant that caused the death of the deceased was committed deliberately and with the reasonable expectation that the death of the deceased or another would result;

(2) whether there is a probability that the defendant would commit criminal acts of violence that would constitute a continuing threat to society; and

(3) if raised by the evidence, whether the conduct of the defendant in killing the deceased in killing the deceased was unreasonable in response to the provocation, if any, by the deceased. (Texas Code Crim. Proc., Art. 37.071(b) (Supp. 1975–1976).

The constitutionality of this approach to guiding jury discretion was affirmed in *Jurek v. Texas* (1976).

[4]However, in *Lockett v. Ohio* (1978), the U.S. Supreme Court ruled that states may not limit the kinds of (continued...)

Also, many capital sentencing systems required bifurcated trials recommended in *Gregg v. Georgia*, (1976:2933–34) or automatic appellate review of death sentences (*Proffitt v. Florida*, 1976:2966; *Gregg v. Georgia*, 1976:2937).

Shortly after the passage of these post-*Furman* statutes, the U.S. Supreme Court considered two constitutional challenges to mandatory sentencing systems (*Woodson v. North Carolina*, 1976; *Roberts v. Louisiana*, 1976), and concluded that they did not overcome the problem of uncontrolled discretion identified in *Furman*. First, the majority noted a clear and distinct historical trend away from the use of mandatory capital punishment:

> At the time the Eighth Amendment was adopted in 1791, the States uniformly followed the common law practice of making death the exclusive and mandatory sentence for certain specified offenses....Almost from the outset [however,] jurors reacted unfavorably to the harshness of mandatory death sentences. The States initially responded to this expression of public dissatisfaction...by limiting the classes of capital offenses.
>
> This reform, however, left unresolved the problem posed by the not infrequent refusal of juries to convict murderers rather than subject them to automatic death sentences...
>
> ...[This difficulty] led the States to grant juries sentencing discretion in capital cases. Tennessee in 1838, followed by Alabama in 1841 and Louisiana in 1846 were the first states to abandon mandatory death sentences...by the end of World War I, all but eight States, Hawaii, and the District of Columbia either had adopted discretionary death penalty schemes or abolished the death penalty altogether. By 1963, all of these remaining jurisdictions had replaced their automatic death penalty statutes with discretionary jury sentencing (*Woodson v. North Carolina*, 1976:2984–5 [citations omitted]; see also *Roberts v. Louisiana*, 3005–06).

Second, because the mandatory sentencing schemes under consideration left undisturbed the jury's power to render a not guilty verdict despite overwhelming evidence to the contrary, the discretion to allow one offender to live while condemning another to death remained essentially uncontrolled and standardless, and thus in conflict with *Furman* (*Woodson v. North Carolina*, 1976:2990–1; *Roberts v. Louisiana*, 1976:3006–07).

Finally, the Court objected to mandatory death penalty schemes because they represented an affront to the notion of individualized justice. The majority observed that the consideration of both the nature of the offense and the characteristics of the offender in order to arrive at a just sentence is typically more a matter of "enlightened policy rather than a constitutional imperative" (*Woodson v. North Carolina*, 1976:2991). However, the extreme and irreversible nature of the death penalty makes its automatic application impermissible under the Eighth Amendment. "In capital cases," wrote Justice Stewart:

> the fundamental respect for humanity underlying the Eighth Amendment requires consideration of the character and record of the individual offender and the circumstances of the particular offense

---

[4](...continued)
mitigating evidence that a judge or jury can consider when deciding the punishment in a capital case.

> as a constitutionally indispensable part of the process of inflicting the penalty of death (*Woodson v. North Carolina*, 1976:2991).

"Guided discretion" sentencing systems have also been challenged (*Gregg v. Georgia*, 1976; *Jurek v. Texas*, 1976; *Proffitt v. Florida*, 1976), but here the Court has concluded that the safeguards present under these statutes were sufficient to prevent the arbitrary and capricious application of the death penalty. First, the Court noted that the "class of offenders" subject to capital punishment had been considerably narrowed in the post-*Furman* statutes (*Gregg v. Georgia*, 1976:2936; *Jurek v. Texas*, 1976:2955; *Proffitt v. Florida*, 1976:2970). Since these provisions were reserved for extremely serious offenders or offenses,

> it becomes reasonable to expect that juries—even given discretion *not* to impose the death penalty—will impose [it] in a substantial portion of the cases so defined. If they do, it can no longer be said that the penalty is being imposed wantonly and freakishly or so infrequently that it loses its usefulness as a sentencing device. (*Gregg v. Georgia*, 1976:2948 [emphasis in original]).

The separation of the trial into a "guilt phase" and a "sentencing phase" was another important safeguard. Because some types of information (such as the way in which the victim was killed) might be irrelevant and prejudicial to the question of guilt, but highly relevant in the determination of an appropriate sentence, bifurcation allows the trial court to exercise some control over the information presented to the jury, preventing them from hearing inappropriate evidence at an inappropriate time (*Gregg v. Georgia*, 1976:2933–34). Essentially, this bifurcation enhanced the adversary nature of the sentencing phase. In this phase, either a judge or jury (depending on the state), must determine whether to impose the death penalty or a sentence of life in prison. The judge or jury must weigh the various mitigating and aggravating circumstances of the homicide and assess the personal characteristics of the offender to make this life or death decision. Naturally, the prosecution will attempt to illustrate the aggravating aspects of the case. He/she may introduce grisly photographs of the victim's body, even though this may not be permitted at the trial phase; it may prejudice the jury. The defense may call expert witnesses to show certain mitigating psycho-social characteristics of the offender. Where death penalty sentencing is done by juries, experts can be called to educate the jury on the routines of prison life and what it means to be a "lifer" within the contexts of both prison subculture and the bureaucratic arrangements of the state department of corrections (parole, good time, classification, *etc.*)[5] Thus, this sentencing phase provides a forum in which the defense can stress youth as a mitigating factor.

---

[5]The second author has served as an "expert" or "corrections specialist" in the sentencing phase of death penalty cases in Louisiana. He was called to inform the sentencing jury about "inmate life" at the state's long term facility. This state is one of six states which has a "natural life" sentence for first degree murderers who are not sentenced to die in the electric chair. That is, natural lifers have no benefit of "probation, parole or suspended sentence." The sentence is mandatory short of an executive pardon (which actually means clemency in this state). In addition to "corrections specialists," social workers, psychologists, clergy, and lay character witnesses have all been called upon in this Louisiana judicial district.

Debates between defense and prosecution about age as a mitigating factor can indeed serve to educate the jury concerning the offender upon whom they are about to impose sentence. But statutes which were supposed to guide such debate have severely criticized. For example, the petitioners in *Gregg*, *Jurek*, and *Proffitt*, all argued that the aggravating and mitigating circumstances specified in the Florida and Georgia statutes (and the three questions the jury had to answer in the Texas scheme) were vague and overbroad and therefore unconstitutional. However, the Court found that, on the whole, they provided jurors with the guidance necessary for rational and consistent sentencing decisions (*Gregg v. Georgia*, 1976:2936–39; *Jurek v. Texas*, 1976:2957–58; *Proffitt v. Florida*, 1976:2967–69).

Finally, guided discretion schemes were acceptable because state Supreme Courts were required to automatically review all capital sentences and vacate any found to be (1) disproportionate in light of the seriousness of the offense or the nature of the offender; (2) atypical in light of past sentencing practice; or (3) imposed because of passion or prejudice (*Gregg v. Georgia*, 1976:2937, 2939; *Proffitt v. Florida*, 1976:2966, 2969–70).

D. Applying the Eighth Amendment: What do the Standards Mean?

So far, the discussion in this section has focused on what the Eighth Amendment prohibits (barbaric punishments, punishments for a status), what it requires (punishments that are proportional and comport with human dignity), and the limits that it places on the process for imposing the death penalty (the use of the "guided discretion" approach is acceptable, but mandatory capital punishment is not). Taken together, the cases presented to this point set out the general constitutional standards that must be met before the death penalty can be imposed; such standards are important because they tell us, in general, what can and cannot be done to other human beings who have broken the law.

However, merely establishing the standards for the constitutional use of the death penalty is not enough; judges are also required to apply these standards in particular cases, and through application, give them meaning. Thus, a number of other capital punishment decisions are important because they elaborate on the general standards outlined above. Some of these cases will be discussed below.

1. When is a Punishment Barbaric?

In *Louisiana ex rel. Francis v. Resweber* (1947), the Court ruled that the Eighth Amendment did not prevent Louisiana from making a second attempt to execute 17 year old Willie Francis after the first attempt failed due to a malfunctioning electric chair. On appeal, Francis argued that a second attempt would be impermissibly cruel. Justice Reed, writing for the majority, responded to this argument as follows:

> The cruelty against which the Constitution protects a convicted man is cruelty inherent in the method of punishment, not the necessary suffering involved in any method employed to extinguish life humanely. The fact that an unforeseeable accident prevented the prompt consummation of the

sentence cannot, it seems to us, add an element of cruelty to the subsequent execution (*Louisiana ex rel. Francis v. Resweber*, 1947:376; *see also*, Inciardi, 1984:536).

2. When Does a Punishment Offend Human Dignity?

The Court has also addressed the requirement that punishments must not be offensive to human dignity. In his concurring opinion in *Furman v. Georgia* (1972:2742–2747), Justice Brennan identified four "principles...[for determining] whether a challenged punishment comports with human dignity." First, to be acceptable, a punishment must not be so severe that it reduces "members of the human race [to the level of] nonhumans, as objects to be toyed with and discarded" (*Furman v. Georgia*, 1972:2743). Second, the punishment must not be arbitrarily inflicted; it must be carried out in the "great majority of cases in which it is legally available" (*Furman v. Georgia*, 1972:2745 [*quoting Wilkerson v. Utah*]). Third, there must be some "objective" evidence that the punishment is acceptable to contemporary society. Finally, the punishment must not be "excessive" in that it involves

> the pointless infliction of suffering. If there is a significantly less severe punishment adequate to achieve the purposes for which the punishment is inflicted, the punishment inflicted is unnecessary and therefore excessive [citation omitted] (*Furman v. Georgia*, 1972:2747).

Justice Brennan's first two principles cover familiar ground—referring, as they do, to the Eighth Amendment's prohibition against barbaric punishments and those used so infrequently that their imposition becomes wanton and freakish. His third principle stands for the notion that a punishment must have a measure of public support in order to comport with human dignity. How is the public support for a punishment to be judged?

It is clear from *Furman* (1976:2746) and *Gregg* (1976:2925) that "objective" criteria are to be used to determine if a sanction is consistent with, or contrary to, contemporary societal values. The sources of information for this judgment include: (1) the history of the punishment; (2) the extent to which its use is authorized by legislatures in other jurisdictions; (3) the extent to which it is actually imposed and carried out in other jurisdictions; and (4) the extent to which the punishment is supported in public opinion (*Furman v. Georgia*, 1972:2746–47, 2756–57, 2774–75, 2778–2793; *Gregg v. Georgia*, 2925–27).

Finally, in his discussion of excessive punishments, Justice Brennan also pointed out that the excessiveness of a penalty was to be judged, in part, in relation to its purpose and its effectiveness: any quantum of punishment above the amount necessary to achieve a valid phenological goal was cruel and unusual (*Furman v. Georgia*, 1972:2747).

3. When is a Punishment Disproportional to the Offense?

In other decisions (*e.g.*, *Coker v. Georgia*, 1977; *Rummel v. Estelle*, 1980; *Solem v. Helm*, 1983), the Court has given additional consideration to the issue of disproportionality in relation to punishment. *Coker* dealt with the question of whether the death penalty could be imposed for the aggravated rape of an adult woman. In a comparatively brief analysis (*Coker v. Georgia*, 1977:2869–2870), a plurality of the

Court found the sentence to be disproportionate to the offense, in part, because rape did not involve taking a human life. *Rummel* concerned the propriety of imposing a life term following conviction for a third non-violent felony. Again without much discussion about why they did not apply (*Rummel v. Estelle*, 1980:1138), the plurality distinguished Rummel's case from prior Eighth Amendment cases because it involved the imposition of a life term, rather than execution, and held that the sentence was not disproportional to the offense. Two years after *Rummel*, the Court held, in *Enmund v. Florida* (1982), that the death penalty for the crime of felony murder was disproportionate when applied to defendants who had not actually participated in the killing.

Solem v. Helm (1983), however, contains a much more comprehensive treatment of the proportionality principle. In 1979, Jerry Solem was convicted in a South Dakota court of uttering a $100 "no account" check. Typically, the maximum penalty for this offense was five years imprisonment and a $5000 fine. But, because of Helm's prior felony record (three third degree burglary convictions, another for obtaining money under false pretenses, and a felony [third offense] drunken driving conviction) he was sentenced instead to life imprisonment without the possibility of parole. On appeal, the U.S. agreed with Helm's contention that the sentence was grossly disproportional and therefore, constituted cruel and unusual punishment, and reversed the conviction.

Tracing the concept of proportionality as far back as the Magna Carta, the Court found it to be a "deeply rooted and frequently repeated" principle in common law, and a longstanding feature of Supreme Court jurisprudence. Consequently, the Court held that it was a basic requirement of each criminal sentence (*Solem v. Helm*, 1983:3006). To determine if a sentence is proportional, courts first must weigh the harshness of the penalty in relation to: (1) the gravity of the offense, as measured by factors such as the harm to the victim, the harm to society, the absolute magnitude of the offense, the offender's role in the crime and whether the crime was attempted or completed; and (2) the offender's culpability, taking into account such factors as the offender's intent and motive. Second, proportionality may be judged by comparing the challenged punishment to the punishments imposed on other offenders in the same jurisdiction.[6] If those convicted of more serious offenses are punished less harshly, then it is likely that the challenged punishment is disproportionate. Finally, the court must compare the challenged punishment to the sanctions for similar crimes in other jurisdictions. Here, disproportionality is likely if many other jurisdictions punish a similar offense less harshly (*Solem v. Helm*, 1983:3010).

In this section we have briefly described the various factors that must be considered in order to determine whether a sanction such as the death penalty is permissible under the Eighth Amendment. To make this decision, a judge must weigh a complex constellation of factors about the offender, the offense, the victim, and the society. Using the framework developed so far, we will now turn our attention to the

[6]For a detailed discussion of alternative methods for comparing similar death penalty cases in the same jurisdiction, see, Baldus, Pulaski and Woodworth (1983).

U.S. Supreme Court decisions focusing on the use of capital punishment in cases involving juvenile offenders.

THE U.S. SUPREME COURT AND JUVENILE EXECUTIONS

A. The Consideration of Age as a Mitigating Factor in Sentencing

As Hoffmann (1989:229–230) notes, the imposition of death sentences against juvenile offenders has been challenged by petitioners on several occasions. Until recently, however, the Court chose to avoid the question by declining to hear some cases (*e.g.*, *Roach v. Martin*, 1985 (see below); also see *Trimble v. State*, 1983; *Cannaday v. State*, 1984; and *Tokman v. State*, 1983), or deciding others without reaching the death penalty issue (*e.g.*, *Bell v. Ohio*, 1978; *Eddings v. Oklahoma*, 1982).

In *Bell*, the petitioner's sentence was reversed because the Ohio death penalty statute prevented the consideration of a defendant's age as a mitigating factor (*Bell v. Ohio*, 1978:2980–81; Hoffmann, 1989:235). This case involved a murder which occurred in the course of a kidnapping. Sixteen–year–old Willie Lee Bell and 18–year–old Samuel Hall abducted a 64–year–old man and eventually shot him with a "sawed off" shot gun. After arrest and indictment, Bell waived his right to a jury trial and opted for trial by a three–judge panel. The panel unanimously found him guilty and, pursuant to Ohio law, ordered a presentence investigation and psychiatric examination of Bell. The psychiatrist found no mitigating factors as defined in the state's death penalty statute. The presentence report, however, contained detailed information about Bell's background, intelligence, prior record, character, and habits. The report noted that Bell had "dull-normal" intelligence, and had been using drugs daily for the three years prior to the murder. It also indicated that Bell "followed" his older co-defendant, Samuel Hall. Bell was also allegedly "scared" of Hall. Bell's teachers testified that he was emotionally unstable and immature for his age. Finally, Bell contended that he cooperated with the police, that there was a lack of proof that he did the actual killing, and that his young age supported a penalty less than death. The three–judge panel concluded that none of the mitigating factors defined in the Ohio statute had been established, and therefore Willie Lee Bell was sentenced to death.

The U.S. Supreme Court ruled that the Ohio law did not adequately allow the consideration of mitigating factors. Bell's death sentence was vacated and he remanded back to court for resentencing (also see *Lockett v. Ohio*, 1978).

Similarly, in *Eddings* (1982:876–877), the petitioner's death sentence was reversed because the sentencing judge refused to consider the defendant's home life, his mental and emotional problems and violent background as mitigating factors, even though Oklahoma law permitted the defense to introduce "any mitigating circumstances."

Sixteen–year–old Monty Lee Eddings was convicted of killing a police officer and was sentenced to death. The U.S. Supreme Court vacated the sentence. Justice Powell explained:

> The trial judge recognized that youth must be considered a relevant mitigating factor. But youth is more than a chronological fact. It is a time and condition of life when a person may be most susceptible to influence and to psychological damage. Our history is replete with laws and judicial recognition that minors, especially in their earlier years, generally are less mature and responsible than adults (*Eddings v. Oklahoma*, 1982:87).

He also reasoned that even the normal 16-year-old customarily lacks the maturity of an adult. Add to this the undisputed fact that the defendant had a neglectful and sometimes violent family life, and it is evident that such mitigating factors must necessarily be given consideration at sentencing. Justice Powell stated that the sentencing court cannot ignore these mitigating factors, but it can decide the amount of weight to give them. This, however, is certainly no guarantee that a sentencing court will not decide that "youth" carry almost no weight in a particular case.

Bell and *Eddings* were reversed on procedural grounds, and this made it unnecessary to decide the constitutionality of juvenile executions *per se*.

B. *Thompson v. Oklahoma*: Persons Under Sixteen Years of Age Cannot Be Sentenced to Death

Three years after *Eddings*, the U.S. Supreme Court reconsidered the question of juvenile executions in *Thompson v. Oklahoma* (1987). Fifteen year old William Wayne Thompson and three older accomplices had been sentenced to death for the murder of Charles Keene, Thompson's brother-in-law. On appeal, Thompson claimed, *inter alia*,[7] that the imposition of a death sentence against a fifteen year old offender constituted cruel and unusual punishment (*Thompson v. Oklahoma*, 1987:2691). While the Court reversed Thompson's sentence by a 5-3 vote, the Justices remained deeply divided over the constitutionality of the death penalty for juveniles. Four Justices—Stevens, Brennan, Marshall and Blackmun—found the death penalty violated the Eighth Amendment when applied to youths under the age of sixteen (*Thompson v. Oklahoma*, 1987:2700; Hoffmann, 1989:237; Note [Ricotta], 1988:921; Note [Jackson], 1988:1000; Note [Simmons], 1989:748). Justice O'Connor concurred in the judgment of the plurality, but wrote a separate opinion (*Thompson v. Oklahoma*, 1987:2706; Hoffmann, 1989:237; Note [Ricotta], 1988:921; Note [Jackson], 1988:1007; Note [Simmons], 1989:748). Three Justices—Scalia, Chief Justice Rhenquist and White dissented (*Thompson v. Oklahoma*, 1987:2711; Hoffmann, 1989:237-38; Note [Ricotta], 1988:934; Note [Jackson], 1988:1008; Note [Simmons], 1989:750).

In their opinions, the Justices in the plurality and those in the dissent exhibited fundamental disagreements over several issues, including: (1) the existence of a national consensus forbidding the execution of juveniles; (2) the extent to which the laws of other Western European nations prohibit or permit the execution of juveniles, and the opinions of "respected professional organizations" (*Thompson*

---

[7]Thompson also argued that the trial court improperly admitted some photographs of the victim's body. Neither the Justices in the plurality, nor Justice O'Connor in her concurrence found it necessary to reach this issue (*Thompson v. Oklahoma*, 1987:2700). The dissent concluded that the nature of the photographs could not, in this case, "form the basis for a constitutional attack..." (*Thompson v. Oklahoma*, 1987:2722).

v. Oklahoma, 1987:2696) should be taken into consideration when deciding on the constitutionality of juvenile executions in the United States; (3) the degree to which juveniles could be held responsible for their actions; (4) whether the execution of juveniles contributed to the retributive or deterrent goals of punishment; and (5) whether the small number of juveniles executed represents the "wanton and freakish" application of the death penalty condemned by Justice Stewart in *Furman* (*Furman v. Georgia*, 1972:2763).

1. Is There a National Consensus on the Issue of Juvenile Executions?

In *Thompson*, those in the plurality, Justice O'Connor, and the dissenting justices acknowledged that the "evolving standards of decency" constituted the proper standard for judging the constitutionality of juvenile executions; there was also agreement that these evolving standards of decency could be accurately measured by state legislative action[8] (*Thompson v. Oklahoma*, 1988:2692, 2706, 2714–15). However, each side conducted its review of state legislation in a different fashion, resulting in opposite conclusions about the acceptability of sentencing young people to death. To support their finding of a consensus *against* the execution of juveniles below a certain age, the concurring justices first divided the states (including the District of Columbia) into three categories: those that abolished the death penalty for any offender (14)[9]; those that authorized the death penalty but did not establish a minimum age for its use (19)[10]; and those that authorized the death penalty and established a minimum age for its imposition (18)[11]; the plurality went on to note that all eighteen jurisdictions in this category set the minimum age for execution at 16 or older at the time of the crime. They then eliminated from consideration the 19 states that authorized execution but set no minimum age for its use, "because they do not focus on the question of where the chronological age line should be drawn" (*Thompson v. Oklahoma*, 1988:2695). Thus, for those in the plurality, nearly two thirds of the states (32 of 51 jurisdictions) have acted to restrict the death penalty in such a way that it cannot be imposed on someone below the age of sixteen, if at all.

In her separate opinion, Justice O'Connor took a similar view of the state legislation. Like the plurality, she combined the number of states that had established a minimum age for execution with those

---

[8]For a critique of the Supreme Courts reliance on legislation as an indicator of contemporary standards of decency, see Note [Ricotta] (1988:939–942).

[9]The jurisdictions in this category are: Alaska, District of Columbia, Hawaii, Iowa, Kansas, Maine, Massachusetts, Michigan, Minnesota, New York, North Dakota, Rhode Island, West Virginia and Wisconsin (*Thompson v. Oklahoma*, 1988:2694–95 n. 25).

[10]The jurisdictions included in this category are: Alabama, Arizona, Arkansas, Delaware, Florida, Idaho, Louisiana, Mississippi, Missouri, Montana, Oklahoma, Pennsylvania, South Carolina, South Dakota, Utah, Vermont, Virginia, Washington, Wyoming (*Thompson v. Oklahoma*, 1988:2695 n. 26).

[11]The jurisdictions in this category include: California, Colorado, Connecticut, Georgia, Illinois, Indiana, Kentucky, Maryland, Nebraska, Nevada, New Hampshire, New Jersey, New Mexico, North Carolina, Ohio, Oregon, Tennessee, Texas (*Thompson v. Oklahoma*, 1988:2696 n. 30).

that abolished it altogether, and concluded that "strong counterevidence would be required to persuade me that a national consensus against this practice does not exist" (*Thompson v. Oklahoma*, 1988:2706–07).

Writing for the dissent, Justice Scalia began his discussion of the evolving standards of contemporary society by noting a trend ignored by the plurality: the fact that several jurisdictions have recently *lowered* the age at which jurisdiction in juvenile cases can be waived to adult court (*Thompson v. Oklahoma*, 1988:2716). He then objected to the plurality's resort to creative accounting in its review of state legislation. "[I]t is beyond me," he writes,

> why an accurate analysis would not include within the computation the larger number of states (19) that have determined that no minimum age for capital punishment is appropriate, leaving that to be governed by their general rules for the age at which juveniles can be held criminally responsible. (*Thompson v. Oklahoma*, 1988:2716 [dissenting opinion]).

To the dissenting Justices, the assessment of contemporary standards regarding capital punishment should focus only on the jurisdictions that have it. When the analysis is restricted to this group,

> ...the Federal Government and almost 40% of the States, including a majority of the States that include capital punishment as a permissible sanction allow for the imposition of the death penalty on any juvenile who has been tried as an adult, which category can include juveniles under 16 at the time of the offense[. I]t is obviously impossible for the plurality to rely upon any evolved societal consensus discernable in legislation (*Thompson v. Oklahoma*, 1988:2716 [dissenting opinion]).

Upon reflection, however, it is clear that the dissent has resorted to some creative accounting of its own in the analysis of state legislation. Justice Scalia's statement to the effect that "...almost 40% of the States... include capital punishment as a permissible sanction [against juveniles tried as adults]" is true as far as it goes: if the 19 jurisdictions that authorize execution without setting a minimum age are combined with the 18 others that authorize executions and set a minimum age, the "...almost 40%" of the jurisdictions apparently do authorize juvenile executions. Reported as a proportion (40%), there does seem to be something of a consensus favoring the capital punishment of juveniles. But, looking only at the raw frequencies used to compute the proportion of "...almost 40%," Justice Scalia's consensus evaporates: of the 37 jurisdictions with capital punishment about half (18) do set a minimum age of at least 16, while about half (19) do not.

To the extent that contemporary societal standards can be judged by a review of capital punishment statutes, it would seem that the plurality's assessment—that a strong consensus exists against the practice of executing people below the age of 16—is the most reasonable one.

2. Are the View of Professional Organizations and Laws in Other Countries Relevant to U.S. Policy on Juvenile Executions?

To further support the assertion that the execution of offenders below the age of 16 was contrary to evolving standards of decency, the plurality also pointed out that the American Bar Association and the

American Law Institute opposed the practice (*Thompson v. Oklahoma*, 1988:2696 n. 32, 33), and that it had been outlawed in many other countries, including the Soviet Union (*Thompson v. Oklahoma*, 1988:2696).

The dissent questioned the relevance of this evidence in a footnote, suggesting that the laws and practices of other nations "cannot be imposed upon Americans through the Constitution." According to the dissent, "the practices of other nations,"

> particularly other democracies, can be relevant to determining whether a practice uniform among our people is not merely an historical accident, but rather so "implicit in the concept of ordered liberty" that it occupies a place not merely in our mores but, text permitting, in our Constitution as well [citation omitted]. But where there is not first a settled consensus among our own people, the views of other nations, however enlightened the Justices of this Court may think them to be, cannot be imposed on Americans through the Constitution. (*Thompson v. Oklahoma*, 1988:2716 n. 4).

Unfortunately, this argument is flawed in two respects. First, Justice Scalia seems to be suggesting that other nations' rejection of juvenile executions is irrelevant to the present case because there is a lack of consensus on the issue in the United States. This appears inconsistent with his previous argument that there is a consensus favoring juvenile executions in the United States, since "almost 40%" of the jurisdictions allow them. Assuming *arguendo* that Justice Scalia's previous statement is correct, and there is a consensus in America on this issue, then the views of the international community become relevant by the terms of his own argument. Once the relevance of other nations' laws have been accepted, it becomes impossible to ignore the fact that these views weigh heavily against the practice of sentencing juveniles to death.

Second, under Justice Scalia's reasoning, it would be necessary to acknowledge the laws and practices of other countries only after a "settled consensus" is discerned in American society. Presumably, the views of other countries would then be used to reinforce this "settled consensus." However, if the fundamental task of the U.S. Supreme Court is the resolution of legal conflict, it seems reasonable to expect that this task would be most effectively carried out when the Court's decisions take into account as much information as possible, including, when necessary, the legislation of other countries. To restrict the Court's view of international legislation to only those laws that are consistent with accepted policies in this country would force a selective perception of reality that would hamper the development of American constitutional law.

3. To What Extent Should Juvenile Offenders Be Held Responsible for Their Crimes?

As discussed above in Section II, the Eighth Amendment requires a rough proportionality between the magnitude of the punishment and the culpability of the offender. Thus in *Thompson*, it was necessary for the Court to decide "whether the juvenile's culpability should be measured by the same standard as that of an adult" (*Thompson v. Oklahoma*, 1988:2698). In consideration of this issue, the plurality, Justice O'Connor, and the dissent all start from a similar premise, but reason to very different conclusions. All discussions of the responsibility issue begin by acknowledging that the punishment for offenders should be directly related to their personal culpability.[12] (*Thompson v. Oklahoma*, 1988:2698; 2708; 2712; 2719). The plurality, however, follows this with the observation that minors cannot vote or exercise other rights, since "the normal 15-year-old is not prepared to assume the full responsibilities of an adult" (*Thompson v. Oklahoma*, 1988:2693 [footnote omitted]). This line of reasoning is then used as partial support for the holding that those below the age of 16 at the time of their crimes cannot be put to death. For the plurality, 16 years of age is a significant "bright line" separating childhood from adulthood, since this is the age (in most states) when minors begin to take on at least some adult responsibilities. Moreover, in all those states that have expressly considered the issue, it represents the minimum age for execution (*Thompson v. Oklahoma*, 1988:2692-96; Appendices A-F).

Justice O'Connor, was less comfortable with such sweeping generalizations about the maturity of minors:

> I agree that "proportionality requires a nexus between the punishment imposed and the defendant's blameworthiness" [citation omitted]. Granting the plurality's other premise—that adolescents are generally less blameworthy than adults who commit similar crimes—it does not necessarily follow that all 15-year-olds are incapable of the moral culpability that would justify the imposition of capital punishment (*Thompson v. Oklahoma*, 1988:2708–09).

Similarly, the dissenting Justices could find "...no rational basis for discerning...a societal judgment that no one so much as one day under 16 can *ever* be mature and morally responsible enough to deserve that penalty" (*Thompson v. Oklahoma*, 1988:2718 [dissenting opinion] [emphasis in original]).

Of these contrasting positions, the plurality's view is untenable for at least three reasons. First, while empirical research based on studies of large numbers of juveniles may demonstrate that many are indeed "less mature and less responsible than adults," "susceptible to influence and to psychological damage," "lack[ing in] experience, perspective and judgment," "more impulsive and less self disciplined" (*Thompson v. Oklahoma*, 1988:2698), such evidence will not support the hasty generalization that these qualities are

---

[12]The plurality's recognition of this premise is explicit ("...it is generally agreed 'that punishment should be directly related to the personal culpability of the defendant'" [citation omitted]) (*Thompson v. Oklahoma*, 1988:2698), as is Justice O'Connor's ("proportionality requires a nexus between the punishment imposed and the defendant's blameworthiness" [citation omitted]) (*Thompson v. Oklahoma*, 1988:2708). Justice Scalia's premise is less clearly stated, but at one point in the opinion he writes:

> I might even agree with the plurality's conclusion if the question were whether a person under 16 when he commits a crime can be deprived of the benefit of a rebuttable presumption that he is not mature and responsible enough to be punished as an adult.

Later, he quotes Justice Powell's statement in *Fare v. Michael C.* (1979:2576 n. 4):

> Some of the older minors become fully "streetwise," hardened criminals, deserving no greater consideration than that properly accorded all persons suspected of crime.

Taken together, these two statements seem to reflect a belief by Justice Scalia that criminal responsibility can vary between individuals.

characteristics of *all* juveniles. Nor would the findings of these studies support the conclusion that any *particular* juvenile is immature, irresponsible, easily influenced, impulsive or lacking in self discipline; any such inference would be an example of what social scientists call the "ecological fallacy" (Nettler, 1984:100–01).

Second, the plurality fails to recognize that state laws preventing those below a certain age from voting, marrying, driving, or purchasing alcohol more possibly spring from the need for administrative convenience rather than a blanket presumption that all minors are too immature to vote, marry, drive, or drink. While there may be some persons below the age of 16 who are responsible enough to vote, marry, drive or drink, it would be impractical to screen the juvenile population in order to find them; a much more plausible solution is to deny these rights to all below a certain age. Therefore, to the extent that these age based restrictions do flow from the need for administrative convenience, they provide little justification for adopting a similar "bright line" rule governing juvenile executions. Since the number of juvenile offenders sentenced to death is vastly smaller than the number who may be potentially responsible enough to vote, marry, drive or drink, the state can afford to conduct a much more detailed examination of each offender to determine if they can, in fact, be held responsible for their crimes (Hoffmann, 1989:281–82; *Stanford v. Kentucky*, 1989:2977).

Finally, the plurality's assumption that all juvenile offenders are irresponsible is problematic because it overlooks the fact that:

> [the] constitutional rules relating to the maturity of minors must be drawn with an eye to the decision for which the maturity is relevant [citation omitted] It is surely constitutional for a State to believe that the degree of maturity that is necessary to fully appreciate the pros and cons of smoking cigarettes or even of marrying may be somewhat greater than the degree necessary to fully appreciate the pros and cons of brutally killing a human being (*Thompson v. Oklahoma*, 1988:2718 n. 5 [dissenting opinion]).

From the passage above, it seems that those in the dissent are distinguishing between: (1) complex situations, in which people must weigh a complicated set of factors before deciding what behavior is appropriate; and (2) simple situations, where the appropriate behavior can be readily determined. According to Justice Scalia, a global presumption that all juveniles are immature is most appropriate in complex situations, since they may not be capable of the sophisticated reasoning the circumstances demand. These situations may also require the imposition of bright line rules applicable to all youths.

On the other hand, a global presumption of immaturity, and bright line rules would be inappropriate in simple situations where the choice of correct behavior is clear cut. For the dissent, juvenile killers face a simple decision, since the laws against killing are well known. Thus, no global presumption of immaturity is required, and the plurality's bright line rule preventing their execution is unnecessary.

4. Do Juvenile Executions Contribute to the Valid Goals of Punishment?

As also indicated above in Section II, punishments that serve no valid purpose are "excessive" under the Eighth Amendment, and cannot be imposed (*Furman v. Georgia*, 1976:2747; *Gregg v. Georgia*, 1976:2929). Later, in *Gregg v. Georgia* (1976:2929–30), the Court considered the death penalty in relation to the accepted goals of punishment. The Court decided that execution served the ends of retribution and deterrence (*Gregg v. Georgia*, 1976:2930–31). Thus, in *Thompson*, the Court had to determine if the execution of juveniles was consistent with these goals as well. In deciding the issue, the plurality took note of "the teenager's capacity for growth, and society's fiduciary obligations to its children" as well as "the lesser culpability of the juvenile offender" (*Thompson v. Oklahoma*, 1988:2699), and concluded that the execution of those who were less than 16 years of age at the time of their crimes could not be justified on retributive grounds. They also concluded that deterrence was an inappropriate justification, since: (1) juveniles, being impulsive, were unlikely to indulge in the cost-benefit analysis of actions that the doctrine presupposes; and (2) the small number of juveniles executed during the 20th Century had reduced the threat of punishment to the point of insignificance (*Thompson v. Oklahoma*, 1988:2700).

Given their previous reluctance to make presumptions about the culpability of all those who committed crimes prior to the age of 16, both Justice O'Connor and the dissent were similarly unwilling to conclude that the execution of such offenders could never further the goals of retribution or deterrence. As a result, neither Justice O'Connor or the dissent was willing to invalidate Thompson's sentence on the grounds that it served no valid phenological purpose (*Thompson v. Oklahoma*, 1988:2708–09; 2718–19).

Thompson's bright line rule, and the plurality's contention that juvenile executions cannot be justified on retributive grounds are criticized in a recent article by Hoffmann (1989). According to Hoffmann (1989:248–50), retributive justice requires *two* types of proportionality: (1) cardinal proportionality, which dictates that punishment be proportional to the harm caused by the crime and the offender's culpability; and (2) ordinal proportionality, which requires that equally culpable offenders guilty of similar crimes receive similar punishments. So far, in Hoffmann's (1989:257) view, the debate about the juvenile death penalty has focused on its cardinal proportionality. Arguably, for a juvenile convicted of homicide, a life sentence would just as easily satisfy the cardinal proportionality requirement as would death. Thus, those opposed to the execution of juveniles have a much stronger argument "if the debate is cast solely in terms of cardinal proportionality" (Hoffmann, 1989:258). In *Thompson*, the discussion of juvenile executions in relation to the principles of retributive justice does focus on cardinal proportionality. Consequently, its justification on retributive grounds becomes difficult, and a bright line rule prohibiting the execution of those under 16 at the time of the crime seems appropriate.

However, if the *Thompson's* bright line rule is considered in light of the concept of ordinal proportionality, a serious flaw becomes apparent. Because juveniles under the age of 16 at the time of their offense cannot be executed, they receive more lenient treatment compared to nonjuvenile offenders who may be just as blameworthy, but who are eligible for the death penalty (*Hoffmann*, 1989:233). From the perspective of retributive theory, injustice flows from *Thompson* because:

> age itself is not the factor that renders the imposition of the death penalty against most juveniles arguably unjust. Rather, age is simply a "proxy," and an imperfect one at that, for a combination of factors that determines the relative culpability of a juvenile murderer. These factors include maturity, judgment, responsibility, and the capability to assess the possible consequences of one's conduct. Because age only imperfectly reflects this complex combination of factors, the adoption of a "bright line" ban on the death penalty for juveniles, fashioned in terms of age, necessarily violates the concept of ordinal proportionality (Hoffmann, 1989:234–35).

Hoffmann (1989:283–84) suggests that guided discretion statutes applied across the board to all offenders, or a set of rebuttable presumptions about culpability based on age, are more consistent with the principles of retributive theory than the bright line rule laid down in *Thompson*.

5. Does the Small Number of Juveniles Executed Make the Death Penalty Wanton and Freakish?

By one estimate, no more than 20 individuals who were under 16 at the time of their crimes have been executed during this century. Bureau of Justice Statistics also show that only five of the 1,393 persons sentenced to death from 1982 to 1986 were under 16 at the time of the crime (*Thompson v. Oklahoma*, 1988:2697). The plurality interpreted these data as objective indicators of jury behavior demonstrating that juvenile executions had little public support, were "cruel and unusual in the way that being struck by lightning is cruel and unusual" and therefore contrary to contemporary standards of decency (*Thompson v. Oklahoma*, 1988:2697).

Justice O'Connor's view of the data was slightly more cautious. While acknowledging that the plurality may be correct, she pointed out that an accurate interpretation could only be obtained by comparing the actual number of executions and death sentences imposed with the number of times prosecutors actually decided to seek the death penalty in juvenile cases. Because an actual execution results from a joint decision of the prosecutor and the jury (and perhaps the judge and others), it is impossible to determine the meaning of sentencing or execution data without first examining the behavior of all those who contributed to the decision (*Thompson*, 1988:2798).

To the dissent, the fact "that no fewer than 5 murderers who committed their crimes under the age of 16 were sentenced to death in five different States between the years 1984 and 1986" (*Thompson v. Oklahoma*, 1988:2717) represented strong public support *for* juvenile executions. Moreover, to the dissent, the small number of juvenile executions resulted from (1) a decline in overall public support for capital punishment; and (2) the movement away from mandatory, automatic death penalty schemes in favor of guided discretion systems that require individualized consideration of each death sentence. Both of these forces, however, were considered irrelevant to the question of whether the execution of juvenile offenders should *ever* be permitted.

The dissent then presented additional statistical data showing that the execution of female offenders was just as rare an occurrence as the execution of juveniles, and pointed out the inconsistency in banning the execution of latter but not the former.

The debate over the meaning of the data on juvenile executions illustrates the difficulties judges encounter when, in the course of interpreting statistical data, they try to crossbreed a precise numerical quantity (5 death sentences of 20 actual executions) with an inexact verbal standard ("cruel and unusual," or "wanton and freakish"). Despite the effort to rely on "objective indicators" to determine the meaning of contemporary standards of decency, and the meaning of "cruel and unusual" punishment, the fact is that these judgments are ultimately subjective. The number of times a punishment is imposed or carried out is a poor way to judge its acceptability: how certainly can anyone say that the imposition of five death sentences in a period of time is wanton and freakish, but more than five is not?

The dilemma judges face is complicated by the distribution of juvenile crime in the population. Whether crime is counted by official statistics (arrest, prosecution or conviction records) or by various "unofficial" measures (self reports), "persistent and grave violations of the law are the experience of a minority" (Nettler, 1884:82). Given that the number of serious juvenile offenders is small to begin with, we would not expect the number of young people to be sentenced to death to be very large under any circumstances.

C. Weighing Mitigating Factors Against Aggravating Factors: Three Cases in Which the Death Sentence[s Initially] Prevailed

In juvenile death penalty cases, judges and juries have are presented with other possible mitigating factors in addition to youth. In three highly publicized cases a wide array of mitigating factors were presented by defense attorneys to no avail. The judge and/or juries decided that the aggravating factors outweighed the various mitigating circumstances. The three respective states represented here are South Carolina, Indiana, and Louisiana. These cases sparked national and international debate. Of course such debates centered on whether an "enlightened society" should resort to the use of the death penalty for juvenile murderers. The debates also addressed the more common mitigating factors raised in juvenile death penalty cases such as backgrounds of severe child maltreatment, mental retardation, the role of peer pressure (or the presence of an adult who encourages the juvenile to murder), and extreme drug and/or alcohol abuse (see Shapiro, 1978; Lemon, 1979; Amnesty International, 1979; Streib, 1987b; Wikberg and Rideau, 1990).

Roach v. Martin, 1986 involved the following facts:

> ...[I]n Fort Jackson, South Carolina, a 17-year-old mentally retarded youth and a 16-year-old companion were living with a 22-year-old soldier in a rented, run-down house...Alcohol, THC, PCP, marijuana, and other drugs were readily available....[A]fter heavy drinking and consuming drugs, the three decided to look for a girl to rape. They drove to a baseball park in nearby Columbia. They parked next to a young couple, a 17-year-old boy and his 14-year-old girl friend. On orders

from the soldier, they shot the boy three times with a high powered rifle, killing him instantly. Then they drove off with the girl to a secluded area where each raped her repeatedly. Finally, they finished her off by shooting her and mutilating her body.

The three were soon arrested by police. The youngest youth agreed to testify against the soldier and the 17-year-old in exchange for a lighter sentence. Both the soldier and the 17-year-old eventually entered guilty pleas and were sentenced to death. After lengthy appeals, the soldier was executed....James Terry Roach, the 17-year-old who killed the boy and the girl and mutilated the girl's body was executed....A crowd cheered outside the prison walls as the execution of Roach occurred (Champion, 1990:437; Streib, 1987b:125-127).

The second case involves 15-year-old Paula Cooper who was convicted of stabbing to death a 78-year-old bible teacher in Gary, Indiana. This occurred while Cooper and three other teenage girls were attempting to rob the woman in her own home. The prosecutor successfully argued that Cooper was the "ring leader," as she actually brought the knife into the teacher's home. The girls took $10.00 and the victim's car. "There was a public outcry....People in Gary wanted Paula Cooper to get the electric chair. There was that element of betrayal, of the girls being a traitor in killing someone who tried to help kids" (*Knoxville News-Sentinel*, January 3, 1988; Champion, 1990:439-440). Cooper was reared in a violent home. Her father routinely required her and her sister to strip so he could whip their bare skin. Cooper also watched her mother get raped, and when she was 9, had joined her mother and sister in a suicide attempt.

While Paula Cooper was on death row, her case took some unusual turns. First, the grandson of the victim has become one of her staunchest supporters. He travelled Europe, attempting to gain support through a petition drive to have Cooper's sentence commuted to life in prison (Champion, 1990:440). [At this writing, it was learned that this drive was successful.]

The third case occurred in Louisiana and involved Dalton Prejean. As a 14-year-old, Prejean killed a Lafayette taxi cab driver during a robbery and was adjudicated in juvenile court. He was sent to a training school and was released early, as the judge felt that he was responding well to treatment programs. At age 17, Prejean and three companions left a night club, and after driving a short distance, were pulled over by Louisiana State Trooper Donald Cleveland. When Trooper Cleveland began to frisk Dalton's brother, Joseph, Dalton shot the Trooper at close range killing him. Dalton Prejean was convicted of first degree murder and sentenced to death (*Prejean v. Blackburn*, 1984:1093).

A series of events served to prolong the execution for 13 years (list is not exhaustive):

- The Trooper's wife sued the juvenile court judge responsible for releasing Prejean from the training school in a wrongful death action. The judge was found not to be liable under the "judicial immunity doctrine."
- Prejean appealed his conviction to U.S. District Court on four grounds: the judge allowed the jury to see grisly photographs of the body; racial composition of the jury (Prejean was black); racial discrimination on the part of the jury in handing down the death penalty instead of life in prison; and youthful age at the time of the homicide—17. Prejean lost all four issues.

- Prejean's age remained an issue through appeals to the U.S. Circuit Court of Appeals and to the U.S. Supreme Court. Again, Prejean's death sentence was not commuted.
- Prejean then applied to the Louisiana Pardon Board for a commutation. "By this time, he had 8 previous 'stays of execution,' 11 lawyers, 20 different legal issues presented to 6 different courts and a total of 35 judges" (Wikberg and Rideau, 1990:28). At the Pardon hearing, defense attorneys emphasized Prejean's mental retardation and the fact that he was an abused child. The Board voted to commute the death sentence, shortly thereafter, Governor Roemer reversed this decision (the Board's role is to make recommendations to the Governor, but this does not bind the Governor in making the final decision). Prejean was executed in May, 1990.

D. Conclusion: Is Proportionality Between Offense and Punishment Really Necessary, or Will Punishment Comporting to Evolving Standards of Decency Suffice?

Like the cases of *Eddings* and *Bell*, the cases of Roach, Cooper and Prejean involved some mitigating factors in addition to youthful age. Why then were Eddings and Bell spared, but Roach and Prejean executed?

A few observations can be made here. The extent and quality of legal representation for the defense is relevant. Many of these attorneys are indigent defenders who earn only a few thousand dollars per year for a single death penalty case while they have a "human life placed in their hands." Still, some anti-death penalty activist groups have adopted the defense's case, providing extensive resources and funding; this occurred in the Prejean case, among others. Naturally, the particular values of the decision maker (judge or jury) are germane, as is the intensity of public outcry for a death sentence.

Ultimately, however, the aggravating aspects of the *Roach* and *Prejean* cases out-weighed the mitigating factors as perceived by the decision makers (judge or jury). While all murders committed by juveniles are shocking due to the youth of perpetrator, the facts in the Roach case were unusually grisly and horrible. The facts in the Prejean case involved the killing of a police officer by a youth who has killed before. Nonetheless, all current death penalty statutes require a judge or jury to weigh aggravation against mitigation; this punctuates the individuality of each case. It is not the legislative intent for such laws to standardize definitions of aggravation and mitigation. Rather, such standards are supposed to reflect the ideological climate and social values of the particular state; that is, "evolving standards of decency." Should satisfaction of these "standards" supplant a proportionality analysis? Will this happen in future Eighth Amendment assessments of juvenile death penalty cases?

The U.S. Supreme Court case of *Stanford v. Kentucky*, 1989[13] may provide some clue. In *Stanford*, two petitioners were convicted in separate homicides: Kevin Stanford was approximately 17 years and four months old at the time of the crime, while Heath Wilkins was about 16 years and 6 months old when he committed his offense. Like most of the other juvenile cases discussed above, Stanford and Heath argued that they were too young to be put to death. The Court disagreed, reaffirming its earlier ruling in

[13] *Stanford* was consolidated with *Wilkins v. Missouri* (1989).

Thompson. *Stanford* is noteworthy not so much for what it says about juvenile executions, but because it may signal a change in how the Court will review future death penalty cases.

Many of the issues considered in *Thompson*—the questions of national consensus, the infrequency of actual executions, the relevance of age-based restrictions on other forms of juvenile behavior, the views of the international community and professional organizations, and the retributive and deterrent value of juvenile executions—were raised once again in *Stanford*.[14] Additionally, however, the Justices seemed to disagree about how an Eighth Amendment analysis should be conducted.[15] The sole focus on the majority's analysis in *Stanford* was whether petitioner's death sentences were consistent with the "evolving standards of decency" test announced three decades earlier in *Trop v. Dulles* (1958). Having decided that the sentences were acceptable, the majority saw no need to go any further and consider, as a separate issue, whether death sentences were disproportionate to the offense. If this interpretation is correct, than the majority has radically altered the way in which death penalty cases will be reviewed. After *Stanford*, it may no longer be true that "the Eighth Amendment demands more than that a challenged punishment be acceptable to contemporary society" (*Gregg v. Georgia*, 1976:2929). This may well become the primary test of the constitutionality of a punishment in the future.

KEVIN N. STANFORD, PETITIONER

V.

KENTUCKY.

HEATH A. WILKINS, PETITIONER

V.

[14]To demonstrate, the following three issues are representative: *Stanford* began with a review of existing capital punishment legislation. Justices Scalia, Rhenquist, White, O'Connor and Kennedy found that 15 jurisdictions set the minimum age for execution at 17 while 12 others set it at 18; they also assumed that 18 states that set no specific minimum age for the operation of their capital punishment statutes would permit executions at age 16, since these jurisdictions permitted 16 year olds to be tried as adults. From this reasoning they concluded that "a majority of the states that permit execution authorize it for crimes committed at age 16 or above" (*Stanford v. Kentucky*, 1989:2975–76).

As they had in *Thompson*, Justices Brennan, Marshall, Blackmun and Stevens combined the 12 jurisdictions that set the minimum age at 18, with 15 others that abolished the death penalty, and three more that prohibited the execution of those under 17 to conclude that a total of 30 jurisdictions would prohibit Wilkins execution; once again they omitted the 18 states that set no minimum age in their capital punishment statutes for the reasons set forth in *Thompson* (*Stanford v. Kentucky*, 1989:2982–83).

The Justices once again considered the infrequency of the punishment itself. For the majority, the low number of juvenile executions occurred because juries appropriately reserved the most extreme punishments for the most extreme juvenile offenders (*Stanford v. Kentucky*, 1989:2977), while the dissent argued that the infrequent imposition made the punishment "unusual" and therefore contrary to the Eighth Amendment.

[15]See extensive annotations in *Stanford v. Kentucky* 106 L.Ed.2d 306, 1989.

MISSOURI.

NOS. 87–5765, 87–6026.

ARGUED MARCH 27, 1989.

DECIDED JUNE 26, 1989.

* * *

SYLLABUS

* * *

These two consolidated cases require us to decide whether the imposition of capital punishment on an individual for a crime committed at 16 or 17 years of age constitutes cruel and unusual punishment under the Eight Amendment.

I

The first case, No. 87–5765, involves the shooting death of 20–year–old Baerbel Poore in Jefferson County, Kentucky. Petitioner Kevin Stanford committed the murder on January 7, 1981, when he was approximately 17 years and 4 months of age. Stanford and his accomplice repeatedly raped and sodomized Poore during and after their commission of a robbery at a gas station where she worked as an attendant. They then drove her to a secluded area near the station, where Stanford shot her point-blank in the face and then in the back of her head. The proceeds from the robbery were roughly 300 cartons of cigarettes, two gallons of fuel and a small amount of cash. A corrections officer testified that petitioner explained the murder as follows: "'[H]e said, I had to shoot her [she] lived next door to me and she would recognize me.... I guess we could have tied her up or something or beat [her up]...and tell her if she tells, we would kill her.... Then after he said that he started laughing.'" 734 S.W.2d 781, 788 (Ky. 1987).

After Stanford's arrest, a Kentucky juvenile court conducted hearings to determine whether he should be transferred for trial as an adult under Ky.Rev.Stat. § 208.170 (Michie 1982). That statute provided that juvenile court jurisdiction could be waived and an offender tried as an adult if he was either charged with a Class A felony or capital crime, or was over 16 years of age and charged with a felony. Stressing the seriousness of petitioner's offenses and the unsuccessful attempts of the juvenile system to treat him for numerous instances of past delinquency, the juvenile court found certification for trial as an adult to be in the best interest of petitioner and the community. Stanford was convicted of murder, first–degree sodomy, first–degree robbery, and receiving stolen property, and was sentenced to death and 45 years in prison. The Kentucky Supreme Court affirmed the death sentence, rejecting Stanford's "deman[d] that he has a constitutional right to treatment" 734 S.W.2d, at 792. Finding that the record clearly demonstrated that "there was no program or treatment appropriate for the appellant in the juvenile justice system" the court held that the juvenile court did not err in certifying petitioner for trial as an adult. The court also stated that petitioner's "age and the possibility that he might be rehabilitated were mitigating factors appropriately left to the consideration of the jury that tried him." *Ibid.*

The second case before us today, No. 87-6026, involves the stabbing death of Nancy Allen, a 26-year-old mother of two who was working behind the sales counter of the convenience store she and David Allen owned and operated in Avondale, Missouri. Petitioner Heath Wilkins committed the murder on July 27, 1985, when he was approximately 16 years and 6 months of age. The record reflects that Wilkins' plan was to rob the store and murder "whoever was behind the counter" because "a dead person can't talk." While Wilkins' accomplice, Patrick Stevens, held Allen, Wilkins stabbed her, causing her to fall to the floor. When Stevens had trouble operating the cash register, Allen spoke up to assist him, leading Wilkins to stab her three more times in her chest. Two of these wounds penetrated the victim's heart. When Allen began to beg for her life, Wilkins stabbed her four more times in the neck, opening her carotid artery. After helping themselves to liquor, cigarettes, rolling papers, and approximately $450 in cash and checks, Wilkins and Stevens left Allen to die on the floor.

Because he was roughly six months short of the age of majority for purposes of criminal prosecution, Mo.Rev.Stat. § 211.021(1) (1986), Wilkins could not automatically be tried as an adult under Missouri law. Before that could happen, the juvenile court was required to terminate juvenile-court jurisdiction and certify Wilkins for trial as an adult under § 211.071, which permits individuals between 14 and 17 years of age who have committed felonies to be tried as adults. Relying on the "viciousness, force and violence" of the alleged crime, petitioner's maturity, and the failure of the juvenile justice system to rehabilitate him after previous delinquent acts, the juvenile court made the necessary certification.

Wilkins was charged with first-degree murder, armed criminal action, and carrying a concealed weapon. After the court found him competent, petitioner entered guilty pleas to all charges. A punishment hearing was held, at which both the State and petitioner himself urged imposition of the death sentence. Evidence at the hearing revealed that petitioner had been in and out of juvenile facilities since the age of eight for various acts of burglary, theft, and arson, had attempted to kill his mother by putting insecticide into Tylenol capsules, and had killed several animals in his neighborhood. Although psychiatric testimony indicated that Wilkins had "personality disorders," the witnesses agreed that Wilkins was aware of his actions and could distinguish right from wrong.

Determining that the death penalty was appropriate, the trial court entered the following order:

"The court finds beyond reasonable doubt that the following aggravated circumstances exist:

"1. The murder in the first degree was committed while the defendant was engaged in the perpetration of the felony and robbery, and

"2. The murder in the first degree involved depravity of mind and that as a result thereof, it was outrageously or wantonly vile, horrible or inhuman." App. in No. 87-6026.

On mandatory review of Wilkins' death sentence, the Supreme Court of Missouri affirmed, rejecting the argument that the punishment violated the Eighth Amendment. 736 S.W.2d 409 (1987).

We granted certiorari in these cases, 488 U.S. ——, 109 S.Ct. 217, 102 L.Ed.2d 208 and 487 U.S. ——, 108 S.Ct. 2896, 101 L.Ed.2d 930 (1988), to decide whether the Eighth Amendment precludes the death penalty for individuals who commit crimes at 16 or 17 years of age.

II

The thrust of both Wilkins' and Stanford's arguments is that imposition of the death penalty on those who were juveniles when they committed their crimes falls within the Eighth Amendment's prohibition against "cruel and unusual punishments." Wilkins would have us define juveniles as individuals 16 years of age and under; Stanford would draw the line at 17.

Neither petitioner asserts that his sentence constitutes one of "those modes or acts of punishment that had been considered cruel and unusual at the time that the Bill of Rights was adopted." *Ford v. Wainwright,* 477 U.S. 399, 405, 106 S.Ct. 2595, 2600, 91 L.Ed.2d 335 (1986). Nor could they support such a contention. At that time, the common law set the rebuttable presumption of incapacity to commit any felony at the age of 14, and theoretically permitted capital punishment to be imposed on anyone over the age of 7. See 4 Blackstone, Commentaries *23–24; 1 M. Hale, Pleas of the Crown 24–29 (1800 ed.). See also *In re Gault,* 387 U.S. 1, 16, 87 S.Ct. 1428, 1437, 18 L.Ed.2d 527 (1967); Streib, Death Penalty for Children: The American Experience with Capital Punishment for Crimes Committed While Under Age Eighteen, 36 Okla.L.Rev. 613, 614–615 (1983); Kean, The History of the Criminal Liability of Children, 53 L.Q.Rev. 364, 369–370 (1937). In accordance with the standards of this common-law tradition, at least 281 offenders under the age of 18 have been executed in this country, and at least 126 under the age of 17. See V. Streib, Death Penalty for Juveniles 57 (1987).

Thus petitioners are left to argue that their punishment is contrary to the "evolving standards of decency that mark the progress of a maturing society," *Trop v. Dulles,* 356 U.S. 86, 101, 78 S.Ct. 590, 598, 2 L.Ed.2d 630 (1958) (plurality opinion). They are correct in asserting that this Court has "not confined the prohibition embodied in the Eighth Amendment to 'barbarous' methods that were generally outlawed in the 18th century," but instead has interpreted the Amendment "in a flexible and dynamic manner." *Gregg v. Georgia,* 428 U.S. 153, 171, 96 S.Ct. 2909, 2924, 49 L.Ed.2d 859 (1976). In determining what standards have "evolved," however, we have looked not to our own conceptions of decency, but to those of modern American society as a whole. As we have said, "Eighth Amendment judgments should not be, or appear to be, merely the subjective views of individual Justices; judgment should be informed by objective factors to the maximum possible extent." * * *

III

"[F]irst" among the "'objective indicia that reflect the public attitude toward a given sanction'" are statutes passed by society's elected representatives. *McCleskey v. Kemp,* 481 U.S. 279, 300, 107 S.Ct. 1756, 1770, 95 L.Ed.2d 262 (1987), quoting *Gregg v. Georgia, supra,* 428 U.S., at 173, 96 S.Ct., at 2925. Of the 37 States whose laws permit capital punishment, 15 decline to impose it upon 16-year-old offenders and 12 decline to impose it on 17-year-old offenders. This does not establish the degree of national consensus this Court has previously thought sufficient to label a particular punishment cruel and unusual. In invalidating the death penalty for rape of an adult woman, we stress that Georgia was the *sole* jurisdiction that authorized such a punishment. See *Coker v. Georgia,* 433 U.S., at 595–596, 97 S.Ct., at 2867–2868. In striking down capital punishment for participation in a robbery in which an accomplice takes a life, we emphasized that only eight jurisdictions authorized similar punishment. *Enmund v. Florida,* 458 U.S., at 792, 102 S.Ct., at 3374. In finding that the Eighth Amendment precludes execution of the insane and thus requires an adequate hearing on the issue of sanity, we relied upon (in addition to the common-law rule) the fact that "no State in the Union" permitted such punishment. *Ford v. Wainwright,* 477 U.S., at 408, 106 S.Ct., at 2601. And in striking down a life sentence without parole under a recidivist statute, we stressed that "[i]t appears that [petitioner] was treated more severely than he would have been in any other State." *Solem v. Helm,* 463 U.S. 277, 300, 103 S.Ct. 3001, 3015, 77 L.Ed.2d 637 (1983).

Since a majority of the States that permit capital punishment authorize it for crimes committed at age 16 or above, petitioners' cases are more analogous to *Tison v. Arizona,* 481 U.S. 137, 107 S.Ct. 1676, 95 L.Ed.2d 127 (1987) than *Coker, Enmund, Ford,* and *Solem*. In *Tison,* which upheld Arizona's imposition of the death penalty for major participation in a felony with reckless indifference to human life, we noted that only 11 of those jurisdictions imposing capital punishment rejected its use in such circumstances. *Id,* at 154, 107 S.Ct., at 1686. As we noted earlier, here the number is 15 for offenders under 17, and 12 for offenders under 18. We think the same conclusion as in *Tison* is required in this case.

Petitioners make much of the recently enacted federal statute providing capital punishment for certain drug-related offenses, but limiting that punishment to offenders 18 and over. The Anti-Drug Abuse Act of 1988, Pub.L. 100–690, 102 Stat. 4390, § 7001(b). That reliance is entirely misplaced. To begin with, the statute in question does not embody a judgment by the Federal Legislature that *no* murder is heinous enough to warrant the execution of such a youthful offender, but merely that the narrow class of offense it defines is not. The congressional judgment on the broader question, if apparent at all, is to be found in the law that permits 16- and 17-year-olds (after appropriate findings) to be tried and punished as adults for *all* federal offenses, including those bearing a capital penalty that is not limited to 18-year-olds. See 18 U.S.C. § 5032 (1982 ed., Supp. V). Moreover, even if it were true that no federal statute permitted the execution of persons under 18, that would not remotely establish—in the face of a substantial number of state statutes to the contrary—a national consensus that such punishment is inhumane, any more than the absence of a federal lottery establishes a national consensus that lotteries are socially harmful. To be sure, the absence of a federal death penalty for 16- or 17-year-olds (if it existed) might be evidence that there is no national consensus *in favor* of such punishment. It is not the burden of Kentucky and Missouri, however, to establish a national consensus approving what their citizens have voted to do; rather, it is the "heavy burden" of petitioners, *Gregg v. Georgia,* 428 U.S., at 175, 96 S.Ct., at 2926, to establish a national consensus *against* it. As far as the primary and most reliable indication of consensus is concerned—the pattern of enacted laws—petitioners have failed to carry that burden.

IV

A

Wilkins and Stanford argue, however, that even if the laws themselves do not establish a settled consensus, the application of the laws does. That contemporary society views capital punishment of 16- and 17-year-old offenders as inappropriate is demonstrated, they say, by the reluctance of juries to impose, and prosecutors to seek, such sentences. Petitioners are quite correct that a far smaller number of offenders under 18 than over 18 have been sentenced to death in this country. From 1982 through 1988, for example, out of 2,106 total death sentences, only 15 were imposed on individuals who were 17 at the time of the crime. See Streib, Imposition of Death Sentences For Juvenile Offenses, January 1, 1982, Through April 1, 1989, p. 2 (paper for Cleveland-Marshall College of Law, April 5, 1989). And it appears that actual executions for crimes committed under age 18 accounted for only about two percent of the total number of executions that occurred between 1642 and 1986. See Streib, Death Penalty for Juveniles, at 55, 57. As Wilkins points out, the last execution of a person who committed a crime under 17 years of age occurred in 1959. These statistics, however, carry little significance. Given the undisputed fact that a far smaller percentage of capital crimes is committed by persons under 18 than over 18, the discrepancy in treatment is much less than might seem. Granted, however, that a substantial discrepancy exists, that does not establish the requisite proposition that the death sentence for offenders under 18 is categorically unacceptable to prosecutors and juries. To the contrary, it is not only possible but overwhelmingly probable that the very considerations which induce petitioners and their supporters to believe that death should *never* be imposed on offenders under 18 cause prosecutors and juries to believe that it should *rarely* be imposed.

B

This last point suggests why there is also no relevance to the law cited by petitioners and their *amici* which set 18 or more as the legal age for engaging in various activities, ranging from driving to drinking alcoholic beverages to voting. It is, to begin with, absurd to think that one must be mature enough to drive carefully, to drink responsibly, or to vote intelligently, in order to be mature enough to understand that murdering another human being is profoundly wrong, and to confirm one's conduct to that most minimal of all civilized standards. But even if the requisite degrees of maturity were comparable, the age-statutes in question would still not be relevant. They do not represent a social judgment that all persons under the designated ages are not responsible enough to drive, to drink, or to vote, but at most a judgment that the vast majority are not. These laws set the appropriate ages for the operation of a system that makes its determinations in gross, and that does not conduct individualized maturity tests for each driver, drinker, or voter. The criminal justice system, however, does provide individualized testing. In the realm of capital punishment in particular, "individualized consideration [is] a constitutional requirement," *Lockett v. Ohio,* 438 U.S. 586, 605, 98 S.Ct. 2954, 2965, 57 L.Ed.2d 973 (1978) (opinion of Burger, C.J.) (footnote omitted); see also *Zant v. Stephens,* 462 U.S. 862, 879, 103 S.Ct. 2733, 2743, 77 L.Ed.2d 235 (1983) (collecting cases), and one of the individualized mitigating factors that sentencers must be permitted to consider is the defendant's age. See *Eddings v. Oklahoma,* 455 U.S. 104, 115–116, 102 S.Ct. 869, 877–878, 71 L.Ed.2d 1 (1982). Twenty-nine States, including both Kentucky and Missouri, have codified this constitutional requirement in laws specifically designating the defendant's age as a mitigating factor in capital cases. Moreover, the determinations required by juvenile transfer statutes to certify a juvenile for trial as an adult ensure individualized consideration of the maturity and moral responsibility of 16- and 17-year-old offenders before they are even held to stand trial as adults. The application of this particularized system to the petitioners can be declared constitutionally inadequate only if there is a consensus, not that 17 or 18 is the age at which most persons, or even almost all persons, achieve sufficient maturity to be held fully responsible for murder; but that 17 or 18 is the age before which *no one* can reasonably be held fully responsible. What displays society's views on this latter point are not the ages set forth in the generalized system of driving, drinking, and voting laws cited by petitioners and their *amici,* but the ages at which the States permit their particularized capital punishment system to be applied.

V

Having failed to establish a consensus against capital punishment for 16- and 17-year-old offenders through state and federal statutes and the behavior of prosecutors and juries, petitioners seek to demonstrate it through other indicia, including public opinion polls, the views of interest groups and the positions adopted by various professional associations. We decline the invitation to rest constitutional law on such uncertain foundations. A revised national consensus so broad, so clear and so enduring as to justify a permanent prohibition on all units of democratic government must appear in the operative acts (laws and the application of laws) that the people have approved.

We also reject petitioners' argument that we should invalidate capital punishment of 16- and 17-year-old offenders on the ground that it fails to serve the legitimate goals of penology. According to petitioners, it fails to deter because juveniles, possessing less developed cognitive skills than adults are less likely to fear death; and it fails to exact just retribution because juveniles, being less mature and responsible, are also less morally blameworthy. In support of these claims, petitioners and their supporting *amici* marshall an array of socioscientific evidence concerning the psychological and emotional development of 16- and 17-year olds.

If such evidence could conclusively establish the entire lack of deterrent effect and moral responsibility, resort to the Cruel and Unusual Punishments Clause would be unnecessary; the Equal Protection Clause of the Fourteenth Amendment would invalidate these laws for lack of a rational basis. See *Dallas v. Stanglin*, 490 U.S.—, 109 S.Ct. 1591, 104 L.Ed.2d 18 (1989). But as the adjective "socioscientific" suggests (and insofar as evaluation of moral responsibility is concerned perhaps the adjective "ethicoscientific" would be more apt), it is not demonstrable that no 16-year-old is "adequately responsible" or significantly deterred. It is rational, even if mistaken, to think the contrary. The battle must be fought then, on the field of the Eighth Amendment; and in that struggle, socioscientific, ethicoscientific or even purely scientific evidence is not an available weapon. The punishment is either "cruel *and* unusual" (*i.e.*, society has set its face against it) or it is not. The audience for these arguments, in other words, is not the Court but the citizenry of the United States. It is they, not we, who must be persuaded. For, as we stated earlier, our job is to *identify* the "evolving standards of decency"; to determine, not what they should be, but what they *are*. We have no power under the Eighth Amendment to substitute our belief in the scientific evidence for society's apparent skepticism. In short, we emphatically reject petitioner's suggestion that the issues in this case permit us to apply our "own informed judgment," Brief for Petitioner in No. 87-6026, p. 23, regarding the desirability of permitting the death penalty for crimes by 16- and 17-year-olds.

* * *

We discern neither a historical nor a modern societal consensus forbidding the imposition of capital punishment on any person who murders at 16 or 17 years of age. Accordingly we conclude that such punishment does not offend the Eighth Amendment's prohibition against cruel and unusual punishment.

The judgments of the Supreme Court of Kentucky and the Supreme Court of Missouri are therefore

AFFIRMED.

STANFORD V. KENTUCKY

1. How did the petitioners make use of the federal law providing for the death penalty for certain drug related offenses? Was this argument successful? Explain.
2. Summarize petitioner's argument that the death penalty for 16- and 17-year-olds should be abolished on the ground that it fails to "serve the legitimate goals of penology."
3. Summarize the psychological report on Wilkins. To what extent should such a social history serve as a mitigating factor in a death penalty case.
4. Discuss the relevance of draft laws, drinking laws, and marriage laws to juvenile death penalty laws.

WILLIAM WAYNE THOMPSON, PETITIONER

v.

OKLAHOMA.

NO. 86-6169.

ARGUED NOV. 9, 1987.

DECIDED JUNE 29, 1988.

* * *

JUSTICE STEVENS announced the judgment of the Court and delivered an opinion in which JUSTICE BRENNAN, JUSTICE MARSHALL, and JUSTICE BLACKMUN join.

Petitioner was convicted of first degree murder and sentenced to death. The principal question presented is whether the execution of that sentence would violate the constitutional prohibition against "cruel and unusual punishments" [footnote omitted] because petitioner was only 15 years old at the time of his offense.

* * *

II

The authors of the Eighth Amendment drafted a categorical prohibition against the infliction of cruel and unusual punishments, but they made no attempt to define the contours of that category. They delegated that task to future generations of judges who have been guided by the "evolving standards of decency that mark the progress of a maturing society." *Trop v. Dulles*, 356 U.S. 86, 101, 78 S.Ct. 590, 598, 2 L.Ed.2d 630 (1958) (plurality opinion) (Warren, C.J.) [footnote omitted]. In performing that task the Court has reviewed the work product of state legislatures and sentencing juries [footnote omitted], and has carefully considered the reasons why a civilized society may accept or reject the death penalty in certain types of cases. Thus, in confronting the question whether the youth of the defendant—more specifically, the fact that he was less than 16 years old at the time of his offense—is a sufficient reason for denying the State the power to sentence him to death, we first review relevant legislative enactments, then refer to jury determinations and finally explain why these indicators of contemporary standards of decency confirm our judgment that such a young person is not capable of acting with the degree of culpability that can justify the ultimate penalty [footnotes omitted].

III

Justice Powell has repeatedly reminded us of the importance of "the experience of mankind, as well as the long history of our law, recognizing that there *are* differences which must be accommodated in determining the rights and duties of children as compared with those of adults." * * * Oklahoma recognizes this basic distinction in a number of its statutes.[16] Thus, a minor is not eligible to vote, to sit on a jury, to marry without parental consent, or to purchase alcohol or cigarettes [citations omitted]. Like all other States, Oklahoma has developed a juvenile justice system in which most offenders under the age of 18 are not held criminally responsible. Its statutes do provide, however, that a 16- or 17-year-old charged with murder and other serious felonies shall be considered an adult [footnote omitted]. Other than the special certification procedure that was used to authorize petitioner's trial in this case "as an adult," apparently their are no Oklahoma statutes, either civil or criminal, that treat a person under 16 years of age as anything but a "child."

The line between childhood and adulthood is drawn in different ways by various States. There is, however, complete or near unanimity among all 50 states and the District of Columbia[17] in treating a person under 16 as a minor for several important purposes. In no State may a 15-year-old vote or serve on a jury. Further, in all but one State a 15-year-old may not drive without parental consent, and in all but four States a 15-year-old may not marry without parental consent. Additionally, in those States that have legislated on the subject, no one under age 16 may purchase pornographic materials (50 States), and in most States that have some form of legalized gambling, minors are not permitted to participate without parental consent (42 States). Most relevant, however, is the fact that all States have enacted legislation designating the maximum age for juvenile court jurisdiction at no less than 16. All of this legislation is consistent with the experience of mankind, as well as the long history of our law, that the normal 15-year-old is not prepared to assume the full responsibilities of an adult.

Most state legislatures have not expressly confronted the question of establishing a minimum age for imposition of the death penalty. In 14 States, capital punishment is not authorized at all, and in 19 others, capital punishment is authorized, but no minimum age is expressly stated in the death penalty statute. One might argue on the basis of this body of legislation that there is no chronological age at which the imposition of the death penalty is unconstitutional and that our current standards of decency would still tolerate the execution of a 10-year-old children. We think it self-evident that such an argument is unacceptable; indeed, no such argument has been advanced in this case [footnote omitted]. If, therefore, we accept the premise that some offenders are simply too young to be put to death, it is reasonable to put this group of statutes to one side because they do not focus on the question of where the chronological age line should be drawn. When we confine our attention to the 18 States that have expressly established a minimum age in their death-penalty statutes, we find that all of them require that the defendant have attained at least the age of 16 at the time of the capital offense.

---

[16]Most of the footnotes in this section of the Court's opinion provide relevant statutory citations as authority for the statements made. In the interest of brevity, these citations have been omitted throughout this section.

[17]Henceforth, the opinion will refer to the 50 States and the District of Columbia as "States," for the sake of simplicity.

The conclusion that it would offend civilized standards of decency to execute a person who was less than 16 years old at the time of his or her offense is consistent with the views that have been expressed by respected professional organizations, by other nations that share our Anglo-American heritage, and by the leading members of the Western European community [footnote omitted]. Thus, the American Bar Association and the American Law Institute have formally expressed their opposition to the death penalty for juveniles. Although the death penalty has not been entirely abolished in the United Kingdom or New Zealand (it has been abolished in Australia, except in the state of New South Wales, where it is available for treason and piracy), in neither of those countries may a juvenile be executed. The death penalty has been abolished in West Germany, France, Portugal, The Netherlands, and all of the Scandinavian countries, and is available only for exceptional crimes such as treason in Canada, Italy, Spain, and Switzerland. Juvenile executions are also prohibited in the Soviet Union.

IV

The second societal factor the Court has examined in determining the acceptability of capital punishment to the American sensibility is the behavior of juries. In fact, the infrequent and haphazard handing out of death sentences by capital juries was a prime factor underlying our judgment in *Furman v. Georgia*, 408 U.S. 238, 92 S.Ct. 2726, 33 L.Ed. 2d 346 (1972), that the death penalty, as then administered in unguided fashion, was unconstitutional.

While it is not known precisely how many persons have been executed during the 20th century for crimes committed under the age of 16, a scholar has recently compiled a table revealing the number to be between 18 and 20.[18] All of these occurred during the first half of the century, with the last such execution taking place apparently in 1948 [footnote omitted]. In the following year, this Court observed that the "whole country has traveled far from the period in which the death sentence was an automatic and commonplace result of convictions..." *Williams v. New York*, 337 U.S. 241, 247, 69 S.Ct. 1079, 1083, 93 L.Ed. 1337 (1949). The road we have traveled during the past four decades—in which thousands of juries have tried murder cases—leads to the unambiguous conclusion that the imposition of the death penalty on a 15-year-old offender is now generally abhorrent to the conscience of the community.

Department of Justice statistics indicate that during the years 1982 through 1986 an average of over 16,000 persons were arrested for wilful criminal homicide (murder and non-negligent manslaughter) each year. Of that group, of 82,094 persons, 1,393 were sentenced to death. Only 5 of them, including the petitioner in this case, were less than 16 years old at the time of the offense [citation omitted]. Statistics of this kind can be interpreted in different ways, but they do suggest that these five young offenders have received sentences that are "cruel and unusual in the same way that being struck by lightning is cruel and unusual." *Furman v. Georgia*, 408 U.S. at 309, 92 S.Ct. 2762, (Stewart, J., concurring).

---

[18]V Streib, *Death Penalty for Juveniles* 190-208 (1987).

V

"Although the judgments of legislatures, juries, and prosecutors weigh heavily in the balance, it is for us ultimately to judge whether the Eighth Amendment permits imposition of the death penalty" on one such as petitioner who has committed a heinous murder when he was only 15 years old. *Enmund v. Florida*, 458 U.S. 782, 797, 102 S.Ct 3368, 3376, 73 L.Ed.2d 1140 (1982) [footnote omitted]. In making that judgment, we first ask whether the juvenile's culpability should be measured by the same standard as that of an adult, and then consider whether the application of the death penalty to this class of offenders "measurably contributes" to the social purposes that are served by the death penalty. *Id.*, at 789, 102 S.Ct., at 3377.

It is generally agreed that "punishment should be directly related to the personal culpability of the criminal defendant." *California v. Brown*, 479 U.S. 538, 545, 107 S.Ct. 837, 841, 93 L.Ed.2d 934 (1987) (O'CONNOR, J., concurring). There is also broad agreement on the proposition that adolescents as a class are less mature and responsible than adults. We stressed this difference in explaining the importance of treating the defendant's youth as a mitigating factor in capital cases:

> "But youth is more than a chronological fact. It is a time and condition of life when a person may be the most susceptible to influence and to psychological damage. Our history is replete with laws and judicial recognition that minors, especially in their earlier years, generally are less mature and responsible than adults. Particularly 'during the formative years of childhood and adolescence, minors often lack the perspective, and judgment' expected of adults. *Bellotti v. Baird*, 443 U.S. 622, 635 [99 S.Ct. 3035, 3043, 61 L.Ed.2d 797] (1979)." *Eddings v. Oklahoma*, 455 U.S. 104, 115–116, 102 S.Ct. 869, 877, 71 L.Ed.2d 1 (1982) (footnotes omitted).

* * *

Thus, the Court has already endorsed the proposition that less culpability should attach to a crime committed by a juvenile than to a comparable crime committed by an adult [footnote omitted]. The basis for this conclusion is too obvious to require extended explanation [footnote omitted]. Inexperience, less education, and less intelligence make the teenager less able to evaluate the consequences of his or her conduct while at the same time he or she is much more apt to be motivated by mere emotion or peer pressure than is an adult. The reasons why juveniles are not trusted with the privileges and responsibilities of an adult also explain why their irresponsible conduct is not as morally reprehensible as that of an adult [footnote omitted].

"The death penalty is said to serve two principle social purposes: retribution and deterrence of capital crimes by prospective offenders." *Gregg v. Georgia*, 428 U.S. 153, 183, 96 S.Ct. 2909, 2929–2930, 49 L.Ed.2d 859 (1976) * * * In *Gregg*, we concluded that as "an expression of society's moral outrage at offensive conduct," retribution was not "inconsistent with our respect for the dignity of men." *Ibid* [footnote omitted]. Given the lesser culpability of the juvenile offender, the teenager's capacity for growth, and society's fiduciary obligations to its children, this conclusion is simply inapplicable to the execution of a 15-year-old offender.

For such a young offender, the deterrence rationale is equally unacceptable [footnote omitted]. The Department of Justice statistics indicate that about 98% of the arrests for willful homicide involved persons who were over 16 at the time of the offense [footnote omitted]. Thus, excluding younger persons from the class that is eligible for the death penalty will not diminish the deterrent value of capital punishment for the vast majority of potential offenders. And even with respect to those under 16 years of age, it is obvious that the potential deterrent value of the death sentence is insignificant for two reasons. The likelihood that the teenage offender has made the kind of cost-benefit analysis that attaches any weight to the possibility of execution is so remote as to be virtually nonexistent. And, even if one posits such a cold-blooded calculation by a 15-year-old, it is fanciful to believe that he would be deterred by the knowledge that a small number of persons his age have been executed during the 20th century. In short, we are not persuaded that the imposition of the death penalty for offenses committed by persons under 16 years of age has made, or can be expected to make, any measurable contribution to the goals that capital punishment is intended to achieve. It is therefore "nothing more than the purposeless and needless imposition of pain and suffering." *Coker v. Georgia*, 433 U.S. at 592, 97 S.Ct. at 2866, and thus an unconstitutional punishment [footnote omitted].

VI

Petitioners counsel and various *amici curiae* have asked us to "draw a line" that would prohibit the execution of any person who was under the age of 18 at the time of the offense. Our task today, however, is to decide the case before us; we do so by concluding that the Eight and Fourteenth Amendment prohibit the execution of a person who was under 16 years of age at the time of his or her offense [footnote omitted].

The judgment of the Court of Criminal Appeals is vacated, and the case is remanded with instructions to enter an appropriate order vacating petitioner's death sentence.

It is so ordered.

THOMPSON V. OKLAHOMA

1. What is the so-called "bright line theory"?

2. Explain the way the idea of "national consensus" was used in *Thompson* to reach a conclusion about the death penalty for juveniles.

3. In *Thompson*, the plurality divided the states into three categories: those that abolished the death penalty for any offender (adult or juvenile); those that set a minimum age for its imposition; and those that permitted the death penalty but did not set a minimum age for its use. Provide pro-con

arguments for each category and then choose the argument which seems to best fit "national consensus."

4. How were international comparisons utilized by the *Thompson* plurality?

5. Address the issue of "personal responsibility" or "culpability" as discussed by Justice O'Connor in the plurality. How was the concept related to the "bright line theory"?

MONTY LEE EDDINGS, PETITIONER,

V.

OKLAHOMA.

NO. 80–5727.

ARGUED NOV. 2, 1981.

DECIDED JAN. 19, 1982.

* * *

JUSTICE POWELL delivered the opinion of the Court.

Petitioner Monty Lee Eddings was convicted of first–degree murder and sentenced to death. Because this sentence was imposed without "the type of individualized consideration of mitigating factors...required by the Eighth and Fourteenth Amendments in capital cases," Lockett v. Ohio, 438 U.S. 586, 606, 98 S.Ct. 2954, 2965, 57 L.Ed.2d 973 (1978) (opinion of BURGER, C. J.), we reverse.

I

On April 4, 1977, Eddings, a 16–year–old youth, and several younger companions ran away from their Missouri homes. They traveled in a car owned by Eddings' brother, and drove without destination or purpose in a southwesterly direction eventually reaching the Oklahoma Turnpike. Eddings had in the car a shotgun and several rifles he had taken from his father. After he momentarily lost control of the car, he was signalled to pull over by Officer Crabtree of the Oklahoma Highway Patrol. Eddings did so, and when the officer approached the car, Eddings stuck a loaded shotgun out of the window and fired, killing the officer.

Because Eddings was a juvenile, the State moved to have him certified to stand trial as an adult. Finding that there was prosecutive merit to the complaint and that Eddings was not amendable to rehabilitation within the juvenile system, the trial court granted the motion. The ruling was affirmed on appeal. *In re M.E.*, 584 P.2d 1340 (Okla.Crim.App.), cert. denied *sub nom. Eddings v. Oklahoma*, 436 U.S. 921, 98 S.Ct. 2271, 56 L.Ed.2d 763 (1978). Eddings was then charged with murder in the first degree, and the District Court of Creek County found him guilty upon his plea of *nolo contendere*.

The Oklahoma death penalty statute provides in pertinent part:

> "Upon conviction...of guilt of a defendant of murder in the first degree, the court shall conduct a separate sentencing proceeding to determine whether the defendant should be sentenced to death or life imprisonment.... In the sentencing proceeding, evidence may be presented as to *any mitigating circumstances* or as to any of the aggravating circumstances enumerated in this act." Okla.Stat., Tit. 21, § 701.10 (1980) (emphasis added).

Section 701.12 lists seven separate aggravating circumstances; the statute nowhere defines what is meant by "any mitigating circumstances."

At the sentencing hearing, the State alleged three of the aggravating circumstances enumerated in the statute: that the murder was especially heinous, atrocious, or cruel, that the crime was committed for the purpose of avoiding or preventing a lawful arrest, and that there was a probability that the defendant would commit criminal acts of violence that would constitute a continuing threat to society. §§ 701.12(4), (5), and (7).

In mitigation, Eddings presented substantial evidence at the hearing of his troubled youth. The testimony of his supervising Juvenile Officer indicated that Eddings had been raised without proper guidance. His parents were divorced when he was 5 years old, and until he was 14 Eddings lived with his mother without rules or supervision. App. 109. There is the suggestion that Eddings' mother was an alcoholic and possibly a prostitute. *Id.*, at 110–111. By the time Eddings was 14 he no longer could be controlled, and his mother sent him to live with his father. But neither could the father control the boy. Attempts to reason and talk gave way to physical punishment. The Juvenile Officer testified that Eddings was frightened and bitter, that his father overreacted and used excessive physical punishment: "Mr. Eddings found the only thing that he thought was effectual with the boy was actual punishment, or physical violence—hitting with a strap or something like this."[19] *Id.*, at 121.

Testimony from other witnesses indicated that Eddings was emotionally disturbed in general and at the time of the crime, and that his mental and emotional development were at a level several years below his age. *Id.*, at 134, 149, and 173. A state psychologist stated that Eddings had a sociopathic or antisocial personality and that approximately 30% of youths suffering from such a disorder grew out of it as they aged. *Id.*, at 137 and 139. A sociologist specializing in juvenile offenders testified that Eddings was treatable. *Id.*, at 149. A psychiatrist testified that Eddings could be rehabilitated by intensive therapy over a 15- to 20-year period. *Id.*, at 181. He testified further that Eddings "did pull the trigger, he did kill

[19]There was evidence that immediately after the shooting Eddings said: "I would rather have shot an Officer than go back to where I live." App. 93.

someone, but I don't even think he knew that he was doing it."[20] The psychiatrist suggested that, if treated, Eddings would no longer pose a serious threat to society. *Id.*, at 180–181.

At the conclusion of all the evidence, the trial judge weighed the evidence of aggravating and mitigating circumstances. He found that the State had provided each of the three alleged aggravating circumstances beyond a reasonable doubt.[21] Turning to the evidence of mitigating circumstances, the judge found that Eddings' youth was a mitigating factor of great weight: "I have given very serious consideration to the youth of the Defendant when this particular crime was committed. Should I fail to do this, I think I would not be carrying out my duty." *Id.* at 188–189. But he would not consider in mitigation the circumstances of Eddings' unhappy upbringing and emotional disturbance: "[T]he Court cannot be persuaded entirely by the...fact that the youth was sixteen years old when this heinous crime was committed. *Nor can the Court in following the law, in my opinion, consider the fact of this young man's violent background.*" *Id.*, at 189 (emphasis added). Finding that the only mitigating circumstance was Eddings' youth and finding further that this circumstance could not outweigh the aggravating circumstances present, the judge sentenced Eddings to death.

The Court of Criminal Appeals affirmed the sentence of death. 616 P.2d 1159 (1980). It found that each of the aggravating circumstances alleged by the State had been present.[22] It recited the mitigating evidence presented by Eddings in some detail, but in the end it agreed with the trial court that only the fact of Eddings' youth was properly considered as a mitigating circumstance:

---

[20]The psychiatrist suggested that, at the time of the murder, Eddings was in his own mind shooting his stepfather—a policeman who had been married to his mother for a brief period when Eddings was seven. The psychiatrist stated: "I think that given the circumstances and the facts of his life, and the facts of his arrested development, he acted as a seven year old seeking revenge and rebellion; and the act—he did pull the trigger, he did kill someone, but I don't even think he knew that he was doing it." *Id.*, at 172.

[21]The trial judge found first that the crime was "heinous, atrocious, and cruel" because "designed to inflict a high degree of pain...in utter indifference to the rights of Patrolman Crabtree." *Id.*, at 187. Second, the judge found that the crime was "committed for the purpose of avoiding or preventing a lawful arrest or prosecution." *Id.*, at 187–188. The evidence was sufficient to indicate that at the time of the offense Eddings did not wish to be returned to Missouri and that in stopping the car the officer's intent was to make a lawful arrest. Finally, the trial judge found that Eddings posed a continuing threat of violence to society. There was evidence that at one point on the day of the murder, after Eddings had been taken to the county jail, he told two officers that "if he was loose...he would shoot" them all. *Id.*, at 77. There was also evidence that at another time, when an officer refused to turn off the light in Eddings' cell, Eddings became angry and threatened the officer: "Now I have shot one of you people, and I'll get you too if you don't turn this light out." *Id.*, at 103. Based on these two "spontaneous utterances," *id.*, at 188, the trial judge found a strong likelihood that Eddings would again commit a criminal act of violence if released.

[22]We understand the Court of Criminal Appeals to hold that the murder of a police officer in the performance of his duties is "heinous, atrocious, or cruel" under the Oklahoma statute. See *Roberts v. Louisiana*, 431 U.S. 633, 636, 97 S.Ct. 1993, 1995, 52 L.Ed.2d 637 (1977). However, we doubt that the trial judge's understanding and application of this aggravating circumstance conformed to that degree of certainty required by our decision in *Godfrey v. Georgia*, 446 U.S. 420, 100 S.Ct. 1759, 64 L.Ed.2d 398 (1980). See n. 3, *supra*.

"[Eddings] also argues his mental state at the time of the murder. He stresses his family history in saying he was suffering from severe psychological and emotional disorders, and that the killing was in actuality an inevitable product of the way he was raised. There is no doubt that the petitioner has a personality disorder. But all the evidence tends to show that he knew the difference between right and wrong at the time he pulled the trigger, and that is the test of criminal responsibility in this State. For the same reason, the petitioner's family history is useful in explaining why he behaved the way he did, but it does not excuse his behavior." *Id.*, at 1170 (citation omitted).

II

In *Lockett v. Ohio*, 438 U.S. 586, 98 S.Ct. 2954, 57 L.Ed.2d 973 (1978), CHIEF JUSTICE BURGER, writing for the plurality, stated the rule that we apply today:[23]

"[W]e conclude that the Eighth and Fourteenth Amendments require that the sentencer...not be precluded from considering, as a *mitigating factor*, any aspect of a defendant's character or record and any of the circumstances of the offense that the defendant proffers as a basis for a sentence less than death." *Id.*, at 604, 98 S.Ct., at 2964 (emphasis in original).

Recognizing "that the imposition of death by public authority is...profoundly different from all other penalties," the plurality held that the sentencer must be free to give "independent mitigating weight to aspects of the defendant's character and record and to circumstances of the offense proffered in mitigation..." *Id.*, at 605, 98 S.Ct., at 2965. Because the Ohio death penalty statute only permitted consideration of three mitigating circumstances, the Court found the statue to be invalid.

As THE CHIEF JUSTICE explained, the rule in *Lockett* is the product of a considerable history reflecting the law's effort to develop a system of capital punishment at once consistent and principled but also humane and sensible to the uniqueness of the individual. Since the early days of the common law, the legal system has struggled to accommodate these twin objectives. Thus, the common law began by treating all criminal homicides as capital offenses, with a mandatory sentence of death. Later it allowed exceptions, first through an exclusion for those entitled to claim benefit of clergy and then by limiting capital punishment to murders upon "malice pretensed." In this country we attempted to soften the rigor of the system of mandatory death sentences we inherited from England, first by grading murder into different degrees of which only murder of the first degree was a capital offense and then by committing use of the death penalty to the absolute discretion of the jury. By the time of our decision in *Furman v. Georgia*, 408 U.S. 238, 92 S.Ct. 2726, 33 L.Ed.2d 346 (1972), the country had moved so far from a mandatory system that the imposition of capital punishment frequently had become arbitrary and capricious.

Beginning with *Furman*, the Court has attempted to provide standards for a constitutional death penalty that would serve both goals of measured, consistent application and fairness to the accused. Thus,

[23]Because we decide this case on the basis of *Lockett v. Ohio*, we do not reach the question of whether—in light of contemporary standards—the Eighth Amendment forbids the execution of a defendant who was 16 at the time of the offense. Cf. *Bell v. Ohio*, 438 U.S. 637, 98 S.Ct. 2977, 57 L.Ed.2d 1010 (1978).

in *Gregg v. Georgia*, 428 U.S. 153, 96 S.Ct. 2909, 49 L.Ed.2d 859 (1976), the principal opinion held that the danger of an arbitrary and capricious death penalty could be met "by a carefully drafted statute that ensures that the sentencing authority is given adequate information and guidance." *Id.*, at 195, 96 S.Ct., at 2935. By its requirement that the jury find one of the aggravating circumstances listed in the death penalty statute, and by its direction to the jury to consider "any mitigating circumstances," the Georgia statute properly confined and directed the jury's attention to the circumstances of the particular crime and to "the characteristics of the person who committed the crime..." *Id.*, at 197, 96 S.Ct., at 2936.[24]

Similarly, in *Woodson v. North Carolina*, 428 U.S. 280, 96 S.Ct. 2978, 49 L.Ed.2d 944 (1976), the plurality held that mandatory death sentencing was not a permissible response to the problem of arbitrary jury discretion. As the history of capital punishment had shown, such an approach to the problem of discretion could not succeed while the Eighth Amendment required that the individual be given his due: "the fundamental respect for humanity underlying the Eighth Amendment...requires consideration of the character and record of the individual offender and the circumstances of the particular offense as a constitutionally indispensable part of the process of inflicting the penalty of death." *Id.*, at 304, 96 S.Ct., at 2991.[25] See *Roberts (Harry) v. Louisiana*, 431 U.S. 633, 97 S.Ct. 1993, 52 L.Ed.2d 637 (1977); *Roberts (Stanislaus) v. Louisiana*, 428 U.S. 325, 96 S.Ct. 3001, 49 L.Ed.2d 974 (1976).

Thus, the rule in *Lockett* followed from the earlier decisions of the Court and from the Court's insistence that capital punishment be imposed fairly, and with reasonable consistency, or not at all. By requiring that the sentencer be permitted to focus "on the characteristics of the person who committed the crime," *Gregg v. Georgia, supra*, at 197, 96 S.Ct., at 2936, the rule in *Lockett* recognizes that "justice...requires...that there be taken into account the circumstances of the offense together with the character and propensities of the offender." *Pennsylvania v. Ashe*, 302 U.S. 51, 55, 58 S.Ct. 59, 60, 82 L.Ed. 43 (1937). By holding that the sentencer in capital cases must be permitted to consider any relevant mitigating factor, the rule in *Lockett* recognizes that a consistency produced by ignoring individual differences is a false consistency.

III

We now apply the rule in *Lockett* to the circumstances of this case. The trial judge stated that "in following the law," he could not "consider the fact of this young man's violent background." App. 189.

---

[24] "[T]he jury's attention is focused on the characteristics of the person who committed the crime: ...Are there any special facts about this defendant that mitigate against imposing capital punishment (*e.g.*, his youth, the extent of his cooperation with eh police, his emotional state at the time of the crime)." 428 U.S., at 197, 96 S.Ct., at 2936.

[25] "A process that accords no significance to relevant facets of the character and record of the individual offender or the circumstances of the particular offense excludes from consideration in fixing the ultimate punishment of death the possibility of compassionate or mitigating factors stemming from the diverse frailties of humankind. It treats all persons convicted of a designated offense not as uniquely individual human beings...." 428 U.S., at 304, 96 S.Ct., at 2991.

There is no dispute that by "violent background" the trial judge was referring to the mitigating evidence of Eddings' family history.[26] From this statement it is clear that the trial judge did not evaluate the evidence in mitigation and find it wanting as a matter of fact; rather he found that as a *matter of law* he was unable even to consider the evidence.

The Court of Criminal Appeals took the same approach. If found that the evidence in mitigation was not relevant because it did not tend to provide a legal excuse from criminal responsibility. Thus the court conceded that Eddings had a "personality disorder," but cast this evidence aside on the basis that "he knew the difference between right and wrong...and that is the test of criminal responsibility." 616 P.2d, at 1170. Similarly, the evidence of Eddings' family history was "useful in explaining" his behavior, but it did not "excuse" the behavior. From these statements it appears that the Court of Criminal Appeals also considered only that evidence to be mitigating which would tend to support a legal excuse from criminal liability.

We find that the limitations placed by these courts upon the mitigating evidence they would consider violated the rule in *Lockett*.[27] Just as the State may not by statute preclude the sentencer from considering

---

[26]Brief for Respondent 55 ("the inference that can be drawn is that the court did not consider petitioner's juvenile record and family life to be a mitigating circumstance"); Tr. or Oral Arg. 36 ("the trial court did not consider the fact of his family background as a mitigating circumstance.... [T]he violent background, which I assume he meant was...[that Eddings] was subject to some slapping around and some beating by his father") (argument of respondent).

[27]Eddings argued to the Court of Criminal Appeals that imposition of the death penalty in the particular circumstances of his case, and in light of the mitigating factors present, was excessive punishment under the Eighth Amendment. But he did not specifically argue that the trial judge erred in refusing to consider relevant mitigating circumstances in the process of sentencing. In rejecting his claim of excessive punishment, the court examined the aggravating and mitigating circumstances and held that Eddings' family history and emotional disorder were *not* mitigating circumstances that ought to be weighed in the balance. The court's holding that these factors were irrelevant to an inquiry into excessiveness was also a holding that they need not have been considered by the sentencer in imposing capital punishment. Similarly, Eddings' argument in his petition for certiorari that imposition of the death penalty was excessive on the facts of this case comprises the argument that the sentencer erred in refusing to consider relevant mitigating circumstances proffered by him at the sentencing hearing. In short, although neither the opinion of the Court of Criminal Appeals nor Eddings' petition for certiorari spoke to our decision in *Lockett* by name, the question of whether the decisions below were consistent with our decision in *Lockett* is properly before us. Our jurisdiction does not depend on citation to book and verse. See, *e.g., New York ex rel. Bryant v. Zimmerman*, 278 U.S. 63, 67, 49 S.Ct. 61, 63, 73 L.Ed. 184 (1928).

Although Eddings' petition for certiorari did not expressly present the *Lockett* issue, his brief in this Court argued it, and the State responded to the argument. Brief for Petitioner 64–67; Brief for Respondent 55–57. The dissenting opinion of THE CHIEF JUSTICE, *post*, at 879, n. 1, states that the courts below were not afforded the opportunity to consider this issue. The fact is, however, that in his petition to the Court of Criminal Appeals for a rehearing, Eddings specifically presented the issue and at some considerable length. See Petition for Re-Hearing and Supporting Brief in No. C-78-325, p. 10 ("This Court, by its interpretation of mitigating circumstances, has effectively limited the scope of mitigation and that limitation renders the Oklahoma death penalty statute unconstitutional"). The Court of Criminal Appeals denied the petition, stating that tit had given it full consideration and had been "fully advised in he premises." See Rule 1.18, Rules of the Court of Criminal Appeals (1980) (court will entertain new arguments upon a petition for rehearing). Cf. *Cox Broadcasting Corp. v. Cohn*, 420 U.S. 469, 476, 95 S.Ct. 1029, 1036, 43 L.Ed.2d 328 (1975). See also *Wood v. Georgia*, 450 U.S. 261, 265, n. 5, 101 S.Ct. 1097, 1100, n. 5, 67 L.Ed.2d 220 (1981);

(continued...)

any mitigating factor, neither may the sentencer refuse to consider, *as a matter of law*, any relevant mitigating evidence. In this instance, it was as if the trial judge had instructed a jury to disregard the mitigating evidence Eddings proffered on his behalf. The sentencer, and the Court of Criminal Appeals on review, may determine the weight to be given relevant mitigating evidence. But they may not give it no weight by excluding such evidence from their consideration.[28]

Nor do we doubt that the evidence Eddings offered was relevant mitigating evidence. Eddings was a youth of 16 years at the time of the murder. Evidence of a difficult family history and of emotional disturbance is typically introduced by defendants in mitigation. See *McGautha v. California*, 402 U.S. 183, 187–188, 193, 91 S.Ct. 1454, 1457, 1460, 28 L.Ed.2d 711 (1971). In some cases, such evidence properly may be given little weight. But when the defendant was 16 years old at the time of the offense there can be no doubt that evidence of a turbulent family history, of beatings by a harsh father, and of severe emotional disturbance is particularly relevant.

The trial judge recognized that youth must be considered a relevant mitigating factor. But youth is more than a chronological fact. It is a time and condition of life when a person may be most susceptible to influence and to psychological damage.[29] Our history is replete with laws and judicial recognition that minors, especially in their earlier years, generally are less mature and responsible than adults.[30] Particularly "during the formative years of childhood and adolescence, minors often lack the experience, perspective, and judgment" expected of adults. *Bellotti v. Baird*, 443 U.S. 622, 635, 99 S.Ct. 3035, 3044, 61 L.Ed.2d 797 (1979).

---

[27](...continued)
Beck v. Alabama, 447 U.S. 625, 631, n. 6, 100 S.Ct. 2382, 2386, n. 6, 65 L.Ed.2d 392 (1980); *Vachon v. New Hampshire*, 414 U.S. 478, 479, n. 3, 94 S.Ct. 664, 665, n. 3, 38 L.Ed.2d 666 (1974).

[28]We note that the Oklahoma death penalty statute permits the defendant to present evidence "as to any mitigating circumstances." Okla.Stat., Tit. 21, § 701.10 (1980). *Lockett* requires the sentencer to listen.

[29]"Adolescents everywhere, from every walk of life, are often dangerous to themselves and to others." The President's Commission on Law Enforcement and Administration of Justice, Task Force Report: Juvenile Delinquency and Youth Crime 41 (1967). "[A]dolescents, particularly in the early and middle teen years, are more vulnerable, more impulsive, and less self-disciplined than adults. Crimes committed by youths may be just as harmful to victims as those committed by older persons, but they deserve less punishment because adolescents may have less capacity to control their conduct and to think in long-range terms than adults. Moreover, youth crime as such is not exclusively the offender's fault; offenses by the young also represent a failure of family, school, and the social system, which share responsibility for the development of America's youth." Twentieth Century Fund Task Force on Sentencing Policy Toward Young Offenders, Confronting Youth Crime 7 (1978).

[30]As Justice Frankfurter stated, "[c]hildren have a very special place in life which law should reflect." *May v. Anderson*, 345 U.S. 528, 536, 73 S.Ct. 840, 844, 97 L.Ed. 1221 (1953) (concurring opinion). And indeed the law does reflect this special place. Every State in the country makes some separate provision for juvenile offenders. See *In re Gault*, 387 U.S. 1, 14, 87 S.Ct. 1428, 1436, 18 L.Ed.2d 527 (1967).

Even the normal 16-year-old customarily lacks the maturity of an adult. In this case, Eddings was not a normal 16-year-old; he had been deprived of the care, concern, and paternal attention that children deserve. On the contrary, it is not disputed that he was a juvenile with serious emotional problems, and had been raised in a neglectful, sometimes even violent, family background. In addition, there was testimony that Eddings' mental and emotional development were at a level several years below his chronological age. All of this does not suggest an absence of responsibility for the crime of murder, deliberately committed in this case. Rather, it is to say that just as the chronological age of a minor is itself a relevant mitigating factor of great weight, so must the background and mental and emotional development of a youthful defendant be duly considered in sentencing.

We are not unaware of the extent to which minors engage increasingly in violent crime. Nor do we suggest an absence of legal responsibility where crime is committed by a minor. We are concerned here only with the manner of the imposition of the ultimate penalty: the death sentence imposed for the crime of murder upon an emotionally disturbed youth with a disturbed child's immaturity.

On remand, the state courts must consider all relevant mitigating evidence and weigh it against the evidence of the aggravating circumstances. We do not weigh the evidence for them. Accordingly, the judgment is reversed to the extent that it sustains the imposition of the death penalty, and the case is remanded for further proceedings not inconsistent with this opinion.

SO ORDERED.

* * *

EDDINGS V. OKLAHOMA

1. What was the rationale of the trial court when it refused to consider youthful age as a mitigating factor in choosing between the death penalty and life in prison for Monty Eddings?
2. What is the difference between a personality disorder and a mental illness, according to the psychiatric professional community? Should the presence of a personality disorder be considered a mitigating factor in juvenile death penalty cases? Explain.
3. Why did the U.S. Supreme Court avoid any direct holding on the constitutionality of the death penalty for juveniles? Of course, this answer will require some speculation.
4. Summarize the holding in the *Eddings* case. Why has this holding served as an important precedent for many lower court rulings involving the possibility of a death sentence for a juvenile?
5. What was the relevance of the *Lockett* case to *Eddings*? Be sure to discuss the issue of judicial discretion.

WORKS CITED IN JUDICATURE ARTICLE

Amnesty International

1983 *The Death Penalty: An Amnesty International Report*. London: Amnesty International.

Baldus, David C., Charles Pulaski, and George Woodworth

1983 "Comparative Review of Death Sentences: An Empirical Study of the Georgia Experience." 74 *Journal of Criminal Law and Criminology* 661.

Bedau, Hugo Adam

1977 *The Death Penalty in America*. (2nd ed.) New York: Doubleday Press.

Berger, Raoul

1982 *Death Penalties: The Supreme Court's Obstacle Course*. Massachusetts: Harvard University Press.

Champion, D.

1990 *Corrections in the United States: A Contemporary Perspective*. Englewood Cliffs, NJ: Prentice-Hall.

Fox, Stanford J.

1970 "Juvenile Justice: An Historical Perspective." 22 *Stanford Law Review* 1187.

Gillers, Steven

1980 "Deciding Who Dies." 125 *University of Pennsylvania Law Review* 1.

Goodpaster, Gary

1983 "Judicial Review of Death Sentences." 74 *Journal of Criminal Law and Criminology* 786.

Hackett, George, Patricia King, and Theodore Stanger

1987 "Indiana Killer, Italian Martyr: A Death Row Cause." *Newsweek* 37 (September 21).

Hamm, Mark

1987 *Attitudes of Indiana Legislators Toward Crime and Criminal Justice*. Terre Haute: Indiana State University.

1989 "Legislator Ideology and Capital Punishment: The Special Case for Indiana Juveniles." 6 *Justice Quarterly* 219.

Hoffmann, Joseph L.

1989 "On the Perils of Line Drawing: Juveniles and the Death Penalty." 40 *Hastings Law Journal* 229.

Inciardi, James A.

1984 *Criminal Justice*. Florida: Academic Press, Inc.

Jamison, Katherine and Timothy J. Flanagan

1989 *Sourcebook of Criminal Justice Statistics—1989*. Washington, D.C.: U.S. Department of Justice, Bureau of Justice Statistics.

Knight, Barbara B. and Stephen T. Early Jr.

1986 ***Prisoner's Rights in America***. Illinois: Nelson-Hall Publishers.

Knoxville News-Sentinel, January 3, 1988.

Lemon, R. II.

1979 "Constitutional Criminal Law—The Role of Mitigating Circumstances in Considering the Death Penalty," ***Tulane Law Review***. 53:608–617.

Mennel, Robert M.

1973 ***Thorns and Thistles: Juvenile Delinquents in the United States, 1825–1940***. New Hampshire: University Press of New England.

Nettler, Gwynn

1984 ***Explaining Crime***. (3rd. ed.) New York: McGraw-Hill Publishing.

Note (Nick Jackson)

1988 "*Thompson v. Oklahoma*: The Law of Averages." 4 ***Detroit College of Law Review*** 999.

Note (Arthur E. Petersen)

1989 "*Thompson v. Oklahoma*: The Mitigating Circumstance of Youthful Capital Offenders." 25 ***Tulsa Law Journal*** 115.

Note (Dominic J. Ricotta)

1988 "Eighth Amendment—The Death Penalty for Juveniles: A State's Right or a Child's Injustice?" 79 ***Journal of Criminal Law and Criminology*** 921.

Note (Susan M. Simmons)

1989 "*Thompson v. Oklahoma*: Debating the Constitutionality of Juvenile Executions." 16 ***Pepperdine Law Review*** 737.

Paternoster, Raymond and Annmarie Kazyaka

1988 "Racial Considerations in Capital Punishment." In Kenneth Haas and James A. Inciardi (eds) ***Challenging Capital Punishment: Legal and Social Science Approaches***. California: Sage Publications.

Platt, Anthony M.

1969 ***The Child Savers: The Invention of Delinquency***. Illinois: The University of Chicago Press.

Ryerson, Ellen

1978 ***The Best Laid Plans: America's Juvenile Court Experiment***. New York: Hill and Wang Publishers, Inc.

Shapiro, H.

1978 "First Degree Murder Statutes and Capital Sentencing Procedures: An Analysis and Comparison of Statutory Systems for the Imposition of the Death Penalty in Georgia, Florida, Texas and Louisiana." ***Loyola Law Review***, 24:709–751.

Skovron, Sandra Evans, Joseph E. Scott and Francis T. Cullen

1986 "The Death Penalty for Juveniles: An Assessment of Public Attitudes." Paper Presented at the Annual Meeting of the American Society of Criminology.

Southern Coalition on Jails and Prisons

1986 "SCJP Poll Results: Don't Execute Juveniles." 13 ***Southern Coalition Report on Jails and Prisons*** 1.

Streib, Victor L.

1986 Testimony on the Death Penalty for Juveniles. Subcommittee on Criminal Justice, U.S. House of Representatives.

1987a Testimony on the Death Penalty for Juveniles. Subcommittee on Judiciary, Indiana General Assembly.

1987b ***Death Penalty for Juveniles***. Indiana: Indiana University Press.

van den Haag, Ernest

1975 ***Punishing Criminals: Concerning a Very Old and Painful Question***. New York: Basic Books.

van den Haag, Ernest and John P. Conrad

1983 ***The Death Penalty: A Debate***. New York: Plenum Press.

Whitehead, John T. and Steven Lab

1990 ***Juvenile Justice: An Introduction***. Ohio: Anderson Publishing Company.

Wikberg, R. and Wilbert Rideau

1990 "Death Watch." ***Angolite***. January-February.

Index